Emerging Leadership in the Pauline Mission

Princeton Theological Monograph Series

K. C. Hanson and Charles M. Collier, Series Editors

Recent volumes in the series:

Richard Valantasis et al., editors
The Subjective Eye: Essays in Honor of Margaret Miles

Anette Ejsing
A Theology of Anticipation: A Constructive Study of C. S. Peirce

Caryn Riswold
Coram Deo: Human Life in the Vision of God

Paul O. Ingram, editor
Constructing a Relational Cosmology

Michael G. Cartwright
Practices, Politics, and Performance: Toward a Communal Hermeneutic for Christian Ethics

David A. Ackerman
Lo, I Tell You a Mystery: Cross, Resurrection, and Paraenesis in the Rhetoric of 1 Corinthians

Lloyd Kim
Polemic in the Book of Hebrews: Anti-Judaism, Anti-Semitism, Supersessionism?

Emerging Leadership in the Pauline Mission

*A Social Identity Perspective on Local
Leadership Development in Corinth and Ephesus*

JACK BARENTSEN

◆PICKWICK *Publications* · Eugene, Oregon

EMERGING LEADERSHIP IN THE PAULINE MISSION
A Social Identity Perspective on Local Leadership Development in Corinth and Ephesus

Princeton Theological Monograph Series 168

Copyright © 2011 Jack Barentsen. All rights reserved. Except for brief quotations in critical publications or reviews, no part of this book may be reproduced in any manner without prior written permission from the publisher. Write: Permissions, Wipf and Stock Publishers, 199 W. 8th Ave., Suite 3, Eugene, OR 97401.

Pickwick Publications
An Imprint of Wipf and Stock Publishers
199 W. 8th Ave., Suite 3
Eugene, OR 97401

www.wipfandstock.com

ISBN 13: 978-1-61097-244-4

Scripture quotations in Greek are from Barbara Aland, Kurt Aland, Matthew Black, et al. *The Greek New Testament*. 4th ed. Stuttgart: United Bible Societies, 1993. Used by permission. All rights reserved.

Scripture quotations in English are from The Holy Bible, English Standard Version® (ESV®), copyright © 2001 by Crossway, a publishing ministry of Good News Publishers. Used by permission. All rights reserved.

Olivier Klein, Russell Spears, Stephen Reicher, "Social Identity Performance: Extending the Strategic Side of SIDE," *Personality and Social Psychology Review* (11:1), p. 41 (figure), copyright © 2007 by SAGE Publications. Chart reprinted by permission of SAGE Publications.

Cataloging-in-Publication data:

Barentsen, Jack.

    Emerging leadership in the Pauline mission : a social identity perspective on local leadership in Corinth and Ephesus / Jack Barentsen.

    p. ; 23cm. —Includes bibliographical references and index(es).

    Princeton Theological Monograph Series 168

    ISBN 13: 978-1-61097-244-4

    1. Bible. N.T. Epistles of Paul—Criticism, interpretation, etc. 2. Christian leadership—Biblical teaching. I. Title. II. Series.

BS2655 L42 B25 2011

Manufactured in the U.S.A.

To the countless and selfless national leaders,
who stepped into the shoes left behind by their missionary heroes
only to realize that these shoes were several sizes too big
but who did their very best
to serve their Lord and their churches

Contents

List of Tables and Figures / x

Foreword by Philip Esler / xi

Preface / xv

Abbreviations / xvii

1. Introduction / 1
   Developing Patterns of Leadership
   Pauline Correspondence to Corinth and Ephesus
   The Social Identity Model of Leadership
   Definitions
   The Plan of the Book

2. The Ideological Challenge of Church Leadership Studies / 16
   Beginnings
   Modern Historical Scholarship and Denominational Ideology
   The Turn to the Social Sciences
   Rethinking Leadership in Terms of the First Century
   Authority and Ideology in a Group Context
   The Challenge to Integrate Social and Ideological Factors

3. The Social Identity Model of Leadership / 32
   Foundations of the Social Identity Approach
   Social Identification Processes
   Leaders as (Competing) Managers of Social Identity
   Developing Leadership Patterns
   Conclusion: The Social Identity Model of Leadership

4 Realigning Emerging Leadership with Christian Social Identity in 1 Corinthians / 75

Situating the Corinthian Correspondence in Paul's Ministry
Social Identification in the Corinthian Community in 55 C.E.
The Corinthian Leaders as Managers of Christian Social Identity
Paul's Leadership as Identity Management
The Development of Local Leadership Patterns at Corinth in 55 C.E.
Conclusions

5 Reestablishing Paul's Leadership as Model in 2 Corinthians / 112

Situating 2 Corinthians in Paul's Ministry
Social Identification in the Corinthian Community in 56 C.E.
The Corinthian Leaders as Managers of Christian Social Identity
Paul's Leadership as Identity Management
The Development of Local Leadership Patterns at Corinth in 56 C.E.
Conclusions

6 Leadership Legitimation and Empowerment in Ephesians / 141

Situating Ephesians in Paul's Ministry
Social Identification in the Ephesian Community in 61 C.E.
The Ephesian Leaders as Managers of Christian Social Identity
Paul's Leadership as Identity Management
The Development of Local Leadership Patterns at Ephesus in 61 C.E.
Conclusions

7 Structuring Leadership and Group Participation in 1 Timothy / 184

Excursus: The Authorship and Social Context of 1–2 Timothy
Situating 1 Timothy in Paul's Ministry
Social Identification in the Ephesian Community in 63 C.E.
The Ephesian Leaders as Managers of Christian Social Identity
Paul's Leadership as Identity Management
The Development of Local Leadership Patterns at Ephesus in 63 C.E.
Conclusions

8   Correcting Leadership Misconceptions and Establishing
    Succession in 2 Timothy / 252
        Situating 2 Timothy in Paul's Ministry
        Social Identification in the Ephesian Community in 66 C.E.
        The Ephesian Leaders as Managers of Christian Social Identity
        Paul's Leadership as Identity Management
        The Development of Local Leadership Patterns at Ephesus in 66 C.E.
        Conclusions

9   Conclusions and Implications: Emerging Leadership in the
    Pauline Mission / 290
        Developing Leadership Patterns in Corinth and Ephesus
        Comparison of Leadership Patterns in Corinth and Ephesus
        Paul's Advocacy of Uniform Patterns of Leadership
        Implications for Further Research
        Paul: Social Strategist, Situational Theologian

Bibliography / 327

Author Index / 347

Subject Index / 355

Scripture Index / 369

Tables and Figures

Table 3.1   Statistics on Identity Research in Religious Studies / 37

Figure 3.2   Identity Performance Cycle / 48

Table 3.3   The Legacy Transferred in Ancient Succession Texts / 71

Table 6.1   Components of Church Office / 175

Table 7.1   Paul's Personal Exhortations as Frame for 1 Timothy / 211

Table 7.2   Components of Office in 1 Timothy / 240

Foreword
by Philip Esler

WHEREVER WE LOOK IN THE NEW TESTAMENT AND ITS WORLD WE ENcounter groups, assemblages of individuals who in some particular manner constitute an "us." We find the most intimate of groups, the family, at one end of the spectrum and large ethnic groups like the Romans, Egyptians, and Judeans at the other. But in between there are also the inhabitants of towns and villages, local aristocracies, military units, trade associations, and people who revere a particular god. These are all groups whose fundamental sense of being an "us" in contrast to non-members who are "them" finds expression, often changing expression, in various ways. The primary group (or groups?) before our gaze in the New Testament are those people motivated by a belief that God has manifested himself in Jesus (the) Christ, a Judean from Nazareth in Galilee, who has revealed a path to salvation but with specific demands on those who would take it. There is no single epithet that captures the identity of these Christ-followers. They transcend the ties of ethnicity by including members from different ethnic groups; they gather in the houses of their members; and they live their lives in a distinctive fashion. While there is a powerful "religious" dimension to their identity, to speak of them as adherents of a "religion" would be anachronistic for this period. Yet it is not just the existence of groups that catches our attention, for it is also impossible to miss relationships between groups and among groups. When Paul says in Gal. 1:13 that "I strenuously persecuted the assembly of God and tried to destroy it," we see an example of intergroup relations (here between the protector of his ethnic group and a new group of a different character) of an extreme type. First and Second Corinthians, on the other hand, are replete with phenomena of an intragroup type. Finally, the New Testament and its world inevitably provide examples of group leadership, where influential members of groups seek to have the membership move in a particular direction, or refrain from doing so, or take a recommended view on some issue, or refrain from taking it.

The abundance of such group data in the New Testament documents and in the context in which they were created poses a dilemma for interpreters. Should we simply rely upon our own experience of, and presuppositions concerning, groups and group phenomena, even if we have been socialised in individualistic North Atlantic cultures very different from those of the Mediterranean world of the first century CE? Or should we take the conscious step of informing ourselves of social-scientific research directly relevant to the group phenomena in these texts and the cultural context in which they were written? This choice first appeared for biblical interpreters in the 1970s with the arrival of the social sciences on the scene and it is with us still, in spite of the dubious claim, occasionally heard, that the job of social-scientific interpretation is done. It is a choice between reliance on folk psychology and the unexamined presuppositions of the interpreter on one hand, or application of readily available social-scientific ideas and perspectives on the other. By use of the social sciences an interpreter not only poses new questions to a biblical text, but is also able to organise the results of that process in a more socially realistic and historically satisfying manner.

In this fine volume, Dr. Jack Barentsen provides notable confirmation of the benefits of social-scientific interpretation, especially in the area of group phenomena. In social identity theory, initially developed by Henri Tajfel at the University of Bristol in the 1970s and now a thriving area of social psychology, he has happily found a resource that allows him to cast new light on a very wide range of Pauline (and arguably Pauline) data. He is especially concerned with the distinctive identities of Christ-following congregations founded by Paul and the ways in which he exercised leadership among them. His particular interest lies in how leadership emerges and is maintained, and in how (we are a long way from modern recruitment processes here!) a leader ensures appropriate succession. Central to the social identity approach to leadership is the need for the leader to be prototypical of group practices, values and beliefs if he or she is to be successful in managing the identity of the group and in influencing it to move in the desired direction. Dr. Barentsen has found a rich seam of data on this topic in the texts he surveys and is fully alive to the aptness of this understanding of leadership for modern ecclesial communities. His results witness to the more general phenomenon that interpreters conducting historical investigations of the New Testament using the social sciences (with the proper methodology) are more likely to return home with discoveries directly applicable to our modern setting than those who do not. In the end, then, Dr. Barentsen has produced a work of notably innovative historical exegesis that will also fertilize contemporary understandings of Christian identity and Christian leadership. It is an admirable achievement.

Preface

DISCIPLESHIP AND TEAMWORK ARE TWO KEY IDEAS THAT HAVE INfluenced my service as church-planting missionary, and teacher of New Testament and Practical Theology. The study of Paul's leadership and the writing of this dissertation are no exception to that. I have grown immensely in my admiration for Paul, not only as theologian (as I was trained to see him), but also as a social strategist in forming his communities, and shaping their leadership amidst opposition from various sources. I have often wished that I had some of Paul's insights in my earlier church-planting ministry. But then, Paul did not start the church-planting ventures that I have studied until he was about the age that I reached somewhere in the middle of this project. Perhaps, then, my journey as a disciple of Paul has only just begun!

This project involved a team of people, even though I spent countless hours alone with my books and my computer. I am deeply grateful to my wife Pat: without her understanding and support, I would have abandoned this project long ago. Thanks to my daughters Laura and Rebecca, budding teenagers when I started but now about to complete their own studies in higher education. They had to do without their dad many an evening and weekend. Thanks also to my parents and in-laws: your prayers and understanding have been very valuable. I also feel deeply grateful to our supporters in the USA, who have given sacrificially to make our ministry and thus also this research possible. Thanks to Martin Webber who as promoter kept on encouraging me to write the next analysis, the next chapter, and the next revision; to Philip Esler whose many NT publications with social identity theory inspired me in my approach and whose expert advice made this a better project; to Alex Haslam whose expertise as social psychologist helped me find my way in another discipline. The Evangelische Theologische Faculteit at Leuven (Belgium) provided a great environment for this project. Among my many colleagues, Gie Vleugels, Armin Baum, Patrick Nullens, and Pieter Boersema were especially helpful in their feedback and encouragement. Thanks to our Leuven group of promovendi who regularly poured over some of my texts, struggling to understand an approach so different from their own. So many other people provided practical help: Heidi McLaughlin, Joe Morell, and Boris Paschke assisted with editing; ETF librarian Marjorie Webber and mission personnel from Biblical Ministries Worldwide collected or shipped my books; mission leadership gave me time to finish the project before new ministry plans could be made; and so many friends from the Baptist Church in Maastricht encouraged and prayed for me. Thanks, finally, to the editorial team of Pickwick Publications, and their vision and guidance in making this study available for a wider audience. Nevertheless, even with all these words of thanks, I did not learn much from Paul if I did not pause here to honor God above everyone else as our Lord, our Provider, and our Sustainer throughout this whole project.

I hope and pray that this research will benefit church leaders everywhere as they struggle with how to contextualize the gospel in their time, place, and culture. How can we influence the group processes that determine how communities will develop? How can we develop local leadership that will grow stronger and more effective when they succeed the leaders that preceded them, whether they represent the foundational missionary leadership or previously established leadership? My research contains some of the answers as we can discover them from Paul. But much remains yet to be done in biblical studies, Practical Theology, and World Missions. The results now lay before the reader. May it encourage discipleship and teamwork in churches everywhere. And if perchance some would be especially interested in advancing research in these areas, you are cordially invited to get in touch.

Abbreviations

AB	The Anchor Bible
AMR	*The Academy of Management Review*
BETL	Bibliotheca Ephemeridum Theologicarum Lovaniensium
BIS	Biblical Interpretation Series
BJM	*British Journal of Management*
BNTC	Black's New Testament Commentary
BTB	*Biblical Theology Bulletin*
COP	Colloquium Oecumenicum Paulinum
DBAG	Danker, Frederick W., et al. *A Greek-English Lexicon of the New Testament and Other Early Christian Literature.* 3rd ed. Chicago: University of Chicago Press, 2000.
DPL	G. F. Hawthorne. *Dictionary of Paul and His Letters.* Downers Grove: InterVarsity Press, 1993
EDNT	Balz, H. R., and G. Schneider. *Exegetical Dictionary of the New Testament.* 3 vols. Grand Rapids: Eerdmans, 1990
EQ	*Evangelical Quarterly*
HTS	*Hervormde Theologische Studies*
HThS	Harvard Theological Studies
ICC	International Critical Commentary
JETS	*Journal of the Evangelical Theological Society*
JMS	*Journal of Management Studies*
JPSP	*Journal of Personality & Social Psychology*
JSNT	*Journal for the Study of the New Testament*
JSNTSS	Journal for the Study of the New Testament Supplement Series
LN	Louw, Johannes P., and Eugene A. Nida. *Greek-English Lexicon of the New Testament Based on Semantic Domains.* 2 vols. 2nd ed. New York: United Bible Societies, 1989
LNTS	Library of New Testament Studies

LQ	*The Leadership Quarterly*
LSJ	Liddell, Henry G., et al. *A Greek-English Lexicon*. 2 vols. 9th ed. Oxford: Clarendon Press, 1996
NAC	The New American Commentary
NICNT	New International Commentary on the New Testament
NIGTC	New International Greek Text Commentary
NT	*Novum Testamentum*
PBM	Paternoster Biblical Monographs
PSPB	*Personality and Social Psychology Bulletin*
PSPR	*Personality and Social Psychology Review*
RQ	*Restoration Quarterly*
SIMOL	Social identity model of leadership
SNTSMS	Society for New Testament Studies Monograph Series
SP	Sacra Pagina
TDNT	*The Theological Dictionary of the New Testament*. 10 vols. Edited by G. Kittel, and G. Friedrich. Translated by Geoffrey W. Bromiley. Grand Rapids: Eerdmans, 1964–76
TB	*Tyndale Bulletin*
WUNT	Wissenschaftliche Untersuchungen zum Neuen Testament

1

Introduction

Developing Patterns of Leadership

IN AN ENVIRONMENT OF MAJOR SOCIAL CHANGE, LEADERSHIP AND group identity become key issues. Without question, the 21st century is such a period of major social change, which impacts every major social, political, and economic institution. The search for a new sense of national or ethnic identities in many parts of the world along with the rise of new international leaders is a sign of this social change. As the church participates in these times of change, renewal movements spark dozens of experimental forms of community and worship, for which traditional leadership structures are not always sufficient. A fresh look at individual communities and their leadership in the NT is needed to assist these renewal movements in their search for new forms of Christian identity and new patterns of leadership.

Traditionally, NT studies on church leadership have focused on church office as it developed in the NT and the few centuries afterwards. These studies often became an apology for the leadership structure of the denomination to which the author belonged. More recently, the application of social science approaches has unearthed a wealth of material about ancient patterns of leadership. Renewed study of NT leadership has pointed to a variety of people, functions, and norms involved, so that a broad scholarly consensus on a normative or apostolic pattern of leadership seems further away than ever. The only agreement seemed to be that the NT does not prescribe any one of these patterns as the universal norm for all churches. However, most of these studies have ignored the dimension of group dynamics in their study of leadership. Newer insights in leadership theory indicate that leadership is essentially a dynamic group phenomenon. These insights have yet to be applied consistently to a study of the first Christ-following communities and their patterns of leadership.

This study aims to contribute to the discussion by approaching leadership as a group phenomenon. A group is understood as a set of persons who all share a sense of "us," of belonging together. This sense of "us" refers to the psychological processes that are at work within individuals as they join others in a group. This sense of "us" is shared, and revolves around group beliefs and norms, which function as the group's ideology. Groups also develop social structures, first because they relate to other groups in their social context, but also because group members relate to one another, and not all group members are equally representative. Thus, some group members may gain more influence than others, occasioning the rise of group leaders and other roles from within the group. Groups are thus a complex mix of group ideology and social structures, which continuously interact with one another in response to changes in their social environment. Since leadership patterns develop within such a group setting, these patterns take shape and change due to social and psychological group processes as groups respond to their (changing) social environment. For the purposes of this study, the social and psychological processes will often be designated as historical and ideological factors, respectively.[1]

This study, then, focuses on patterns of leadership as they develop within Pauline groups or communities. These developing patterns can be fruitfully studied by analyzing leadership emergence, maintenance, and succession. Leadership emergence refers to the ways a regular group member comes to be a group leader. Leadership maintenance discusses the ways established leaders maintain their influence, whether or not in competition with others. Leadership succession relates to the ways established leaders empower new leaders to emerge, either joining the established leaders or taking their places.

The study aims to trace the development of these leadership patterns by studying the social and psychological mechanisms that drive

---

1. The psychological processes could also be designated as theological factors, which is the more common term in NT studies. However, in the context of group theory the term "ideology" refers to the central beliefs and values of a group, that is, it refers to both theological beliefs and their social location in a community (Bar-Tal, "Group Beliefs," 99–101). Thus, "ideology" describes the perspective of this study more precisely than "theology."

this development. The study aims to answer questions like, "How did leaders relate to each other and to the community?" "How did leaders come to be in positions of leadership and authority?" "What processes were at work in the community to legitimate the authority and power differential between leaders and followers?" "What processes allowed leaders to transfer their authority or position to new leaders?" These questions will point out how leadership patterns changed over time, and what social and psychological processes brought about these changes. The result is a portrayal of how these leadership patterns developed.

In sum, this study contributes to the ongoing reflection about church identity and leadership by focusing on developing patterns of leadership in some Pauline communities. The project is undertaken in the hope that it will contribute to a greater consensus in the field. A recent review, commenting on leadership in terms of ministry and church order, has noted:

> Continued debate over the origin, shapes, and historical development of ministry and order in the early church appears to be as much an inevitability as death and taxes. Perhaps this is to be expected with an issue in which all ecclesial communions have such pronounced self-interests in justifying their own ecclesial orders. At the same time, the diverse and numerous exegetical, historical, social, and theological factors involved, combined with the less than fully clear nature of the literary sources, virtually guarantees a plethora of differing reconstructions, none of which has led yet to an overall consensus.[2]

Such is the challenge of the current study.

Pauline Correspondence to Corinth and Ephesus

The aim to study the development of patterns of leadership over time and across space requires a clearly defined chronological and geographical range. The geographical range is defined by the Pauline communities at Corinth and Ephesus, which offer a number of advantages for this study. First, Corinth and Ephesus represent two major locations of Paul's Aegean ministry, where he and his missionary team founded new churches. This avoids difficult questions regarding, for

---

2. Elliott, "Elders as Honored Household Heads," 2.

instance, Antioch or Rome where Paul was involved, but where other founders could have significantly affected the available leadership strategies. Second, Paul's work in these locations can be considered as his more mature efforts, coming almost twenty years after his conversion and at a time when he had at least ten years of cross-cultural ministry experience behind him. Third, these cities, located across the Aegean Sea from one another, represent major urban areas with many cultural, political, and religious links to Rome, to their own region, and to one another. This benefited the work of Paul's missionary team, since they appear to have been in communication with most of the churches in the Aegean region (i.e., in Achaia, Macedonia, and Asia Minor) while ministering in any one of these locations. Both locations seem to have functioned as hubs in Paul's Aegean network. Fourth, these social networks established by Paul, his coworkers, and other traveling believers imply that significant developments in one location most likely did not escape notice in the other locations. In Corinth, they heard of some of Paul's difficulties in Ephesus, while the Ephesian community undoubtedly followed Paul's involvement in the Corinthian troubles with great interest. Fifth, the Corinthian and Ephesian communities are the recipients of several Pauline letters, 1–2 Corinthians, and Ephesians and 1–2 Timothy. Sixth, with the recent increase of interest in socio-historical methods, inscriptions, and archaeology, the cultural landscape of these cities has been extensively studied, reflected in commentaries and with handbooks now readily available for more general use.[3] Finally, these two locations have not often been compared in scholarly studies of the last few decades, providing an opportunity to study development across a geographical range that has not received significant attention of late. Of course, a significant obstacle for comparing these two Pauline communities is that the Pauline letters addressed to Ephesus are often considered post-Pauline, which leads to a clearer definition of the next parameter for this study.

The chronological range is defined by the date of composition of the letters to the locations, in this study taken to date from 55 through 66 CE. The dating of 1 and 2 Corinthians is generally not

---

3. For Corinth, see for instance Murphy-O'Connor, *St. Paul's Corinth*; and Schowalter and Friesen, *Urban Religion in Roman Corinth*; for Ephesus, see Koester, *Ephesos*; Scherrer, *Ephesus*; and Murphy-O'Connor, *St. Paul's Ephesus*.

problematic, except for an occasional multiple source theory for 2 Corinthians. However, the scholarly consensus on the authorship of Ephesians is about equally divided between Pauline and second generation post-Pauline authorship[4]; the scholarly consensus on 1 and 2 Timothy holds predominantly to third generation post-Pauline authorship, although this is vigorously contested in a series of recent English commentaries.[5] Remarkably, only the Asian side of the Pauline corpus is often considered pseudepigraphal. Different authorship proposals date 1–2 Timothy in the middle '60s, the '80s–'90s or even the 120–40s. Since the Ephesian community was founded in 52-53, these proposals date 1–2 Timothy some 10–15, 30–40 or even 70–90 years later. Although these differences may not seem much in two millennia of church history, relative to the founding date they are huge and result in significantly different reconstructions of community and leadership development. Since this study engages questions concerning social structures and developing patterns of leadership, a relatively secure date for the sources is imperative. Since, moreover, this study is based on the minority position of Pauline authorship of Ephesians and 1–2 Timothy, some basic argumentation will be provided to indicate the evidential support for this view, sufficient to undergird the credibility of the social reconstructions built upon it, but without attempting to argue the matter exhaustively.[6]

These geographical and chronological limitations have some disadvantages. The study does not take into account the earlier stages of Paul's ministry from Antioch to Galatia, nor does it consider Romans with its rich understanding of leadership, and even some of the Pauline sources from his Aegean ministry (i.e. 1–2 Thessalonians, Philippians, Colossians, Philemon, and Titus) remain unaddressed. In addition, issues concerning the role of women in Paul's leadership strategies receive attention only when they appear to affect the overall pattern of leadership, without focusing especially on the issue. Given

---

4. Hoehner, *Ephesians*, 15–19.

5. See the response to this trend by Herzer, "Abschied vom Konsens," 1267–80.

6. An alternative strategy is to avoid the authorship discussion altogether and to chart development in terms of a Pauline trajectory, regardless of authorship and date. However, it will be argued that differences in authorship and date may result in widely divergent social reconstructions, so that removal of this constraint merely avoids one set of difficulties at the expense of introducing a different set that turns social reconstruction into a very dubious venture. See the excursus in chapter 7.

the sensitivities around this issue, this is better left to more dedicated studies.

The research question for the study can now be formulated as follows:

> "According to the Pauline letters addressed to Corinth and Ephesus, what were the leadership patterns in these early Christ-following communities, and how did the communities as well as Paul influence the development of these patterns?"

The Social Identity Model of Leadership

Typically, studies on leadership in the Pauline letters consider the historical and ideological factors separately. Either they focus on the socio-historical structures of Pauline leadership by comparing it to other ancient leadership structures, or they focus on the ideological aspects of Pauline leadership by studying Paul's principles, methods or theology of leadership.[7] The relationship between the historical and ideological factors has not yet been systematically analyzed, nor has it been adequately recognized how one factor influences and shapes the other.

This study employs the social identity model of leadership to study this interaction between historical and ideological factors. Social identity theory is a widely accepted academic theory from the disciplines of social and cognitive psychology, which uses both qualitative and quantitative research methods. It spans a wide variety of group-related phenomena and variables, providing a sufficient methodological basis for the study of leadership. The social identity model of leadership (SIMOL) describes the social position of group members relative to one another, and thus of the leader(s) relative to other group members. The model also describes the psychological processes that underpin the development of social positions within the group. Although SIMOL does not directly analyze organizational structures (as a sociological study might do), it analyzes the social and psychological processes that underpin such structural developments. It was on this basis that this chapter opened with the proposition that

---

7. A striking case in point are two publications by Clarke, the first investigating the historical component (*Serve the Community of the Church*) and the second the ideological component (*A Pauline Theology of Church Leadership*).

leadership is a dynamic group phenomenon that related to group or social identity.⁸

SIMOL offers a number of ways to integrate various aspects of leadership research into NT studies. First, SIMOL brings innovative research models from social psychology and leadership theory into biblical studies. An independent familiarity with these theories is necessary to apply the model, since applications so far are rare in NT studies. Second, SIMOL has shown that groups and their leaders are very sensitive to social context. Thus, SIMOL benefits from the wealth of socio-historical and cultural information about the first century that has been discovered and analyzed in recent decades; without such information, the social context would remain too undefined to be able to apply SIMOL. Third, SIMOL analyzes the connections between social reality and psychological processes, and thus offers a method to study the interaction between Pauline rhetoric and the social reality he addresses. Hermeneutically, this implies that it is possible to derive socio-historical information from Paul's ideological rhetoric with SIMOL as a guide.

In biblical studies, only a handful of scholars have taken notice of the social identity theory and related theories from social and cognitive psychology. Those who have done so have found that it shed new light on the subject under investigation.⁹ More recently, interest in questions regarding early Christian identity has received a significant impulse from some research projects in Scandinavian countries.¹⁰ The current study fits well within this burgeoning field.

An important aspect of methodology is critical reflection on the personal pre-commitments of the researcher. From the preface, it is evident that this project approaches Paul from the perspective of a sympathetic reader. This will no doubt influence the project along the way. The challenge is not so much to achieve a disinterested point of view, which is generally acknowledged to be impossible,¹¹ but to

---

8. Judge was, as far as I know, the first to apply the term "social identity" to early Christian communities in a seminal essay from 1980 ("The Social Identity of the First Christians," 201–17).

9. Most notably Esler in *Galatians*, and in *Conflict and Identity in Romans*.

10. See for instance Luomanen et al., *Explaining Christian Origins and Early Judaism*; and Holmberg and Winninge, *Identity Formation in the New Testament*.

11. As indicated in the familiar and often repeated phrase that "facts are always theory-laden" (Alvesson and Sköldberg, *Reflexive Methodology*, 6).

account adequately for one's pre-commitments so that they do not as unquestioned presuppositions dictate the results obtained. In many ways, this is in itself an exercise in social identification: does the researcher consider himself as belonging to the types of communities Paul founded? A positive answer indicates that he is predisposed to value Paul's perspective on the social identity of these communities, while a negative answer likewise predisposes the scholar to be critical of Paul's vision of social identity. In our social universe, we only have these two options: to belong to the ingroup or the outgroup, but with varying levels of identification and commitment.[12] The challenge in research is not to seek a detached scholarly stance (which by its very nature implies an outsider perspective), but to reflect adequately on one's own presuppositions and group memberships in order to discern its effect on our scholarly stance. Whether or not a researcher identifies with Paul, the level of scholarship is defined by the level of critical reflection on the historical sources as well as on one's pre-commitments and group memberships, not necessarily by the level of criticism of Paul's vision of social identity.[13]

Definitions

A few matters of definition are needed to keep the discussion clear.

Significant debate surrounds the labels "Jew," "Christian," and "church." In modern usage these labels indicate two distinct religions, but this is hardly what first century "Jews" and "Christians" had in mind. Thus, Esler argues for labels like "Christ-believer" or "Christ-follower" instead of "Christian," which he considers a Latin label by outsiders for Christ-believers. Furthermore, he argues that Ἰουδαῖοι should be translated as the ethnic "Judeans," not as "Jew" with its anachronistic religious overtones, and that ἔθνη should be translated as "foreigner" or, when used by a Judean, as "heathen." The early church

---

12. Shkul takes this kind of argument much further. She discusses the possibility of various reading positions and identifies her own reading of Ephesians as an examination of difficulties in the text as well as in various interpretations, but has no interest in establishing "what *the* meaning of the text is" (Minna Shkul, *Reading Ephesians: Exploring Social Entrepreneurship in the Text*, 76–77).

13. This is a key argument in Alvesson and Sköldberg's presentation of reflexive methodology (*Reflexive Methodology*, 8–10).

is labeled as "Christ-movement."[14] Campbell voices similar concerns and proposes slightly different labels.[15] Runesson, however, argues that modern Jewish and Christian groups are sufficiently continuous with the earlier groups thus labeled, so that the use of the labels "Jew" and "Christian" remains defensible as long as they are situated in the right context.[16] Since this study does not have relationships between Jewish and gentile Christ-believers or between the church and the synagogue as its main subject, these labels are of less importance. Occasionally, "Christ-follower" and "Christ-movement" will be used to avoid prejudging questions about community formation and group identity, while "Jew" and "gentile" will be retained as ethnic markers. The term "Christian" will frequently appear in "Christian social identity" since "the social identity of the Christ-movement" is too cumbersome.

Another matter of definition relates to the distinction between leadership *office* and leadership *position*. Leadership structures may be instituted as a formal organizational office, which is a theoretical organizational slot that a group member (or even an outsider) may occupy, by virtue of which he or she has authority to direct the group. This slot usually involves provisions for appointment, ordination, duration, payment, and abdication in the language of church or canon law. The office and its occupant(s) are generally perceived as divinely legitimated to serve the community.[17] Although office is an important aspect of the Pauline patterns of leadership, it indicates little about the early development of these patterns and is not the exclusive focus of this study. On the other hand, this study frequently refers to certain leaders and their position of social influence within their particular group. Their leadership may be legitimated in various ways and may be exercised with significant social power, so that the leader occupies a definable social position within that group. Interactive group processes between more and less prototypical group members generate this position of influence; the position does not necessarily exist as an abstract slot in the organizational structure apart from such processes. It is possible but not necessary that such a position of social influence

14. Esler, *Conflict and Identity in Romans*, 12–13.

15. Campbell, *Paul and the Creation of Christian Identity*, 12–13.

16. Runesson, "Inventing Christian identity," 64–73.

17. Brockhaus, *Charisma und Amt*, 123; Merklein, *Das kirchliche Amt nach dem Epheserbrief*, 280.

is formalized in the group by some or all of the features that constitute an organizational office. Thus, the study focuses on the social position of leadership, which is a broader category than leadership office.

Finally, in a study on developing leadership, gendered references may be particularly sensitive. As a matter of convention, this study uses the third person masculine form "he" to refer to individuals generically without gender distinction, instead of randomly alternating between "he" and "she" or using the cumbersome "he or she" or even "s/he."

The Plan of the Book

This study proceeds as follows. Chapter 2 reviews the history of scholarship on church leadership. Monepiscopacy was considered the normative pattern of church leadership until the Reformation when the debate divided along denominational lines. Scholars often discovered their own denominational leadership structure in the sources so it was suspected that, in spite of progress in historical research, the debate was often unintentionally guided by denominational ideology. When the debate changed to more social-scientific approaches, the initial result was that sociological models replaced the earlier denominational ideology, projecting modern sociological instead of denominational views onto ancient sources. As social-scientific approaches matured, notably in the area of cultural anthropology, much fruitful research was done on the Mediterranean culture of the first century, analyzing its community and leadership structures. In the last two decades, theories from social and cognitive psychology have been tested to study ancient community structures in their Roman, Jewish, and Christian contexts. This sets the stage for the present study, building on the accomplishments of historical research and on the theoretical advances of social and cognitive psychology, to study leadership as a dynamic group phenomenon.

Chapter 3 presents the particular theoretical model used, the social identity model of leadership (SIMOL). From its origins in the late 1960s, social identity theory has become a broadly accepted research model, spilling over in and connecting with identity research in the fields of organizational psychology, organizational identity and behavior, and sociology. Leadership theory is one of several beneficiaries of this fruitful and continuing expansion.[18] The model is presented in two stages. The first stage presents the concept of social identity, which refers to a person's sense of "us," of belonging to a particular group. Social identities take shape through social comparison, which often center on stereotyped or "prototypical" representatives of these groups. Social identification is a dynamic process in which individuals identify with a particular group, depending on the comparison outgroup and on the characteristics considered prototypical in that situation. The identity narrative of a group provides cohesion over time, enabling members to maintain, deepen or weaken their commitment to the group. Their level of commitment influences to what extent group members conform to group norms for the way they think and behave. The second stage presents leadership as the ability to manage social identity and to embed people in that identity. Leaders *emerge* in a group if they embody the group's values and serve its interests more than other members, i.e. if they are more prototypical than others. Leaders *maintain* their leadership by managing the group's social identity, and by mobilizing and empowering group members so that they become embedded in that identity. Successful leaders are viewed increasingly as charismatic, which earns them the social power to initiate *succession* by similar, prototypical leaders, and which extends their influence beyond their own span of leadership.

Chapters 4 through 8 apply SIMOL to a study of the selected sources, 1–2 Corinthians, Ephesians, and 1–2 Timothy. Each chapter introduces the letter and briefly situates the letter in Paul's ministry. Group and leadership aspects of the letter are studied afresh with social identity theory as an investigative framework to shed new light on the existing debate about patterns of leadership. First, the processes of social identification are surveyed in each letter to discern the group processes taking place (as Paul understood them). Second, the role of the leaders is studied in how they shaped these processes of identification, discussing both local and Pauline leadership. These considerations make it possible, third, to describe more clearly the processes of leadership emergence, leadership maintenance, and leadership succession. This leads finally to conclusions about the patterns of leadership (in terms of people, functions, and norms) at the time of the

---

18. See the textbook: Haslam, Reicher, and Platow, *The New Psychology of Leadership*.

composition of each letter, which can then be fruitfully compared with earlier studies on Pauline patterns of leadership.

As these chapters proceed, the pictures of social identification and of patterns of leadership in Corinth and Ephesus are increasingly developed. In Corinth (chapter 4), the emergence of local leaders in a harmoniously functioning collegial group failed initially. Local leadership became divided because of the formation of subgroups parallel to cultural conventions, which marginalized Paul. Other cultural values caused conflicts of interest between Christian and non-Christian social identities. Even their basic community activities, such as the Lord's Supper and broad participation were threatened by these factors. Paul's letter to correct the situation (1 Corinthians) was probably not effective, since it arrived at about the same time as itinerant Jewish teachers, who responded to the same difficulties by offering a more Jewish vision of social identity (focusing on Moses) and who functioned in a more culturally acceptable leadership model (letters of recommendation, accepting patronage) (chapter 5). Apparently, the local leaders did unite, but around this more Jewish vision of social identity, which almost completely sidelined Paul. Through a personal painful visit, a lost tearful letter, and the mediation of Titus, Paul negotiated reconciliation with the Corinthian church, including restoration of his role as founding apostle and teacher of the gospel. Another letter (2 Corinthians) reflects the content of the negotiations, written just before Paul could personally arrive to put the reconciliation into effect. Paul's confidence in the reconciliation suggests that local leaders had now unitedly rallied to Paul's support, although a few opponents remained. With Paul's apostleship and leadership finally accepted in Corinth, he could serve as model for these united local leaders as their leadership stabilized in Corinth around Paul's gospel and vision of Christian social identity.

The study of Ephesians (chapter 6) begins with a brief review of arguments for Pauline authorship and an Ephesian destination to help locate this letter in its social environment. Paul's stature as charismatically legitimated leader grew especially in Ephesus, as the community observed his successful negotiations in Corinth. This empowered Paul to write from a Roman prison, surrounded by symbols of Roman ideology, to the Ephesian church. From that social and geographical distance, Paul portrayed a stable local leadership subgroup in Ephesus that had established titles and functions, and that was divinely legitimated in their functions of teaching and oversight. Their leaders maintained the unity and cohesion of the community, as they lived out Paul's vision of Christian social identity, which was defined and expanded to empower group members to live out their identity in a context with competing Jewish identities, and Greco-Roman institutions and ideology.

The study of 1–2 Timothy (chapters 7 and 8) required a more extensive review of the debate about their authorship and date, since this significantly affects the socio-historical setting, which is the basis for a social identity analysis. The self-testimony of the letters and their external attestation unanimously point to Pauline authorship. The ancients considered pseudepigraphy forgery and dedicated much of their literary criticism to verifying authorial claims to guard against such deception. The scribal practice of authors to keep personal copies even of their letters, as well as the oral traditions about authorship accompanying 'published' works provided additional safeguards, making it very unlikely that the Pastoral Epistles would have escaped detection if they were non-Pauline. A number of important differences between the Pastorals and Paul's early letters are reviewed next. Recent linguistic theory indicates that the observed literary differences could be classified as a more literary style in the Pastorals compared to a style closer to speech in the earlier Paulines. Theological differences can be credibly attributed to differences in contextualization at Corinth and Ephesus. Historical differences are most likely complementary to the data from Acts and Paul's other epistles. This review is sufficient to warrant the position of the present study that the Pastorals are Pauline and can be situated towards the end of Paul's life and ministry.

After his release from prison, Paul visited Ephesus again and left Timothy as long-term delegate, perhaps because of lessons learned in Corinth (chapter 7). Even though some deviance in leadership remained (unlike the portrayal in Ephesians), Paul instructed Timothy mainly (in 1 Timothy) in how to maintain local leadership, by keeping it aligned with God's mission with the church, and by providing procedures for appointment, payment, and impeachment. This suggests a functioning subgroup of local leaders (the *presbyterion*), functioning on a collegial level with one another, where the main issues are how to provide for their faithful continuity and maintenance, alongside other subgroups (notably widows) who also participate in the community. Paul instructs Timothy in leadership function to provide a model of leadership in a setting where Greco-Roman and Jewish identities continue to compete for influence. It was shown in the concluding summary that 'overseer' and 'elder' referred to the same leader from different perspectives, and that 'overseer' and 'deacon' were fully constituted offices, although they were still mostly connected with the person providing the leadership than with an abstract organizational slot. The role of women in leadership was limited to the household sphere.

Finally, Paul writes Timothy again (2 Timothy), once more from a Roman prison, to effect leadership succession (chapter 8). Paul's high status as apostolic leader raises Timothy's leadership status, because of his close association with and similarity to Paul, a process that Paul intentionally boosts by portraying Timothy's relationship to himself as parallel to Joshua's relationship to Moses. Paul's instructions to Timothy, to teach his gospel to new leaders and to serve as a gentle model to the community in his leadership, do not so much inform Timothy as they provide a model for local leaders as well as an indirect critique of some deviant local leaders. Thus, Paul guides the maintenance and institutes the succession of local leadership through the mediation of Timothy as delegate and successor. Thus, Paul did not write 1–2 Timothy to instruct the recipient, but to vindicate him before his critics and to mobilize the community as well as the critics to accept Timothy. The rhetorical setting of these letters also indicates that they focus on the concerns of the leadership subgroup, not those of the whole church, which explain the use of stereotypes and of household metaphors.

With chapters 4 through 8 thus completed, chapter 9 summarizes the results, compares the leadership patterns in Corinth with those in Ephesus, and offers the conclusions to this study. The comparison suggests several observations that further refine the above picture of the developing patterns of leadership. First, Paul worked generally with whatever cultural forms of leadership were available, but consistently redefined leadership as self-sacrifice for the community in the service of the gospel, aligning it with the beliefs and values of Christian social identity. Second, in both locations local leaders were repeatedly corrected in their construction of Christian social identity and their leadership, although tension and damage from Jewish teachers and Greco-Roman identity were more severe in Corinth than later in Ephesus. Third, the Corinthian and Ephesian communities both developed a similar pattern of collegial leadership, although the available evidence indicates stages of leadership emergence in Corinth and stages of leadership maintenance and succession in Ephesus. It will be argued that this is to be interpreted as successive stages of leadership formation in Paul's Aegean mission. Fourth, the charismatic leadership, increasingly attributed to Paul as his communities observed his successful identity management gave him the social power to guide the maintenance and succession of local leadership in Ephesus through Timothy's agency, steps that were impossible earlier in Corinth although 1 Clement suggests this occurred in Corinth as well.

These final observations lead to the conclusion that Paul attempted to establish some uniform patterns of leadership for his churches, and that he was already partially successful in his efforts. Thus, the thesis of this study is that Paul instituted uniform patterns of leadership for those levels of leadership, which sustained the consistent communication of Paul's gospel in each community in alignment with other churches in the Pauline network. Paul advocated such uniform patterns as cross-cultural norm to enhance the future stability and cohesion of the Christ-following communities and their social identity. It is doubtful that the specific historical structures and titles were also intended as a cross-cultural norm, although many scholars read Paul this way. Moreover, Paul's practice of succession through Timothy may well have encouraged the development of monepiscopacy. However, it is doubtful that the later hierarchical developments, so natural in the Roman world, fully reflect Paul's intentions for his communities.

2

The Ideological Challenge of Church Leadership Studies

LEADERS HAVE A DISPROPORTIONATELY LARGE INFLUENCE IN A GROUP and exercise significant control over the group's identity. Indeed, leadership and authority are an integral part of group identity, which explains why Christian communities have always shown such keen interest in these features of their community life. It is no surprise then, that leadership, authority, and office have been and continue to be hotly debated issues, not merely as a matter of scholarly pursuit, but as a way of clarifying, justifying, and protecting the identity of one's Christian community in a pluralistic, competitive world.

This chapter tells the story of this long-standing debate by reviewing a representative selection of scholarly studies on church leadership patterns and their development. The review will trace the development of the debate, which showed significant traces of denominational ideology until the middle of the 20th century. The advent of social-scientific studies in the 1970's led to an increasing diversity of contributions from linguistic, sociological, cultural, and psychological perspectives, in which ideology was disconnected from denominational loyalties. This diversity in leadership studies testifies to the fragmented nature of the current debate, with few attempts to integrate these findings into a homogeneous picture of leadership development in the early church. The current state of the debate suggests to many scholars that the reconstruction of a homogeneous leadership structure originated mainly from denominational ideology, while the historical evidence testifies instead to an original diversity.

It is too soon, however, to conclude that uniform leadership structures represent an ideological fiction, over against an original diversity in the historical sources. In the attempt to chart differences and similarities in leadership patterns from one location and time to another, discontinuities as well as continuities are discernable. Local or temporal diversity does not necessarily exclude the possibility of translocal homogeneous development, nor does a measure of homogeneous development exclude the possibility of local variation. Recent trends in sociological and psychological research on identity provide ways to distinguish ideological from social factors and to study their interaction in historical sources. This chapter tells the story of the debate up to that point. The remaining chapters continue the story, but with a more comprehensive approach to study the interaction of social and ideological factors in developing patterns of leadership.

Beginnings

From the very start, authority and leadership were key issues in early Christian communities. Paul vigorously defended his authority on several occasions, while the Pastoral Epistles advocated the selection and appointment of qualified overseers/elders and deacons by one of Paul's trusted associates. By the end of the first century, traditions had arisen about the apostolic appointment of bishops (*1 Clement* 42–44), while over the next several centuries, debate ensued whether the apostles considered *presbyteros* and *episkopos* to be interchangeable terms.[1] Throughout this period, the apostolic authority of duly appointed church leaders functioned as guarantee of the trustworthiness of the gospel message these leaders proclaimed. From the fourth century onwards, beliefs about the primacy of the Roman bishop emerged, providing a vision of hierarchical leadership that formed the basis for the construction of church office for over a millennium.

Modern Historical Scholarship and Denominational Ideology

Since the Reformation, Protestant scholars vigorously debated the question of the origins of church office. They paid increasing attention to extra-biblical leadership patterns from which church offices could have derived. In 1696, Campegius Vitringa traced the origins

---

1. See Lightfoot's discussion of Irenaeus and Maier's discussion of Jerome (Lightfoot, *Philippians*, 228–29; Maier, *Social Setting*, 1).

of church office to the synagogue.² Two centuries later, Edwin Hatch argued that the office of *presbyter* had some Jewish roots, but that it paralleled more closely the office of a presiding officer of the *collegia*, the ancient voluntary associations.³ Adolf von Harnack suggested that the Christian use of *presbyter* derived from the synagogue, while the Christian use of *bishop* arose more or less spontaneously from several sources such as the Septuagint and municipal administrations.⁴ Additional debate surrounded the relationship between the offices of *presbyter* and *bishop*. Joseph Lightfoot proposed that initially the terms referred to the same officer, while the bishop arose from the midst of the elders as their presiding officer.⁵ Harnack, on the other hand, claimed that the authority of the apostles was transferred to the local bishop by way of apostolic succession.⁶

Evaluating the rise of church office more critically, Heinrich Holtzmann contrasted the church organization in the uncontested Pauline letters with the one represented in 1 Timothy. The letters to Corinth portrayed a fluid manifestation of the Spirit's powers, devoid of settled leadership relationships, while 1 Timothy spoke of the *presbyterion* as a closed college of elders. Holtzmann described this contrast as an original law-free Paulinism ("ursprünglich gesetzesfreie Paulinismus") that was later overshadowed by the legalistic Christianity ("gesetzlichen Christentum") of the Apostolic Fathers. The freer organizational forms of Greco-Roman associations were replaced by stricter Jewish synagogue structures.⁷ In 1892, Rudolph Sohm expanded Holtzmann's position by arguing for an original charismatic church order that was later replaced by the threefold ministry of bishop, elders, and deacons to protect the church against false prophets and safeguard the purity of the eucharist.⁸ Holtzmann and Sohm observed the dialectic between spirit and structure, as Harnack had

---

2. Vitringa, *De synagoga vetere libri tres*, 467ff. and 609ff. as cited in Maier, *Social Setting*, 10.

3. Hatch, *Organization of the Early Christian Churches*, 26–54.

4. Harnack, *The Constitution and Law of the Church*, 58.

5. Lightfoot, *Philippians*, 192–96.

6. Harnack, *Constitution*, 58, 124–25.

7. Holtzmann, *Die Pastoralbriefe*, 203.

8. Sohm, *Kirchenrecht I*, 28–51, as cited by Maier, *Social Setting*, 3.

also recognized,⁹ but they neglected evidence for leadership structure in the early Pauline letters as well as evidence for charisma in the later epistles. Unaware of their denominational ideology, they pictured historical development as structure replacing the Spirit, which they interpreted in terms of the theological antithesis between gospel and law, or between Paul's law-free and (Jewish) legalistic Christianity. Harnack criticized Sohm's understanding of the relationship between religion and law as superficial, wondering how Sohm's concept of the church as "a purely religious and spiritual entity" devoid of any earthly realities, "can then be anything but *a mere idea, in which each individual Christian in his isolation believes.*"¹⁰ Harnack's insistence that *"the social and corporate element cannot be sundered from the sublimest conception of the Church"*¹¹ anticipates the later applications of social-scientific analysis in biblical scholarship by almost a century.

Ecclesiastical interests are readily apparent. The Holtzmann-Sohm hypothesis, with its development from charisma to office, became entrenched in German scholarship. The German Lutheran Hans von Campenhausen (1953) and the Swiss Reformed Eduard Schweizer (1959)¹² suggested that the later ecclesiastical development of the threefold ministry formed a departure from an original apostolic church order. This reflects Sohm's classic analysis of Catholicism as a development from original Christianity (one suspects he saw this as the pre-cursor of Lutheranism) towards ecclesiastical law and legal structures. British scholarship with its Anglican orientation generally took a much friendlier view of church office, defending monepiscopacy as the normative church order at the close of the apostolic age.¹³ Roman Catholic scholars defended their tradition by arguing for a more unified development of ecclesiastical authority,¹⁴ often on

---

9. "The whole constitutional history of the Church can also be represented with the conflict between spirit and office as its framework" (Harnack, *Constitution*, 43).

10. Ibid., 210–11 (emphasis original).

11. Ibid., 213–14 (emphasis original). For more extended criticism, see pp. 242ff.

12. Campenhausen, *Ecclesiastical Authority and Spiritual Power*; Schweizer, *Church Order in the NT*.

13. E.g. Gore, *The Church and the Ministry*; Dix, "The Ministry in the Early Church," 183–303.

14. E.g. Schnackenburg, *Kirche im Neuen Testament*; Hainz, *Ekklesia*.

theological grounds.[15] Holtzmann and Sohm were not the only ones influenced by their denominational ideology.

Some scholars resisted the ideological implications of the debate. Anglican scholar Burnett Hillman Streeter (1929) noted the tendency for each scholar to "discover" his own ecclesiastical tradition in the sources and claimed instead that developments were so diverse in different regions and at different times that it was impossible to speak of an apostolic church order.[16] Streeter believed that this removed a major obstacle for the ecumenical movement in which he was involved. Hans Küng, the well known Roman Catholic rebel, adopted a version of the Holtzmann-Sohm hypothesis to diminish the emphasis on the primacy of Rome, also desiring to open ecumenical doors from Rome to other traditions.[17] This line of reasoning was taken up by Dutch theologian Geurt Smink, who advocated openness to monepiscopacy with worldwide ecclesiastical structures, quite revolutionary for the Reformed churches he represented.[18] While many scholars interpreted the evidence for church office in defense of their own ecclesiastical tradition, these authors interpreted the same evidence as a cause for relativizing their own tradition in order to build ecumenical bridges to other traditions. These scholars recognized the role of denominational ideology in the debate and countered it by an ecumenical ideology of their own. Ideology was not brought to the surface as an explicit part of research, but remained more or less hidden behind the historical argumentation being offered, which resulted in a stalemate between various denominational and ecumenical positions.

The Turn to the Social Sciences

In this stalemate, the Holtzmann-Sohm hypothesis often represented the scholarly consensus for much of the 20th century debate on church order.[19] This is by no means the self-evident outcome of the described ecclesiastical debate. Several factors combined to give this hypothesis such a dominant status. First, from 1831 onwards, Ferdinand Christian

---

15. Sullivan, *From Apostles to Bishops*, esp. 217–30.
16. Streeter, *The Primitive Church*, 75–76.
17. See Küng, *Strukturen der Kirche*, and many of his later works as well.
18. Smink, *Het kerkelijk ambt naar een nieuw paradigma*.
19. See Brockhaus, *Charisma und Amt*, 7–94.

Baur's approach to early Christianity left a legacy where development was seen in terms of conflict and opposition, often between Christianity as a universal, spiritual religion and particularistic, legalistic Judaism.[20] This conflict scenario was adapted towards a more pluralistic vision in Walter Bauer's famous *Orthodoxy and Heresy* (1934), which continues to exercise significant influence in British and American scholarship through the 1971 English translation.[21] These influences provided a scholarly environment within which the Holtzmann-Sohm hypothesis continued to thrive. Second, the rise of pseudepigraphy as the majority scholarly opinion for the authorship of the Pastoral Epistles has reinforced the consistent later dates for leadership structures as required by the Holtzmann-Sohm hypothesis. Numerous monographs on the Pastoral Epistles thus take this hypothesis as the historical reference point against which their own research must be measured.[22] Third, in an ironic accident of history Sohm's views on charisma have been absorbed and transformed by Max Weber in his sociological analysis of authority and institutionalization,[23] which in turn has greatly influenced the first wave of social-scientific studies on early Christian conceptions of church office. Even though Weber altered Sohm's conception of charisma, the denominational ideology present in the Holtzmann-Sohm hypothesis became part of these new sociological approaches. Thus, early in the 20th century the Holtzmann-Sohm hypothesis emerged as the scholarly consensus in studies on church office and frequently functioned as the assumed reference point for further research. Its influence is still felt today, although it is now strongly contested.

John Schütz is critical of Weber in his landmark study on Paul's authority. He focuses on why and how authority is exercised, and locates authority in a group process where both the person exercising authority and those subordinating themselves to it desire to be

---

20. See Campbell, *Paul and the Creation of Christian Identity*, 15–17.

21. Bauer, *Orthodoxy and Heresy in Earliest Christianity*.

22. Monographs by Aageson (2008), Fiore (1986), Merz (2004), Richards (2002) and Verner (1983) are among them. They will be discussed in more detail in chapters 7 and 8 on 1–2 Timothy.

23. See Weber's remarks about Sohm in Weber, *Wirtschaft und Gesellschaft*, 124 and 753–54. Haley demonstrates "the magnitude of Weber's intellectual debt to Sohm, and . . . how Weber's generalization of it has yielded a vastly altered idea of charisma" (Haley, "Rudolph Sohm on Charisma," 185).

part of the group and willingly acknowledge a different status for the authority.[24] Schütz criticizes Weber for confusing power, authority, and legitimacy, which Schütz believes to be the coordinates that locate the apostolic office in the communities of the early church.[25] Thus, Schütz adopts Weber critically, while situating authority in the context of the community.

Bengt Holmberg adapts and enhances Weber's views. Holmberg proposes that local leadership consisted of a group of teachers and another group with sufficient wealth to accommodate church meetings and traveling missionaries, but he sees no trace of the supposed opposition between charisma and office.[26] Holmberg is critical of Weber's idea that the charisma of the founder is incorporated only in later institutional structures, since basic community structures are already evident in the charismatic community.[27] Most significantly, Holmberg identifies the fallacy of idealism, which he defines as the mistaken view that theology and ideas are the sole and sufficient cause for social structures; instead, he advocates an historical approach that acknowledges the dialectical relationship between theology and the social structures in which theology is located,[28] echoing Harnack's criticism of Sohm. Holmberg's study thus presents a sound critique of the Holtzmann-Sohm hypothesis in his adaptation of Weber, and he points out that ideology was an important but often unacknowledged influence in much earlier research.

Margaret MacDonald, the third and last author to mention here, incorporates at least five major sociological and anthropological methodologies to study institutionalization in Pauline churches.[29] She argues, among other things, that the basic structures of the household were already visible in the early days of Paul's churches, and that the second and third generations institutionalized these structures in household codes (Colossians/Ephesians) and church offices (Pastorals). She is mildly critical of the Holtzmann-Sohm hypothesis, but in the

24. Schütz, *Paul and the Anatomy of Apostolic Authority*, 11.
25. Ibid., 20–21.
26. Holmberg, *Paul and Power*, 116–21.
27. Ibid., 146–47.
28. Ibid., 201–4. The significance of the book is acknowledged by its 2004 Wipf & Stock reprint.
29. MacDonald, *The Pauline Churches*.

main, she accepts it as the unquestioned historical-critical consensus and simply fleshes out its developmental scenario. Unfortunately, she benefits little from Schütz's and Holmberg's earlier criticism of Weber.[30] Moreover, she applies the church-sect model, which is derived from the study of how Protestant sects broke away from the "mother church," anachronistically to the much different social context of the first century church,[31] but that is an understandable risk of new methods.

Thus, the early application of social science approaches yielded new approaches, but often the dominance of the Holtzmann-Sohm hypothesis merely transformed earlier denominational ideologies into newer sociological ideology. The increasing awareness of the ideological factor in the debate was a welcome development, along with the rising stream of criticism of the Holtzmann-Sohm hypothesis. However, the risk of anachronistic interpretations also increased with the advent of modern sociological models and a better methodological focus on the first century was needed.

Rethinking Leadership in Terms of the First Century

First Century Community Structures

During the 1980s, cultural anthropological approaches revolutionized the study of the first century world,[32] resulting in a wealth of information about ancient communities and their leaders. First, it is now generally acknowledged that the ancient household provided both the physical and organizational structures for Paul's churches, even though analogous leadership patterns were visible in the synagogue or in associations.[33] Some debate continues about whether the Pastorals indicate a transfer of the supreme authority of the householder to his

---

30. Brockhaus, who also offers an excellent exegetical criticism of the Holtzmann-Sohm hypothesis, is not even listed in her bibliography (see *Charisma und Amt*, 210–18).

31. Holmberg, *Sociology and the New Testament*, 108–14.

32. Malina's 1981 *The New Testament World* is the classical introduction in this field.

33. Gehring, *House Church and Mission*, 196–210, and 192.

leadership role in the church,[34] but this depends on the social context proposed for these letters.

Second, the role of elder is now recognized to be largely an honorary function in a community, based on seniority and status within the family or other group, and not necessarily based on a defined office.[35] Initially, church leaders served in the honorary role of elder while functioning as overseer of their house church, but by the time of the Pastorals these elders functioned collectively as a college.[36]

Third, the synagogue still appears as a major influence on church organization. The structure of a bishop with assisting deacons and a college of elders paralleled synagogue structures, even though the nomenclature for the offices differed.[37] This, however, reflected a typical Jewish practice to differentiate themselves from other groups, even when basic community structures were similar. These synagogue structures could be readily adapted to the Greco-Roman world, since diaspora synagogues were thoroughly Hellenized.[38]

Fourth, patronage is now often seen as a basic social structure in early Christian leadership, although its values were contested. The Corinthian problems of status, honor, and divisions, manifested a cultural application of patronage in leadership,[39] which Paul corrected by presenting a different leadership model.[40] Leaders were to behave as benefactors, expecting nothing in return, and were to participate in the life of the community, unlike the patron in other forms of ancient association. Such different leader behavior may well have occasioned disrespect from group members, unlike the honor they would have normally bestowed on patrons.[41]

---

34. Verner, *The Household of God*, 148–52, and 182.
35. Campbell, *The Elders*, 131.
36. Gehring, *House Church and Mission*, 279–80.
37. Burtchaell, *Synagogue*, 228–338.
38. See Clarke, *Serve the Community*, 166–67.
39. Chow, *Patronage and Power*, 113–66.
40. Clarke, *Leadership in Corinth*, 109–28
41. Schmeller, *Hierarchie und Egalität*, 61–62.

First Century Leadership Practice

While socio-historical studies situated leadership more firmly in the context of first century community structures, several literary studies refocused the study of leadership in terms of first century leadership practice.

The role of leadership example in Paul's letters compares well with similar usage in ancient kingship literature, hortatory letters, and the Socratic letters. These documents generally present a senior official instructing his juniors in how to carry out their duty and usually claim a broader application than only the immediate occasion. This compares especially well with the role of Timothy and Titus as Paul's juniors in the Pastoral Letters.[42]

The evaluation of a leader's character plays a prominent role in ancient leadership practice. The *cura morum* referred to censoring or inspecting the lives of subordinate leaders in order to maintain their integrity and wholesomeness.[43] The maxims of the Delphic Canon contained ethical instruction for the *epheboi*, young men preparing for leadership.[44] Such leadership evaluation used character or quality lists that were familiar in many parts of the ancient world. Thus, character lists like the ones in 1 Tim 3 and Titus 1 would have been familiar to many Christ-followers, especially to their leaders.

Another key dimension of ancient leadership is succession, which can be defined as the passing of a particular object of succession from a predecessor to a successor, along with a desired result. A father may pass his inheritance to his sons in order to provide for his family; a philosopher may pass his teaching to his friends in order to assist them in leading virtuous lives or he may pass the leadership of his school to a trusted disciple in order to provide for continuity in teaching and continued institutional vitality.[45] Seen in this light, the Pastoral Epistles would have been received as leadership succession documents.

These studies of ancient leadership practice complement the earlier studies of leadership structure. These studies have unearthed a wealth of socio-historical information, which is increasingly difficult to

---

42. Fiore, *The Function of Personal Example*, 76–77, 193–95.
43. Paschke, "The *cura morum* of the Roman Censors," 117–19.
44. Harrison, "Paul and the Gymnasiarchs, 177–78.
45. Stepp, *Leadership Succession*, 18–59.

integrate. With a healthy caution, if not a suspicion towards ideological motives, many scholars refrain from suggesting such an integrated, uniform pattern of leadership and simply observe the variety in organizational and leadership structures evident in Paul's communities.[46]

Authority and Ideology in a Group Context

The initial turn to the social sciences had now borne fruit in more specific studies on first century communities and their leadership. Increasing awareness of the role of ideology in leadership studies, as well as new developments in social theory, opened up new ways to study NT leadership the interaction of power, authority, and ideology.

Paul turns out to be a skilled power broker. Elisabeth Castelli discerns in Paul's language of imitation an asymmetrical power relationship with his churches, in which Paul "*claims* the position of the privileged speaker for these nascent Christian communities." In light of Foucault's deconstruction of power, she interprets this claim as a totalitarian principle that suppresses all other truth claims as deviant.[47] She resists this totalitarian principle by dismissing Paul's authorial intent, which she considers a legitimate hermeneutical maneuver; she argues instead against Paul's call for unity and pleads for openness to diversity.[48] Castelli may be credited for discerning the ideological force of Paul's claim to authority, but appears unaware of the ideology that motivates her own disagreement with Paul.

Sandra Hack Polaski also studies Paul's language of power, focusing on his apostolic call and his use of the concept of grace. "Couched in the language of 'grace', Paul claims an unassailable position of power, an authority over his correspondents, which is his alone precisely *because* he is the subject of the undeserved favor of a powerful God."[49] Polaski is more willing than Castelli to accept the legitimacy of Paul's claim to power.[50] Curiously, both Castelli and Polaski are sensitive

---

46. Clarke, Serve the Community, 207. This parallels the development of practical theology as a discipline in its own right, in response to the crisis of authority experienced in the 60's and 70's in the West, as described for instance by Heitink, Praktische theologie, 14–15.

47. Castelli, Imitating Paul, 14–15, 28–42. The quote is from p. 36.

48. Ibid., 119, 32.

49. Polaski, Paul and the Discourse of Power, 122.

50. Copan likewise interprets Paul's use of power as beneficial for the spiritual

to Paul's claims of authority and show how Paul uses his authority to present his beliefs as group ideology to urge group members to comply. Yet, they do not take the group context sufficiently into account, nor do they give an adequate account of their own ideological stance in overturning or respecting Paul's ideology; they appear to be influenced by a particular attitude toward feminist concerns.[51] A social identity perspective suggests that agreement with Paul's leadership and group ideology qualifies one as ingroup member of Paul's communities, while disagreement reveals one's position as a deviant or even outgroup member, a suggestion that portrays the delicate relationships between Paul, NT scholarship, and various group ideologies—but this is getting ahead of the analysis.

David Stagaman's analysis of power shifts the focus from authority as something that a leader uses to authority as a form of social practice that binds leader and followers together in a community. Authority and power can be abused, but this practice of authority gives the community its identity.[52] A similar perspective is proposed by Kathy Ehrensperger, who completed the most comprehensive investigation of Paul's dynamics of power to date. In Pauline communities, power is used so "that those members of the Christ-movement who have become Christ-followers through Paul be empowered to grow and deepen in their understanding and embodiment of the message of the gospel." Power as empowerment, based on trust, emerges as a core dimension, while power that dominates in order to maintain control or to protect one's position out of self-interest "is not true to the message they proclaim."[53] If authority, then, serves to undergird the identity of the community, it does so by empowering members to absorb and abide by the community's ideology as represented by its authority.

These studies point out how power and authority relate to ideology in a group context. The analysis can be advanced by extending it to the whole Pauline corpus, since even Ehrensperger's comprehensive

---

growth of the addressees (*Saint Paul as Spiritual Director*, 182–218).

51. Similarly, Ehrensperger critiques Polaski's discussion of Paul's use of power as a discussion still based on a theological instead of a social reading of Paul's language of grace; however, Ehrensperger does not refer to a group context (ancient or modern) within which theology plays its role (*Paul and the Dynamics of Power*, 65–67).

52. Stagaman, *Authority in the Church*, 31–35. The quote is from p. 37. See also Turner, "Explaining the Nature of Power," 18.

53. Ehrensperger, *Paul and the Dynamics of Power*, 197–98.

study only dealt with Paul's uncontested letters. The issues become more complex in the Pastoral Epistles with their considerable claims to power, but this is to be expected since they closely reflect ancient leadership practice as outlined above. Ideology plays a central role in these epistles, since either Paul claimed authority to safeguard the gospel he taught or else a later generation claimed his authority to defend their particular interpretation of Paul's heritage. Both scenarios assume competition from individuals or groups making similar authority claims. Clearly, authority is used to buttress or undermine certain ideological truth claims, an aspect of leadership that the current project must also take into account.

While some scholars focused on power and ideology, others applied group and leadership theory to the Pauline corpus. An early attempt at integrating group theory into biblical studies is Alfred Schreiber's commentary on 1 Corinthians, which described group and leadership formation in the Corinthian congregation.[54] Only a few years later, Allen Chapple was the first to combine group and leadership theory in a study of NT leadership, devoting most of his dissertation to a detailed exegesis of 1 Thess 5:14–22, 1 Cor 16:15–18, and Phil 1:1, 4:2–3.[55] His method remains unparalleled, although his unpublished results have since been confirmed in other studies.

Several other studies use leadership (but not group) theory, and are less successful than Chapple in their analysis. Brian Dodd sets out to study Paul's missionary leadership, and finds that few studies offer a thorough examination of leadership in terms of "succession planning, organizational management, management of personnel and finance, vision casting and goal setting."[56] However, he fails to develop an adequate leadership theory so that his study is mainly a theological exposition of Paul's leadership principles, with a selection of texts based apparently on preconceived notions of leadership. John Hiigel appears equally reluctant to use leadership theory in his study on leadership in Corinth. In his socio-historical study, he interacts neither with ancient nor with modern models of leadership, but simply draws out seven defining categories for leadership from an initial survey of 1 Corinthians. Since the model of leadership is drawn directly from the

---

54. Schreiber, *Die Gemeinde in Korinth*, 12–32.
55. Chapple, "Local Leadership."
56. Dodd, *Paul's Paradigmatic "I"*, 13–14.

main source being studied without further methodological argument, this essentially begs the question about the nature and definition of leadership.[57] Studies such as these effectively contain any discussion of Pauline patterns of leadership to the already known (or preconceived) contours of his theology.

Efrain Agosto offers a better basis of leadership theory with his review of Weber, Greenleaf, and a few other theorists, while he is careful to situate the leadership of Jesus and Paul in their first century Greco-Roman context.[58] Remarkably, he argues that Paul's letters in their entirety are an exercise in leadership. Agosto thus advances previous research on leadership, although his leadership theory is not fully convincing and he only studies Paul's undisputed letters, content to repeat the Holtzmann-Sohm hypothesis in a few comments on the Pastoral Epistles.[59]

Surprisingly, the best use of group and leadership theory to date is in Philip Esler's commentary on Romans. Esler raises the question of Paul's authority in Rome, since Paul wrote Romans presumably to influence Roman believers towards some course of action even though he had not founded the community.[60] For this, Esler turns to the social identity theory of leadership, which assists him in understanding various aspects of Romans as an exercise of leadership in Rome. For instance, Paul is seen to establish common ground with the Roman believers in Rom 1 and 16, while the "I" voice in Rom 7 positions Paul as model and spokesman for Jewish and gentile believers whose Christian experience he exemplifies.[61] Thus, Esler characterizes Romans as Paul's bid for leadership in Rome.[62] Although not intended as a contribution to the debate about patterns of church leadership, Esler's commentary on Romans offers one of the best models to date of an integrated methodology that includes ancient historical data, an up-to-date and independent acquaintance

---

57. See Hiigel, *Leadership in 1 Corinthians*, 5–7.
58. Agosto, *Servant Leadership: Jesus and Paul*, 3–7.
59. Ibid., 209.
60. Esler, *Conflict and Identity in Romans*, 33ff.
61. See Ibid., chapters 5, 6 and 10.
62. Ibid., 138, 96 and 226. See also Barentsen, "Pre-Pauline Leadership in the Roman Church," 589–610.

with suitable social science methods, and the exegesis of a complete text instead of only a few selections.

This section shows that adequate group and leadership theories bring new appreciation for Paul's letters not just as containing a few nuggets of information about leadership, but as in themselves instruments of leadership. The letters may be studied for evidence of leadership structure and leadership style, but their intention was to establish, affirm or correct social structures in the communities addressed; that is, Paul exercised his leadership, at least in part, through his letters. Paul's letters were ideological tools to bring about the social change needed to develop his communities and their leadership according to his own vision of Christian social identity. This opens up new approaches to study the development of leadership patterns in Paul's churches.

The Challenge to Integrate Social and Ideological Factors

This chapter reviewed scholarly studies on church leadership patterns and their development. Many puzzling pieces of Paul's developing patterns of leadership have been assembled and studied, and the variety of leadership aspects discovered can at times be overwhelming. Now that the Holtzmann-Sohm hypothesis, which provided a standardized pattern of historical development, has mostly faded, Streeter's proposal of an original variety of structures and offices seems to have been ahead of its time. Undoubtedly, additional pieces of the historical puzzle of NT leadership remain to be discovered, but another approach is required and is now possible[63] to arrange the already assembled puzzle pieces into a coherent overall portrait.

Such integration is far from simple. One of the most accomplished researchers in the field, Andrew Clarke, provides an overview of Pauline leadership in two separate stages. His first full-fledged study of church leadership compared the church with organization and leadership structures in ancient communities—only a final chapter dealt with issues of leadership style such as authority and ministry as service.[64] His second full-fledged study investigates Paul's theology or

---

63. Clarke, *Leadership in Corinth*, xiv–xvii, also notes this potential in his 2006 preface to the second edition.

64. Clarke, *Serve the Community*.

style of leadership thematically by studying the titles, status, power, task, and tools of leadership.⁶⁵ Clarke contributes significantly to the study of ancient leadership, but his separate studies on leadership structure and leadership style demonstrate the difficulty of integrating the data. It is indeed difficult to integrate issues of structure and style, for the former is usually analyzed in terms of sociology or anthropology, the latter in terms of theology or ideology. Clarke's studies, then, do not present a fully integrated perspective, but rather a juxtaposition of the social and ideological perspectives.

This study advances the debate by analyzing the social and ideological components of ancient leadership patterns in their group context. It was shown above that ancient leadership structures and the ancient practice of leadership have received significant attention. It also became evident that authority and ideology in the context of community have become explicit subjects of research, which reflects a growing awareness that "historical investigation should self-critically engage in discerning and peeling off the influence from ideological perspectives and time-bound ideas."⁶⁶ SIMOL provides the investigative framework within which these aspects can be analyzed in an integrative fashion in self-critical fashion. This is the subject of the next chapter.

---

65. Clarke, *A Pauline Theology of Church Leadership*, 1–7 and later chapters.

66. Holmberg, "The First Hundred Years of Christian Identity," 30. Although Holmberg uses 'ideology' in a more pejorative sense of a dominant belief system that hinders objectivity, his point about ideological bias in reconstructing early Christian identity is well-taken. Moreover, this use of 'ideology' still relates to a group context, now to be located within the circles of modern NT scholarship rather than in ancient Pauline communities.

3

The Social Identity Model of Leadership

MOST OF THE PRELIMINARY GROUND HAS NOW BEEN COVERED. Chapter 1 presented the project, its approach, and limitations. Chapter 2 provided a history of research, which showed that group and leadership theories need to complement socio-historical studies to be able to chart the development of leadership patterns in the Pauline churches at Corinth and Ephesus. This chapter presents the methodology to be used, the social identity approach.

The chapter begins with the foundations of the social identity approach. These include the origin and basic concepts that provide an overview of the position this theory occupies within the larger field to which it belongs. The application of such a social-scientific method in biblical studies raises some issues that will be addressed briefly. Next, the approach is presented as an heuristic model that will be used in the succeeding chapters to analyze the Pauline correspondence to Corinth and Ephesus. This model consists of three stages. The first stage reviews a number of processes of social identification in a community. The second stage presents leadership as the hard and often competitive work of managing the social identity of the group. The third stage explains how leadership patterns develop as a result of the identity management of the more influential members of the group.

Foundations of the Social Identity Approach

Already in 1983, Thomas Best argued that scholars who use a social-scientific approach, must move beyond a favorite-teacher or most-interesting-theory approach, and look instead for the best theory in a particular field.[1] Thus, it is necessary to present an independent

1. Best, "The Sociological Study of the New Testament," 191.

overview of the field from which the selected method derives; it is not sufficient merely to adapt a theory that other NT scholars have also used. This chapter, therefore, reviews the social identity model of leadership from a study of its primary sources.

The Origins of the Approach

During the late 1960's and early 1970's the discipline of social psychology was in crisis. Both insiders and outsiders criticized the scientific status, methodological adequacy, testing procedures, and the societal applicability of social psychology.[2] One area of difficulty was the study of groups, which had only been studied as a collection of individuals without recognizing the effect that group membership had on individual behavior. This led to a loss of interest in group dynamics. The resolution to this crisis led to multiple research programs and to the resurrection of the group. A major European response resulted in the social identity approach, while a significant American response resulted in the social cognition approach.

Henri Tajfel (1919–82), of Polish-Jewish heritage, is considered the originator of the social identity theory. His survival of the holocaust led him to initial insights into group membership.[3] Shortly after assuming a chair in social psychology at Bristol (UK), Tajfel introduced the concept of social identity in a study of discrimination. He conducted his famous minimal group experiments in which participants were assigned to two groups based on very minimal criteria (for instance, the toss of a coin or shirt color). He discovered that when people categorized themselves as group member, their behavior changed to favor individuals they now considered fellow group members and to discriminate against others who were considered to be members of other groups. It became evident that group behavior was more than an

---

2. Hogg and Grieve, "Social Identity Theory and the Crisis of Confidence in Social Psychology," 79–80.

3. Reicher, "Biography of Henri Tajfel (1919–1982)." Tajfel survived German prisoner-of-war camps because the Germans never discovered his Jewish identity. "These experiences shaped his subsequent career in three ways. First, he developed an abiding interest in prejudice; second, he recognised that his fate was tied entirely to his group identity; third, he understood that the Holocaust was not a product of psychology but of the way in which psychological processes operate within a given social and political context."

addition of individual psychological processes.⁴ "Groups are not only external features of the world, they are also internalized so that they contribute to a person's sense of self."⁵

Social identity theory began as an intergroup theory that focused on the dynamics between groups. Further questions arose about why people define themselves as member of one instead of another group and how social identification produces consensus and social action. In response to these questions, John C. Turner, one of Tajfel's doctoral students and early colleagues, developed self-categorization theory in the 1980s.⁶ Using the resources of cognitive psychology, Turner hypothesized that one's self-concept can be defined along a sliding scale ranging from personal to social identity. Towards one end of the scale, individuals categorize themselves in terms of their personal identity and interact with others on the basis of a personal relationship. Towards the other end of the scale, individuals categorize themselves in terms of a social identity and interact with others on the basis on their common or different group membership. In each social context, individuals 'switch' to the relevant identity. When individuals align themselves with several others as members of a common group, group behavior becomes possible.⁷

As a sign of strength, the social identity approach by Tajfel and Turner crossed over into organizational psychology with a seminal essay in 1989 by Ashforth, professor of management and Mael, then a doctoral candidate in industrial psychology.⁸ In 2001 Haslam, professor of social and organizational psychology at Exeter (UK), and one of Turner's former doctoral students, authored the first full scale textbook on organizational psychology from a social identity perspective. Although the book seemed premature to some, experimental work

4. Tajfel, *Differentiation between Social Groups*, 101ff. For a collection of Tajfel's work, see Tajfel, *Human Groups and Social Categories*. For a celebration of his work, see Robinson, *Social Groups and Identities: Developing the Legacy of Henri Tajfel*.

5. Haslam and Ellemers, "Social Identity in Industrial and Organizational Psychology, 41.

6. Turner, "Cognitive Redefinition of the Social Group"; Turner et al., *Rediscovering the Social Group*.

7. Alexander Haslam, *Psychology in Organizations*, 19 ff. The situation is actually more complex. For more sophisticated models, see Worchel et al., "A Multidimensional Model of Identity," and Capozza and Brown, "New Trends in Theory and Research," 184–85.

8. Ashforth and Mael, "Social Identity Theory and the Organization," 20–39.

advanced so significantly in the new millennium that a revised second edition was published only 3 years later.⁹ The book covers a wide range of organizational topics, of which leadership, conflict management, and power are the most relevant for this study. Each chapter reviews the history of research on a particular topic in organizational studies to demonstrate how social identity theory resolves earlier difficulties and provides theoretical advances. Social identity research and theorizing represent a robust scholarly discipline, and continue to generate fruitful lines of research in new areas of study.

The cross-over into organizational psychology was remarkable considering the different research styles in each discipline. Social psychology preferred the carefully controlled laboratory for quantitative experimental analysis, while organizational psychology depended on field surveys and qualitative studies of organizational functions. Yet, social psychology has its proponents for more qualitative research, among whom Tajfel earns a prominent place.¹⁰ This diversification of methods presents an opportunity for the use the social identity approach in historical research, which is dependent largely on qualitative research.

A key reason for selecting the social identity approach as research framework is that it approaches leadership as a group phenomenon and integrates relevant aspects of group dynamics and social identity. This relatively new trend dates from around the turn of the millennium and involves interdisciplinary research in various branches of social and organization psychology.¹¹ During the above mentioned crisis in social psychology, small group research declined and leadership received little attention. Leadership research moved instead towards organizational psychology. When the social identity approach crossed over into organizational psychology, it provided an integrative framework for the study of leadership in the context of the group.¹²

---

9. Haslam, *Psychology in Organizations*, xxiv–xxv.

10. See for instance Tajfel, *Human Groups and Social Categories*, 18–23; for a recent proposal in this direction, see Cornelissen et al., "Social Identity, Organizational Identity and Corporate Identity," 10.

11. For an indication of the relationship of the social identity model of leadership to the history of leadership research in the 20th century, see Haslam, *Psychology in Organizations*, 40–45; and Hogg, "A Social Identity Theory of Leadership," 184–86.

12. See the literature overview in van Knippenberg et al., "Leadership, Self, and Identity," 829–41.

The 2001 publication of Hogg's study "A Social Identity Theory of Leadership" was a landmark,[13] although Haslam and Platow published three research articles on leadership and social identity in the same year.[14] Since then, research into the correlation between social identity and leadership has increased substantially, so that leadership is once again a key topic in social psychology. The first scholarly textbook on leadership from a social identity perspective appeared only in 2011.[15]

Initial research in groups and identity consisted of two lines: a European tradition in social identity research and a north-American tradition in social cognition. In the 1990's, growing mutual interest lead to the merging of these traditions into the social identity approach.[16] During this decade, the approach grew in influence beyond social psychology, and it continues to grow. Several researchers have noted that articles on identity related issues in journals for social and organizational psychology have increased exponentially over the last several decades.[17] A survey of representative collections of online social science and religion journals confirms this exponential increase, since the number of articles with "identity" or "social identity" in the title has nearly doubled every five years since 1981.[18] Social identity research is part of a broader stream of identity research in social psychology as well as in sociology.[19]

---

13. See also his other studies that same year, "From Prototypicality to Power"; "Social Identification, Group Prototypicality, and Emergent Leadership"; and with Reid, "Social Identity, Leadership, and Power."

14. Haslam and Platow, "Social Identity and the Romance of Leadership," "The Link between Leadership and Followership," and "Your Wish Is Our Command."

15. Haslam et al., *The New Psychology of Leadership*.

16. Abrams and Hogg, "Social Identity and Social Cognition," 1–12; and Operario and Fiske, "Integrating Social Identity and Social Cognition," 26–31.

17. Haslam et al, "More Than a Metaphor," 357–59; Brown, "Social Identity Theory," 745–46.

18. Sage Online Journals (http://online.sagepub.com/); Proquest Philosophy and Religion Database (http://proquest.umi.com/login), and Atla Serials Religion (http://web.ebscohost.com), accessed July 7, 2011. The search was limited to scholarly, full text journal articles.

19. See Burke and Stets, *Identity Theory*; Lawler, *Identity: Sociological Perspectives*; and Cornelissen et al., "Social, Organizational and Corporate Identity," S1–S16.

Table 3.1: Statistics on Identity Research in Social Science and Religious Studies

	Sage - Social Sciences		Proquest Religion		Atla Serials Religion	
	Identity	Social Id.	Identity	Social Id.	Identity	Social Id.
2006–2010	1504	45	396	5	201	4
2001–2005	1117	46	335	2	245	6
1996–2000	762	28	182	3	155	4
1991–1995	353	18	31	0	89	0
1986–1990	174	11	6	0	45	0
1981–1985	117	5	0	0	21	0

One promising aspect of the discipline is its increasing focus on process. Besides studying the nature of social and organizational *identities*, research focuses increasingly on social and organizational *identification*,[20] which presents the opportunity for this study to focus on the processes of social identification and developing leadership patterns, rather than only on the social identity of Paul's communities, and the position and function of their leaders.

One danger of the popularization of the concept of identity is the potential for misunderstanding and misapplication. A spate of literature reviews in the last decade signals this development and offers correctives.[21] They provide useful overviews of the field, clarifying definitions, charting developments, and setting the agenda for future research.

Overall, social identity theory is a robust field of experimental and theoretical research, with a healthy level of criticism and rebuttal. It has

---

20. Reicher and Hopkins, "Psychology and the End of History," 401.

21. Abrams and Hogg, "Social Identity and Social Cognition" (1999); Operario and Fiske, "Integrating Social Identity and Social Cognition" (1999); Brown, "Social Identity Theory" (2000); Reicher and Hopkins, "Psychology and the End of History" (2001); Abrams and Hogg, "Metatheory: Lessons from Social Identity Research," (2004); Reicher, "The Context of Social Identity," 2004; Haslam and Ellemers, "Social Identity in Industrial and Organizational Psychology" (2005); Cornelissen et al., "Social, Organizational and Corporate Identity" (2007); Hornsey, "Social Identity Theory and Self-Categorization Theory," 2008; Alvesson et al., "Identity Matters," 2008.

crossed over from its host discipline of social psychology into a number of related disciplines with fruitful results. This builds confidence that a cross-over into biblical studies offers potential for fresh analyses.

Basic Concepts

Social Identities in (Competing) Hierarchies. Identity has become a common concept in both popular and academic language, but its definition proves slippery. In this study, identity is understood as people's sense of who they are, as their subjective self-concept.[22] This definition interprets identity as a subjective psychological experience and not as an objective entity, that is, not as referring to what a person or group really is deep down inside, independent of the circumstances of the moment.

People usually perceive their *personal identity* as a relatively stable core or essence, but it is more like a psychological reality that is constructed through the influence of "cognitive, affective, and social interaction processes, occurring within particular cultural and local contexts."[23] Personal identity tells an individual that he is different from other individuals. One could describe oneself as the son of X in one context, as a lover of Bach in another, and so forth, all of which relate to one's personal identity.[24]

Social identity refers to a person's sense of 'us', of belonging to a group. It is defined as

> that part of an individual's self-concept which derives from his knowledge of his membership of a social group (or groups) together with the value and emotional significance attached to that membership.[25]

Social identity is in focus when one describes oneself by one's nationality, family or membership of a sports club or church.

Social identity, then, implies group membership. *Groups* are defined by what distinguishes one group from another, by how a group compares itself to other similar groups. Such a comparison involves

---

22. Haslam, *Psychology in Organizations*, 21.
23. Vignoles et al., "Beyond Self-Esteem," 309.
24. Hogg and Abrams, *Social Identifications*, 24–25.
25. Tajfel, *Differentiation between Social Groups*, 63, as cited in Brown, *Group Processes*, 311.

only a few aspects or dimensions, which vary with the context of the comparison. A soccer team compares itself with rival teams in terms of skills and scores. However, several rival soccer teams see themselves as one group in comparison with, for instance, field hockey or volleyball teams, in which case the particular rules of the sport are the likely dimension of comparison. The comparison dimension changes again when a soccer team compares itself with a trade union or a theological faculty, where the comparison dimension focuses on the general activity of each group: sports, worker representation or theology. Groups are thus defined along several dimensions of comparison in relation to other groups.

Such different comparisons suggest that individuals identify with different social identities depending on which group is the focus of the comparison: family, gender, job, socio-economic class, religion, sports fan, ethnicity, nationality, and much more. People identify with one or another of these social identities, which provides a sense of self in that particular context. This in turn determines particular styles of behavior and interaction. When people attend a soccer match, they think, feel, and behave differently from when they participate in a family gathering; people are very flexible in how they identify with different groups in different contexts.[26]

Social identities interface in complex ways. Some function in hierarchical layers. For instance, someone belongs to a Bible study group, which is part of a local church, which is part of a denomination, which is part of a national association of churches. In such a situation, each level in the hierarchy of identities fully encompasses the lower levels. The lower level social identities are nested as subgroups in the higher level, superordinate identities. Other social identities cut across two or more identity hierarchies. For instance, an individual is member of a department at work, a neighborhood association, and a hobby club, neither of which fully overlaps with or encompasses the others. The interests of one such social identity may conflict with the obligations of another. A typical example of *cross-cutting social identities* is a working mother who balances demands from work and family in situations that often bring tension. A typical example of *nested social identities* is interdepartmental competition

---

26. Cf. Brown, *Group Processes*, 311 ff., for a similar exposition of SIT.

in a large firm, where subgroups compete against one another at the expense of the firm as a whole at the *superordinate* level.[27]

Prototypes and Stereotypes. Generally, group members see themselves as relatively similar to other ingroup members and as quite different from members of the outgroup. However, this perception does not necessarily represent an objective comparative judgment. It has been shown that group members tend to maximize (overemphasize) their similarities with ingroup members while minimizing their mutual differences; conversely, they minimize their similarities and maximize their differences with outgroup members. Different social contexts change these perceptions: soccer fans of team A highlight their differences with rival team B, while in comparison with field hockey teams, both soccer teams would emphasize their similarities to one another and their differences with the field hockey team. This principle means that similarities and differences within and between groups are not judged independently and on their own merit, but always in a comparative context.[28]

This comparison process also influences how group members evaluate one another's position within the group. Members are not considered on the basis of their personal attributes, but on the basis of their similarity to what the group stands for.[29] Common features that describe and define the group function as the *ingroup prototype*. The prototype represents that which best epitomizes what group members have in common and makes them different from the outgroup. The *outgroup stereotype*, by contrast, represents that which magnifies the differences with the ingroup and minimizes the similarities.[30] This prototype is not an abstract, idealized representation of the group, but is embodied by certain group members who best represent the group and its vision of social identity in a particular comparison situation. The degree to which a group member corresponds to this prototype is one's *prototypicality*, which functions like an intragroup sliding scale

---

27. See Hogg et al., "The Social Identity Perspective," 261.

28. In the literature of social psychology, this is called the *principle of meta*-contrast (Hornsey, "Social Identity Theory," 208 and Haslam, *Psychology in Organizations*, 31–33).

29. Haslam, *Psychology in Organizations*, 30 ff. This process is referred to as *depersonalization*.

30. Haslam et al., *The New Psychology of Leadership*, 66.

measuring one's social distance from the ingroup prototype.[31] Thus, group members who are considered to be most prototypical in a particular situation often function as the reference point of the group, by which members measure how well other group members fit the group's social identity. Such prototypical members gain a position of influence and social attraction in the group, simply by virtue of how well they embody the group's identity. For instance, most pastors teach and preach in their church, but those who do so better or for larger audiences or whose books sell better, are often perceived to be more prototypical than other pastors. The line-up of speakers at a pastor's conference usually reflects the sense that certain pastors function as reference points for their peers (= fellow ingroup members), at least on the issue (comparison dimension) being addressed.

To sum up, groups define their social identity along a few dimensions in comparison with other groups in a particular context, and as a result, group members see themselves as similar to one another and as very different from members of the other comparison group(s). Usually, these similarities and differences are measured by reference to one or a few group members who embody the group's identity most of all, and who are thus considered to be most prototypical.

Use in NT Studies

After sketching the theory's development and explaining some of its most basic concepts, it is necessary to indicate how the social identity approach can be applied to biblical studies. Its first application in NT studies dates already from 1996, while it is only now beginning to gain some recognition.[32] The social identity perspective is a hermeneutical tool that belongs under the umbrella of social-scientific criticism, where it keeps company with rhetorical, narrative, and literary criticism, to name but a few. Together, they study a broad range of social, historical, and literary features of the biblical text.[33]

---

31. Oakes et al., "The Role of Prototypicality," 75–76.
32. Esler, "Group Boundaries in Galatians," 215–40, culminating in his *Galatians*. Esler supervised several dissertations using social identity theory, of which the most relevant is Keay, "Paul the Spiritual Guide." For a somewhat broader perspective, see Luomanen et al., *Explaining Christian Origins*.
33. Elliott, "From Social Description to Social-Scientific Criticism," 29–30.

Social science approaches have been criticized on several counts. Some approaches are reductionistic in their concern to discuss social phenomena at the expense of the supernatural dimension of the biblical text.[34] However, with the increasing use of such approaches, this danger is increasingly recognized so that more mature applications are now possible.

More generally, modern social science methods have been developed through the collection of data through quantitative and statistical research, which cannot be directly applied to historical texts. NT historical data often are fragmented, from one perspective only, and with very limited resources to carry out a cross-check with other locations or times.[35] However, more first century data are available today than ever before because of numerous comparative studies using literary, archaeological, and inscriptional evidence. These studies provide the contextual data needed for the application of the social identity theory. Moreover, social identity research now also supplements its traditional quantitative lab research with qualitative case studies, which provide "an important means of 'filling in the gaps' and triangulating findings that have been obtained using other methodologies."[36] A case study approach does not overcome all the obstacles of data collection for the current study. The evidence is still mostly limited to Paul's side of the conversation, with very limited ability to cross-check the data. Even with these limitations, a case study is the best approach to the available data.

The cross-cultural applicability of social science models is a notorious problem, as was evident in some of the anachronistic applications of social science models noted above.[37] A key factor in cross-cultural studies is the individualism versus collectivism dimension,[38] which determines whether a culture is oriented more towards individual or collective identity. Triandis observed that conformity is important in

---

34. Berding, "The Hermeneutical Framework of Social-Scientific Criticism," 12–13.

35. Best, "The Sociological Study of the NT," 188.

36. Haslam and Reicher, "Social Identity and the Dynamics of Organizational Life," 139–40.

37. Crook, "Culture and Social-Scientific Models," 515.

38. Other dimensions of culture are power distance, uncertainty avoidance, time orientation and gender, which are less relevant for the present study. See Chryssochoou, *Cultural Diversity*, 139–41.

collectivist societies, with clear norms and strong censure of deviant behavior, while "doing your own thing," creativity and innovation are more valued in individualist societies. Collectivists emphasize people, so group behavior is an all pervasive influence and norm; individualists emphasize task and independence, so group behavior has only superficial and specific influence.[39] Collectivists automatically obey ingroup authority, and are willing to sacrifice to maintain ingroup integrity even at personal cost; individualists decide for themselves, and will compete and sacrifice for personal goals.[40] Mediterranean cultures, past and present, are considered predominantly collectivist,[41] and a quick scan of the Pauline corpus, with its emphasis on conformity, group norms, personal sacrifice, and authority structure, suggests such a collectivist orientation. This presents a challenge to most scholars who operate from a western, individualist perspective. Thus, social identity theory is able not only to analyze the collective group identities of the ancient Mediterranean world, but also to assist the western scholar in properly accounting for his own individualist perspective.

In the competitive collectivist world of the NT, the social identity approach is a useful tool for analysis. Like other social science approaches, it is not without its pitfalls, but it is particularly well suited to analyze intergroup relationships and intragroup differentiation, which played such an important part in the formation of Paul's churches and their leadership.

The previous sections explain the development of the social identity perspective and its basic conceptual framework, which has already proven useful in its application to NT studies in spite of some general obstacles and cautions. The present study uses this perspective as a heuristic tool to ask new questions about the leadership patterns in the Pauline communities at Corinth and Ephesus, in order to provide a more comprehensive and persuasive interpretation of the development of these leadership patterns than is possible with the methods used thus far.

The analysis of a community and its social identity needs to progress through three stages to arrive at such developing leadership patterns. The first stage describes the social identification processes

---

39. Triandis et al., "Individualism and Collectivism," 324–25.
40. Triandis and Gelfand, "Converging Measurement," 509.
41. Malina, *The New Testament World*, 58–80.

in a group, since from a social identity perspective leaders are group members who influence and manage these processes. Such a description provides insight into Christian community formation in Corinth and Ephesus. The second stage analyzes how leaders manage these processes of social identification, which provides insight into how local leaders as well as Paul managed the social identity of their communities. The third stage then considers how this identity management leads to the emergence, maintenance, and succession of leaders, which provides insight into the developing leadership patterns in Corinth and Ephesus. These stages build towards a more comprehensive interpretation of Pauline leadership patterns, which can then be compared with the current reconstructions in the literature reviewed above.

Social Identification Processes

The first stage of the present study describes the processes of social identification in groups, for which this section presents the model. Social identification means that people come to share a common social identity. When that happens, social relations are transformed, which allows these people to work together, trusting and supporting each other. Moreover, members generally attempt to verify their own understanding of group definition and seek to conform their behavior to it.[42] The question that this section seeks to answer is how people identify themselves with one social identity or another.

On Being Socially Distinct

Social identity in the first century world was typically defined by kinship and ethnicity, patronage and social status, and also by trade, city, and religious belief. Social identification seems fairly unproblematic with such group identities, since social customs often predetermine which groups one is expected to identify with. But what happened when a new social identity was introduced, such as when Paul assembled people together in what he envisioned as a stable and enduring community of Christ-followers? How did this new social identity relate to already existing social identities? Which beliefs and values determined the group's identity as compared to these other social

---

42. Haslam et al., *The New Psychology of Leadership*, 143–44.

identities? What kind of behavior was to be characteristic of members of this new community? What resources did the group offer to cope with social pressure to leave (i.e. disidentify from) this new community or to change some of its key characteristics? Since the new community lacked a local history, could it connect with similar groups and their social history elsewhere to gain social status locally or to serve as guide for local development? Clearly, social identification is much more than simply sharing certain characteristics of sociological groups, such as kinship, ethnicity, trade or gender. Group identity and group membership are a matter of psychology as it interacts with social reality.[43]

Individuals are diversely motivated to identify with a particular group. One motivation is reduction of uncertainty and of social tension. Group membership is a way of ordering one's social world, creating a sense of order and allowing people to determine their own place within it. This reduces social tension and the subjective feelings of uncertainty that accompany it.[44] A second motivation is a sense of distinctiveness. People often identify with groups that reflect positively on their self-conception, identifying with groups that contribute to a sense of distinctiveness—although different cultures express this differently.[45] Third, individuals may be motivated to identify with a group because of its foundational beliefs and values,[46] which is significant for the study of Christian social identity. Further motivations may be a sense of belonging or increased efficacy.[47] Several of these motivations are visible in the Pauline corpus, becoming visible mostly through processes of comparison.

Matching Social Identity with Reality

Social identification, then, is not simply a matter of sharing certain characteristics with other individuals, or of simply joining a particular group of people. Rather, it concerns the psychological process that is involved in one's evaluation of the perceived differences and similarities with individuals and groups that one encounters. One's motivation

43. Ibid., 132–35.
44. Grieve and Hogg, "Subjective Uncertainty," 936–37.
45. Vignoles, "The Motive for Distinctiveness," 494–95.
46. Bar-Tal, "Group Beliefs," 110–13.
47. Deaux, "Models, Meanings and Motivations," 12.

for social identification determines which similarities and differences are considered to be significant, and which can be overlooked (or which will be maximized and which minimized; see pp. 38ff). This leads an individual to identify with one social identity and not with another, depending on the social context encountered. Thus, social identification is an ongoing psychological process of comparison, where an individual continually compares his understanding of social identity with his perceptions of social reality.

This comparison process is guided by several mechanisms. One mechanism considers which social identity fits best in a particular context (principle of *comparative fit*).[48] For instance, math teachers will likely identify with other math teachers at a large teacher training conference, rather than with other kinds of teachers or with students. However, at a tournament these same math teachers will likely identify with anyone from their school (all teachers and students), rather than with their colleagues at the rival school. Depending on context, teachers identify themselves with their colleagues generally, with their specialty or with their school. How well a particular social identity fits in a comparative context is a mix of observed social characteristics and psychological processes of evaluation. A good comparative fit facilitates social identification.

A second mechanism compares one's expectations of a particular social identity with one's observations (the principle of *normative fit*).[49] In other words, the observed behavior of group members is expected to match fairly consistently with how they are expected to behave based on their social identity. If group members behave in ways inconsistent with these expectations, normative fit is lacking and identification with this group may become problematic.

A third and final mechanism of comparison considers how readily people use a particular social identity to identify themselves (the principle of *category accessibility*).[50] This mechanism is concerned with whether an individual has pre-existing categories and a social history for identifying with one or another social identity. For instance, a student who has never watched or attended a soccer tournament has no mental category for this experience and may behave unexpectedly,

---

48. Haslam, *Psychology in Organizations*, 34.
49. Ibid., 34–35.
50. Ibid., 36.

such as by discussing his next assignment with the professor seated next to him on the bleachers. Thus, this lack of category accessibility leads to a lack of normative fit as perceived by others, who may then wish not to identify with this student in this situation.

These three mechanisms together determine which social identity people consider fitting. Does a particular social identity fit the situation better than another (comparative fit)? Do people with whom they may identify behave according to their expectations of that social identity (normative fit)? Is that social identity a readily accessible mental category, based on their experience and social history? These principles reveal important aspects of social comparison that determine why individuals identify with a particular social identity.

Social Identity Performance

Being socially distinct by being "one of us" in various contexts brings a sense of order to one's social life. The sections above discussed various motivations for social identification in different contexts, and several mechanisms of comparison which people use in the identification processes. Once people identify with a social identity (comparative fit), their behavior changes. They begin to act and speak in a way that conforms to the expectations of their social identity (normative fit). This is referred to as identity performance, which can be defined as "the purposeful expression (or suppression) of behaviors relevant to those norms conventionally associated" with a particular social identity.[51] It concerns the visible, public expression of behavior and norms with which "individuals strive to communicate each of their identity elements to others in everyday life."[52] "Performance" here is not to be interpreted as in the world of theater where "performance" means "acting as someone I am not," but as in the world of music where "performance" makes the music into what it is. Thus, identity performance is the visible, social expression of one's sense of belonging to a particular group.

Social identification and identity performance are mutually reinforcing: social identification leads to identity performance, which in

---

51. Klein et al., "Social Identity Performance," 30.
52. Vignoles et al., "Beyond Self-Esteem," 320.

turn influences further social identification.[53] Initially, identification with a particular group leads to a change in attitude, beliefs, feelings, and behavior as one aligns oneself with the ingroup prototype. Such changes result in identity performance, which demonstrates the degree to which these changes have been absorbed by the group member. This performance in turn affects all group members in their social identification with the group.

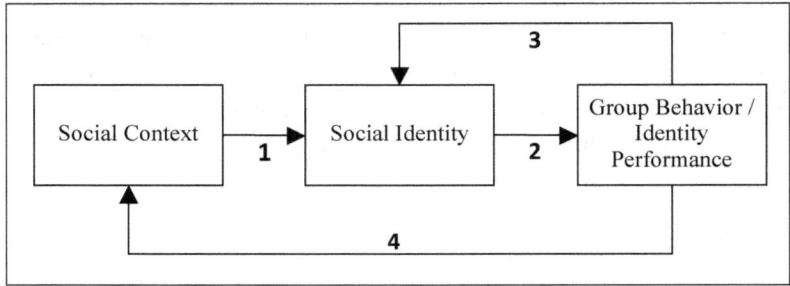

Figure 3.2: Identity Performance Cycle

Observed identity performance tends to affirm and strengthen individual and group identities. The observed performance signals to other ingroup members the extent to which the beliefs and values of their common social identity have been absorbed by the performing ingroup member. This *consolidates* the social identity for the group as well as for the acting individual. Initiation rituals and other rites of passage often function this way. Observed identity performance serves to persuade other ingroup members to adopt similar behavior, and thus *mobilizes* them to similar identity performance. Personal example and modeling often serve this function. When identity performance takes place in the presence of outgroup members, i.e. for an outgroup audience, it is often experienced as a *celebration* of ingroup identity and may well function to either mobilize outgroup members on behalf of the ingroup (as in evangelism) or to demobilize their resistance to the ingroup (as in apologetics or political lobbying).

Thus, social identification leads to identity performance, which in turn leads to further levels of identification (or sometimes disidentification). This cyclical process is pictured in figure 3.2.[54] The relevant social identity in a particular social context leads to certain

---

53. This section follows Klein et al., "Social Identity Performance," 28–45.
54. Ibid., 41, figure reprinted by permission of SAGE Publications.

types of group behaviors or identity performance (arrows 1 and 2 in the diagram). This identity performance leads to consolidation of the relevant social identity and mobilizes others for this social identity (arrow 3). Identity performance for an outgroup audience may result in mobilizing outgroup members on behalf of the ingroup, thus shaping and changing the social context (arrow 4), which influences subsequent social identification, etc.

Identity performance before an outgroup audience always aims to highlight or "celebrate" the positive character of one's own social identity.[55] If this is unsuccessful, individuals may leave one group and join another, referred to as *social mobility*. But such mobility is frequently considered undesirable and may even be impossible. When individual mobility is not an option, groups may engage in *social competition* to try to enhance their social status and better their lot. Thus, the group would seek to change social reality to improve the status of their own group. But even that is not always possible, for instance when a dominant outgroup does ot tolerate social challenges without serious consequences. Minority groups in such a position cannot engage in social competition without severe consequences so they are more likely to change their perspective on the situation, portraying what looks like a negative situation instead as positive for group members. This is referred to as *social creativity*: instead of changing social reality, a group adjusts their thinking about this reality by changing their strategy of social comparison. In effect, the group changes their definition of social identity to match the social reality they face. Thus, the subordinate group may change the *dimension* along which they compare themselves to others. When a soccer player comments, "we may not score as well as team X, but our teamwork is much better," he adjusts his social identity by changing the comparison dimension from score to teamwork. The subordinate group may change the *value* by portraying a particular dimension of comparison as positive instead of negative. The same soccer player comments, "we may not have as large a fan club, but we know our most loyal fans personally," which portrays their smaller fan club in a positive light. Again, the subordinate group may change the *comparison group*, as when the player says, "We cannot compare with the champion, but compared to team Y we

---

55. This section follows Reicher, "The Context of Social Identity," 932, and Haslam, *Psychology in Organizations*, 23–27. See also Esler, *Galatians*, 49–55.

are doing quite well."⁵⁶ Since Pauline communities generally were low status, minority communities without the resources to challenge the status quo of other groups in their social environment, strategies of social creativity are abundant in Paul's letters.

Identity performance is a necessary component of social identification. Without identity performance, the relevance of a particular identity is reduced and it may cease to influence the attitudes, thinking, and behavior of individuals in a given situation. On the other hand, persistent identity performance will strengthen social identification at the individual and group levels, and will encourage others to adopt similar behaviors. When identity performance takes place before an outgroup audience, the celebration of ingroup identity seeks to portray its positive qualities and may lead new individuals to join the group. Such identity performance may also seek to mobilize help for or reduce resistance to the ingroup. Where a dominant outgroup is generally unreceptive to a minority group, their identity performance will usually focus on changing the perception of ingroup members in order that they see and experience as positive what would otherwise be considered a negative situation.

Constructing an Identity Narrative

Throughout such processes of comparison and social adjustment, groups create and maintain an identity narrative, which can be defined as the social memory of the group, shared in the form of narratives or discourses.⁵⁷ This involves a group member's personal history, but also shared social memories of the group's history and traditions. The ingroup prototype is informed by memories about boundary definitions and previous experiences of social identification, and often by exemplars, persons from past or present who embody the ingroup prototype in particularly meaningful ways.⁵⁸ The collection, interaction, and merging of these discourses and narratives describe the vision of 'who we are,' of social identity. Thus, clear identity narratives

---

56. Blanz et al., "Responding to Negative Social Identity," 697–729; Niens and Cairns, "Explaining Social Change and Identity Management Strategies," 489–509.

57. Lawler, *Identity: Sociological Perspectives*, 10ff.

58. Further analysis of the relation between prototype and exemplar, as well as some explanations of these phenomena from cognitive psychology and neuroscience, see Luomanen, "The Sociology of Knowledge," 217 ff.

significantly enhance category accessibility for ingroup members, which assists new group members in deepening their social identification. A coherent identity narrative provides a sense of individual and collective continuity, and thus contributes to long-term group stability and cohesion.

However, identity narratives not only reveal a group's social identity, they also construct it. These narratives provide portraits of social identification from the group's history, which orient group members to current challenges to envision how they might change and adapt while maintaining a consistent group identity.[59] In times of social stability, new experiences are easily integrated into the community's identity narrative, but in times of change and discontinuity, "the identity narrative is actively explored, defended or modified."[60] In most organizations various versions and interpretations of the identity narrative circulate, which allows the organization to engage flexibly with its current challenges.[61] This also suggests that the seeds for diverse developments are always present, which may at times lead to intragroup competition about which version of the identity narratives is most applicable, or which interpretation most viable.

In summary, identification with a particular social identity involves alignment with the beliefs, values, and behaviors of that social identity, and distancing oneself from conflicting beliefs, values, and behaviors. Social identification involves a cyclical process of social comparison and identity performance, which results in maintenance or adaptation of one's self-conception as group member and sometimes in an adaptation of the group's social identity. In this process, an individual negotiates his relationship with the group with reference to the intergroup comparative context. These negotiations center on matching one's understanding of social identity with social reality. Social identification with the group is expressed in identity performance, which consolidates the group's social identity and mobilizes others to similar performance. Social identification is guided by the identity narrative, which utilizes the group's social history to provide a

---

59. Ibid.; Ashforth et al., "Identification in Organizations," 339–45.
60. Alvesson and Willmott, "Identity Regulation as Organizational Control," 633.
61. Brown, "A Narrative Approach to Collective Identities," 739.

sense of individual and collective continuity, and to provide direction for future challenges.[62]

Leaders as (Competing) Managers of Social Identity

The previous section outlined the first stage of a social identity model for studying developing leadership patterns in Pauline churches. It focused on social identification processes in a group, to be applied to Christian community formation in Corinth and Ephesus. This section outlines the second stage of the model and considers how leaders manage these processes of social identification. It provides the tools to analyze how Paul engaged with local leaders as well as their congregations to manage their social identity.

A Definition of Leadership

Defining leadership is no small task. Bass and Stogdill review over two hundred definitions of leadership covering each decade of the 20th century in their classic handbook on leadership.[63] After a ten-page discussion of the various types of definitions, they conclude that a definition of leadership depends on the purpose of the analysis and suggest the following definition as starting point:

> Effective leadership [is] the interaction among members of a group that initiates and maintains improved expectations and the competence of the group to solve problems or attain goals.[64]

---

62. For a similar exposition of the circular process of social identification from an organizational point of view, see Ashforth et al., "Identification in Organizations," 339–47.

63. Bass et al., *Handbook of Leadership*, 17. The history of leadership research falls outside the limitations of this study. A number of contributions show the relevance of the history of leadership research for social identity theory (e.g. Haslam, *Psychology in Organizations*, 40–45; Hogg, "A Social Identity Theory of Leadership," 184–86). Chemers offers a more extensive review, organized by leadership function (*An Integrative Theory of Leadership*, 17–114), while Northouse discusses the historical phases of research as various parallel approaches for the study of leadership today (*Leadership: Theory and Practice*, 15–206). Bass et al., *Handbook of Leadership*, remains the standard work.

64. Bass et al., *Handbook of Leadership*, 25–26.

This general definition includes the elements of the group and goals. Followers are only implicitly referred to as "the group" while the leadership process is seen mostly as interaction. Clarifying these elements, the definition becomes:

> Leadership is a process whereby an individual influences a group of individuals to achieve a common goal.[65]

Leadership as influence is broader than but includes leadership as interaction, while the goals to be attained are clearly connected to the group as common goals. A missing element in these definitions is that leadership is "a social perception ... that produces an influence increment for the perceived leader."[66] Some group members are perceived more as leaders than others, and are consequently granted more opportunity and credibility in the process of social influence. Thus, influence, group, common goals, followers, and perception represent important elements of leadership in a variety of leadership approaches.

Since a definition of leadership depends on the purpose of the analysis, a definition of leadership as a dynamic group phenomenon needs to be considered. Three questions clarify how influence as the key process of leadership relates to the dynamics of the group.[67] First, who is influential in a group? In a group setting, the more prototypical group members function as reference point for the group's behaviors and norms; they have more influence in the group than other members. Second, who is open to such influence? Leading group members are influential by virtue of their prototypicality, which only relates to the ingroup and not to other groups. Thus, only ingroup members, who look towards prototypical members as reference point, are open to their influence. Third, what is influential? Group members are generally not open to just any influence from prototypical group members. Their influence relates to their prototypicality, and thus they are only authoritative on issues relating to their common group identity. Finally, social identification varies with specific contexts, which is reflected in definitions of leadership that emphasize its situational nature.[68] Thus, the definition of leadership for the current study is:

---

65. Northouse, *Leadership*, 3, who sees influence, groups, goals and followers as the four key components of leadership.
   66. Lord et al., "System Constraints on Leadership Perceptions," 283.
   67. Haslam et al., *The New Psychology of Leadership*, 144ff.
   68. E.g. Northouse, *Leadership*, 91–112, "Chapter 5: The Situational Approach."

> Leadership is a process of social influence through which an individual, perceived to be more prototypical and influential than other group members in a particular social context, empowers and mobilizes other group members to solve collective problems or to attain collective goals.

Power and Agency

How do these leaders mobilize other group members to attain collective goals? How do they obtain the power to do so? Older conceptions of power typically conceive of the leader as someone with control over resources, which gives him power over others who desire these resources but have no access to them.[69] Control over resources thus leads to power, which in turn generates a leader's influence. In this perspective, the greater the power of a leader, the less the power of the followers. That is, the agency of the leader is enhanced at the expense of the agency of the followers. Although in certain contexts this use of power can be observed, it has been shown that precisely the opposite is often the case.[70] A prototypical member is influential because he is perceived as exemplary in how he embodies the group and serves its interests. Through his example, he influences other members to embody the group and serve its interests in similar fashion. Thus, a prototypical member enhances the agency of other group members to carry out group goals. This leads to the principle that the agency of the leader is enhanced when he succeeds in recruiting the agency of his followers. A leader's social power to accomplish goals does not increase to the extent that the power of his followers decreases, but precisely the opposite. The more a leader empowers group members and activates their agency on behalf of the group, the more social power he gains to mobilize the group for united social action.[71]

This theory proposes that social influence in the group leads to power, which in turn leads to a greater access to resources.[72] At the basis

---

69. French and Raven, "The Bases of Social Power," 153ff. See also Raven's recent update on these earlier findings and their developments since then in "The Power/Interaction Model of Interpersonal Influence."

70. Haslam, *Psychology in Organizations*, 139ff.; and Simon and Oakes, "Beyond Dependence," 106ff.

71. Simon and Oakes, "Beyond Dependence," 112 ff.

72. Turner, "Explaining the Nature of Power," 10–14.

of power, then, is a prototypical leader who influences group members through his understanding and performance of their common social identity (*informational power*).[73] Group members tend to align their thinking, attitudes, and feelings most with the group's prototypical leaders (*referent power*). These leaders represent the collective beliefs and values of the group, strengthening the meaning attached to the group's social identity ('we are like this'), and weakening the meaning attached to competing social identities ('we are not like that') (*expert power*).[74] When a leader's influence is perceived as legitimate, it functions in accordance with group beliefs and values, and the leader gains in social status relative to other group members (*legitimate power*). When a leader's influence is perceived as illegitimate, the leader is not (or is no longer) prototypical and presents a deviant or perhaps even an outgroup social identity (in which case, group members may be enticed to act against group goals with *reward or coercive power*). Thus, the power of a leader depends largely on his prototypicality. Group members internalize group norms and values as embodied by the leader, and respond positively and voluntarily to his leadership as long as it is perceived as prototypical.[75]

Three Dimensions of Identity-Based Leadership

This description of identity-based leadership suggests that leaders exercise influence by virtue of their ability to direct the social identification process of other community members. This may simply be because they are exemplary group members, but established leaders can be more proactive. For instance, they may adapt the group's vision of social identity as an offer to guide the group through social change. Whether such an offer will be accepted or not, depends in part on the availability of alternative offers by competing leaders. Leadership is thus exercised in a process of identity management, which has three dimensions: a cognitive, a performative, and a behavioral dimension. Haslam, Reicher, and Platow describe them as follows: a leader who

---

73. This social identity analysis can be fruitfully connected with French and Raven's earlier research on the bases of power, cited above. The terms in parentheses refer to their theory of power.

74. Ashforth et al., "Identification in Organizations," 339–42. Reicher et al., "Social Identity and the Dynamics of Leadership," 563–65.

75. Tyler, "The Psychology of Legitimacy," 336.

successfully manages the social identity of his group must be an artist of identity in the vision he creates, an impresario of identity in directing group activities that express his vision, and an engineer of identity in mobilizing group members to turn his vision into social reality.[76]

First, leaders are *artists* of identity. Leaders exercise their influence by directing the social identification of group members, so they create and present a vision of social identity as a compelling cognitive alternative to the status quo. This presentation is generally accomplished rhetorically, although a leader's example may also serve as symbol for his vision of social identity. Identity-based leaders use language creatively to express their vision of social identity in terms that are relevant to the social context, that are compelling in their motivational force, and that are culturally rooted in the history and daily experiences of the group.

Second, leaders are *impresarios* of identity. Leaders not only paint a verbal picture of social identity, they also engage group members in activities by which they experience and express their social identity. For instance, a politician speaking at a national convention makes a compelling presentation of his vision of social identity, of how he proposes to change society with his policies. The ensuing debate with competing candidates and the vote form the ritual, which embeds the elected politician's followers in his vision of social identity. In religious communities, rites of passage such as baptism fulfill this function, since they usually celebrate the social identity of the community and enlist the group commitment of new members while reaffirming the commitment of already established members. These community activities and rituals represent, as it were, the choreography of the leader to encourage and affirm the affective attachment of group members to his vision of identity.

Third, leaders are *engineers* of identity. Presenting a vision of social identity and orchestrating community activities are not enough to maintain viable communities. Leaders need to mobilize group members in turning their vision of social identity into social reality, which demonstrates the day-to-day value of their social identity. Politicians need to mobilize their supporters not only to get elected but also to

---

76. See Haslam et al., *The New Psychology of Leadership*, 171–92. This is the first full length textbook on leadership research and theory from a social identity perspective.

implement their political vision. Religious communities not only celebrate community rituals but also provide structure for daily life and for influencing the larger social environment. This requires structures to facilitate coordination and focus the activity of the community, so that leaders are initiators of identity-embedding structures. This also involves demobilizing any opposition, which may hinder the implementation of the leader's vision or even cause it to fail altogether. Thus, leaders mobilize their followers to use the energies of the group to reshape social reality, which in the end demonstrates the value of their vision of social identity in their social identity and thus validates the leaders as effective.[77]

These three aspects, a vision of social identity, rituals with which to embed members in that vision, and mobilization for social action to turn that vision into reality, are all necessary for successful identity-based leadership. This is based on the observation that leaders are prototypical group members who are more influential than other group members. They influence or even purposely direct the processes of social identification. In creating a vision of social identity, they appeal more than others to the group's motivations for identification. They choose the dimension of comparison that they consider most relevant for the social context of their group. In orchestrating the group's activities, leaders usually play a central role in meetings and rituals. In mobilizing the group for social action, their own example sets the standard for appropriate identity performance. Their example and rhetoric maintain and enhance the identity narrative of the group, with the aim to provide long-term stability and cohesion, also beyond their own time of leadership.[78]

77. These leadership dimensions interact with the cognitive, affective and evaluative dimensions of social identity which Tajfel's proposed originally, but they are broader: leaders attempt to shape and change the way group members see and experience their social identity, which is indicated by the terms used: artist, impresario and engineer. For the three dimensions of social identity, see Tajfel, *Differentiation between Social Groups*, 28–29. For the use of these three dimensions in NT studies, see Esler, *Galatians*, 42ff.; and "Social Identity, the Virtues, and the Good Life," 53ff.

78. It is not difficult to point out parallels between this perspective on leadership and the earlier schools of leadership research. For instance, the following observations can be made by comparing Haslam et al., *The New Psychology of Leadership* with Northouse, *Leadership*. The leader as artist relates to conceptual, rhetorical and interrelational skills with which the social situation of the group is addressed. The leader as impresario relates to traits such as self-confidence and integrity, and to the leader's ability to transform the thinking and behavior of group members to align

Developing Leadership Patterns

The model now proceeds to the third stage of analysis. The first stage focused on social identification processes in a group; the second stage described leadership as identity management, including three dimensions of such leadership. The third stage now outlines how social identification and the leaders' identity management lead to the emergence, maintenance, and succession of leaders in the community. This is to be applied later to an analysis of the developing leadership patterns in Corinth and Ephesus.

Leadership Emergence

Leadership means that some group members are disproportionately influential. The emergence of a group member into leadership generally depends on two aspects.[79] First, an emerging leader comes to be seen as "one of us," which refers to his prototypicality. More prototypical members are more representative of the group and have greater social influence.[80] A prototypical group member often acts as opinion leader and reduces uncertainty, serving as a model for the social identification of other group members. Such a member may thus emerge as leader in certain situations and is seen as "one of us."[81] The ingroup

---

with his presentation of social identity. The leader as engineer relates to traits like determination and sociability, to technical skills in designing identity-embedding structures, to a leader's ability to work out a vision in terms of goals and objectives. Successful "engineering" will provide group members with a sense of value of and pride in their group membership in exchange for their teamwork. A fuller exploration of the connections between social identity leadership and earlier leadership schools is beyond the scope of this study, but these observations suggest that such well known leadership theories as the trait and skill approaches, situational leadership, path-goal theory, leader-member exchange theory, and transformational leadership all have signicant parallel with the social identity theory of leadership. Haslam, Reicher and Platow present their theory as a more integrative perspective on leadership than has thus far been possible.

79. Hogg lists the processes of social influence, social attraction, leadership attribution and trust as mechanisms for leadership emergence. For the purposes of this study, these processes are simplified in terms of prototypicality. See "A Social Identity Theory of Leadership," 188–91, and "Social Identification, Group Prototypicality, and Emergent Leadership," 200–6.

80. Knippenberg and Hogg, "A Social Identity Model of Leadership Effectiveness," 250–51.

81. Haslam and Platow, "Your Wish Is Our Command," 218.

prototype, however, does not remain constant, but responds flexibly to changing contexts. For instance, in 1940 Winston Churchill was elected as prime minister for the strength and determination he embodied in a context of war. In 1945, the very different Clement Atlee was surprisingly elected. Why? The comparative context had shifted dramatically from war to rebuilding, and the prototype changed accordingly. Thus, in a context where social identity is relevant, prototypicality provides a basis for the rise of leadership in groups, while the comparative context influences the way the prototype is perceived.

Second, an emerging leader is marked by his group-oriented behavior and comes to be seen as "doing it for us." Such an emerging leader displays greater favor towards group members than towards outsiders, sacrifices on behalf of the group and engages in other significant identity performance. Such group-oriented behavior builds the members' trust in the group orientation of the leader, especially if he is perceived as treating all group members fairly.[82] Non-prototypical group members need to engage more often than prototypical members in identity affirming behaviors to secure group membership and build trust, while leaders can use these behaviors to gain endorsement from other group members.[83] Thus, the leader is seen as "doing it for us."[84]

Leadership Maintenance

Once a prototypical member emerges as group leader, he can adopt more proactive leadership strategies to influence and lead the group, similar to leaders whose position is structurally defined and established. However, those who are prototypical in one situation may decline in prototypicality when the situation changes, which often results in a "redistribution of influence within the group."[85] In such a changing context with a shifting ingroup prototype, proactive leadership strategies become important in order to maintain one's leadership

---

82. Van Knippenberg and Hogg, "A Social Identity Model of Leadership," 245–47 and Van Knippenberg and Van Knippenberg, "Leader Self-Sacrifice and Leadership Effectiveness," 26–28.

83. Platow and Knippenberg, "A Social Identity Analysis of Leadership Endorsement," 1516.

84. Haslam and Platow, "Social Identity and the Romance of Leadership," 195.

85. Hogg, "A Social Identity Theory of Leadership," 190–91.

role. This essentially requires an effective performance in each of the three dimensions of leadership described above.

As artist of social identity, an effective leader succeeds in maintaining the relevance of the group's vision of social identity in the changing social context. He may accentuate the existing ingroup prototype in order to maintain his own prototypical position within the group in spite of social change. This may be accomplished by narrating the leader's self-sacrifice on behalf of the group but also by stigmatizing deviant group members or demonizing members of a relevant outgroup. Alternatively, the leader may conform himself to the shifting prototype, adopting his views and behavior to maintain his alignment with the changing prototype. However, leaders often redefine the prototype as they seek to address the changing social environment.[86] Overall, then, the leader seeks to keep his own rhetoric and behavior aligned with the (shifting) ingroup prototype to maintain his own prototypicality and thus his leadership.

As impresario of identity, an effective leader regularly succeeds in orchestrating the participation of group members in meaningful events, expressing their social identity. The "meetings, parades, celebrations, memorials and more besides should, in miniature and in the here and now, stand in anticipation of the world to come."[87] In these events, group members are not mere spectators; they participate frequently and thus reinforce their commitment to the group while particularly meaningful events become part of the community's identity narrative. These events provide a sense of continuity. An effective leader is able to direct these community events to meet the demands of a changing social context while maintaining this sense of continuity. In this way, the leader enlists, renews, and celebrates the commitment of his followers to his vision of social identity.

As engineer of social identity, an effective leader succeeds in directing the group's energy to effect social change. The group's vision of social identity is often a vision of "what we want to become" or "what we want society to become," which is only imperfectly reflected in current reality. Effective leaders turn the group's vision of social identity into reality by mobilizing members to appropriate

---

86. Hogg, "Social Identification, Group Prototypicality, and Emergent Leadership," 205, 211.

87. Haslam et al., *The New Psychology of Leadership*, 179–80.

identity performance and by initiating identity-embedding structures that facilitate these expressions of social identity. The degree to which a leader is successful in transforming the group's vision into reality determines the leader's effectiveness and affirms his position.[88] Without this achievement, or at least a significant movement towards the desired reality, "even the most eloquent of constructions and the most elaborate of performances then become an empty show that have no relationship of any sort to the structure of social reality."[89] If a leader succeeds as engineer of identity, he has successfully raised the status of their social identity in the perception of group members as well as in the perception of many outsiders.

Leadership Succession

Thus far, this overview of developing leadership patterns has presented the processes of leadership emergence and leadership maintenance. The next stage is to review the process of leadership succession, which is more than simply the emergence of new leaders to join or succeed established leaders. This section answers the question when and how established leaders can move new leaders into positions of influence. It also analyzes how and when the leader's vision of social identity or his identity management strategies can be transferred to new leaders, not just in personal contact and training, but also in a group setting so that the legitimacy of the predecessor transfers to the successor.

Unfortunately, the social identity literature consulted to date hardly refers to succession. From a cognitive perspective, only Ritter and Lord have devoted any attention to it, showing that group members' expectations of a new leader are likely transferred from their experience and expectations of an old leader, if the new leader is similar to the old one.[90] They analyze succession by studying follower perceptions of new leaders. No model is yet forthcoming to study the complete process of leadership succession. Although the personal

---

88. Reicher et al., "Social Identity and the Dynamics of Leadership," 562.

89. Haslam et al., *The New Psychology of Leadership*, 188–89.

90. Ritter and Lord, "The Impact of Previous Leaders on the Evaluation of New Leaders," 1683–93. In a 1999 study, Lord touched on the topic of mentoring, while in a 2000 study, he suggested succession as a topic further study (Lord et al., "Understanding the Dynamics of Leadership," 187; Lord and Emrich, "Thinking Outside the Box by Looking Inside the Box," 568–69).

relationship between old and new leader, as a leader-subordinate or mentor-trainee, play an important role, succession takes place in the context of the group. Thus, social identity issues are relevant in an analysis of leadership succession.[91]

Succession and Leadership Perception

Since succession is relatively under-investigated in social identity research, the present leadership model needs to be expanded to provide a theoretical account of succession. The point of departure will be Ritter and Lord's work on new leader perception, supplemented with Stepp's study of succession in the Pauline world.[92] The resulting account of succession will be integrated with the previously discussed three dimensions of leadership.

Ritter and Lord analyze the effect of the old leader or predecessor on the acceptance of a new leader or successor. The situation envisaged is broader than only succession but includes it as well. They demonstrate that memories of significant others, such as a former teacher, a parent or a close friend, often determine how new individuals are categorized. This is the case especially in a context where memories of these significant others are called to mind so that they overwhelm the generic image of teachers, parents or friends. Thus, individuals who are exposed to a new leader rely on their memory of the previous leader to assess the expected effectiveness and treatment by the new leader. If the new leader is similar to the previous leader, similar effectiveness and treatment are expected. If the new leader is not similar to the previous one, or if an individual has no personal experience of a previous leader, a generic image of a leader will be used for the assessment. In other words, in certain contexts the previous leader as exemplar will overrule a more generic leadership image in assessing new leaders.

In succession, complex interactions take place between the predecessor, the successor, and the group. Ritter and Lord focus on the perception of effectiveness, which appears as a quality of leadership

---

91. Ashforth et al., "Identification in Organizations," 350–51; Sluss and Ashforth, "Relational Identity and Identification," 17, 27.

92. Ritter and Lord, "The Impact of Previous Leaders," 1691–93 and Stepp, *Leadership Succession*, 55–59 and 88–90.

that is transferred from predecessor to successor. For the purposes of this study, this quality is interpreted as the heritage or legacy of succession. This results in an analysis of succession where predecessor, successor, and legacy are considered in the context of social identification. More specifically, this involves an analysis of:

- the ingroup status and effectiveness of the predecessor as he initiates the process of succession,
- the presentation and subsequent ingroup status of the successor as direct beneficiary of the process of succession, and
- the content of the legacy bequeathed and its purpose to provide continuity for the group involved as the indirect beneficiaries of the process of succession.

This portrayal of succession has clear links with the social identity model of leadership. An effective leader will incorporate his succession initiative into his vision of social identity, which involves both predecessor and successor as artists of social identity. The ease with which the predecessor can institute succession depends on his status and effectiveness as prototypical leader of the group. Next, succession involves the presentation of the successor to the group as well as a community activity or ritual to effect the succession, which involves both predecessor and successor as impresarios of social identity. Finally, succession aims at certain kinds of continuity in the transfer of the predecessor's legacy, so that succession involves the institution of identity-embedding structures for the long-term stability and cohesion of the community. This involves both predecessor and successor as engineers of social identity.

Succession as Component of a Leader's Vision of Identity

The first point of analysis is the ingroup status and effectiveness of the predecessor as he initiates the process of succession. The social identity perspective implies that succession is not merely the replacement of personnel, but a way of providing continuity for the group and its vision of social identity. Since prototypical leaders function as reference point for the group, and are among the group's best presenters of this vision, succession moves a new leader into prominence with the expectation that he will function similarly as reference point and presenter for the group's social identity. Succession, then, is not just a coincidental affair in the life of the group, but instead forms an important aspect of long-term social stability for the community. Therefore, as artist of social identity, an effective leader will incorporate succession into his vision of social identity.

According to Ritter and Lord, the status and effectiveness of the predecessor are important indicators for how his successor will be received. Applying this insight to succession, this suggests that status and effectiveness determine a predecessor's social power to initiate succession. The more effective the predecessor and the higher his status, the more likely it is that the group will accept his proposal for succession, especially if the successor is similar to himself and a prototypical group member as well. Lack of status or ineffective leadership reduces the social power of the leader to initiate succession, since his proposal for succession is less likely to be accepted. In such a situation, the successor will likely come from outside his direct sphere of influence or even from among those group members with a competing vision of social identity. The status and perceived effectiveness of a leader are thus important predictors of his effectiveness in initiating succession.

Leadership status is a measure of leader effectives, as explained by the concept of *leadership attribution*. As group members experience the influence of a highly prototypical member and respond by accepting his suggestions, they attribute greater popularity and status to this member. Over time, the perceived difference between this influential member and other group members increases so that the prototypical member is seen as distinctive, standing out from the rest of the group. Before long, group members ascribe this distinctiveness not to prototypicality, but to inherent leadership qualities; they begin to see and treat him as a "natural" leader.[93] Thus, a leader's higher status within the group results from his effective influence which derives from his prototypical position within the group, while in the eyes of group members this influence derives from his natural leadership qualities which in turn justify his higher intragroup status.

This process of leadership attribution is an aspect of leadership perception, on which Ritter and Lord's work was built. Leadership attribution is stronger when a leader effectively leads through social

---

93. Hogg, "A Social Identity Theory of Leadership," 190; van Knippenberg and Hogg, "A Social Identity Model of Leadership," 252.

turmoil or when he performs extreme sacrifices for the group, which will result in the attribution of charismatic leadership. Although "charismatic leadership" commonly refers to someone's effective leadership as a rare "gift," this is a function of leadership attribution. Since the twins of charisma and leadership have a long history in the debate on church leadership (see the literature review in chapter 2), this phenomenon merits extra attention.

Succession and Charismatic Leadership Attribution

In typical overviews of leadership research, charismatic leadership is classified with transformational leadership, sometimes called the "new leadership," which rose to popularity in the late 1980s and 1990s.[94] Its roots are much older, originating with Sohm's theological analysis at the end of the 19th century and Weber's sociological analysis in the early 20th century. Since the 1980s, there has been a resurgence of interest in Weber's concept of charismatic leadership, based on the assumption that the mystique around charisma should be studied as a behavioral process. Leaders are considered charismatic because of their ability to inspire change through their vision, their self-sacrifice, and their innovative change strategies.[95] The most relevant elements in current charismatic leadership research are the collective identity of leader and followers, the reverence for and trust of the charismatic leaders, and the ability of the leader to (re)define group norms and goals.[96]

Weber's analysis of charismatic authority provides a starting point for modern research on charismatic leadership. First, Weber insists that a leader's charismatic claims fail when they are not

---

94. For an in-depth overview of research on charisma and charismatic leadership, see Sashkin, "Transformational Leadership Approaches," 171–96, who integrates aspects of the trait, skill and situational leadership theories into his review of charismatic leadership. The present study integrates charismatic leadership with its group context. For a more limited overview, see Paul et al., "The Mutability of Charisma in Leadership Research," 192–99; and Northouse, *Leadership*, 175–206.

95. Kanungo and Conger, "Charisma: Exploring New Dimensions of Leadership Behaviour," 25; Conger and Kanungo, "Toward a Behavioral Theory of Charismatic Leadership," 639–45.

96. Conger et al., "Charismatic Leadership and Follower Effects," 749–53 and 760ff.

recognized by the followers.[97] "What is alone important is how the individual is *actually regarded* by those subject to charismatic authority, by his 'followers' or 'disciples.'"[98] Weber acknowledges that charismatic leadership depends upon follower perceptions of the leader, and thus upon the leadership attribution process. In social identity research, this representative character of charisma is recognized: "It is those who best embody who we are . . . to whom we will attribute charisma. In this way, charisma may, indeed, be a special gift, but it is one bestowed on group members by group members for being representative of, rather than distinct from, the group itself."[99]

Second, Weber also acknowledges the charismatic leader's ability to shape and redefine group goals and values. In the introduction to Weber's selected writings on charisma, Eisenstadt summarizes Weber's ideas that charismatic leaders bring about social change in times of social transformation by "the recrystallization of the centers of a society." They redefine "the central charismatic symbols" and "the modes of participation in them."[100] Although the terminology is different, this is similar to a prototypical leader who redefines the ingroup prototype to adapt to a changing social context and enlists other group members to adopt his redefinition. A prototypical leader may "fundamentally redefine followers' goals, values, and aspirations."[101] Thus, the way Weber conceives the relationship between the charismatic leader and his followers offers significant links for the later developments in cognitive and social identity theories of leadership.

Third, Weber's concept of charisma has "some inherent antinomian and anti-institutional predispositions,"[102] which reflect his beliefs that charisma goes beyond the demands of everyday routine, is never permanent, and lacks orderly procedures for appointment and dismissal; it is founded upon an inner sense of personal mission that drives social change.[103] These beliefs contain strong reminiscences of

---

97. Weber and Eisenstadt, *Max Weber on Charisma*, 20.

98. Ibid., 48, emphasis added.

99. Platow et al., "A Special Gift We Bestow on You," 317.

100. Eisenstadt, "Introduction," in Weber and Eisenstadt, *Max Weber on Charisma*, xlv–xlvi.

101. Haslam and Platow, "Your Wish Is Our Command," 214.

102. Eisenstadt, "Introduction," xix.

103. Ibid., 18–19.

Sohm's radical opposition between a law-free gospel, and the later institutionalized and legalistic religious structures, but it also reflects a dimension of charismatic leadership that social identity research describes as follows. When a prototypical group member gains influence and begins to be seen as leader through the leadership attribution process, he gains greater freedom to redefine group identity when the group is confronted by social challenges. If successful, the perceived 'natural' leadership qualities are magnified as manifesting charismatic leadership. When that occurs, the group willingly follows the member they now perceive as charismatic leader into uncharted social territory, even if some of the group's established patterns and traditions are set aside. Thus, Weber's observations about the antinomian and anti-institutional tendencies of charismatic leadership align—at least in part—with social identity research, which indicates that in socially ambiguous situations, prototypical members are most likely to take the lead.[104] Weber pointed to aspects of charismatic leadership that have often seemed heroic and even mysterious, but which can now be analyzed as the result of an extended process of leadership attribution. Indeed, such a framework meets the challenge of Weber's work that Eisenstadt already indicated in the 1960s.[105]

To sum up, charismatic leadership arises as a result of processes of intragroup differentiation and leadership attribution. Prototypicality and group-oriented behavior increase the social influence of a prototypical group member, which enhances the leadership attribution process whereby this member is perceived as, and thus turned into a leader. If in times of social change this leader represents the group's vision of identity with compelling force and sacrifices to turn the group's vision into reality, he will most likely be perceived as a charismatic leader. Charisma is therefore not an organizing and structuring principle of intragroup differentiation and leadership formation, but it is instead the result of such processes. In turn, it can add its weight to further intragroup differentiation and group structuring, further raising the status of such leaders relative to other group members.

104. Van Knippenberg et al., "Who Takes the Lead," 213.

105. Eisenstadt wrote, "We know as yet very little either about conditions of development of such entrepreneurial, charismatic people, of their psychological and behavioral attributes, and about the conditions under which they may be capable of implementing their vision. . . These aspects still constitute an essential part of the challenge of Weber's work for modern sociological analysis" ("Introduction," xl–xii).

This perspective is only now gaining clarity in sociology and social psychology, so the discussions of developing leadership structures in the early church have not yet benefited from it. As reviewed briefly in chapter 2, the early 20th century consensus proposed a development from pristine charismatic beginnings to later institutionalized forms, with charisma as the key organizing principle of the early Christian groups. Thus, charismatic qualities were thought to be most evident in the Corinthian community, while structuring and institutionalization were thought to take center stage in Ephesus. However, the above perspective on charismatic leadership suggests that the Corinthian community struggled with leadership emergence and maintenance since Paul's leadership was as yet strongly contested, while his (and Timothy's) leadership in the Ephesian community may well be qualified as 'charismatic leadership' because of their increased leadership status. Possibly, a retrieval of Weber's theory of authority as seen through social identity theory may lead to better results as compared with earlier analyses of charisma and office. The later chapters on Ephesians and 1–2 Timothy will take special note of these questions.

To bring this discussion of charismatic leadership back to the issue at hand, a leader as an artist of social identity will incorporate succession into his vision of social identity. His status in the community is a strong predictor of how well received his proposals for succession will be. If leadership attribution has advanced far enough to portray the leader as charismatic, more than likely his succession proposals will be broadly accepted within the community. Meanwhile, the (potential) successor is likely to adopt the predecessor's vision of social identity, since it legitimates his succession. The more the predecessor is perceived and revered as charismatic leader and the closer the successor is associated with the predecessor, the more the successor's status in the community will increase and the faster his leadership will be consolidated. The successor, too, emerges as an artist of identity. Thus, leadership succession within a particular community is a process of providing the group with a viable interpretation of reality in terms of its social identity with the new leader as model and prototype.[106]

---

106. Alvesson et al., "The Charismatization of Routines," 344–45.

The Predecessor's Presentation of the Successor

The second point of the analysis of succession is the presentation and subsequent ingroup status of the successor as direct beneficiary of the process of succession. When succession becomes part of the group's vision of social identity, it affects the beliefs, attitudes, and motivations of group members towards the new leader, but it does not yet realize the actual succession. This involves more than a newly emerging leader who exercises increasing influence and an old leader who steps down from an acknowledged position of leadership. Although succession does occur in this fashion, this usually leads to competition among the new leaders for dominance. Thus, effective leaders will usually use or design a community activity to ritualize the transfer of leadership from predecessor to successor. Since both predecessor and successor play their part in the ritual, both are perceived by the community as impresarios of social identity.

The predecessor presents the successor to the community in a way, which highlights his prototypicality and group-oriented behavior. In effective succession, the successor is usually portrayed as an excellent representative of the group's beliefs and values, with a history of serving the group. Also, the successor is presented as similar to the predecessor in terms of his vision of social identity and his commitment to serve the group. Research indicates that modeling and socialization play an important role in effective succession,[107] so that the successor is often portrayed as the faithful follower of the predecessor. Thus, ingroup prototypicality and leader similarity are important factors in how the successor is presented to the community.

A number of contextual constraints influence the presentation of the successor.

- If the predecessor is seen as effective, and the group situation is stable, the successor is expected to be effective especially if he is similar to the predecessor. The presentation of the successor will likely focus on the successor's similarity, while his prototypicality is mostly assumed.

- If the predecessor is seen as ineffective, the similarity of the successor may actually work against the proposed succession. The presentation of the successor will likely focus on the succes-

---

107. Hart, "Leader Succession and Socialization," 451.

sor's prototypicality as assurance that he has the community's interests at heart, while it may even emphasize the successor's dissimilarity to indicate that he will serve differently from his ineffective predecessor.

- If the community experiences or is about to experience significant social change, the presentation of the successor will focus again on the successor's prototypicality as assurance of his fit with the group, since in such a situation previous effectiveness offers no assurance of future effectiveness.

- If succession takes place in a situation with rival bids for leadership, currently or in the near future, the presentation of the successor likely focuses on both the successor's prototypicality and his similarity, the first as assurance that he is really 'one of us,' and the second as indication that he would defend the group like the predecessor against these rivals and their alternative visions of social identity. The group is led to expect the successor to engage in the same denunciation of ingroup deviants and appropriate outgroups as the predecessor.

- Finally, if the predecessor is seen as charismatic leader, the presentation of the successor will likely include elements that attribute charismatic qualities to the successor. Thus, the predecessor uses his social power to facilitate his proposal for succession by encouraging the group to attribute charismatic leadership to their new leader. So rather than leader charisma being diffused in succession and institutionalization, a predecessor may instead 'charismaticize' the process of succession by a ritual transfer of charisma to the successor.[108]

Thus, contextual constraints influence the presentation of the successor, depending on the effectiveness of the previous leader, the similarity of old and new leader, and the social change—including competing bids for leadership—which the community may expect.

The predecessor presents the successor as the preferred new leader who will lead by his vision of social identity and his direction at community events. This context-sensitive presentation of the successor aims to raise group expectations of continued stability and cohesion in their particular circumstances. Such a presentation solicits the

108. Alvesson et al., "The Charismatization of Routines," 333–35.

group's approval of the successor, which can then be publicly affirmed in an activity or ritual, which includes both a transfer of leadership to the new leader and an affirmation of the group's commitment to the new leader. This ritual of succession involves both predecessor and successor in their roles as impresarios of identity.

The Legacy of and Structures for Succession

After analyzing the ingroup status and effectiveness of the predecessor, and the presentation and subsequent ingroup status of the successor, the third point of analysis concerns the legacy bequeathed and its purpose to provide continuity for the group involved as the indirect beneficiaries of succession.

A legacy implies continuity from predecessor to successor as they lead and serve the group. The transmission of this legacy through the process of succession ensures the continued stability and cohesion of the group. This suggests that the content of the legacy can be distinguished from its social function, as Stepp's research on succession in the Pauline world has demonstrated. He found the following relationships between the content and function of a legacy.[109]

Table 3.3: The Legacy Transferred in Ancient Succession Texts

1. When the legacy consists of possessions, succession ensures *continuity of ownership*
2. When the legacy is a characteristic attitude or action shared by predecessor and successor, succession promotes *continuity of manner*
3. When the legacy consists of an institution, succession ensures *continuity of institutional vitality*
4. When the legacy consists of a task, succession ensures either that the task be completed (*realization of effect*), or that the results of the task be maintained (*continuity of effect*)
5. In Jewish and Christian literature, Stepp also found that when the legacy consists of a task or office, succession functions to secure *the legitimacy of a particular successor*.

Function 1 is of little importance for the analysis of leadership, but functions 2–5 can be related to social identity as follows.

109. Stepp, *Leadership Succession*, 55–56, 89.

(2) Continuity of manner relates to the similarity of successor and predecessor. Similarly, (4) realization and continuity of effect seek to ensure that the successor will continue to function in the same way, doing the same things, as the predecessor. This similarity in manner and effect (or task) from predecessor to successor is not merely an aspect of the presentation of the successor, as discussed above, but must be embedded in the leadership structures of the community to ensure continuity for at least some time after the succession ritual. (3) Continuity of institutional vitality relates to the leader's vision of social identity, which is passed on in succession to ensure that the new leader continues to articulate the same vision. This relates to the prototypicality of both predecessor and successor, a quality that assures the community that the new leader is also representative of the group and committed to serve its best interests. Finally, (5) the ritual of succession designates certain successors as legitimate, while the absence of such ritual delegitimates other claimants to succession. Thus, succession functions to provide continuity in the vision of social identity from one leader to the next, as well as to provide continuity in leadership style and function.

The enduring effect of such a legacy must become anchored in the community through identity-embedding structures. This involves the leadership dimension of engineer, initiating structures for succession that accord with and provide continuity for the group's social identity. Generally, the predecessor initiates these structures, while the successor is the beneficiary of the instituted structures, which he subsequently maintains. Both are involved in their function as engineer of social identity.[110]

In summary, leadership succession is a yet underdeveloped area in social identity research. The current theoretical account found that leadership succession is very amenable to an analysis from a social identity perspective since it concerns not only a relationship between two leaders but also with the community as a whole. Succession could therefore be defined as a particular process of identity management in which not one but two leaders interact, the one as established leader who is possibly phasing out, the other as the emerging leader joining

---

110. This structuring of succession is informed by succession practices in the ancient Mediterranean world and may not be transferrable to the modern, western world. That may be an obstacle for current social identity research on succession, but it fits well in the present study.

or succeeding the established leader. As an artist of social identity, the predecessor incorporates succession into his vision of social identity, which is adopted and maintained by the successor. As impresarios of identity, the predecessor and successor design and participate in a succession ritual whereby leadership is transferred (or shared), and which mobilizes group members to celebrate succession as a critical event in successful social identity maintenance. As an engineer of identity, the predecessor initiates leadership structures that facilitate succession by (generally) similar and prototypical successors, who readily accept and develop these structures.

This theoretical account of leadership succession is based only on basic initial research of the process. The challenge for social identity research is to turn this account into hypotheses that can be tested, while the current study proposes to test it in an analysis of Paul's letters.

Conclusion: The Social Identity Model of Leadership

This concludes the review of the analytical model to be used in the rest of this study. The first stage concentrates on the processes of social identification that shaped the first Christ-following communities in Corinth and Ephesus. These processes were initiated through the missionary activities of Paul's team, which were often followed up by mutual visits and correspondence. The communities blended Pauline input with their previous understanding and experience of Greco-Roman and Jewish social identities to explore and find appropriate and consistent expressions of their new social identity as a Christ-following community. Usually, these expressions were not very successful on the first (or second, or third) try, which invited further input from Paul and now also from local leaders. The second stage, then, focuses on these leaders as—sometimes competing—managers of social identity. The three dimensions of such leadership are the leader as artist (creating a vision of social identity), as impresario (conducting community rituals celebrating its social identity), and as engineer (mobilizing group members to turn the vision of social identity into reality). This second stage analyzes how the processes of social identification in Corinth and Ephesus were influenced and directed by Paul as well as by local leaders and their community in order to guide the communities in consistently expressing their social identity. The third stage describes how these processes of social identification and identity management led to the development of leadership patterns in these communities. This stage analyzes the development in terms of the leadership emergence, maintenance, and succession. Leaders emerge on the basis of their prototypicality and group-oriented service; leaders maintain their leadership by successful performance in each of the three dimensions of leadership; and leaders arrange for succession (following the same three dimensions of leadership) to ensure that their legacy of identity management is preserved to bring stability and cohesion to future generations of the Christ-following communities. These three stages build towards a more comprehensive interpretation of Pauline leadership patterns, which will be tested against the reconstructions in the literature that were reviewed in chapter 2.

The study now turns to an analysis of Pauline correspondence to Corinth and Ephesus with a social identity theory of leadership as an heuristic tool.

4

Realigning Emerging Leadership with Christian Social Identity in 1 Corinthians

THE PRELIMINARY INVESTIGATIONS ARE NOW COMPLETE. THE LITERAture review traced the history of the debate on early church leadership, which pointed out the need for an integrative method to connect social structure and theological or ideological factors into an overall analysis of leadership in a group context. An adequate method to account for these factors is the social identity theory, and so a social identity model of leadership was presented. The study now turns to an analysis of the Pauline communities in Corinth and Ephesus. The study of Corinth focuses on 1–2 Corinthians, the study of Ephesus on Ephesians, 1 and 2 Timothy, to be treated in the stated order since that represents both their chronological order of composition and the increasing ages of the communities to which they were addressed. This chapter focuses on 1 Corinthians.

Since the 1970s, the Corinthian correspondence has been the favored subject of socio-scientific analysis, beginning with Theissen's seminal essays.[1] The intensive engagement of Paul's missionary team with Corinth, out of which this correspondence arose, is evident on every page of these letters, which provide a great deal of information about the social situation being addressed. First Corinthians especially treats so many different problems, that an entire range of social, religious, political, and literary considerations are necessary to reconstruct the situation. Consequently, this letter has been designated, somewhat superficially, as a problem-oriented letter,[2] but its genre continues to be

---

1. Now collected in Theissen, *The Social Setting of Pauline Christianity*.
2. Chapple, "Local Leadership," 296–98, 334–35.

debated.³ Many of the earlier studies on Corinth did not address leadership in the church.⁴ This changed with the dissertation by Chapple, who studied local Corinthian leadership through a detailed exegetical analysis of 1 Cor 16:15-18.⁵ Castelli focused mostly on Paul's leadership in her study of Paul's mimetic language and the alleged authority claims this involved.⁶ Clarke's first leadership study focused directly on local leadership in 1 Cor 1-6 and situated it in its cultural context; his work is now frequently cited in major commentaries.⁷ The present chapter builds on these studies, but expands previous approaches by surveying the whole letter and by incorporating insights from both ancient Mediterranean culture and modern leadership theory.

Situating the Corinthian Correspondence in Paul's Ministry

Although Paul's letters often figure as individual literary sources in their own right, the social reality of the Pauline ministries in Corinth and Ephesus suggests that the letters to these communities are intimately connected. The church in Corinth had been started during an 18-month ministry in 50-51 as part of Paul's Macedonian and Achaian tour (see Acts 16:11—18:18).⁸ Just prior to arriving in Corinth, the Thessalonian church had been started and it is likely,

---

3. For a recent discussion, see Thiselton, *First Corinthians*, 41ff.

4. For instance, a prominent 2004 collection of essays, intended as a representative selection of scholarly work on the Corinthian church during the second half of the 20th century, does not contain any article on or index reference to leadership (Adams and Horrell, *Christianity at Corinth*). The same is true for Theissen's collection, referred to above. An older commentary, such as the one by Barrett, contains only one reference to leadership in the introductory pages (*First Corinthians*, 23).

5. Chapple, "Local Leadership," 393-444. Unfortunately, this study is not well known even in NT studies on leadership.

6. Castelli, *Imitating Paul*, 98-115.

7. Clarke, *Leadership in Corinth*, 41-128. The book was reprinted in the Paternoster Biblical Monograph series in 2006 (second edition). Clarke's work is extensively cited in newer commentaries such as Thiselton, *First Corinthians*, and Garland, *1 Corinthians*.

8. This study reads Acts as on the same level as the best of ancient historiographers like Thucydides and Polybius, and accept the reports as essentially historical and trustworthy. For argumentation, see Fitzmyer, *Acts*, 124-29 and Witherington, *Acts*, 2-39.

given the frequent contacts between these churches, that the Pauline team made use of the lessons being learned in community formation in Thessalonica to strengthen their developing ministry in Corinth, and vice versa. Similarly, the second half of Paul's ministry in Ephesus coincided with his intensive engagement with developing problems in Corinth, out of which the Corinthian epistles arose (cf. 1 Cor 16:8–9), dated around 55–56 CE[9] Here, again, it is likely that many of the painful lessons learned in Paul's engagement with the Corinthian church would have been taught and implemented in Ephesus and the surrounding region by Paul's team—just as Paul shared some of his painful ministry experiences in Ephesus with the Corinthians (2 Cor 1:8–11, cf. Acts 19:23ff).

These social connections are evident in the address of each letter. The first letter emphasizes that the Corinthian believers are embedded in an extensive social network of similar Christian groups throughout the world (πᾶσιν τοῖς ἐπικαλουμένοις . . . παντὶ τόπῳ, "with *all* those in *every* place," 1 Cor 1:2), while the second letter more specifically highlights the multiplication of churches throughout Achaia (σὺν τοῖς ἁγίοις πᾶσιν τοῖς οὖσιν ἐν ὅλῃ τῇ Ἀχαΐᾳ, "with *all* the saints who are in the *whole* of Achaia," 2 Cor 1:1). The parallel phrases suggest that Paul not only associates the Corinthian believers with other groups,[10] but also that the letters are addressed to these broader audiences. Apparently, Paul expected these letters to travel beyond the congregation of Corinth,[11] which makes likely that they were also known in Ephesus, especially since Paul wrote the first letter before leaving Ephesus, a copy of which would have been available for others to consult and even copy before his departure.[12]

These social connections across Paul's Aegean ministry suggest that the processes of social identification and developing leadership

---

9. For the chronology and circumstances see DeSilva, *Introduction to the New Testament*, 555–66, and McDonald and Porter, *Early Christianity and Its Sacred Literature*, 368–71, 429–41.

10. See Thiselton, *First Corinthians*, 78.

11. Donfried observes: "surely when Paul writes a letter to the church in Corinth, 'including all the saints throughout Achaia' (2 Cor 1,1), there had to be procedures and structures in place for such transmission and communication". ("Rethinking Scholarly Approaches to 1 Timothy," 160).

12. See the excursus in chapter 7 for a discussion of ancient scribal practices and their importance for understanding Paul's habits of correspondence.

patterns would have been broadly shared in the region, though likely with local variation. One should expect Paul's correspondence, as a small part of this social reality, to reflect some of the connections between these two locations. In fact, if such social connections are completely absent, one may doubt that they ever existed, implying that the correspondence to Ephesus would date from a time much beyond Paul. This concern will be increasingly relevant in analyzing the later correspondence of Ephesians and 1–2 Timothy, studied in chapters 6–8, but it is appropriate at this point to situate the Corinthian correspondence in Paul's ministry.

Social Identification in the Corinthian Community in 55 CE

The Corinthian church had been in existence for about six years when 1–2 Corinthians were written, and had significantly expanded in numbers. Consequently, the missionary team is no longer dealing with the initial formation of Christian social identity in Corinth, but with the next stage of group formation.[13] Intragroup differentiation, external obligations, and cultural patterns created uncertainty about their social identification, which resulted in internal conflict and poor identity performance. A key to interpreting the difficulties addressed in 1 Corinthians is to approach them as the growing pains of early and quick expansion from this perspective of social identification.[14]

The first major difficulty concerns how the subgroups, which had developed in Corinth, related to one another, whether as a loose collection of competing groups or as subordinate groups coordinated within one superordinate group. This can be interpreted as a problem with how to evaluate the relevance of nested identities in relation to the superordinate group (1 Cor 1–4). The oral report of divisions and strife (σχίσματα and ἔριδες, 1:10–11), with the accompanying mottoes ("I follow Paul," etc.) indicate that subgroups had formed which centered on loyalty to Paul or Apollos as valued missionary leaders, or

13. According to Malina's application of group formation theory, this stage would probably be labeled 'storming' ("Early Christian Groups: Using Small Group Formation Theory," 104).

14. See more elaborate studies that apply social identity theory to 1 Corinthians, see Keay, "Paul the Spiritual Guide"; Hansen, *'All of You Are One'*; and Tucker, *'You Belong to Christ.'*

to Peter or Christ as valued founders of the movement (1:12). All of these men were Jews from outside Corinth. Paul can still address the church as a whole, so that the situation has apparently not yet resulted in a final schism. The divisions represent subgroups or parties within the church.

Beginning with F. C. Baur, scholars have often identified the cause of these parties with doctrinal divisions.[15] Paul's gospel was thought to differ from the gospels of Apollos and Peter, while the mention of a Christ party was allegedly for rhetorical effect. However, in these chapters, Paul does not contrast his theology with that of Apollos or Peter, nor does he engage in any competitive strategy with the other named party leaders. Rather, Paul aligns himself with Apollos and Peter, while Christ is raised to the level of supreme example. Instead of taking sides, Paul characterizes these divisions as jealousy and strife (ζῆλος καὶ ἔρις, 3:3), regardless of the party involved, and he equates them with fleshly thinking (3:1–4). The alternative, he argues, is humility and unity in thinking. This call for unity is based on the absolute priority of divine wisdom (1:18–25) and the gospel of Christ crucified (2:1–5), with respect for the contribution of various leaders in its proclamation (3:5–9). Thus, these subgroups represent not theological divisions, but social phenomena.

The social character of these divisions has been explained against the background of patronage[16] and of traveling sophists.[17] Patronage with its values of social status and honor competition was a feature of almost every level of community life in Corinth. Paul refuses to be acknowledged as the community's patron, but describes himself as an agrarian worker and a household servant (3:5–9; 4:1–5), deliberately inverting the typical status-based leadership expectations in Corinth.[18] Instead, God is the community's patron or benefactor (3:9–10, 16,

15. See the extensive discussion in Thiselton, *First Corinthians*, 121–33.

16. Independently of one another, Chow and Clarke describe the function and impact of patronage in the Corinthian community, based mostly on inscriptional evidence (Chow, *Patronage and Power* and Clarke, *Leadership in Corinth*).

17. Winter discusses Alexandrian and Corinthian sophists and applies his findings to 1 Cor 1–4 and 2 Cor 10–13 (*Philo and Paul among the Sophists*). For a more detailed analysis, see Barentsen, "Destabilisatie van opkomend leiderschap," 197ff.

18. Clarke, *Leadership in Corinth*, 133. Williams describes the status of the 'steward' (*oikonomos*) as ambivalent, since the position is usually filled by a slave, but the proximity to the patron gives him a higher status than the patron's clients (*Stewards, Prophets, Keepers of the Word*, 76–77).

22–23).[19] Paul's reversal of the cultural norms of honor, status, and competition indicate the patronage background of the problem with subgroups. Traveling sophist teachers were dependent on the sponsorship of patrons who in turn sought to gain honor by association with a famous teacher. A patron's clients would often compete with another patron's clients (sometimes to the point of fistfights) to attribute the highest honors to their patron and his learned guest. The rivalry of subgroups over famous Jewish teachers like Paul, Apollos, Peter, and Christ runs parallel to these cultural patterns. Paul downplayed his use of rhetorical strategies and "eloquent wisdom" (1:17; 2:1), and emphasized instead his weakness and uncertainty (2:3) as well as the perceived foolishness of the message (1:18), indicates his awareness of sophist conventions in Corinth.[20]

The social character of these divisions can be further explained as a problem with comparative fit. Christian social identity was still relatively new in Corinth, so that even the first converts still experienced a steep learning curve in their social identification. In the short life of the church, at least two famous teachers, Paul and Apollos, had preached there, resulting in mixed allegiance of believers to their favored teacher. The church's expansion probably included the addition of several house churches. The Corinthians then expressed their distinctive loyalty to their Jewish teachers through competitive intergroup rivalries, typical of their culture. They distinguished themselves not from outgroups by demonstrating loyalty to Christ instead of to other gods or temples, but from other ingroups by rivalry over the distinctive teacher they sought to honor. Paul essentially argued that this was an inappropriate social identification for expressing their distinctive identity in Christ (problem of comparative fit), even though he recognized that it was culturally the most accessible identity category (problem of category accessibility).[21]

The second major difficulty concerns how obligations from the socio-economic sphere of a few higher status believers influenced the community, which resulted in conflicting interests due to cross-cutting

---

19. For an extensive study, see Neyrey, "God, Benefactor and Patron," 465–92. For the difference between patronage and benefaction, see Batten, "The Patron-Client Institution."

20. See Winter, *Philo and Paul*, especially chapters 8 and 9.

21. For a more extensive analysis of social identity in these chapters, see Tucker, *'You Belong to Christ.'*

social identities (1 Cor 5–10). Several issues relate to these conflicting interests. The first issue relates to a bizarre incest case (5:1–13), while the Corinthians continued in sophistic arrogance and boasting (5:2, 6).[22] Apparently, the Corinthians considered their internal competition more important than such a trivial case of immorality ("a little leaven," 5:6).[23] This indicates a problem with comparative fit, since intergroup competition is valued more highly as an aspect of group identity than moral purity. But the case is more complicated. Chow has argued convincingly that believers were unable to deal with the incest offender, because he was one of the patrons who supported the community with his status and wealth.[24] Chow's argument can be extended further. Although a fellow patron (i.e. one of the few higher status believers) could raise his own status by challenging the incest perpetrator, he would be constrained by the relatively low number of patrons in even a city like Corinth. Believing patrons would probably meet one another in several different settings, both Christian as well as political and civil. Could a social peer publicly shame a fellow believer-patron in a Christian context by correcting and even expelling him for what would usually be considered a minor misdemeanor, while in political and civil contexts normal obligations needed to be maintained? This could result in very awkward situations for the patrons involved and even bring the entire Christian community in disrepute. This implies that the conflicting interests of a few members of higher status hampered the church's ability to deal with the incest case. Such conflicting interest arose due to cross-cutting social identities, where the offender's higher civic identity was given priority above his social identity as Christ-follower.

The second issue of cross-cutting social identities relates to the legal conflict between believers. The courts were accessible mostly to people of higher status, and the proceedings often involved partiality, bribery, and manipulation in order to gain honor at the expense of

---

22. For this section, see also Barentsen, "Destabilisatie van opkomend leiderschap," 203–5.

23. The Corinthians are probably not proud *of* the incest, but *in spite of* it. For interpretations about the relationship between incest and pride, see Clarke, *Leadership in Corinth*, 74–77.

24. See "Patronage and the Law Court" in Chow, *Patronage and Power*, 75–80 and also 130–41.

the opponent who would be publicly shamed.²⁵ Higher status believers who considered themselves wise and influential enough to go to court did not consider the believing community, to which they themselves belonged, wise enough to mediate (6:5). These believers considered the privileges and obligations of their civic social identity as more relevant in such a case of conflict then the resources of their Christian social identity, another case of conflicting interests due to cross-cutting social identities. A third issue relates to marriage (7:1ff.), which embeds two individuals in one new social identity with its own set of behaviors and obligations. As cross-cutting identities, these too presented difficulties for Christian social identity. Paul instructed the community that group members should maintain the social status they had before their conversion, applying his general principle about circumcision and slavery (7:17–24) to marital status. Where marital status conflicts with Christian identity, Christian social identity is to be given priority. A fourth and final issue of cross-cutting social identities relates to the disunity regarding eating sacrificial meat (8:1, 13).²⁶ Some believers had no trouble eating such meat, even at a sacrificial meal in a pagan temple (8:10). Some believers, converted from idol worship, could only conceive of such eating in terms of idolatry, so it weakened their Christian social identification to see other believers participate in it. Only wealthier people enjoyed the privilege of eating any meat at all, so Paul speaks about renouncing his privileges to address this conflict of interest.²⁷ This, too, is a conflict due to cross-cutting social identities, since a key issue is the social privilege of some (cf. 9:1–27), which undermined the cohesion and stability of the whole community.

Paul addressed various problems with cross-cutting identities and comparative fit, which often made the Christian community ineffective in its identity performance. Believers were uncertain how to reconcile the interests and obligations of their Christian social identity with other social identities, but with increasing longevity and expansion of the community, group members needed to deepen their identification with the believing community and with Christ while they

---

25. In Ibid. and Thiselton, *First Corinthians*, 420–21.

26. Thiselton, *First Corinthians*, 617–20.

27. Theissen, *Social Setting*, 122–27. Others argue that the knowledge and privilege claimed by some Corinthians was unrelated to status; see Witherington, *Conflict and Community in Corinth*, 195; Anderson, *1 Korintiërs*, 117, cf. 159–61.

stayed connected with the rest of their social world. As the community had grown and developed, tension arose over such cross-cutting social obligations. The Corinthians often resolved this tension by rating the value of Christian social identity lower than their (higher status) civic or political identities, following the normal expectations of social rank in Corinth.

A third major area of difficulty relates to disorder in the community's internal activities and identity narrative, which had been affected by the same social tension from the handling of nested and cross-cutting social identities (1 Cor 11–15). These activities had been clearly informed and shaped by earlier teaching traditions, but had come into conflict with cultural values relating to gender roles, community meals, and religious expressions and beliefs. The concentration of tradition terminology in 11:2[28] suggests that previous discussions related to issues that were generally not covered by Pauline teaching traditions. In other words, the issues of nested and cross-cutting social identities reflected unforeseen developments of social identification processes, while from 11:2 onwards, Paul affirmed and clarified previously taught traditions in order to reaffirm their identity narrative and realign their community ritual to rescue them from the disorder of inappropriate social identification.

A first point of disorder is the tension caused by the participation of some women in worship. The social background for Paul's instruction that women pray and prophesy with their head covered (1 Cor 11:2–17) is very difficult to pinpoint. It has been suggested that it reflects an overrealized eschatology that seeks to eradicate the traditional male/female distinctions,[29] and that it reflects Roman tendencies towards greater freedom for elite women.[30] Both suggestions accords well with the context of recurring problems with higher status believers.[31] The passage reflects "the jostling for power

---

28. See Paul's terminology relating to his teaching tradition in this section: παράδοσις ("tradition," 11:2), παραδίδωμι ("to deliver," 11:2, 23; 15:3, 24) and παραλαμβάνω ("to receive," 11:23; 15:1, 3).

29. Meeks, *The First Urban Christians*, 88–89.

30. Winter, *Roman Wives, Roman Widows*, 77–96. Garland evades the search for the appropriate background and simply deals with Paul's prohibition (Garland, *1 Corinthians*, 506–7).

31. Thiselton, *First Corinthians*, 799, who lists 80 scholarly works for his discussion of this issue.

and authority amongst the leading families" so that Paul counteracts the behavior of some of the elite women in the church.[32] Paul appealed to "nature" (ἡ φύσις, 1 Cor 11:14), i.e. the culturally accepted[33] standard for female behavior and to the creation narrative, applying again the principle to maintain one's social status from before conversion. Quite possibly, some elite women justified their unconventional behavior through an overrealized understanding of Paul's eschatology, causing tension in the community about female participation in basic community events.[34]

A second issue of disorder is the disunity experienced in their common meals. Although both rich and poor participated, the distribution of food and drink was unequal, with divisions and even disease or death as a result (11:18–19, 30). This reflected both the dining customs and the dining quarters of the rich.[35] Social tension was inevitable since their common meal became an expression of social inequality rather than of mutual concern. The community lacked the cognitive and material resources to structure their meals appropriately, indicating that even the practice of such a basic community ritual as a meal (the Lord's Supper) was negatively affected by inadequate identification with their Christian social identity.

Disorder and disruption of community ritual was also evident in the unequal participation in the life of the community. Paul's concern to downgrade the phenomenon of pneumatic speech (12:8–10; 28–30; 13:1; 14:1–4), and to upgrade group members of little honor (12:21–25), follows the logic of earlier chapters, where status and honor were

---

32. Gill, "The Importance of Roman Portraiture for Head Coverings," 260.

33. Thiselton discusses the meaning of ἡ φύσις αὐτὴ, "nature itself" (11:14) extensively and concludes that it refers to the commonly accepted order of things at the time and context of writing (*First Corinthians*, 844–46), contra Barrett, *First Corinthians*, 256 who argues that Paul refers to the natural state as God created it.

34. This may be the background to the difficult passage about the silence of women in 1 Cor 14:34–36, but a discussion of the passage will not shed additional light on social identification and will thus be omitted.

35. Witherington, *Conflict & Community in Corinth*, 191–95. The rich generally invited social peers and favored friends to eat with them in the *triclinium*, a dining room with reclining couches that fitted up to 10 people, while clients and lesser public dined in the atrium with a noticeably lower quality of food and drink. Such homes were designed to reflect these dining customs and could not easily accommodate larger groups to share equally in a common meal, and such material limitations strongly resist alternative social identifications.

downplayed, and lower status believers received recognition.[36] It suggests that in their community assemblies, their pagan background[37] as well as their cultural values of honor and status were significant influences that undermined proper Christian identity performance.

A final issue of disorder in Christian identity performance is the deviant belief "that there is no resurrection" (15:12). Earlier Pauline teaching and a still earlier apostolic tradition (15:5–7) had established the resurrection as a foundational group belief[38] and essential part of their identity narrative (15:1–4), but this still did not prevent difficulties. Garland argues that the Corinthians were honestly confused about this belief,[39] which is certainly possible due to the lack of any parallel to this Christian belief in Greek or Jewish thinking.[40] This suggests at least a lack of category accessibility. Witherington, however, points out important social dimensions of this difficulty, since those who disbelieved in the resurrection apparently took it as occasion to "eat and drink, for tomorrow we die" while the warning that "bad company ruins good morals" (15:32–33) is reminiscent of the conflicting interests due to cross-cutting social identities discussed above.[41] Most likely, this is again a difficulty with social elites adjusting the beliefs and values of Christian social identity to legitimate their elite behavior, instead of renouncing their privilege and status on behalf of the community. Thus, it appears that cultural beliefs and social pressure

---

36. Martin concludes that tongue-speaking was exercised by the high status members in Corinth to further highlight their distinctiveness in the community, which shows the same type of argumentation as in chapters 5–6, 8–10 and 11 ("Tongues of Angels and Other Status Indicators," 579–80). See also Esler, "Glossolalia and the Admission of Gentiles into the Early Christian Community."

37. Forbes considers the attempt to discover parallels between Christian glossolalia and the Hellenistic oracle cult unsuccessful and even misleading ("Early Christian Inspired Speech," 268), while Winters argues at great length that the spirit-inspired speaker seeks personal honor by saying "Jesus accurse [you]," Winter's alternative translation of "Jesus is accursed" (*After Paul Left Corinth*, 174–76).

38. Cf. Bar-Tal, "Group Beliefs," as discussed in chapter 3.

39. Garland, *1 Corinthians*, 678.

40. For a study of these discontinuities of Christian resurrection belief as compared to the surrounding culture, see Wright, *The Resurrection of the Son of God*, with key arguments briefly summarized in Wright and Crossan, "The Resurrection," 16–21.

41. Witherington, *Conflict & Community in Corinth*, 292–98.

overruled this core expression of Christian social identity, in spite of its demonstrated centrality for the Christ-believing community.

To summarize, although 1 Corinthians describes many problems, it is not simply a problem-oriented letter.[42] A different perspective commends itself after the analysis of social identification, which demonstrates that many problems can be traced to a lack of comparative fit and category accessibility, which reflect a young and rapidly expanding community with increasing social complexities. First Corinthians deals not so much with a resistant or rebellious church, but rather with the normal growing pains of social identification in the relatively complex world of a Greek city like Corinth. The addition of various house groups led to normal subgroup formation, but then rivalries arose between these subgroups over loyalty to favored Jewish teachers, parallel to the cultural patterns of patronage, honor competition, and traveling sophists. The character of the subgroups as nested social identities relative to one superordinate Christian social identity was not yet properly appreciated. Conflicts of interest arose between Christian and non-Christian social identities, which resulted from the increasing social complexity of the church. The lower priority of cross-cutting social identities relative to Christian social identity was not yet fully understood, due to a lack of comparative fit. Even basic identity rituals, anchored in well known teaching traditions, were expressed imperfectly. Participation in these community activities as well as belief in the resurrection suffered from misplaced cultural values, often due to the influence of a few higher status group members.

The Corinthian Leaders as Managers of Christian Social Identity

The previous section analyzed the social identification processes addressed in 1 Corinthians. This section asks the question that is hardly addressed in the scholarly literature,[43] what role the local Corinthian leaders played in influencing and addressing the challenges in social

---

42. See Chapple, "Local Leadership," 296–98, 334–35, who designates 1 Thessalonians as a progress oriented letter.

43. But see Hiigel, *Leadership in 1 Corinthians*, 129–42, who speaks of "adjudicatory" leadership and the leader's charge to articulate and foster the community's values.

identification. At first sight, this seems an impossible task, since a few known leaders in Corinth are mentioned only in the letter opening and closing (1:1-16; 16:15-18), while the rest of the letter is addressed to the community. Yet, the letter provides several indications of local leadership.

Identifying the Local Leadership Subgroup[44]

Seven named individuals in Corinth likely form part of the local leadership.[45] Sosthenes and Crispus (1:1, 14) are converted former synagogue rulers (Acts 18:17 and 8, respectively), a good indicator of their wealth and relatively high social status.[46] Gaius and Stephanas are both converted householders who used their homes in service of the church (1:14 and Rom 16:23; 1 Cor 1:16 and 16:15, respectively). Fortunatus and Achaicus, part of the Corinthian delegation to Paul (16:17), are most likely independent delegation partners instead of dependents of Stephanas' household, since Paul instructs believers to also submit to them (ὑποτάσσησθε τοῖς τοιούτοις, 16:16). Given the expense of travel, their membership in the delegation may be an indication of some wealth. Finally, Chloe seems to be a female householder, whose dependents have reported the divisions to Paul (1:11). In addition, Paul mentions Phoebe as patroness of the church in Cenchreae (Rom 16:1),[47] and Erastus, Corinth's city treasurer (Rom 16:23).[48] Compared to the majority of Corinthian believers (1 Cor 1:26), these named individuals are almost certainly people of relative wealth and high social status, who played an influential role due to the way they used their relative wealth and status. The specific commendation of those who labor on behalf of the community (16:17),

---

44. For a more extensive discussion, see Barentsen, "Destabilisatie van opkomend leiderschap," 194-97.

45. See chapter 4, "Christian Leaders in Secular Corinth," in Clarke, *Leadership in Corinth*, 41-56; Ellis, "Paul and His Coworkers," 183-99; Theissen, *Social Setting*, 54-57.

46. Clarke, *Serve the Community*, 128.

47. According to DBAG, προστάτις (*prostatis*) means "Protectress, patroness, helper," while LSJ refers to the male form προστάτης (*prostatēs*) with the meaning, "one who stands before, a front-rank-man, a chief, a ruler." The word διάκονος (*diakonos*) usually refers to a representative of a person of higher status (Collins, *Diakonia*).

48. For discussion of Erastus, see also Theissen, *Social Setting*, 85-93.

indicates that these people functioned as local leaders, although their exact function and title remain unspecified. Most likely, their mention in 1 Corinthians is not coincidental, but serves to highlight Paul's positive estimate of their leadership in a climate where leadership threatened to divide the church.

The gift lists of 1 Cor 12 give a second indication of local leadership. In the second list (12:28–30) Paul lists the trio of apostles, prophets, and teachers, whom God "appointed" (ἔθετο, 12:28). Although Paul's ranking them as first, second, and third is not to be construed as a hierarchy, it does indicate the primacy of apostolic leadership,[49] next to prophets and teachers as persons given to the church in certain functions. After the trio, the list switches to an unnumbered list of gifts, which includes "helping, administrating" (ἀντιλήμψεις, κυβερνήσεις, 12:28), two items which Thiselton translates as "kinds of administrative support" and "ability to formulate strategies."[50] The evidence is insufficient to conclude that these two terms are precursors of "deacon" and "elder," much less that they refer offices in the institutional sense, but it certainly points in the direction of leadership with its needed support staff, however informal its arrangements.[51]

The third and last indication of local leadership comes from Paul's specific commendation of some (16:15–18). Stephanas and his household are singled out as first converts in Achaia (ἀπαρχὴ, 16:15), a term that White has shown to refer to people first dedicated to a particular service.[52] The reference to his household is significant, since social studies have shown that innovators are rarely low status persons. Rather they are sufficiently socially rooted to face the inevitable challenges to their leadership in innovation.[53] Paul requires recognition

---

49. See Chapple, "Local Leadership," 388–89.

50. See his thorough overview of papyri in determining this meaning (Thiselton, *First Corinthians*, 1019–21).

51. See also Bruggen, *Ambten in de apostolische kerk*, 153ff. Brockhaus proposes on the basis of these passage that in 1 Cor leadership *office* functioned from the start, with all the key elements involved: duration, authority, title, legitimation, and being set apart (Brockhaus, *Charisma und Amt*, 123).

52. White, *Die Erstlingsgabe im Neuen Testament*, 201. See also Aune, "Distinct Lexical Meanings of ἀπαρχή" and Delling, "ἄρχω, ἀρχή, ἀπαρχή, ἀρχαῖος, ἀρχηγός, ἄρχων," Chapple still prefers "first convert" although his emphasis on being the first baptized and founding member of the church comes close to White's proposal (Chapple, "Local Leadership," 398).

53. Malina, *Timothy: Paul's Closest Associate*, 77. A few pages later, Malina adds:

of and submission to Stephanas and other such group members, significantly raising their leadership status before the community. Their devotion to serving the group and their function as "fellow worker and laborer" (συνεργοῦντι καὶ κοπιῶντι, 16:16) classify them as group members loyal to Paul and prototypical in their service of the believing community. Paul here endorses a leadership pattern that is already operative in Corinth. Unfortunately, Paul does not tell us whether they fit in the category of "helping" and "administrating," whether they functioned as prophet or teacher, or both.[54]

The Role of the Corinthian Leaders in the Corinthian Problems

One of the leading puzzles about the role of local Corinthian leaders is what were they doing to resolve the problems Paul addressed in his letter. Nine leading individuals from Corinth are identified in the letter, with some of their leadership functions probably mentioned in the gift lists, and some even specifically commended for their leadership. They were presumably familiar with the difficulties Paul addressed, so why did they not resolve these difficulties themselves? Did they lack insight or were they powerless in the face of conflicting social forces? Does Paul intervene on their behalf or does he intervene over their heads, perhaps even correcting them implicitly? Alternatively, could these leaders perhaps have caused the difficulties because of an inappropriate style of leadership?

It is unlikely that the named leaders had caused the problems, since Paul mentioned them with approval. Sosthenes functioned as co-author (1:1); Chloe's people reported on the divisions (1:11); Crispus and Gaius are mentioned uncritically as believers that Paul baptized who were likely involved from the foundation of the church (1:14); and Stephanas, Fortunatus, and Achaicus were recommended for their leadership (16:17–18).

"Cross-cultural studies of first adopters indicate that as a rule they control adequate material and personality resources to absorb the possible failure should the innovation prove unsuccessful" (p. 92).

54. Chapple also observes that Paul values prophets and teachers as key leaders in 1 Cor 12 while he recommends patronal leadership in 1 Cor 16 (as in 1 Tess.) (Chapple, "Local Leadership," 440).

It is also unlikely that these leaders represented the Paul party, even though they appear to be loyal to Paul. If that were the case, Paul's arguments for unity would in effect have been an argument for unity as the 'Paul party.' Paul would have chosen sides in the rivalries and exacerbated the jealousies. Members of other subgroups would have perceived Paul as an outgroup member and would have interpreted his argument for unity as an exercise of coercive power against their subgroup interests. Obviously, Paul would not have succeeded in unifying the various subgroups on this basis.[55]

Perhaps the Corinthian problems implicated some of the unnamed local leaders. The subgroups may well have formed around households or patronage groups whose leaders encouraged boasting to maintain the unity for their subgroup. The role of higher status believers in the incest and court cases, in the difficulties with eating sacrificial meat, and in the disorder with the Lord's Supper and the community's activities, all implicate some, probably unnamed, local leaders in these problems.

Thus, part of the explanation for the relative inaction of the local leaders is their ambivalent role in the difficulties. They appear to be divided amongst themselves, some implicated in the difficulties, others loyal to Paul. This is also reflected in the fragmented nature in which reports on Corinth reached Paul: by letter (7:1, 8:1 etc.), from Chloe's people (1:11), from the delegation (16:17–18) and from his trusted delegate Timothy (4:17, 16:10).

Another factor in their relative inaction is the tenacity of cultural patterns of intergroup interaction. The Corinthian church consisted of a number of households with householders as its most influential leaders.[56] In this context, cultural conventions about households, patronage, honor competition, and traveling sophist teachers were so strong, that alternative styles of interaction and leadership were very

---

55. In research on schism in groups, Sani found that the perception of identity subversion plays a significant role in forming schismatic intentions and that the opportunity to voice dissent is an important factor in defusing such intentions (Sani, "When Subgroups Secede," 1076ff). In other words, if Paul had merely approved his own party, he would have reinforced the perception of identity subversion and squelched the expression of dissent, thus propelling the group towards schism. Instead, Paul emphasized the superordinate nature of Christian social identity with respect for subgroups, which defused schismatic intentions.

56. Gehring, *House Church and Mission*, 134–41.

difficult to maintain over against these cultural stereotypes.[57] This not only helps to understand the internal division of the local leaders; it also suggests that the named leaders whom Paul approves have insufficient social influence to resolve the Corinthian difficulties successfully. These named leaders were probably members of some of the house groups that were involved in the problematic social competition, perhaps even as householder or patron, but even then, they were probably unable to break fully with these cultural patterns without external intervention.

Finally, the leaders were not completely inactive, for at least an important cross-section of leaders had initiated a delegation to Paul, along with a letter from the congregation with some key questions to be addressed. This probably indicates that at least the named delegation members had sufficient influence in the church so that they could "avoid being so identified with the pro-Pauline group as to have their proposal rejected out of hand by the other groups."[58]

The Identity Management of the Corinthian Leaders

This scenario suggests that the Corinthian leaders were not yet able to lead by identity management as Paul envisioned and modeled. As *artists* of social identity, they regularly mistook cultural comparison dimensions as defining features of Christian social identity. Wisdom, status, and honor must have functioned as relevant dimensions of Christian social identity in Corinth, as is evident from Paul's rejecting them. Thus, their vision of Christian social identity was still imperfectly developed since at least some cultural values were not yet sufficiently transformed. This lack had serious consequences for the other two areas of their leadership.

As *engineers* of social identity, the Corinthian leaders were caught in or even encouraged subgroup formation. Even if this was intended as a way to provide stability and cohesion for the subgroups under their leadership, it actually undermined appropriate identity performance. In the cases of incest and legal proceedings, the involved

---

57. Harland points out that models of leadership in associations often replicated leadership pattern of their city or the empire (*Associations, Synagogues, and Congregations*, 102–3). Such a process of replication seems to have taken place also in Corinth.

58. Chapple, "Local Leadership," 414.

leaders seemed unaware of the disastrous consequences of their behavior, which incurs Paul's strong censure. In the cases of marital status and sacrificial meat, leaders seemed as concerned as the rest of the community about how to align their identity performance with Paul's vision of identity, since they wrote Paul about it. Even then, they did not yet resolve the situation by initiating adequate structures for Christian social identity; they remained dependent on Paul.

As *impresarios* of social identity, the local leaders predictably showed similar weaknesses. Their expression of loyalty to Jewish teachers disintegrated in a competitive display of strife and jealousy. Their sensitivity to status and honor turned their common meals and even the Lord's Supper into a shameful discrimination of the poorer members, while the gifts of the Holy Spirit, intended for all, became an occasion for competitive boasting. Even such a basic error as the denial of the resurrection could find a platform within the community, without the local leaders able to root it out.

It is no surprise, that the local leaders faced shortcomings in their identity management of the community. Without a fully developed vision of Christian social identity, local leaders were unable to help community members consistently to live out their Christian identity in various other social relationships, while they themselves often gave priority to a social identity other than their Christian social identity. Naturally, the internal activities and rituals of the community reflected this inadequate vision and identity performance. Yet, it must not be forgotten that these difficulties had arisen at least in part because of the continuing expansion of the church, with new house groups and new leaders being added. Existing leaders, even those who had been believers since the founding of the church, had as yet insufficient experience and resources to be able to navigate the community through such times of growth and social change.

Paul's Leadership as Identity Management

In times of social change through expansion, social identification often lags behind reality, unless guidance is available from earlier experiences with expansion. It is evident that the Corinthian Christ-following community could not draw on such experience locally, which explains the imperfect development of social identification at this stage. The neighboring churches in Philippi, Berea or Thessalonica were not very likely sources of such experience, since they had been founded within the same year as the church in Corinth, which moreover had been the primary location for Paul's ministry in the region for 18 months (cf. Acts 16:11—18:17). If anything, these churches would have faced similar challenges in social identification then or in the near future if they expanded at rates similar to the church at Corinth. The intervention of Paul's missionary team was necessary to help the Corinthians match their social identification with their current social reality of an expanded community with a number of house groups and their individual leaders. Paul's intervention was most likely intended to benefit the other churches in Macedonia and Achaia as well, since Paul addressed not only the Corinthian believers in this letter (1 Cor 1:2).

This section analyzes how Paul engaged these challenges in social identification, and how he competed with the local leaders for the right to define their vision of Christian social identity and to determine which behaviors were appropriate for the group. Paul's rhetoric not only influenced the community, but it also affected the leadership status for himself and the local leaders. If he proved effective in matching their social identification with social reality, his leadership status would significantly increase and earn him the social power to shape the developing local leadership group. If he would not prove effective, he would lose status and the Corinthian church would either divide or look for alternative proposals for social identification that would move the church in a different direction than Paul had envisioned. Clearly, much more was at stake than merely the resolution of a few local difficulties. The future of the Corinthian church as part of the Pauline mission hangs in the balance and with it probably the future of Paul's entire mission in Macedonia and Achaia.

Attaching Corinthian Values to Foundational Beliefs

Paul first clarified and adapted his vision of Christian social identity, parallel to the leader's role as artist of social identity. He tailored his vision of Christian social identity to address the issue of comparative fit (1:20—2:16). The Corinthians viewed wisdom as important comparison dimensions, so Paul adopted the label of "wisdom" from its Greek context and attached it to his gospel of Christ crucified, which—by way of social creativity—attributed value and distinctiveness to their Christian identity. Likewise, Paul adopted the pejorative value of the label 'foolishness' but attributes it to the outgroup.[59] Thus, God's provision of salvation is wisdom for all believers but foolishness to unbelievers (1:18, 23–24). Moreover, God's calling grants all believers the status of being chosen by God and in Christ Jesus (1:26–30),[60] while the elite of this world have no status with God but "are doomed to pass away" (2:6–8). Wisdom and status, properly applied, are not categories for intragroup differentiation, but boundary markers for differentiation between believers and unbelievers. Thus, Paul associated the treasured values of wisdom and status with the foundational beliefs of Christian social identity, which delegitimized any comparison of wisdom and status between himself, Apollos or Peter. In this way, Paul sought to convince all subgroups that his alternative for defining their Christian social identity was a better comparative fit than the various subgroup perspectives.

Reclaiming the Corinthian Identity Narrative

Furthermore, Paul retold the story of the Corinthian ministry as well as of his own broader ministry to reclaim the identity narrative in support of his vision for Christian social identity (3:1—4:21). He narrated his own role in founding and Apollos' role in developing the church (3:5–9, 12–15; 4:1–5), downgrading their role of preachers and leaders as subordinate to God's work. Moreover, the church is pictured as God's "field" and "building" (3:5–9), a "temple" for his Spirit (3:16–17), upgrading the value of their superordinate social identity as a unified community consisting of all subgroups. Paul did not deny the value of

---

59. As Ehrensperger remarks, the division wisdom/foolishness marks a radical difference between the Christian community and the world (*Paul and the Dynamics of Power*, 170). She does not take into account, though, that the actual social differences were too small in Paul's evaluation, and that Paul strongly argued for a more radical perspective. His use of "wisdom" attaches positive emotional value to the gospel, while his use of "foolishness" attaches negative emotional value to the Corinthian search for eloquent rhetoric and philosophical knowledge.

60. Tucker concurs, although from a slightly different methodological framework: "It is possible to describe ἐν Χριστῷ as Paul's preferred overarching social identity position, a position that does not obliterate previous social identities but reprioritizes them" (Tucker, *'You Belong to Christ,'* 122).

the subgroups,[61] but argued that the higher level superordinate social identity encompasses them all. Paul also sketched his own broader ministry, including much suffering, which must have appeared as "scum" and "refuse" to the Corinthians who pretended to "have become kings" (4:8–13, 18). Such boasts are, or course, preposterous and Paul counted on the Corinthians to realize the absurdity of their competitive behavior through his rhetorical exaggeration.[62] A key to Paul's intricate rhetoric is that his narrative reappropriates and reinterprets the past differently from the Corinthian perspective, which interpreted the past as basis for varieties of Christian social identity. Paul reclaimed the past not out of historical interest,[63] but out of concern to shape the group's social memory as a foundation for different behavior. His retelling of his ministry experiences in Corinth and elsewhere, parallel to the ministries of others like Apollos and Peter, served to reorient the Corinthian's identity narrative to support Paul's vision of Christian social identity.

Paul's identity management in handling the subgroup divisions shows that the problem is neither purely social nor purely theological or ideological; instead, social and ideological factors interact upon one another, each shaping and being shaped by the other. Thus, both the older exegesis that these divisions are primarily theologically motivated and the modern exegesis that these divisions are mostly socially structured are rooted in historical reality, but each represents only a partial perspective on the whole. This social identity analysis shows how social structure and (both local and Pauline) ideology interact.

---

61. A strategy confirmed in modern social identity research on conflict management (Hornsey and Hogg, "Assimilation and Diversity," 153.

62. Thiselton connects Paul's use of irony with a problem of overrealized eschatology and conversion experiences in local cults (Thiselton, *First Corinthians*, 357). The exact background is for the present purpose less important than how Paul uses this literary feature to reshape the identity narrative.

63. Williams notes the memory remains connected with foundational persons and events (see Williams, *Stewards, Prophets*, 154), but this memory can still be interpreted differently to legitimate different practices in the present.

Restructuring Social Reality to Match Christian Social Identity

Besides clarifying his vision of Christian social identity, Paul assisted the Corinthians in adjusting their social relationships with ingroup and outgroup members to match this identity. In dealing with the incest offender, Paul considers intragroup moral discernment of higher value for Christian social identity than maintaining respect for kinship relationships of group members with outsiders. Thus, Paul stigmatized the offender as deviant and instructed the Corinthians to expel him (5:3-5). The intragroup judgment which this requires (5:12-13) is based on moral purity and not on status and wisdom which had occasioned the subgroups. He links the handling of deviance with Christ's sacrifice and the Passover narrative, incorporating it into the group's identity narrative. Intragroup moral discernment also takes precedence over the civic interests of some higher status members who were embroiled in lawsuits. Paul reinterprets these legal proceedings as a lost cause already (6:7) in which the high status plaintiff perpetrates new injustices (6:8). Conversely, all believers have a high religious status and are considered competent to judge righteously (6:1-3). Paul argued that, if it sounded preposterous to patrons to have clients render judgment over their affairs, it was even more preposterous to appoint an unbelieving judge as judge over believers, which is a clear violation of ingroup integrity and priority. The comparative fit for believers is defined by comparing not with social peers but with fellow believers. Paul links this downgrading of social status with an appeal to the coming judgment, in which believers will judge the world (6:2) and to their status in Christ as sanctified and justified (6:11), also incorporating this issue in their identity narrative.

A further restructuring of social relationships concerns sacrificial meat and common meals. Paul's permission of eating of sacrificial meat in some circumstances (10:25-27) acknowledged the broader relationships of the few wealthier believers, while his prohibition against eating meat in a pagan temple ritual (10:20-22) likely affected both high and low status believers. Paul thus accepted that social status differentiated believers from one another, but he argued that mutual support, personal sacrifice, and winsomeness were relevant comparison dimensions for Christian social identity, not status and privilege. Paul supports his argument with his personal example in self-sacrifice and with Jewish warnings about idolatry from the life of Moses, incorporating his advice into their identity narrative. Similarly, Paul accepted that status differences influenced their common meals (some provided space and food while others apparently came empty-handed, 11:21), but he argued that they should participate as a community (probably proposing for equal access to the food regardless of social status, 11:29, 33). The narrative about the Lord's Supper supports Paul's contention and embeds this manner of participation in their identity narrative. Thus, parallel to the leader's role as engineer of social identity, Paul restructured the Corinthian social conventions significantly to match their relationships with his vision of Christian identity.[64]

Ordering the Activities of the Community

Paul's restructuring of social relationships generally is also reflected in his ordering of the community's internal activities, which had been mismanaged because of the social tension from nested and cross-cutting social identities. Paul consistently reordered these activities by narratives, which strengthened their foundational beliefs and values, and thus their social identity. Paul shaped female participation partly by reference to the creation narrative (11:7–12), which connects male and female to God as part of his community. He guides respectful and equal participation in the Lord's Supper by narrating the instituting traditions of the Lord's Supper (11:23–26), which anchored the ritual in core identity elements. Equal participation of every group member is fashioned in various ways: a narrative about the Trinity's direction of community activities (12:4–11) connects participation with every member of the Trinity; the body metaphor (12:12–26)[65] connects equal honor for all with diversity and cohesion; and the ode to love (1 Cor 13) demonstrates that status and honor with their resulting jealousy and conflict are opposed to the mutual respect and concern needed for the community's functioning. In these community activities, cultural traditions about gender roles, meals, and differentiated participation

---

64. Hiigel interprets these passages as a call for adjudicatory leadership but does not address the wider social consequences (Hiigel, *Leadership in 1 Corinthians*, 129–35).

65. Witherington, *Conflict & Community in Corinth*, 254.

clashed with Christian identity. Finally, Paul encourages participation in the collection for the church in Jerusalem by referring to the Galatian churches (16:1–4). Generally, Paul encourages compliance by emphasizing the common traditions in the network of churches within which the church in Corinth is embedded (4:7, 7:17, 10:32, 11:16, 14:33; cf. 16:19). Paul infuses the community's internal activities with meaning from Christian identity narratives about creation, about the institution of the Lord's Supper, and about the divine calling and ordering of the community, and by embedding them within his larger network of communities, thus ordering their activities and aligning them with his vision of Christian social identity.

Paul's Social Power and the Agency of the Corinthian Believers

This raises the question of how Paul's identity management would have been received in the Corinthian church, especially in light of Paul's strong authority claims. He hands people over to Satan (5:5), shames them (6:5, 15:34–36), posits his own practice as rule (9:1–27; 11:16, 14:32), diagnoses sickness and death as caused by sin (11:30), and pronounces a curse on all who do not share his love for Christ (16:22). Does Paul have the social power necessary for his authoritative claims to be accepted? What are the implications for the agency of the believers?

Taylor argues that Paul's leadership was not being contested in Corinth when 1 Corinthians was being written.[66] Yet, the above analysis indicates a degree of competition between Paul and local leaders as is evident from their differences of opinion about the definition and performance of Christian social identity in changing social circumstances. Considering the social tensions that accompany group expansion, this competition represented not so much a purposeful attack on Paul and his authority, but a contest over how to resolve the normal tensions and conflicts of the advancing social identification processes. Such differences could very well harden into community divisions or intentional opposition, including direct attempts to undermine Paul's influence, but such was likely not yet the case in 1 Corinthians. Paul's rhetoric was aimed to prevent such hardening from taking place

---

66. Taylor, "Conflict as Context for Defining Identity," 934.

by convincing local leaders of his vision of Christian social identity without engaging in open conflict such as seems to have occurred in 2 Corinthians.

On the other hand, Paul's leadership has been criticized as tending towards authoritarianism and hierarchy,[67] or for its exclusion of females or the poor.[68] In spite of a number of authoritative pronouncements, Paul's leadership style can be seen to be participatory and empowering. When addressing the subgroup difficulties, Paul downplayed his own apostolic role, not because it was contested but because it could be misunderstood. He refused to shame anyone (4:14), focused on humility instead of boasting (1:29, 3:21), and emphasized the equal value of all 'parties.' However, in the ensuing discussion Paul spoke freely on his own authority, excommunicating the offender (5:4–5) and shaming suing believers (6:5). Evidently, Paul was sensitive to the context in how to wield his authority. Paul's rhetoric in 1 Cor 1–4 aimed to regain the loyalty of all subgroups to one common vision of Christian identity, while Paul's authoritative assertions of 1 Cor 5–6 indicate that he believed his authority would at that point prove acceptable to all Corinthian believers, so that he could directly mobilize them to administer correction and adjudicate internal conflict.[69] Moreover, incest was a clear moral case that cut across all party allegiances, so that Paul could immediately move the discussion away from parties and speak authoritatively without being seen as self-serving. Thus, instead of being authoritarian, he first presented his case for one superordinate Christian social identity, which then empowered them to act as one whole body in these important issues.

In subsequent discussions, Paul remained sensitive to the social context in his expressions of authority. In addressing various marital situations (1 Cor 7), Paul wielded his authority in a more nuanced way. He gave advice as a wise counselor, showed concern for the believers, and negotiated an acceptable solution, thus empowering believers to make their own choice. In the delicate issues surrounding the eating of meat, Paul seemed to first side with the rich in their privilege and "knowledge" (8:1–3, 7). The narratives about his own denial of privilege

---

67. Castelli, *Imitating Paul*, 75, 96, 116–17; Polaski, *Paul and the Discourse of Power*, 16, 119.

68. Tamez, *Struggles for Power in Early Christianity*, 33–56.

69. Hiigel, *Leadership in 1 Corinthians*, 93–95.

(9:1–27), and about idolatry under Moses' leadership (10:1–13) created strong points of identification for the Corinthian leaders, eliciting a favorable response to his prohibitions against participating in pagan cultic rituals, which was perhaps especially critical of the elite. In emphasizing the foundational beliefs, Paul referred to traditions that he himself had simply passed on (11:23; 15:3–8), while he spoke in the first person singular to identify himself with the Corinthians in their learning process (13:1–3, 11–12; 14:6, 11, 14–15, 18–19), moderating the sharpness of his rebuke. Even when he referred to his privileged position in the apostolic tradition, he moderated his exceptional status by picturing himself as unworthy and working harder than the other apostles (15:8–10). Though Paul expected the Corinthians to comply with his instructions because he was their founder and apostle, he did not do so highhandedly but downplayed his authority and focused instead on motivating the Corinthians in their processes of social identification.

Surprisingly, the discussion of such a central belief as the resurrection is placed nearly at the end of the letter. Paul first reestablished his leadership as prototypical for the whole congregation to avoid the disastrous perception that his view on the resurrection might be merely a subgroup distinctive. He next empowered the Corinthians to resolve social tension from cross-cutting identities conflict. Then he moved to common teaching traditions, which united the whole congregation, anchored in sources beyond Paul. Once all these pieces were in place, Paul confidently corrected the resurrection doubters, knowing that this would not be mistaken for party-politics. The relative ease with which Paul can argue at this stage in the letter comes from careful preparation for the reception of his arguments.

Paul is very sensitive to the social context within which he practices his leadership. As a manager of Christian social identity, he skillfully enables group members to identify with their common vision. Each situation requires an adjustment of Paul's rhetoric to motivate group members to deepen their Christian identification and to perform their Christian identity with confidence. Paul's agency as apostle does not turn Corinthian believers into passive receivers of his directives, but empowers them (or so at least Paul argues) to strong identity performance.

Summary

As Paul encourages continuing Christian social identification among the believers in Corinth, he is clearly aware of the internal and external social pressures that his readers are experiencing. He intentionally engages those experiences and shows the desired outcomes for all parties, often by minimizing the implications of social status and honor for the few wealthier believers, and by highlighting the implications for every member of the community. Paul does not preach an abstract message of identification, but he contextualizes it and tailors it to his audience, so that it interacts with other sources of identification in their environment and will have the greatest positive effect on their Christian identification.

Contrary to the Holtzmann-Sohm hypothesis, 1 Corinthians does not present a theological ideal of equality for all in a Spirit-led charismatic community, which in succeeding generations succumbed to the pressures of social and cultural accommodation. Paul is critically aware that his communities are not a complete alternative society in themselves, but that they function in a hierarchical society full of injustices and inequalities. At least some of the values of the Christian community are different, namely those that represent relevant dimensions of comparison, but in many respects his communities are similar to other contemporary cultural expressions of community and religion. First Corinthians is an excellent source to document the early development of Christian social identity, which empowers community members in deepening their social identification and performing their social identity in internal rituals and external relationships.

The Development of Local Leadership Patterns at Corinth in 55 CE

This section draws out the implications of the preceding analyses for the developing leadership patterns in Corinth. The basic situation is as follows. After five or six years of development, the expansion of the church presented local leadership with the need for additional levels of coordination than they had provided up to that point. Without outside assistance from Jewish teachers such as Paul or Apollos, local leadership opted for the best comparative fit for their situation, and demonstrated their loyalty to their Jewish teachers by Corinthian patterns of boasting and competition. This practice generated intragroup rivalry, and reduced the cohesion and stability of the community rather than enhancing it, which was not generally recognized as problematic and destructive since this strategy represented an accepted and readily accessible category for them. Moreover, these leaders wrestled with how to balance their outside obligations with their commitments to the Christian community, and often gave priority to these outgroup relationships. This even influenced the internal functions of the community, so that internal activities such as the Lord's Supper or teaching about the resurrection resulted in subgroup formation and internal divisions.

In this context of expansion and social change, Paul's influence was not only marginalized to a subgroup, but no longer considered effective by significant sections of the Corinthian church—even if they considered him important for their founding period—for several reasons. First, the Corinthians evidently did not recognize that Paul's gospel contained within itself the resources to navigate through this period of social change. Second, if Paul was at this time embroiled in Ephesian affairs (2 Cor 1:8–10), he was not readily accessible for them. Some local leaders even counted on Paul not visiting again (4:18). Third, Paul's model of leadership had significant countercultural components, such as his refusal to participate in honor competition and his self-sacrifice in supporting himself through manual labor.[70] In many ways, Paul would have been perceived by those of higher status as socially located among manual laborers and slaves, which suggests Paul led from a "position among the lower class."[71] Thus, Paul's leadership model caused problems with category accessibility and comparative fit, since the leaders had no one locally with whom to compare themselves. Fourth, in situations of social change, the ingroup prototype often shifts because the challenges from the outgroup have changed or because internal dynamics require different types of input (or both). Typically, leaders need to redefine the prototype or conform themselves to the shifting prototype to maintain their influence and leadership. Paul evidently had not been available to do this, so that as the ingroup prototype shifted towards influential local group

---

70. Judge and Scholer, *Social Distinctives*, 165 and 173 respectively.
71. Williams, *Stewards, Prophets*, 82–83.

members, Paul's influence shifted away from the center of the group towards its margins.

In effect, this created a leadership vacuum which the local leadership filled by reverting to familiar leadership models, resolving the tension over category accessibility and comparative fit. They still maintained loyalty to their Jewish teachers, and were able to provide cohesion and stability for the Christian community on the level of the household. This was, of course, the level of oversight and leadership that local householders had already provided for the past 5 or 6 years, so they merely continued it, in spite of the increasing complexity of the developing community. Over time, other tensions arose. Some group members observed that this arrangement led to intragroup jealousy and strife. This was not reported in the letter, but only orally, so this observation was probably not broadly shared. Similarly, the tensions caused by moral impurity and legal proceedings seem not to be broadly recognized, probably because the incest problem related to just one subgroup, while the legal proceedings involved householders of two different subgroups in social obligations beyond their subgroup. Without a level of coordination that provided oversight for all the subgroups jointly, such problems seemed limited to small pockets here and there, without seriously affecting other subgroups. And yet they influenced the entire community, for their common meals, the Lord's Supper, and their regular meetings were all affected, since the subgroups still regularly met together in larger assemblies (e.g., 1 Cor 11:17, 14:26, cf. Rom 16:23). Evidently, the familiar leadership models in Corinth did not provide an adequate model to navigate the community through these difficult social changes, however well intentioned they might have been employed.

Without Paul or Apollos as key figures to unite the church by their presence, local leadership styles had led them to division. Some apparently realized that a different leadership model was needed or that another level of leadership coordination needed to be added. As they wrestled with the implications of their Christian social identity as they understood it, they at least succeeded in uniting the church to send a delegation and a letter to Paul to address these difficulties. Not all agreed about these difficulties, so that some were reported orally rather than in writing. This began the process of finding coordinating leadership mechanisms to unite all the house groups in the city, with the house group leaders joining in a collegial level of oversight, which had thus far failed to develop.

This is a likely scenario for the patterns of leadership in Corinth just before the writing of 1 Corinthians. How did the processes of leadership emergence, maintenance, and succession function in this context?

Leadership Emergence. Clearly, local leadership functioned already with moderate effectiveness in Corinth, but it was slipping. The changing social context changed the ingroup prototype, which not only marginalized Paul's leadership, but affected local leadership as well. Not all who did well in overseeing a subgroup would be effective when leading larger groups that encompassed several households. Different skills and a different vision were needed. Thus, Paul's commendation of the hardworking Stephanas and others like him is not merely a passing comment in closing the letter (16:15–17), but actually brings closure to the arguments. After 16 chapters of careful argumentation, exercising and often defending his own leadership, Paul's commendation of certain leaders at once enhanced their leadership status in Corinth.

The leadership implications of this passage are contested. The identification of Stephanas and his household as the firstfruits of Achaia is usually interpreted as referring to the first Achaian conversions,[72] but instead this identification honors them as 'charter' members of the church and as Paul's first local coworkers.[73] Thiselton believes that their self-appointed service (εἰς διακονίαν τοῖς ἁγίοις ἔταξαν, 16:15) cannot refer to an assigned task or office, since that implies "the very self-centered forwardness that troubles Paul." It must therefore refer to a "self-imposed duty."[74] The recognition which Paul commends (ἐπιγινώσκετε, 16:18) is understood "in the sense of appreciation."[75] Garland advances Thiselton's argument by insisting that Paul is not lobbying for authority for these men since he refers to their labors, that their devotion does not denote their role as leader, and that Paul emphasized the mutuality in his relationship with his coworkers to

---

72. For instance, Garland, *1 Corinthians*, 767.

73. On the meaning of 'firstfruits' as 'first dedicated workers,' see pp. 88–89.

74. Thiselton, *First Corinthians*, 1339, referring to ὑποτάσσω (16:16) merely in passing.

75. Ibid., 1342.

root out the patronage system in the Corinthian church.⁷⁶ Their concern to avoid any implications of a leadership role seems motivated by the belief that if Paul were to commend someone in a formal role or office, he would be guilty of the same honor competition for which he criticized other Corinthian leaders. They correctly perceive that Paul blames the Corinthian honor competition for many of their problems, but they misunderstand the way Paul connects leadership role and honor in presenting Stephanas to the community.

However, Paul's identification of Stephanas as firstfruit indicates a leadership role, which presents Stephanas as the ingroup prototype of the community. Paul's commendation of Stephanas' labors highlights his self-sacrificial and group-oriented behavior. Thus, Paul encouraged the community to see Stephanas "as being one of us" and "as doing it for us," the two key factors that guide the emergence of new leaders in a group according to the social identity model of leadership. Moreover, Paul also positions Stephanas as his coworker, affirming his leadership status within the community. To what extent this leadership role had been formalized is not clear, but that does not affect the argument. Paul's exhortation to "obey" (ὑποτάσσησθε, 16:16) and "recognize" (ἐπιγινώσκετε, 16:18) such believers clearly directs the group to attribute leadership status to him and similar group members. Paul is not concerned to avoid all appearances of leadership and honor, since he regularly portrayed himself as exemplary leader and founding apostle; rather, he seeks to recast leadership in terms of modeling group values, group-oriented behavior, and seeking God's honor.⁷⁷ The social identity model of leadership makes finer distinctions between intragroup positions of social influence and leadership, rather than only focusing on the formal side of "office" and "appointment," and thus allows for a more nuanced interpretation of this passage.

Stephanas, of course, was not a new leader, since he had been involved from the founding days of the community, nor did Paul

---

76. Garland, *1 Corinthians*, 768–69, citing Winter, *After Paul Left Corinth*, 193 in support of his claim about patronage.

77. Also, Paul cannot root out patronage as a basic societal structure, but he redefines some dimensions of how patronage functioned to make it compatible with his vision of Christian social identity. This allowed Paul to build his communities, at least to some extent, on patronage structures, since those with the means to facilitate a group in their home became important community's sponsors and were *de facto* its leaders.

advocate a new leadership model, since it was a reapplication of his own model of self-sacrifice and suffering to Stephanas. However, Stephanas is the first one mentioned from the Corinthian delegation that visited Paul (the others being Fortunatus and Achaicus, 16:17), whose name also appears—almost as an afterthought—in 1:16 with the list of important people in Corinth. As leader and most likely (co) sponsor of the delegation to Paul, Stephanas probably was one of the innovating leaders necessary in Corinth to move leadership from its focus on household to a collegial focus on the whole community. Thus, Paul's recommendation of Stephanas not only commended him for his effort in visiting Paul, but affirmed leaders like him who emerged to form a collegial level of oversight over the entire community. Paul's recommendation presented Stephanas as a prototypical leader, worthy not only of respect and a following within the community, but also of imitation by other leaders.

Leadership Maintenance. This recommendation of a new level of leadership, however, takes place at the end of 1 Corinthians, and for good reason. With Paul's leadership marginalized and the ingroup prototype shifting, Paul first had to reestablish his own leadership before he could make such a recommendation. He used several strategies to maintain his leadership in Corinth.

First, he consistently presented himself as a model to imitate, even though he downplayed his status as apostle and emphasized his servanthood.[78] His exhortations to imitate him (4:16–17; 11:1) refer back to Paul's example in preaching (2:1–5), in suffering (4:8–13), and in voluntarily renouncing personal privilege (9:3–19). By exhibiting his self-sacrifice, Paul solicited endorsement for his leadership, which would enhance the perception of leadership effectiveness on his part. Also, Paul's ode to love was based on his personal example (13:1–7). He spoke hypothetically in the first person singular, "If I speak . . ." (13:1), but all knew that Paul spoke in tongues (14:18), had great prophetic gifts, and had sacrificed all but his life. Paul's self-sacrifice illustrated all the characteristics of love, which he presented as a model for the community. Thus, Paul clarified his vision of Christian social identity for the Corinthians by demonstrating how he himself embodied its foundational beliefs and core values.

---

78. For the importance of this modeling function in ancient hortatory leadership literature, see Fiore, *Personal Example*, 26–164.

Second, Paul reminded the Corinthians of his own role as founding father. He had brought the gospel to Corinth (2:1–5) and had baptized several leading men and their households (1:14–16). He considered himself the spiritual father of the whole church (4:15) and planned to send Timothy as his representative to implement his advice (4:17; 16:10). Paul also reminds them how he had taught them their key traditions (11:2, 23; 15:1–3). He served as "servant" and "steward" of God's mysteries in Corinth (4:1), presenting himself as God's ambassador[79] and power broker.[80] These roles emphasized the priority of Paul's leadership over other leaders in the Corinthian church, which legitimated Paul's right to accentuate or redefine the prototype for their Christian social identity.

Third, Paul also indicated structures of leadership that moved him as apostle back to first place. His second gift list (12:28–30) emphasizes that God appointed "first apostles, second prophets, third teachers" and mentions "helping" and "administrating" (ἀντιλήμψεις, κυβερνήσεις[81]), leadership functions often provided by patrons and householders, as items six and seven, with only tongue-speaking listed lower. Although Paul's ranking of gifts seems incongruous in this chapter,[82] it is no accident that apostles come first and tongues last, while functions that relate potentially to patrons rank near the bottom. Paul did not aim to encourage honor competition for the highest gift, as is evident from his use of the body metaphor; rather he subtly signaled that priority of his apostolic leadership over the leadership as exercised by householders even as he argues for equal participation and honor in the life of the community. This parallels his earlier argument when he aligned himself with Apollos as "servants" and "workers" of God (3:6–9), while claiming priority as community founder in the same breath (3:10). From a social identity perspective, equal participation in the community does not rule out intragroup differentiation, so that Paul's emphasis on equality is not in conflict with his unique role as

---

79. Collins, *Deacons and the Church*, 77.

80. Anderson, *1 Korintiërs*, 61; Williams, *Stewards, Prophets*, 76ff.

81. Witherington argues that this word is not simply "administrating" but refers to "those who give guidance or wise counsel" (Witherington, *Conflict & Community in Corinth*, 261), thus adding support to the notion that this represented a leadership function.

82. For instance, Fee argues that this cannot represent a ranking of gifts (*First Corinthians*, 619).

apostle. Thus, in a curious way, Paul's argument for equality within the body can be used simultaneously to claim priority for his own leadership as apostle in order to reestablish his leadership in Corinth.

These references to the Corinthians' memory of Paul's leadership have a polemical burden. Paul's appeal to their social memory served to correct and even rebuke the church for its lack of respect for Paul and to reintegrate Paul as founder and apostle into their identity narrative. Paul, as it were, maneuvered himself back to the center stage of leadership in Corinth. Castelli well summarizes, "Paul's discourse of mimesis . . . reinforces both Paul's own privileged position and the power relations of the early Christian communities as somehow 'natural.'"[83] Castelli's Foucauldian perspective makes her suspicious of such use of power, but a social identity perspective suggests that this maneuver aimed to restore Paul's social power as leader in Corinth, which in turn would restore the agency of the local believers and their leaders in bringing cohesion and vitality to their community.[84]

Thus, Paul not only exercised identity-based leadership on behalf of the Corinthians, but he expertly wove a defense of his apostleship into his other proposals for the social identity of the Corinthian congregation. At each turn, Paul showed how his foundational role in the church was for their benefit, both in his self-sacrifice and in the revelations he received. His claim to authority was cast in competition with the alternative but gradually ineffective proposals of local leaders in order to regain the social power he had lost. Paul could only revitalize his vision of Christian social identity in Corinth if he could regain this social power, which would allow him to realign Corinth's emerging leadership with that vision.

Leadership Succession. With his position of apostolic leadership thus secured, at least in his argument, Paul assumed he had the social power to recommend local leaders like Stephanas, both for their service as well as for their function as leadership model. However, this was not yet a permanent handover of leadership, as expected in leadership succession. Even though Stephanas and his delegation

---

83. Castelli, *Imitating Paul*, 116.

84. Cf. Ehrensperger who writes, "The transformative empowering dimension of power . . . has emerged as a decisive aspect for understanding how Paul and other leaders of the early Christ-movement relation to the communities, whether as 'weak' apostles, 'nursing fathers' and 'teaching mothers,' models to imitate, and messengers who transmit God's call to response-ability" (*Paul and the Dynamics of Power*, 179).

probably carried Paul's letter back with them, Paul did not leave the implementation of his instructions solely to them. He likely evaluated their leadership status as too unstable and their social power as too weak, so that they would not be able to implement the letter without outside assistance from Paul and his team. Thus, Paul sent Timothy ahead, to arrive shortly after the letter itself (4:17; 16:10) and planned to visit soon afterwards to set things in order and confront some other local leaders (4:19). Paul's sense of instability and risk proved only too right, considering the subsequent events leading up to the writing of 2 Corinthians, but he did what he could to provide adequate leadership in his absence. The instability of the situation would render any succession proposal fruitless, since not even Paul himself was certain of his leadership status and social power, so instead Paul focused attention on Timothy as an acceptable delegate and intermediary.

The theoretical account of succession (see pp. 61ff.) proposed that as *artist*, a leader should incorporate succession into his vision of social identity, the success of which depended on his own leadership status. Paul's recommendation of Stephanas is the closest to succession that is evident in this letter, since Paul's own leadership status was uncertain. This is rather ironic, since Paul's leadership is usually portrayed as charismatic precisely in this city. Thus, Robertson considers Paul's charismatic claims to be the basis of his leadership in Corinth.[85] However, from a social identity perspective, charismatic leadership is not a matter of self-presentation but of follower perception. Paul's claims of divine authority were certainly significant, but his followers accepted them initially because of his self-sacrifice and group-oriented behavior of which he reminded them frequently in this letter. However, in this situation, Paul's influence was reduced because the ingroup prototype had shifted and subgroups had formed. He was not considered effective by significant portions of the Corinthian community and thus he was not perceived as charismatic leader in Corinth. He did not have the status or social power necessary to initiate succession. Only if Paul's vision of Christian social identity proved relevant and effective in guiding the Corinthian community as they expanded, would Paul be perceived as a leader with some status, which over time

---

85. He cites as evidence: Paul claims to be an apostle called of God, founder of the church, endowed with pneumatic gifts as well as a *pneumatikos* authority endowed, focusing on the cross and serving in weakness (see Robertson, "Paul's Claim to Authority in 1 and 2 Corinthians," 71ff.)

and with more success might grow to the status of charismatic leadership. However, at the time of writing of 1 Corinthians, this is certainly not the case.

The best Paul could do was to send Timothy, a trusted coworker already known in Corinth, to implement Paul's instructions in his absence (4:18–19). Assuming for the moment that his arguments for his leadership status were effective—which was yet to be confirmed—Paul presented Timothy as a prototypical leader, similar to himself. This is comparable to how an effective leader as would present his successor. Timothy is portrayed as "my beloved and faithful child," able to remind the Corinthians of Paul's ways (4:17), which indicated his similarity to Paul. Timothy was also "doing the work of the Lord" just like Paul (16:10–11), which indicated his prototypicality for the community. This presentation positioned Timothy as Paul's assistant, and empowered him to implement Paul's solution for the subgroup divisions and to resist those who oppose it. Paul hereby sought to prevent a dissimilar or non-prototypical leader from rising up and establishing himself, which is a possible outcome in a situation where the predecessor is perceived as ineffective.

This is as far as Paul could go with his uncertain leadership status: to recommend some local leaders and present a temporary delegate as similar and prototypical. He was not yet able, as *engineer* of social identity, to initiate structures for succession, nor was this needed with Paul's upcoming visit. However, if the local leaders proved effective in the near future, the community would attribute leadership to them and they could emerge from Paul's and Timothy's shadow. Alternatively, if Timothy proved successful in the social turmoil at Corinth, even as temporary delegate, he would be seen as a significant leader in his own right. From the vantage point of Paul as author of 1 Corinthians, local leaders as well as Timothy could thus emerge as candidates for succession from this situation. That, however, was dependent on the reception and implementation of Paul's letter—which proved less fortuitous than any of the parties anticipated at this point.

Conclusions

The stability of local leadership suffered because of the described tensions in social identification. Several Corinthians named in the letter appear influential in the congregation, as indicated by their relative wealth and social status. It is probably correct to identify these people as local leaders that were loyal to Paul, while some passages indicate the presence of other unnamed leaders. As the social situation grew more complex and Paul's (and Apollos') absence was prolonged, local leadership shifted increasingly to familiar cultural patterns of patronage and traveling sophists, resolving social tension through the more familiar comparative fit and category accessibility. The local leaders provided subgroup cohesion and maintained their loyalty to Jewish teachers following these cultural patterns, to the detriment of the cohesion of the community as a whole. These leaders failed to adapt to collegial leadership overseeing the entire community, and fragmented into leadership over subgroups.

Paul acknowledged that leadership is shaped by familiar cultural structures, since he acknowledged leaders who have the status and wealth to offer their services to the church. However, Paul clearly did not legitimate their leadership by the cultural norms of honor and competition, but by Christian ingroup norms of self-sacrifice, personal involvement, and group-oriented service. In this letter, Paul demonstrated his sensitivity to social identification processes and how his exercise of authority is related to his prototypicality in any given situation at any given time. His commendation of Stephanas and others is not based on office, training or on official recognition but on their ability to serve in order to navigate the community through this stage of growth and instability. The letter does not indicate any interest in precise structures of authority, in defining the nature and extent of a leadership office, or in constructing a leadership hierarchy. However, the existence of differentiated intragroup leadership roles is plain, even if the precise structural features were unsettled in this climate of social growth and change.

5

Reestablishing Paul's Leadership as Model in 2 Corinthians

SECOND CORINTHIANS LAGS BEHIND 1 CORINTHIANS IN ATTRACTING attention for its socio-cultural background, and it attracts even less attention as evidence of local leadership patterns. Sumney's groundbreaking study on Paul's opponents in 2 Corinthians[1] moved scholarship in this direction, so that discussions on Paul's leadership style and on his confrontation with his opponents are easily found in the literature. Most of these discussions, however, still focus on perceived divisions in early Christianity between Paul and his opponents, without investigating traces of local leadership in Corinth. Clarke's second leadership study advances the debate by showing from 2 Corinthians how a sophist model of leadership had become the pattern for local leadership in Corinth.[2] Ehrensperger recently added that 2 Corinthians presents evidence that strategies of domination intruded into local leadership patterns.[3] This chapter continues this line of argument and aims to describe more fully the patterns of local leadership that are reflected in 2 Corinthians.

Situating 2 Corinthians in Paul's Ministry

The social background of 2 Corinthians is notoriously difficult to reconstruct. First, little of the content of 1 Corinthians returns in 2 Corinthians. The first letter deals mostly with cultural influences in the

---

1. See Sumney, *Identifying Paul's Opponents*, later expanded in Sumney, *'Servants of Satan,' 'False Brothers' and Other Opponents of Paul*.
2. Clarke, *Serve the Community*, 185–89.
3. Ehrensperger, *Paul and the Dynamics of Power*, 114.

community, while the second deals with an intragroup conflict over leadership. Second Corinthians also contains contradictory themes: joy and harmony with reconciliation close at hand versus open conflict with itinerant teachers whose identity remains obscure. Second, the chronology of numerous events reported in 2 Corinthians remains unclear: the punishment of an offender (2:6), the arrival of deviant teachers (11:4–6), Paul's painful visit from Ephesus to Corinth (1:23—2:3), a tearful letter (2:3; 7:12), Titus' mission (2:13; 7:6, 13; 12:18), a cancelled visit (1:15–23), the sending of 2 Corinthians (13:10), and Paul's renewed plans for a third visit (12:14; 13:1–2).[4] Third, the time period between the letters is relatively short, roughly estimated at about eighteen months.[5] These factors render any socio-historical reconstruction tentative.

One way to resolve these difficulties is to propose that the abrupt transitions of the letter (2:13–14; 6:13–14; 7:1–2, 4–5; 8:1; 10:1)[6] reflect different situations at different times, so that 2 Corinthians is a collation of several separate letters.[7] However, although the literary unity is disputed, it is not without its supporters.[8] Furthermore, without manuscript evidence to support this proposal, such a solution creates a new set of difficulties. Therefore, in this study the unity of the letter is the basis for the analysis.

Another way to resolve these difficulties is to propose a major disruptive incident between 1 and 2 Corinthians combined with a social identity analysis of Paul's changing tone between the first and last sections of 2 Corinthians. A major disruptive incident is indicated by Paul's painful second visit, frequent change of travel plans, and tearful

4. For extended argumentation, see Harris, *Second Corinthians*, 54–59.

5. Harris suggests the spring of 55 and the fall of 56 for the delivery of our 1 and 2 Corinthians respectively. (Ibid., 101–5). Martin situates them about a year earlier, but with the same approximate time between the letters (*2 Corinthians*, xxxiv–xv).

6. See the summary in Lambrecht, *Second Corinthians*, 9–11.

7. See for instance Martin, *2 Corinthians*, xxxiv and the extended discussion in Furnish, *II Corinthians*, 29–54.

8. Bieringer, "Plädoyer für die Einheitlichkeit des 2. Korintherbriefes," 131–79; Bieringer also provides an extensive history of research on partition and unity theories in two articles preceding his own plea for unity. See also Blomberg, "The Structure of 2 Corinthians 1–7," 3–20; DeSilva, "Measuring Penultimate against Ultimate Reality," 41–70; Hall, *The Unity of the Corinthian Correspondence*, especially chapters 4 and 5; Long, *Ancient Rhetoric and Paul's Apology*; Stegman, *The Character of Jesus*, 5–25 and Vegge, *2 Corinthians, A Letter about Reconciliation*.

letter. Considering Paul's sensitive handling of the subgroups and other social identification issues in 1 Corinthians and Timothy's familiarity with and acceptability in Corinth, it is unlikely that either the letter or Timothy's arrival caused serious disruption without other aggravating circumstances. Most likely, unexpected complications arose about when 1 Corinthians and Timothy arrived. Two complications can be suggested. First, Paul's painful visit seems to be occasioned by an offender who is ready to be restored at the time when Paul wrote 2 Corinthians (2:1–6). Whether this offender represents the incest perpetrator of 1 Cor 5,[9] an outsider who lead a revolt against Paul,[10] or a believer who stole money from the collection,[11] remains unclear, but this confrontation resulted in much turmoil. However, since this person is ready to be restored (cf. 7:12), this disruption is not likely connected with the opposition from several individuals addressed in chapters 10–13. It appears that this confrontation added to the turmoil but is insufficient by itself to account for large sections of the letter.

Thus, a second suggestion should be considered, namely that the turmoil resulted from the unexpected arrival of itinerant Jewish-Christian teachers in Corinth (11:4–6, 22–23).[12] These itinerant teachers were of Jewish origin, but they adapted their leadership style to the Greco-Roman forms of patronage and sophist honor competition.[13] They presented another solution to the Corinthian challenges in social identification and probably succeeded in uniting the community and its local leadership under their banner, much like Paul and Apollos had done when they had ministered in the city. This created a situation of intensive competition between different solutions and different versions of social identity, presented both by the itinerant Jewish-Christian teachers and by Paul, Timothy, and Titus. It appears that Paul rushed to Corinth to intervene in this uneven debate, but that his visit was not effective. As a result, 1 Corinthians was probably rejected initially in Corinth, since Paul's humble and suffering leadership could not compete with the strong leadership of the itinerant teachers, who moreover promoted Jewish traditions and the Mosaic

---

9. Garland, *2 Corinthians*, 118–19, as also in most ancient commentaries.
10. Barrett, *Second Corinthians*, 89, 93.
11. Thrall, *Second Corinthians*, 1:68–69.
12. Harris, *Second Corinthians*, 743–44.
13. Cf. Clarke, *Serve the Community*, 188–89.

law more strongly than Paul was willing to do. Soon after the painful visit, Paul appears to have followed up with a severe letter, carried by Titus who returns from Corinth to meet Paul in Macedonia (2:3–13; 7:8–12). He reports that the Corinthians have repented and are ready to be reconciled, which would be officially sealed as soon as Paul could arrive. This accounts for the joy of reconciliation in the early parts of the letter, combined with the strong warnings against remaining dissenters in the latter sections lest the Corinthians change their mind before Paul arrived and the prospect of reconciliation proved to be an empty hope.

For the purposes of this study, these few paragraphs are sufficient to indicate important connections between 1 and 2 Corinthians.[14] The suggestion then is that 2 Corinthians addresses new issues, primarily because intruding Jewish-Christian leadership provided an alternative proposal to Paul's instructions in resolving the social identification issues in Corinth. Thus, 1 Corinthians failed to accomplish its purposes. These complications and the widely divergent emotions they involved are reflected in the different topics and tone of the various letter sections. The task is to analyze the processes of social identification visible in the letter and to study the processes of identity-based leadership.

Social Identification in the Corinthian Community in 56 CE

Second Corinthians shows signs of intense competition for leadership. The previous chapter showed that this was already the case in 1 Corinthians where Paul competed with local leaders who were struggling with expansion and social change. The competition was unequal, since the local leaders were far less knowledgeable and experienced about Christian social identity than Paul. Paul's concern was to inform these leaders more fully and to complement their vision of social identity, so that they could grow from household based leadership to collegial leadership overseeing all subgroups in the city. However, in 2 Corinthians Paul competed with accredited Jewish-Christian leaders arriving from elsewhere, with an alternative vision of social identity and a leadership style to match. This competition

---

14. For further discussions of the introductory issues, see deSilva, *Introduction to the NT*, 575–86; and McDonald and Porter, *Early Christianity*, 441–48.

was also unequal, but now Paul was at a disadvantage because his leadership was at odds with important dimensions of Jewish as well as Greco-Roman social identities with which these Jewish-Christian leaders were much better aligned.

The community's social identification processes are somewhat eclipsed by this leadership competition. The Christ-believing community in Corinth formed the audience before which this leadership competition took place. Ultimately, they decided which leaders would triumph. The stakes were high since Paul had almost lost his position as apostolic leader in Corinth so that the entire Corinthian congregation might have been lost as hub in Paul's Aegean network. The dominant concern in 2 Corinthians focuses on who emerged as winner of this leadership contest, since the winner would have the right to define Christian social identity and direct the Corinthians in their identity performance. Yet, in the background, sufficient traces of social identification are visible to point out important developments that connect with the situation addressed in 1 Corinthians. These social identification processes relate to a conflict for which Titus had already negotiated reconciliation at the time of writing. However, since Paul had not yet personally consolidated this reconciliation, he presented his team's perspective on the conflict in writing to affirm what Titus had already communicated orally. In other words, 2 Corinthians reveals social identification processes of a conflict that had for the most part already been resolved.

Second Corinthians shows two key dimensions of change in social identification. The first dimension is shift towards Jewish identity with greater respect for Jewish traditions and descent. Paul used Jewish traditions in a way, which suggests that they rose to prominence in Corinth due to the influence of his opponents. For instance, Paul's discourse about the new covenant (3:5–18) is introduced by a clear reference to the opponents (3:1–2).[15] Avemarie argues that Paul defends the legitimacy of his apostolic ministry by demonstrating that his ministry surpasses the ministry of Moses in order to regain Corinth's approval.[16] But why would Paul compare himself with Moses, if the

15. Cf. Sumney, 'Servants of Satan,' 128.

16. Avemarie, "The Notion of a 'New Covenant' in 2 Corinthians 3," 3 and 8. Grindheim analyzes this discourse only in theological terms and interprets it in terms of the traditional law-gospel dualism. He completely misses any link with the argumentative structure of 2 Corinthians and with how this passage functioned in Paul's

Corinthians had accepted his earlier teaching about the Mosaic law? Barnett suggests that Paul's new covenant defense is a response to the "newly arrived ministers [who] had been commending the ministry of the old covenant."[17] That is, Paul's opponents forced the covenant theme upon him, which also explains some of the "un-pauline" features such as the lack of reference to the Abrahamic covenant. Thus, the new covenant discourse is not only a theological battle; rather, Paul uses it to undermine the social influence of his opponents who had won the allegiance of almost the entire Corinthian congregation in presenting themselves as ministers of old covenant.

Another possible instance of Jewish traditions is the passage 6:14—7:1, with Scripture quotations that Paul used nowhere else, and with typical Jewish views on purity and idolatry.[18] The passage seems to interrupt Paul's argumentation in 6:11—7:4 and is often considered non-pauline.[19] Yet, its function in the argument of 2 Corinthians fits well as an appeal to dissolve ties with Paul's opponents and to renew loyalty to Paul.[20] Perhaps some of the vocabulary, style, and Scripture citations, that seem so un-Pauline, were also forced upon Paul by his opponents, or else represented familiar Jewish traditions current in Corinth.

By the time Paul wrote these words, the conflict with Corinth had essentially been resolved and he fully expected them to agree with his presentation. However, before resolution was achieved, the Corinthians had apparently accepted the increased emphasis on Jewish traditions. How might this have happened? It is likely that the development of subgroups in Corinth gradually came to be seen as problematic, not least due to Paul's input through 1 Corinthians and Timothy. They needed a new rallying point for all the groups, which Paul provided with his countercultural vision of Christian social identity as superordinate. As the Corinthians considered Paul's option, the newly arrived Jewish-Christian teachers presented an alternative. They advocated renewed loyalty to Moses and Jewish tradition, of which

arguments about apostolic ministry ("The Law Kills but the Gospel Gives Life," 97ff).

17. Barnett, *Second Corinthians*, 178.

18. For an extended discussion, see Furnish, *II Corinthians*, 359–83.

19. Betz even proposed that the passage is anti-pauline in origin ("2 Cor 6:14—7:1: An Anti-Pauline Fragment," 89–90).

20. DeSilva, "Recasting the Moment of Decision," 16. See also Bieringer, "2 Korinther 6,14–7,1 im Kontext des 2. Korintherbriefes," 551–70.

they were eminent representatives, judging by their Jewish descent (11: 22) and their letters of recommendation (3:1–2; 10:12, 18). They capitalized on the Corinthian loyalty to Jewish teachers, which caused the division in subgroups in the first place (see pp. 78ff.) and united the community by taking up local residence like Paul and Apollos at an earlier stage. Perhaps the Corinthians expected Paul to appreciate this increased emphasis on Jewish traditions, since they had witnessed Paul's own use of such traditions to construct their identity narrative.[21] Moreover, this resolved their problem with nested identities in a practical way around physically present Jewish representatives, rather than through activating their social memories of Paul's example and his teaching, which they found difficult to contextualize. Little did they realize that the subtle shift towards a more Jewish form of social identity represented regression to an earlier stage of development where the physical presence of an esteemed Jewish leader served as rallying point, rather than progression towards a more mature level of cooperation between the local leaders and their subgroups on the basis of shared social identification around Paul's gospel.

The second dimension of change is a shift towards Greco-Roman identity with an acceptance of patronage and sophist conventions in spite of Paul's strong challenge against them. Paul defended himself against charges of "unskilled in speaking" (11:6, cf. 10:10) and argued that the arguments or sophistries[22] (10:4–5) of his opponents destroyed the true knowledge of God. Paul portrayed the boasting of the intruding teachers (10:12–13; 11:18–19) as the boastful practices of the charlatan and false leader.[23] Moreover, he also defended himself against charges that he lacked love (11:11) because he did not accept patronage for his teaching (11:7; 12:14–15), and argued instead that patronage for the intruding teachers amounted to being dominated and exploited by them (11:20).[24] Paul focused not on these teachers, who are referred to in the third person,[25] but on how their self-presentation had been received by the Corinthians. They had received

---

21. For instance "Christ, our Passover lamb, has been sacrificed" (1 Cor 5:7), "You shall not muzzle an ox" (9:9) and "all were baptized into Moses" (10:2).

22. See DBAG, s.v. and LN, 30.11, taken up by Garland, *2 Corinthians*, 436.

23. Martin, *2 Corinthians*, 300.

24. Harris, *Second Corinthians*, 784–87.

25. Such as the five times repeated εἴ τις ("if someone . . .," 11:20), or the plural τινες ("some," 3:1, 10:2).

the preaching of an alternative Jesus, Spirit or gospel "readily enough" (11:4) and considered themselves "wise" (11:19), so that their reception of these teachers "forced" Paul to play the fool (12:11).[26] Thus, in Paul's judgment, the boasting about rhetorical skill and the obligations of patronage sponsorship had not only been features of the ministry of the intruding teachers but they had also been accepted uncritically by the Corinthian community.

Again, the question arises how this could have happened. The problem with nested identities was relatively easy to discern, and a change in social identification was sufficient to restructure the community internally. The problems with cross-cutting identities, however, were more difficult to resolve, since group members functioned in various social settings, which continually challenged their Christian social identification. Basic social structures such as patronage relationships and home architecture could not simply be changed with the stroke of a pen. Moreover, Jewish communities in Israel and diaspora were strongly Hellenized, which is evident for instance in the use of patronage for synagogue building construction and in their leadership structures.[27] This suggests that such teachers likely believed that these Greco-Roman social structures were irrelevant with respect to Christian social identity. Thus, while the visiting teachers may have intentionally introduced a greater emphasis on Jewish traditions, they probably accepted these Greco-Roman social structures as a simple matter of course. As argued above, the Corinthians had accepted these values as well, probably not because the teachers had attempted to convince them, but simply because they represented shared and unchallenged values. It is a case of good comparative fit because of the high degree of category accessibility.

In summary, the problem with nested social identities, evident in 1 Cor 1–4, was resolved by a greater focus on Jewish traditions and a shift towards Jewish identity. The presence of accredited Jewish-Christian teachers was sufficient to unite the various subgroups. Moreover, since these teachers shared unquestioned values about patronage and boasting with the Corinthians, Paul's way of being distinct appeared inappropriate and unhelpful. Resolving the subgroup problem may have softened some of the problems with cross-cutting

---

26. Martin, *2 Corinthians*, 301.
27. Clarke, *Serve the Community*, 124–26 and 36–37.

identities, but without Paul's proposals, they would have continued to undermine the cohesion of the Corinthian community.

The Corinthian Leaders as Managers of Christian Social Identity

The leadership situation in Corinth has become more complex.[28] The local leaders described in 1 Corinthians are not mentioned in this letter, but they were certainly key individuals in receiving the recently arrived teachers who quickly rose to dominance. This section describes both the local and the visiting leaders in their role as managers of Christian social identity. The identity management of the visiting teachers has already been described briefly above to chart the general social identification processes in Corinth, but more can be said about their leadership.

It was argued above that the visiting teachers gained influence because of their comparative fit with the Corinthian congregation, but the timing of their visit plays a crucial role in their quick acceptance. Paul had carefully planned the reception of 1 Corinthians. He had proposed solutions to their difficulties of social identification to enable them to continue to expand, he had commended local leaders like Stephanas as model for the new kind of leadership needed, and had sent Timothy to support the implementation of his instructions. With such careful social engineering, Paul rightfully expected to have resolved the social tensions in Corinth. Thus, these Jewish-Christian teachers from Israel could not have arrived long after the delivery of 1 Corinthians, for by then Paul's proposals would have been implemented and the social instability would have been resolved. A new level of collegial leadership would be in place, which would have resisted destabilizing the entire community with competing solutions for what had already been resolved. Their arrival must have come at a time when the social tension and instability of their sense of social identity

---

28. It should be noted that Paul's rhetorical strategy in 2 Cor 10–13 cannot be read as a disinterested, 'objective' portrayal of these teachers, since Paul uses a strategy of vilification which is a form of "deviancy labeling, or as it was known in the rhetorical schools, vituperatio" (Taylor, "Conflict," 938), as Thurén has recently argued in connection to opponents in Galatians, Colossians and 2 Timothy ("The Antagonists," 85–86). Care must be taken to avoid overinterpreting the evidence in the next few pages.

were still acutely felt, and when these difficulties still created doubts about Paul's effectiveness as apostolic leader. This instability presented the opportunity for leadership dissimilar to Paul to take the initiative.

If these intruding leaders are to succeed in swaying the community, they must present a relevant vision of Christian social identity (the leader as artist of social identity). However, the content of their message is notoriously difficult to define. Thrall summarized the variety of scholarly proposals in three main categories: "the opponents preach a Judaizing gospel; they propound a christology different from Paul's own; the attack on his apostleship implies the advocacy of an alien gospel."[29] Not fully content with these proposals, she added her own that the rival missionaries were Jewish Christians who operated on the basis of the universalistic mission of Matt 28:16-20 without respect for the territorial limitations of the Jerusalem agreements in Gal 2:9.[30] The advantage of Thrall's own proposal is its focus on social more than theological issues. Scholarship on the subgroups of 1 Cor 1-4 converges on the position that these divisions were socially rather than theologically motivated, while even the difficulty with such a core element of theology as the resurrection is likely to have social roots (see pp. 78ff). If the intruding leaders succeeded in bridging the social divisions of the subgroups that arose in spite of a common theology, as suggested in the analysis above, it is unlikely that they did so primarily by presenting a different theology (whether in Jewish, Hellenistic of gnostic form). However, although the territorial limitations of the Jerusalem agreement might play a role in Corinth (cf. 2 Cor 10:13-16), social causes unique to Corinth were not further investigated by Thrall. It appears, then, that the intruders' vision of Christian social identity differs from Paul's more on its social than its theological dimensions.

After reviewing this debate, Stegman concluded that the evidence of 2 Corinthians is too limited to identify the opponents and suggested that the christology of Paul and not of the opponents is the key to interpreting the letter.[31] Although still moving within the arena of theology, this proposal has the advantage of focusing on Jesus Christ, which

---

29. Thrall, *Second Corinthians 8-13*.

30. Ibid., 669-70.

31. Stegman, *The Character of Jesus*, 40-42. Stegman summarized the debate in five categories: Gnostics, divine men, Judaizers, Jerusalem apostles and pneumatics (Ibid., 25-40).

is evidently of major concern to Paul who blamed the intruders for teaching "another Jesus" (11:4). In the main part of his work, Stegman demonstrated that the character of Jesus was Paul's central concern in 2 Corinthians, that Paul presented himself as embodying Jesus' character, and that Paul exhorted the Corinthians to do likewise.[32] Paul participated in Christ's victory not as champion but as captive prisoner (2:14–16),[33] and although believers are being transformed in the image of Christ (3:18), Paul emphasizes that this includes suffering as participation in Christ (4:7–14).[34] Stegman's helpful work, though, does not consider sufficiently the social dimension of his thesis. These dimensions of suffering, humility and shame had already proven difficult for the Corinthians before, considering Paul's emphasis on the foolishness of the gospel (1 Cor 1:18—2:5) and his ironic contrast between the kingly Corinthians and the suffering apostles (1 Cor 4:8–13). Paul's extended comments on these issues in 2 Corinthians (4:7—5:5; 6:4–10; 11:21–29) suggest that this difficulty had not yet been resolved. Very likely, the intruding teachers had conformed to the Corinthians at this point, emphasizing the more glorious aspects of Christ's ministry, which "would have been highly congenial to them—not something that required toleration."[35] This is not to say that the intruders presented a different christology, but rather that, as artists of identity, they selectively emphasized those aspects of Christ's ministry that allowed them to affirm the Corinthians in their faith without challenging them to reform their community in its attitudes towards honor, rhetoric, and patronage in the way Paul had advocated. In other words, as leaders they conformed themselves to the vision of Christian social identity that was already prevalent in Corinth; this provided a good normative fit with the Corinthians, and allowed them to gain a position of social influence and leadership in the community.

Besides presenting Jesus in a fashion suitable to Corinth, the intruding teachers claimed legitimacy for their leadership role (the leader

32. Ibid., 117–377.

33. Ibid., 263–64. See also Hafemann, *Suffering and Ministry in the Spirit*, 16–34, who sketched the historical background of this metaphor based on first century sources.

34. Stegman, *The Character of Jesus*, 233–58.

35. Thrall, *Second Corinthians*, 2:669. See also Thiselton's proposal that over-realized eschatology accounts for many of the Corinthian difficulties ("Realized Eschatology at Corinth," 107–18).

as impresario). Aware that the Corinthian subgroups had formed as an expression of loyalty to significant Jewish teachers, they presented themselves as 'pure' Israelites (11:22), personally acquainted with the early Jesus (10:7; 11:13, 23) and authorized by letters or recommendation (3:1–2; 10:12).[36] In this they demonstrated better comparative fit than Paul, who was only a diaspora Jew without personal experience of the earthly Jesus, who came without letters of recommendation which could be interpreted as a lack of esteem for instance in Israel; Paul's defense indicates that these teachers had influenced the community to voice similar criticisms of Paul. Moreover, these teachers appear to have made good use of rhetoric in their self-presentation and their teaching, while they shared a critical attitude with the congregation towards Paul's physical and rhetorical weakness (2 Cor 10:10; 11:6). These practices demonstrate the same competitive attitude of these teachers to "rivals" that the Corinthians had demonstrated towards Paul, Apollos, and Peter, which enhanced their normative fit. Such self-presentation harmonized well with their somewhat greater emphasis on Moses, which was thus also legitimated.

Finally, these intruding teachers adapted to social structures already in place in Corinth (the leader as engineer). First, it appears that Paul's rivals willingly accepted the financial support of Corinthian patrons (11:7–9), although Paul stigmatized their financial dependence as "devouring" their following (11:20). Second, their letters of recommendation (10:12; cf. 3:1) not only legitimated their leadership but also incorporated Corinth in a social network that originated with the Christ-following communities in Israel, far beyond the Aegean network within which Paul had included Corinth. Although these leaders did not create social structures to fit their Christian social identity, as Paul had done, they deftly employed the existing structures to their advantage, and were thus able to compete successfully against Paul for the leadership of the Corinthian community.

To summarize, itinerant Jewish-Christian teachers shifted their emphasis towards the more honorable parts of Christ's life as a strategy to adapt their vision of Christian social identity to Corinth to indicate their normative fit. They legitimated themselves as better situated than Paul to assist the Corinthians in this stage of community development, based primarily on their Jewish roots, which indicated their

---

36. Harris, *Second Corinthians*, 794–95 and Garland, *2 Corinthians*, 441.

comparative fit. Moreover, they adopted pre-existing social structures to accommodate Corinth. Admittedly, their physical presence did not resolve all issues of social identification, but it brought a new sense of unity, status, and honor. Their leadership performance was perceived as equal to or better than Paul's on every count, precisely because ironically these leaders were more Hellenized than Paul. Thus, for most Corinthians it must have seemed self-evident that these Jewish-Christian teachers succeeded Paul in leadership. Paul may have been effective as founder, but his guidance in further community development had not effectively resolved their social tension. For that, they needed to go back to the original source of their Christian social identity with these Jewish-Christian teachers from Israel.

Little did they realize that in this fashion, the agency of the higher status believers was enhanced at the expense of the agency of the majority of lower status believers. The renewed acceptance of dominating cultural values of rhetoric and patronage without physical weakness or suffering, favored the few wealthier believers, who could more fully participate in this way of structuring their social identity. However, it disenfranchised the majority of believers, who had no rhetorical training, no means to support these kinds of teachers, and who experienced their daily share of weakness and suffering while living on the edge of poverty. This admittedly conformed to the normal social structures of Corinthian society, so that it reduced the social tension that especially the richer believers must have experienced in their Christian social identity. However, what little social power the believers of lower status might have gained in the Christian community was taken away from them, so that they could not initiate any changes to return to the values and structures Paul had advocated. Furthermore, this also decreased the agency of all believers in maintaining their teaching traditions, since the emphasis on the pure Jewish descent of the new teachers put all other teachers at a disadvantage. It created the kind of dependency on teachers from Israel that Paul had sought to avoid. Essentially, the social tension with which the Corinthians had wrestled was resolved by accommodating to traditional Corinthian values, which turned most group members into passive participants in the Christian community.

With the identity management of the intruding teachers described, the influence of local Corinthians leaders needs to be briefly considered. No local believers are named in 2 Corinthians in contrast to 1 Corinthians. Paul portrayed Christ and his own ministry as models of leadership, but did not take the occasion to recommend Stephanas again as example of the kind of collegial leadership he sought to establish. It is possible that Stephanas had also been influenced by the intruding teachers, but there is no evidence to support or deny that. Instead, by the time Paul writes 2 Corinthians, the resolution of the difficulties had already been negotiated by Titus, and the majority of local leaders had renewed their allegiance to Paul. Thus, an explicit recommendation of one from their midst as suitable model for leadership is no longer necessary, since the majority is already on Paul's side. Following the analysis of 1 Corinthians in chapter 4, presumably the local leaders are now willing to lead together in the collegial fashion Paul had aimed for with 1 Corinthians.

Paul's Leadership as Identity Management

The reconciliation to be negotiated in Corinth was perhaps Paul's greatest challenge to date. He needed to present a vision of Christian social identity that was more compelling that the vision of the Jewish-Christian teachers in order to win back the community. What resources did Paul have? He had no riches or social status in Corinth, he did not want to accept patronage support nor did he want to earn credit by rhetorical display. He could not and would not erase the presence of weakness and suffering in his ministry, nor could he match the claims of Palestinian Jewish descent or of personal knowledge of the earthly Jesus. In other words, he could not and would not compete with the Jewish-Christian teachers on their terms, a contest he had lost already. He could only win by changing the terms of the debate to his favor, which is exactly what Paul does throughout 2 Corinthians.

Since Paul had lost most or even all support in Corinth, he first reaffirmed common ground. His suffering resulted in salvation for the Corinthians, while the comfort he received comforted them (2 Cor 1:5–7). Thus, Paul displayed his self-sacrifice as group-oriented behavior ('doing it for us'). Moreover, Paul suffered to the point of death, but was raised to life by "God who raises the dead" (1:9). This implicit comparison with Christ turned Paul into a prototypical group member par excellence, since his identification with Christ extended much further than that of the average Corinthian believer. He also presented an apology for his cancelled visit[37] to remove any remaining doubts about his leadership. Thus, Paul established common ground as a fellow ingroup member, highlighting his prototypicality and group-oriented behavior to correct their perception of his leadership and to inspire renewed trust in his leadership.

(Re)Defining Christian Social Identity in Terms of Suffering

Paul's main concern was to reaffirm his vision of Christian identity (the leader as artist). He consistently reinterprets suffering and weakness as important dimensions of identity. For instance, he used a strategy of social creativity to argue that his suffering was in fact a sign of victory: he shared in Christ's triumph, even though he played the role of "the conquered slave exposed to public ridicule."[38] The Corinthians are drawn into this triumph as spectators who see Christ's aroma on display through Paul "as commissioned by God" (2:16–17; cf. 4:1), even though they would find it very difficult to identify with such a symbol of Paul's leadership among them. Second, Paul claims that the ministry of the Spirit for which he is commissioned is far superior to the ministry of Moses (3:5–18); he thus undermines the Jewish-Christian claims about Moses. Third, rather than boasting about this privilege, he characterized his ministry as one marked by suffering and weakness (4:7—5:5), which were not presented as unfortunate circumstances but rather as essential qualities that embodied the death of Jesus while eagerly anticipating the new life of the resurrection (4:10, 14).[39] Paul includes the Corinthians in this transformation from death to life since "we all" are being transformed into the glorious likeness of Christ through the ministry of the Spirit (3:18) and since God "has shone in our hearts" with "the light of the gospel" (4:4–6). Paul thus

---

37. Which was not to be taken as a sign of fickleness (ἐλαφρία, 1:17) and lack of commitment, but instead as a sign of faithfulness and care for the community in line with God's own faithfulness (1:18–19). For similar comments, see Malina, *Timothy: Paul's Closest Associate*, 85–86.

38. Martin, *2 Corinthians*, 46–47. See also Nguyen who remarks that "Paul thanks God . . . for displaying him and the other apostles in this lowly position as captives who are doomed to death," (*Christian Identity in Corinth*, 154ff).

39. Stegman, *The Character of Jesus*, 250–52. The themes of suffering and weakness occur frequently in Paul's 'foolish discourse' (11:16—12:10), but here they are less connected with Paul's vision of Christian social identity and more with the legitimacy of his role of apostle in proclaiming this vision.

affirms a vision of Christian identity where the reconciled Corinthian believers and the missionary team are equal members of the community, while Paul's critics are implicitly included in this outgroup. This highlights the social dimension of Paul's plea for reconciliation (5:18–20), since they are reconciled not only with God, but also with Paul as well as with one another regardless of social status. With this vision, Paul identified himself especially with the lower status believers who would be intimately familiar with suffering and weakness in their daily lives; Paul provided a rallying point that empowered the whole congregation and not only a few higher status members in their Christian identity performance.[40]

Paul spends considerable effort to legitimate his presentation of Jesus as the community prototype for every community member (the leader as impresario). Some of his credentials were incorporated into his vision of identity: his imitation of Christ in his suffering (1:5; 4:10, 14), his commission as minister of a more glorious covenant than the Mosaic (2:17; 4:1), and his privileged role as ambassador of Christ to proclaim the message of reconciliation (5:18–20). Other credentials are voiced when Paul switched to the "I" voice in 10:1 to deal more directly with the criticisms of his legitimacy as apostle.[41] He belonged to Christ (10:7) and was of Jewish descent (11:22), just like his critics claimed for themselves. He was the first one to reach the city with the gospel (10:13–15), so that the Corinthians are his letters of recommendation instead of needing such letters to gain acceptance (3:1–3; cf. 12:11). He claims to have had visions of Christ and paradise (12:1–4), far superior to any knowledge of the earthly Jesus which his critics boasted about. Finally, Paul demonstrated his apostolic powers

40. Ngyuen demonstrated that Paul's criticisms parallel the writings of Epictetus and Valerius Maximus as they critique the Roman preoccupation with the public *persona*, that is, with the overdone concern by the elite for one's public image of honor and status of leaders. Although Paul's criticism was differently motivated, it was not unique. See Nguyen, *Christian Identity in Corinth*, especially 209–14.

41. This switch from the first person plural in the first 9 chapters to the first person singular in chapters 10–13 is one of the literary discontinuities that are considered problematic for the literary unity of the letter (see e.g. Furnish, *II Corinthians*, 32. However, Paul's vision of identity in chapters 1–7 was shared by his missionary team (including Timothy and Titus), reflected in the 'we'-voice, while the attack on Paul's apostolic ministry also had a very personal dimension, reflected in Paul's passionate defense in the 'I'-voice. Moreover, the 'I'-voice is already dominant in 1:15—2:13, so that the discontinuity is not as great as is sometimes supposed. Thus, there is no need to explain this discontinuity by resort to literary partition theories.

through miracles (12:12). Thus, Paul endeavors to reestablish his credibility as Corinth's apostle.

(De)Legitimating Claims to Apostolic Leadership

Paul not only defended his own legitimacy, but he also strongly criticized the legitimacy of the intruding teachers. He accused them of presenting a different Jesus (11:4), and demonized them as false apostles and servants of Satan (11:12–14). Paul vilified their leadership as enslavement and exploitation, and their claim to know Christ and be from pure Palestinian Jewish descent as putting on airs (11:20). Such a tactic is familiar as a "status degradation ritual."[42] The resulting portrayal would have surprised and even shocked the Corinthians in their pre-reconciliation perspective. Paul's rhetorical strategy here is not always understood. Taylor suggests "that Paul is unable to repudiate the credentials of his opponents on any objective basis."[43] However, deviance labeling is hardly effective if other arguments are lacking. Instead, vilification is a way of stereotyping the outgroup and the motivation for agreeing with it is a matter of social identification. The Corinthians had formerly accepted these teachers as prototypical ingroup members and perceived their leadership as serving the group. Their influence was considered beneficial, as is evident from the community's willingness to dissociate themselves from Paul. Paul, however, perceived these same leaders as outsiders and therefore experienced their behavior quite differently. Financial requests from deviant outsiders are seen as extortion, their teaching as deception and their leadership away from Paul as manipulation. Given the reconciliation already negotiated by Titus, Paul could assume that the Corinthians had again adopted his vision of Christian social identity, including his role in proclaiming and defending it, so that Paul's evaluation of his critics became a reference point for their group's perspective. Thus, Paul's ritual of vilification or status degradation was not so much an argument for the Corinthians to change their perspective, but reflected their changed perspective on the intruding teachers as well as their renewed acceptance of Paul's credentials as their apostle.

---

42. See Malina and Neyrey, "Conflict in Luke-Acts: Labelling and Deviance Theory," 107; Pietersen, *The Polemic of the Pastorals*, 139.

43. Taylor, "Conflict," 938.

(Re)Structuring Social Networks

It remained for Paul to consolidate the promised reconciliation in appropriate community structures (the leader as engineer). Paul ended this section with the repeated plea that the Corinthians open their hearts wide for him (6:13, 7:2), which framed his appeal to not be unequally yoked (6:14—7:1). As argued above, this passage is not a digressive appeal as is often noted.[44] Instead, this chiasm contained Paul's positive and negative appeals for their restoration. Their social relationships with Paul were to be strengthened to reflect their renewed allegiance to Paul, while their social ties with the intruding teachers, including any patronage obligations, were to be dissolved. Paul had already provided them with arguments to answer his critics (5:12) and his vilification in later sections (10:1ff.) added urgency to his request. Here he exhorts them to structure their social network to reflect their renewed acceptance of Paul's vision of and role in Christian social identity.

Paul's arrangements for the collection (8:1—9:15) also aimed to restructure the social network of the Corinthians. Paul boasted about Macedonia's performance in the collection to the Corinthians (8:1ff.), as he had boasted about the Corinthians to the Macedonians (9:2-3). In a strategy of social creativity, Paul redirected the Corinthian drive for honor competition to compete for honor in sacrificing for the benefit of other communities in their network. In this way, their competitive spirit would express and affirm their place in Paul's Aegean network of Christ-following communities. More significantly, their participation would change their network relationship with Jewish-Christian communities Jerusalem. The giving of gifts represents the establishment or continuation of a social exchange relationship.[45] Jennings argues that Paul uses the language of patronage to reinforce the social connections between the community as God's client, God as Patron, and himself as patron-proxy who services the Corinthian clients.[46] Jennings overlooks the fact that such a set of relationships seems to have been established by the visiting Jewish-Christian teachers, who accepted the patronage

---

44. Harris, *Second Corinthians*, 14–25. See also Bieringer, "2 Korinther 6,14–7,1"; and deSilva, "Recasting the Moment of Decision."

45. Joubert, *Paul as Benefactor*, 70–72.

46. Jennings, "Patronage and Rebuke in Paul's Persuasion in 2 Corinthians 8-9," 126–27.

of some Corinthian believers in exchange for their teaching.[47] Paul's understanding of this relationship was clearly that it is hierarchical: the teachers devoured and exploited their clients. The Corinthians in turn had become dependent, since these teachers united the community through their physical presence and their teaching about Moses, but without providing the needed mechanisms of social identification to enable them to function independently. Thus, Paul is critical of such a hierarchical patronage relationship and advocates the type of exchange relationship where both parties should benefit equally.[48] This interpretation advances significantly over older perspectives on the collection as an exercise in benevolence for needy believers, and as a demonstration of Paul's good will towards Jerusalem.[49] However, these newer interpretations need to be pushed further for their relevance to Paul's leadership in Corinth and his network of communities. Paul's exhortation to dissolve ties with the intruding teachers in effect released them from the hierarchical relationship with these teachers and their senders, which had maintained their dependence. Conversely, his exhortation to join in the collection for Jerusalem connected the Corinthian community in a network of mutuality with Jerusalem, together with Paul's other communities. In this way, Paul embedded the Corinthians' renewed allegiance in new internal relationships between local leaders, their subgroups, and himself, and in renewed external relationships with Paul's other communities and with Jerusalem.[50]

47. It is likely that the Corinthians' participation in the collection was hampered by this patronal relationship, since they may well have reasoned that they already fulfilled their patronage obligations towards Jerusalem in this way and that this was more beneficial than Paul's project, which would cost a great deal without any direct benefits for themselves—conveniently overlooking that they had already received benefits through the proclamation of the gospel through Paul's Jerusalem agreement. Furnish proposes instead that the Corinthians distrusted Paul's motives and therefore delayed their participation (Furnish, *II Corinthians*, 45–46), but even if the intruding teachers encouraged such mistrust, it would have mainly served the preservation of their preferred social network, a factor which Furnish overlooks.

48. As demonstrated by Joubert, *Paul as Benefactor*, 140. Ehrensperger argues similarly that Paul redefined the gift, not as a benefaction that creates the obligation of reciprocity, but as an expression of mutuality, i.e. of mutual concern for each other and for all in the network of the Christ-movement (*Paul and the Dynamics of Power*, 69–70).

49. Barrett, *Second Corinthians*, 25–28.

50. It is significant that Paul did not append these collection instructions to the end of the letter, as he had done in 1 Cor 16:1–4. Instead, Paul pressed the need for

Summary

In competition with the intruding teachers, Paul reestablished common ground with the Corinthians. He reaffirmed his vision of Christian social identity, including suffering and weakness as important dimensions, which allowed especially the lower status believers to identify with Paul as their champion. Paul elaborately displayed his many credentials to legitimate his leadership as founding father and apostle for Corinth, and he downgraded the leadership status of his rivals. Finally, Paul indicated appropriate social structures with which the Corinthians were to express their renewed allegiance, which included their release from patronage relationships with the intruding teachers and their inclusion in Paul's network of communities in a relationship of mutuality with Jerusalem. It was suggested that the key problem with the intruding teachers was not a different theology, but at the most that they emphasized some dimensions of Christ's life and ministry more than others. However, their most objectionable practices were the acceptance of patronage and use of rhetorical conventions, which favored the higher status believers, and disenfranchised those of lower status believers. This model of leadership was not congruous with the message of reconciliation through a suffering Savior. It may well be that the "different Jesus," of which Paul accused his rivals, represents Jesus as a Roman savior who promised benefits to the elite to keep them connected to and dependent on the emperor, but whose benefits hardly reached the lower status citizens which included 98% of the empire. This was visible more in the behavior of these intruding teachers than in their teaching.[51]

---

restructured relationships that had become evident in 2 Cor 1–7, before embarking on the status degradation ritual that would add urgency to his proposals.

51. Martin argues that for the opponents Jesus "is the figure of charismatic power, the θεῖος ἀνήρ of the early miracle-stories, and essentially κατὰ σάρκα (5:16)... As they patterned their ministry on the Jesus-figure who resembled the Moses of Philonic Judaism, they claimed that they were the mouthpiece of divine revelation in the new age of eschatological fulfillment (13:3)" (Martin, *2 Corinthians*, 339). The strength of Martin's argument is that it shows how an increased emphasis on the role of power in Jesus' ministry could lead to a lopsided view of Jesus. The argument needs to be pushed further, though, to recognize the social dimension: the portrayal of Jesus by the intruding teachers was especially congenial to elite leaders since it affirmed their quest for status and power, and it perpetuated existing social dichotomies. Paul's portrayal of Jesus, on the other hand, appealed broadly to all group members since it bridged the social dichotomies which it strongly criticized. Thus, Paul's Jesus un-

The Development of Local Leadership Patterns at Corinth in 56 CE

The previous two sections analyzed how Jewish-Christian leaders as well as Paul (and his team) competed intensely to fill the leadership vacuum that had arisen in the Corinth community due to expansion and the development of subgroups. Local leadership was hardly addressed in 2 Corinthians and seems to have disappeared from the scene, but it must have continued to function as the basic social structure within which the Jewish-Christian leaders as well as Paul intended to function. Apparently, local leadership was initially united by the intruding teachers in their admiration for Moses and disapproval of Paul. A little while later, Titus' reports about reconciliation implied that Paul was once again accepted in his imitation of Christ by the local leaders who now shared his disapproval of the Jewish-Christian teachers. This evidently influences the processes of leadership emergence, maintenance, and succession.

Restoring the Agency of the Local Corinthian Leaders. An important question about Paul's leadership and his use of power is how he could engage in such a strong polemic, vilify his opponents so sharply and threaten to rebuke the sinners, and still expect to bring unity instead of further division. A social identity analysis of power[52] proposes that power exercised by a prototypical, ingroup leader is usually experienced as beneficial and legitimate, but when exercised by an outgroup member it is usually considered illegitimate and coercive. Thus, if Paul exercised such authority at a time when most Corinthians perceived him as marginal or even as outsider, as had almost certainly been the case at some time between the writing of our 1 and 2 Corinthians, this would have been experienced as illegitimate and coercive. However, Titus had just reported that all was prepared for reconciliation. Evidently, Paul's relationship with the community was (about to be) restored, and he was again perceived as a prototypical ingroup leader and as authoritative reference point for the group. When Paul denounced these intruding teachers, the Corinthians would have

---

dermines the usual social hierarchy as well as privileges of status and power of the relatively wealthier believers. Witherington also points to social rather than theological aspects (see Witherington, *Conflict & Community in Corinth*, 348).

52. See Simon and Oakes, "Beyond Dependence," 112ff.; and Turner, "Explaining the Nature of Power," 10–14, as discussed in chapter 3.

perceived this forceful rhetoric as a beneficial and legitimate exercise of power.⁵³

This resolves the difficulty of how the householders would have responded to Paul's rhetoric if they were still actively sponsoring these opposing teachers. If they had not yet been convinced of Paul's rightful place and by implication of the deviant or even outgroup character of the opposing teachers, Paul would have entirely estranged the local leadership of the Corinthian community through this epistle. Only after receiving Titus' report is Paul willing to engage in such strong rhetoric, and that must imply that Paul estimated his chances for a good reception as very high, unless we are ready to conceive of Paul as a very clumsy communicator.⁵⁴ Moreover, a process had already started in Corinth whereby the opposing teachers were being marginalized, which probably included the withdrawing of patronage support. Paul's rhetoric confirms their marginalization, and empowers the householders to complete this process and to express their renewed loyalty to Paul publicly.⁵⁵

The opposing teachers, on the other hand, are not very likely to have accepted Paul's portrayal of themselves, their motives, and their teaching, at least not without a change of mind about their teaching and their leadership style. Paul's argument gives them only two options: repent and accept Paul's vision of Christian identity, with Paul as primary leader for Corinth, or be treated as outsider (and loose their funding). This is another application of Paul's earlier strategy, when Paul, as ambassador of the glorious ministry of reconciliation, offered the Corinthians the same choice: accept Paul's call for reconciliation

---

53. Garland helpfully distinguishes various kinds of power used in leadership, and argues (with respect to 2 Cor 10:5–6) that Paul used integrative power in dealing with the Corinthians and the opponents, instead of coercive of manipulative power (Garland, *2 Corinthians*, 439).

54. This reconstruction suggests that Paul could employ the strong rhetoric of vilification of ch. 10–13 precisely because the reconciliation had been prepared, as indicated by the conciliatory tone of ch. 2–7. Thus, there is no need to argue with Harris (Harris, *Second Corinthians*, 43–45, 105) that the change of tone is caused by fresh, independent and later information from Corinth, apart from Titus' favorable report; rather, the conciliatory and vilifying tone reflect the same underlying social situation of a community reconciled to Paul, willing to accept his evaluation of the opponents without questioning his motives.

55. Cf. 2 Cor 5:12, where Paul explicitly writes that he aims to empower the Corinthians to answer his opponents.

including his primary place as apostle, or be treated as outsider. With his vision of Christian social identity restored and his role as apostolic founder reestablished, Paul had regained the social power necessary to reinstitute local leadership according to patterns that were consistent with their restored Christian social identity.

Leadership Emergence. Leadership emergence is essentially a process of coming to be seen "as one of us" and "doing it for us." This is likely how Paul's competitors emerged in Corinth as leaders. As pointed out above, they conformed to cultural values in their appreciation of rhetoric, in their acceptance of financial support and in interpreting Paul's suffering as a sign of ineffective leadership. Moreover, they were properly credentialed from Israel and demonstrated greater loyalty for Jewish traditions in their treatment of Moses, which conforms to Corinthian expectations about itinerant teachers. In their bid for leadership in Corinth, they benefited from a better normative fit and category accessibility than Paul and his team. Perhaps they had even responded to reports about the Corinthian difficulties by traveling all the way from Israel, while Paul had not found time to come from Ephesus, demonstrating their greater commitment to Corinth. The Corinthians would be duly impressed by their prototypicality as key reference points in Christ-following communities, and by their group-oriented behavior to come to their assistance so quickly. Apparently, such a process took place quite quickly, since they appear to have emerged as acknowledged leaders soon after the arrival of 1 Corinthians.

This would have significantly impacted the local leaders, some of whom would have sponsored these Jewish-Christian teachers. This suggests that the disunity of local leadership as reported in 1 Corinthians, had been resolved by these visiting teachers in a new form of unity centered on their leadership. This probably reminded the Corinthians of their previous experiences where Paul and afterwards Apollos, also Jewish-Christian teachers, united the local leadership under their leadership in Corinth. Somehow, Paul's critics had succeeded, not merely in influencing one or more subgroups in Corinth, following the pattern of the divisions recorded in 1 Corinthians, but in influencing the majority of the congregation and its leadership to follow their teaching.[56] Even local leaders that previously were loyal

---

56. See also White's explanation of the two levels of leadership in Corinth with

to Paul appear to have been swayed by Paul's critics. In other words, these Jewish-Christian leaders had been able to move local leadership to a level of collegial coordination and leadership, providing the next move in leadership development that Paul had also envisioned, but under their own supervision. Thus, leadership structures seem to have developed to the level of collegial cooperation and coordination, even though Paul clearly denounces the leadership style, which they now had adopted.

Leadership Maintenance. It should not come as a surprise that Paul's first priority was to reestablish himself as prototypical leader, commissioned by God to bring the gospel, and sacrificing on behalf of the group to found and develop the community. His leadership had been marginalized and maligned to such an extent that Paul needed to retrace the steps of leadership emergence again, before any further leadership development could be initiated. As analyzed above, Paul directed the congregation to consolidate their association with himself and to dissociate themselves from his critics. He restored his vision of Christian social identity and regained his role as apostolic founder. This provided the social power Paul needed to restore the functioning of local leadership to patterns that were consistent with their restored Christian social identity. Thus, Paul maintained his leadership in Corinth by refreshing their social memory about his previous emergence as their community apostle, and by integrating his role as authoritative proclaimer in their identity narrative.

Paul's success in regaining his role as apostolic leader coincided with his success in uniting local leadership. Although Paul's strong denunciation of his opponents seems to suggest continuing divisions, several observations point to this opposite conclusion. First, studies of deviance show that deviants attract a disproportionate greater share of group communication, and that the intensity of denunciation correlates with the perceived level of danger posed by the deviant.[57] Thus, neither the amount of such communication nor its intensity can be used as evidence for the number of opponents in Corinth. Second, it was argued above that Paul voiced his denunciations only when he expected the community to receive it positively in order to avoid causing new divisions. Third, a distinction should be made between local

---

which Paul has to contend (White, "Social Authority in the House Church," 219–20).

57. Brown, *Group Processes*, 141–42.

Corinthian antagonists who were at one time critical of Paul but had now repented and (some) itinerant teachers who continued their opposition.[58] It is likely that Paul had won the allegiance of the majority of the Corinthian community, while the itinerant teachers attempted to retain their influence and thus their financial support. Paul's strong denunciations warn the community about the danger of this continuing deviant influence as long as their social networks were not restructured to express their renewed loyalty to Paul; thus, they underline the urgency of his instructions to "not be unequally yoked" and to rejoin the collection project. With Paul's leadership in Corinth restored, he used his social power to unite the local leaders around his own vision of Christian identity.

In all likelihood, Paul expected not merely to restore local leadership to its former state, but also to transform it to the collegial level of city-wide oversight that he had aimed to institute when he wrote 1 Corinthians and sent Timothy to follow up. A specific leadership model such as Stephanas was no longer needed to motivate this transformation, since their crisis experience taught them the value and function of this level of leadership, albeit it with the wrong values and with an inappropriate model of supervision by the intruding teachers. The local leaders were ready not only to accept Paul's leadership, but also to adopt a new level of leadership under Paul's banner of Christian social identity.

Leadership Succession. If succession was difficult to envision at the end of 1 Corinthians, it is all the more so at the end of 2 Corinthians. At great personal cost, Paul had been able to reestablish his vision of Christian social identity with his own apostolic role as the acknowledged exemplar. Without having finalized the reconciliation through his personal visit, Paul could not yet assume that he had the leadership status necessary to recommend any local leaders, as he had done at the end of 1 Corinthians. If the visit went well, that would have given him the status and social power necessary to arrange succession as he spent the winter in Corinth—but any such events remain beyond the horizon of the letter.

As Paul presented Timothy as trusted delegate in 1 Corinthians, so he presented Titus in 2 Corinthians without explaining this switch.

---

58. On the identification of two groups of critics, see Long, *The Compositional Unity of 2 Corinthians*, 178ff.

Perhaps the events following Timothy's visit to Corinth to follow up on Paul's letter (4:17; 16:10) prevented so soon a return. Thus Paul, as impresario, presented Titus as someone with "the same earnest care" for the Corinthians as himself (8:16), and as his partner and fellow worker (κοινωνὸς . . . συνεργός, 8:23), who likewise did not accept sponsorship (12:18). Titus is thus presented as a prototypical leader, similar to Paul, who will faithfully discharge his task as Paul's delegate, similar to how Timothy was presented in 1 Corinthians. Paul takes all possible care to keep the reconciliation going in the right direction, and Titus' arrival as similar, prototypical leader ahead of Paul is an added precaution against renewed influence from Paul's critics. Thus, Titus' mission and role have certain affinities with what would ordinarily be accomplished through succession, but with Paul's impending personal arrival in Corinth, he operates only in Paul's shadow as a temporary delegate.

Conclusions

The above social identity analysis demonstrates that a study of leadership in 2 Corinthians can be pushed much further than a study of Paul and his opponents, and of their competing leadership styles. Significant conclusions can be drawn about the broader patterns of local leadership as they developed in Corinth.

In the situation described in 1 Corinthians, Paul's leadership was marginalized to a subgroup and most likely considered ineffective by some in the community and by its leaders. This delicate social situation is visible in the progress of Paul's argumentation throughout the letter, and left the community with a leadership vacuum. Paul aims to protect the community from leadership succession by dissimilar and/or non-prototypical leaders who could take advantage of this delicate situation, so he dispatches 1 Corinthians, in which he presents Timothy as a similar, prototypical leader to stabilize the situation as delegate until he can arrive personally. One of the aims would be to assist the local Corinthian leadership to move to a new level of collegial cooperation and coordination, something that Stephanas modeled which earned him Paul's recommendation.

Unfortunately, Paul's plans did not succeed and itinerant Jewish-Christian teachers from Israel took advantage of the vulnerable situation not just to gain a foothold but also to take over the leadership of the community. Their leadership model was culturally more aligned with Greco-Roman values, while their vision of social identity was more aligned with Jewish traditions. They denigrated Paul for not being of 'pure' Palestinian descent. They also interpreted his lack of rhetorical skill, his physical weakness, and frequent suffering as signs of dishonor and failure, and accused him of lack of love because of his unwillingness to accept the patronage of Corinthian believers—which ironically shows them to be more Hellenized in their leadership style than Paul. Nevertheless, it appears that the local Corinthian leaders were convinced to support these Jewish-Christian teachers, providing hospitality and sponsorship, which gave them the platform to promote their teaching. As a result, the local leaders experienced a new sense of unity and coordination under their leadership, reminiscent perhaps of earlier days when Paul and Apollos had provided this type of coordination. In other words, a collegial level of leadership cooperation and coordination developed as Paul had also advocated, but under the supervision of the itinerant teachers with a deviant vision of social identity.

Paul, therefore, objected against this leadership transformation, but not because of the changes in structure. Rather, the shift towards Jewish traditions changed essential comparison dimensions of Paul's vision of Christian social identity, while the shift towards Greco-Roman values transformed the ingroup prototype to conform to the higher status members. Paul did not consider these changes as identity-neutral adaptations to local culture, but portrayed them as centering on a "different Jesus." Therefore, Paul endeavored to reestablish his leadership. He revisited the basics of leadership emergence to emphasize his prototypicality and sacrificial service on behalf of the community. He accentuated Christ as model of suffering and victory, and portrayed his own ministry as parallel with Christ; he narrated the story of his commission as bearer of the gospel and as ambassador of divine reconciliation. Paul already knew that his portrayal was, broadly speaking, acceptable to the Corinthians since they had declared their loyalty and repented of deserting Paul. In 2 Corinthians, no local leaders are commended, but this was no longer necessary since most had declared their loyalty to Paul. Thus, they can be assumed to move towards collegial leadership under Paul's supervision, and a specific model of such type of leadership, such as

Stephanas in 1 Corinthians, no longer needed explicit recommendation. The few remaining critics needed not to be named, since the Corinthians knew them all too well. Thus, Paul was restored to his role as apostle and founder, with the local leaders adapting to the new social situation under his supervision. Since Paul's status still needed to be officially affirmed upon his arrival, his leadership status was yet too insecure to allow him to initiate succession.

Later evidence (1 Clem. 44:3–6) suggests that Corinthian elders, appointed by the apostles, operated on the level of collegial oversight, which suggests that Paul was ultimately successful in his attempts to develop new levels of leadership in Corinth under the banner of his own gospel and apostleship. This has significant ramifications for how Paul was perceived in Corinth and elsewhere, since Paul had been able to navigate the Corinthian community successfully through times of very threatening social turmoil. The Corinthian community almost lost its place as hub of Paul's Achaian network of communities, but Paul had succeeded in regaining his leadership position, reclaiming the community, and aligning their local leaders in collegial coordination. In such a situation, charismatic leadership attribution is likely to take place, so that Paul probably emerged from the Corinthian struggles as acclaimed charismatic leader.

Finally, did Paul institute succession during his winter in Corinth after the reconciliation was effected? The cited traditions from 1 Clement indicate at least that Paul appointed some of the Corinthian leaders as bishop(s) and elders. How would a situation arise where a 'younger' generation deposed some of the older leaders, without indications of moral or ideological deviance? This is, of course, another step in the study of first century church leadership: it appears that succession from Paul to local leadership went well, but that further succession faltered. Undoubtedly, the strenuous difficulties surrounding the initial succession from Paul to local leaders and their growth to collegial leadership became embedded in their identity narrative. The intensity of these memories may well have resulted in a 'freezing' of further development of leadership in order to safeguard the leadership structures that had been established at such great cost.[59] Moreover, the

---

59. This phenomenon is known as the reification of social identity and its social processes. See Reicher and Hopkins, "Psychology and the End of History," 401; Haslam and Ellemers, "Social Identity in Industrial and Organizational Psychology," 94–95; and Cornelissen at al., "Social, Organizational and Corporate Identity," 10.

Corinthian values of honor and seniority may have reasserted their hold on the community so that the appointment of younger leaders next to older leaders was considered dishonorable and was thus resisted. Did the established leaders, then, hesitate too long to initiate the next installment of succession in order to protect their history and their seniority? Perhaps they had not learned sufficiently from Paul how to incorporate succession into their vision of Christian social identity and how to create community rituals that would enable their successors to function effectively with the support of the community. It is precisely these issues, which form part of Paul's agenda in his correspondence with Ephesus.

6

Leadership Legitimation and Empowerment in Ephesians

ALTHOUGH EPHESIANS CONTAINS IMPORTANT PASSAGES ABOUT COMmunity leadership, it does not often feature prominently in leadership studies. For instance, Holmberg and Burtchaell include only a few references to Ephesians, mostly in their broader discussion of apostles and prophets,[1] while Campbell's study on eldership as seniority hardly refers to the letter at all.[2] However, Merklein devotes a lengthy monograph to "office" in Ephesians, while MacDonald allots one chapter to governance in Colossians and Ephesians taken together.[3] One factor that explains the relative absence of Ephesians in leadership studies is that many consider it deutero-Pauline.[4] Thus, even Chapple and Clarke who are inclined towards a more canonical approach to the letter, exclude it from their socio-historical study of leadership structures.[5] Another factor is that Ephesians is very generic, so that

---

1. Holmberg, *Paul and Power*, 97–101 and Burtchaell, *Synagogue*, esp. 300–3.

2. Campbell, *The Elders*, 109–10, but of course the term 'elder' does not occur in the letter.

3. Merklein, *Das kirchliche Amt*; and MacDonald, *The Pauline Churches*, 123–38.

4. Brown estimates that 70–80% take this position (Brown, *Introduction to the New Testament*, 629), but Hoehner's survey of almost 300 commentaries finds that a slight majority favors Pauline authorship (*Ephesians*, 19–20).

5. Chapple, "Local Leadership," who focuses on 1 Thess 5:12–13, 1 Cor 16:15–18 and Phil 1:1, and Clarke, *Serve the Community*, 173–208 offers no chapter on leadership in Ephesians as he does for the uncontested Pauline letters, but in his later study on leadership style he includes the entire Pauline corpus (*A Pauline Theology of Church Leadership*, 4ff).

social issues are at best vaguely visible against a remote background.[6] Shkul, therefore, argues that "there is no need to reconstruct particular socio-historical causes" in her reading of Ephesians.[7] However, even an ideological text such as Ephesians—to use Skhul's terminology—remains connected with its social setting. A third factor relates to the destination and addressees of the letter, since the words "in Ephesus" (1:1) are uncertain and a Jewish presence within the community is disputed. These uncertainties about the author, date, and destination influence the perception of the Ephesian leadership passages, so that they are investigated for qualitative aspects of leadership such as style and function, rather than for concrete social patterns of leadership.

Since the present study focuses on concrete leadership patterns, a brief consideration of these factors is necessary. Pauline authorship of Ephesians was unanimously accepted in the early church, but over the last few centuries, the many known differences between Ephesians and the other Paulines have caused doubt. A representative summary of the argumentation is as follows. First, Ephesians portrays Paul's apostolic role in very lofty language, without the weaknesses and suffering so prominent in 1–2 Corinthians. This "reads far more like the estimate of Paul's apostleship on the part of someone looking back than like Paul talking about himself."[8] However, considering Paul's earlier claims to be a divine ambassador of reconciliation (2 Cor 5:20) and to have received heavenly visions (2 Cor 12:1–4), there is no intrinsic reason why Paul could not present himself in this way. It was suggested above that after his successful management of the Corinthian crisis, he was perceived as charismatic leader, and it will be argued below that Ephesians reflects circumstances where Paul judged it beneficial to refer to this perspective. Second, Ephesians highlights Christ's resurrection and His cosmic lordship over all cosmic powers as well as over the universal church, unlike the emphasis on Christ's death in Paul's

---

6. Lindemann proposes that time in Ephesians comes to a standstill in Christ (Lindemann, *Die Aufhebung der Zeit*, 106–92), cited in Yee, *Jews, Gentiles, and Ethnic Reconciliation*, 19.

7. Shkul, *Reading Ephesians*, 7–9.

8. Lincoln, *Ephesians*, lxiii. This section follows Lincoln's argumentation as representative. Less comprehensive argumentation along the same lines can be found in MacDonald, *Colossians and Ephesians*, 15–17; and Talbert, *Ephesians and Colossians*, 7–11.

earlier letters and his focus on particular local assemblies.[9] However, considering that—from the traditional perspective—Paul wrote from a Roman prison when he was confronted daily with Roman imperial dominance, and reflected on his network of churches in Asia Minor that had expanded in spite of Roman opposition, Paul's references to cosmic lordship, evil forces, and a universal church are not very surprising at all.[10]

Third, the language and style of Ephesians differ significantly from other Pauline epistles. For instance, Lincoln notes that Ephesians contains 40 hapax legomena and 51 other words not found in the Pauline corpus although present elsewhere in the NT.[11] However, Hoehner aptly juxtaposes the same statistics for Galatians. Citing Morgenthaler's statistical analysis of NT vocabulary, Hoehner identifies 31 hapax legomena and 80 other unique words in Galatians, which no exegete finds troublesome for Pauline authorship.[12] Fourth, the style of the letter is less direct, without the "incisive argumentation of the earlier letters. This is replaced by a heavier, pleonastic style."[13] This debate still seems to be captive to theological categories, since scholars usually correlate differences in language and style directly with theology and authorship. However, linguistic theories of composition suggest that greater social distance (writing from Rome, five years after his last visit to Ephesus) decreases the specificity and the directness of argumentation, and more available time (house arrest) increases the literary level of writing.[14] In addition, Paul's theology has been found to interact intimately with its social context.[15]

---

9. Lincoln, *Ephesians*, lxiii–lxiv.

10. Hoehner also notes that the death of Christ is hardly absent from Ephesians nor is the universal church absent from 1–2 Cor (*Ephesians*, 49–55). See also the discussion of eschatology as another area of theological difference in Hoehner, *Ephesians*, 56–58 and Lincoln, *Ephesians*, lxiv.

11. Lincoln, *Ephesians*, lxv.

12. Hoehner, *Ephesians*, 24, citing Morgenthaler, *Statistik des neutestamentlichen Wortschatzes*, 194ff.

13. Lincoln, *Ephesians*, lxv.

14. For more detailed argumentation, see the excursus on the authorship of the Pastoral Epistles in the next chapter.

15. Cf. Holmberg, who identified the failure to recognize how theology and social context interact as the fallacy of idealism (*Paul and Power*, 201–4).

These all too brief remarks[16] show that more comprehensive social and linguistic analyses are able to explain these differences as from the pen of one author. Even without such methods, traditional exegetical methods[17] and more recent studies of ancient compositional techniques[18] have been ably employed to demonstrate that such differences do not necessarily lead to a conclusion in favor of pseudonymity. Thus, in the absence of conclusive evidence for pseudonymous authorship, it seems best to respect the indications of the text and early church tradition and to proceed on the presupposition of Pauline authorship. A social reconstruction of the setting of the letter in Paul's ministry may be more difficult than in the case of 1–2 Corinthians, but must nevertheless be attempted.

A second factor, which influences the perception of Ephesians with regard to patterns of leadership, is the identity of the addressees. The words ἐν Ἐφέσῳ ("in Ephesus," 1:1) do not occur in some of the best manuscripts of the Alexandrian text (P46, ℵ and B) nor in a few ancient fathers, but they are found in other Alexandrian and in all Byzantine and Western texts. Considering the unanimous early church tradition in favor of the Ephesian destination, the UBS Committee decided to retain ἐν Ἐφέσῳ, but enclosed in square brackets with a "C" rating.[19] Since the contents of the letter are very generic, Perkins interprets this textual and internal evidence as indication that the words ἐν Ἐφέσῳ were initially absent, and that the letter was "addressed to Christian churches in general."[20] However, O'Brien points out that the manuscripts, which omit the phrase, put nothing in its place. Even if the letter was intended as circular letter, no copy survives with another place name besides Ephesians.[21] O'Brien then concludes that the words

---

16. For instance, the difficulties raised by the literary relationship between Colossians and Ephesians was not considered, though Lincoln, *Ephesians*, lxvi considers them very weighty evidence in favor of pseudonymity. Also, ancient perceptions of pseudepigraphy were not reviewed, though they present weighty evidence in favor of authenticity (see the excursus on authorship in the next chapter).

17. See for instance Barth, *Ephesians 1–3*, 4–50 and Hoehner, *Ephesians*, 2–61. For an able summary, see DeSilva, *Introduction to the NT*, 716–21.

18. Richards, *Secretary*; Klauck, *Die antike Briefliteratur und das Neue Testament*.

19. Metzger, *The Text of the New Testament*, 532.

20. Perkins, *Ephesians*, 16–17.

21. O'Brien, *Ephesians*, 85–86. Even though Marcion listed Ephesians as the letter to the Laodiceans, this suggestion did not find its way into the manuscripts.

were likely not original but that the letter is nevertheless correctly connected with Ephesus by early church traditions.[22] However, considering that even the Alexandrian text is divided in its witness, the textual evidence favors the words as original.[23] Thus, letter's connection with Ephesus will be retained, although this connection is evidently less personal and direct as compared with other Pauline epistles. This may indeed indicate that the letter was to be distributed in a broader circle than only in Ephesus, a practice already known from 1–2 Corinthians, which were addressed to a wider audience than only the Corinthians, while the letters to the Colossians and the Laodiceans were to be exchanged.[24] If Paul himself did not envision Ephesians as a circular letter, it would have been but a small step for Ephesian believers to propose that 'their' letter should also circulate in the region, which may account for the omission of the words in only a small segment of the manuscript tradition.

Situating Ephesians in Paul's Ministry

A third factor influencing the debate about leadership in Ephesians is its general character. The letter refers to Paul's imprisonment and thus likely dates to the close of Paul's first imprisonment in Rome.[25] It presents a social context where Paul is at a greater distance from the community he writes to: a distance in location because he was not readily accessible for the Ephesian believers, a distance in time because he had left Ephesus about 5 years prior and a distance of social development because the church had expanded since his departure. Thus, the letter's style and theology appear more generic and standardized than the earlier letters.

This generic character not only reflects the greater social distance between Paul and the Ephesian community, it also reflects the overall development of Paul's Aegean mission.[26] In an oral society with the

22. Ibid., 47–49 and 86–87.

23. See also Hoehner, *Ephesians*, 78–79.

24. See 1 Cor 1:1, 2 Cor 1:1–2 and the discussion above in chapter 4. See also Col 4:16.

25. O'Brien, *Ephesians*; deSilva, *Introduction to the NT*, 723. For further discussion of Paul as prisoner, see below.

26. See also Trebilco's discussion of the position of Ephesians in the Pauline corpus (*The Early Christians in Ephesus*, 90–93).

close networks Christians maintained, the lessons learned in one Christian community soon found their way to other Christian communities. Thus, Paul probably taught in Corinth what he wrote to Thessalonica, as he later taught in Ephesus what he wrote to Corinth. Moreover, common scribal practice suggests that local leaders probably would have had access to Paul's various letters,[27] so that any additional correspondence could focus on new issues. Due to community expansion, increasing complexity, and involvement of local leaders, it is only to be expected that Paul's concern as apostolic leader move from the specific to the more general. In other words, Paul's growing network would drive Paul to more generalized and overarching concerns to continue to provide leadership to the network. This is reflected in Ephesians.

Social Identification in the Ephesian Community in 61 CE

The generic character of Ephesus makes it difficult to reconstruct the social background.[28] Issues of social identification play a major role in this letter, as is evident from several recent monographs on Ephesians that use social identity theory. Shkul, for instance, reads Ephesians for its social entrepreneurship, and identifies such strategies as identity construction (Eph 1), social memory and legitimation (Eph 2–3), and communal social orientation through prototypes and antitypes (Eph 4–6). She is, however, skeptical of attempts at social reconstruction.[29] Tellbe acknowledges that authors construct the world in their text ("textual identities"), but believes that careful reconstruction of the socio-historical realities "in and behind the ancient text" is possible.[30]

---

27. For further detail, see the excursus on the authorship of 1 Timothy in the next chapter.

28. MacDonald comments that the "the opaque and idealizing language of Ephesians" makes it difficult to situate the letter historically ("The Politics of Identity in Ephesians," 419).

29. Shkul, *Reading Ephesians*, 7–9, 28. Lieu is equally skeptical (*Christian Identity*, 9 and 61).

30. Tellbe, *Christ-Believers in Ephesus*, 47–52, and "The Prototypical Christ-Believer," 119–20. Tellbe agrees with Trebilco (*The Early Christians in Ephesus*, 10), but faults him for not distinguishing between the perspective of the author and the social life of the community 'behind' the text.

Darko does not explicitly address the issue, but mentions it as an issue for further study in his conclusions.[31] Roitto is most positive, arguing with social identity theory that texts and social circumstances are connected in the normal cognitive processes of understanding, and that minimal historical reconstruction is possible and even necessary to understand the text.[32]

These arguments can be strengthened in favor of historical and social reconstruction. The social entrepreneurship evident in Ephesians suggests that the author aimed to provide leadership for the community. Although Shkul does not address this, such an aim implies a measure of leadership status within the community addressed; that is, ingroup leadership status depends on prototypicality and group-oriented behavior, so that the leader's vision of social identity is received as relevant for the group and its concerns. Using the social identity model of leadership maintenance, such a vision relates to the existing group context in one of the following ways: (1) it either *accentuates* the existing ingroup prototype and portrays the leader as embodying this prototype; (2) it *conforms* to the existing prototype and portrays the leader as adapting himself to embody this prototype; or (3) it *changes* the existing prototype to conform to the leader's vision and argues that the group should conform to the leader as a better prototype for the social context of the group than the current ingroup prototype. These three ways of leadership maintenance help to determine the relationship between a leader's construal of social identity and the group's experience of social identity.

How closely is the rhetoric of identity in Ephesians connected with the experience of the Ephesians? The letter shows few signs of concrete problems or social stresses, although they are discussed from a general perspective. It is unlikely, then, that Ephesians presented a different ingroup prototype to resolve these social stresses as Paul had done in 1–2 Corinthians (option 3). The identity management in 1–2 Corinthians demonstrates that Paul did not simply accommodate

---

31. Darko, *No Longer Living as the Gentiles*, 132, cf. 34.

32. Roitto, *Behaving*, 35–40, 127–35. He proposes that the historical reality can be assessed by answering three questions from a social identity perspective: "(1) Does the author seem to be ingroup for the recipients? . . . (2) Does the author seem to be prototypical in the eyes of the recipients? . . . (3) Does the message in the text seem to take its starting point in the recipients' current cognition?" (Ibid., 38–39). This study uses the social identity model of leadership for its historical assessment.

himself to the Corinthians' local vision of social identity, but aimed to change their vision to match his own on vital dimensions of Christian social identity. Thus, Paul was unlikely to conform himself to an Ephesian version of social identity with respect to these vital dimensions (option 2).[33] This leaves option one that Paul likely affirmed the ingroup prototype as he had previously taught and explained it during his Aegean ministry. This does not to deny that Paul's letter contained anything new for the Ephesians; it may well have strengthened, expanded or revitalized the Ephesian perception of their Christian social identity. What is argued is that the vision of social identity as presented in Ephesians matches relatively closely the historical and social reality being addressed, without ignoring that leaders aim to construct reality through their rhetoric and texts.[34]

Ephesians defines Christian social identity not case by case as in 1–2 Corinthians, but more generically in competition with Greco-Roman and Jewish identities. Ephesus was the most important city of Asia Minor with dominant Roman influence, which the letter reflects in its use of Roman military language and in its portrayal of Christ as Lord over all in competition with the emperor.[35] The letter challenges the pagan world with its emphasis on evil spiritual powers. This reflects only partly the worship of Artemis as the dominant religious

---

33. If Ephesians is pseudepigraphal, the same three options are available as leadership strategy. Such strategies would generally aim to legitimate the author's perception of the Pauline tradition and portray the author as true follower of Paul; that is, these strategies amount to the claim "I am of Paul" for various different social scenarios in Ephesus. However, since a pseudonymous author hides behind the stated author Paul, he would have remained invisible and would not have gained leadership status within the community. Considering the ingrained habits of honor competition in the ancient world, it seems highly unlikely that someone with the status and means to compose and distribute a pseudonymous letter would have been content to hide behind Paul and forego a rise in leadership status. He might, of course, have accepted Paul's anti-honor rhetoric and portrayal of self-sacrificial leadership, but then it is highly unlikely that he would have presumed to write the church on behalf of a long-deceased Paul. Even if this transpired, Christian tradition would most likely have attached his name to the letter in memory of his loyalty to Paul, as occurred with 1 Clement and the letters of Ignatius. Thus, if Ephesians is rightfully considered with Shkul as a text of social entrepreneurship, it seems that pseudonymous authorship presents acute difficulties for social reconstruction contra Shkul. Her skepticism about social reconstruction allows her to skirt this issue, but she has missed an important aspect of social identity theory in how rhetoric relates to reality.

34. Similar to the argument of Roitto, *Behaving*, 127ff.

35. MacDonald, "The Politics of Identity," 424–27.

orientation, since other forms of idolatry, including emperor worship, were also present in Ephesus.[36] The city also had a substantial Jewish community,[37] compared to which the Christ-following community must have seemed small. The Christian community thus had to define its social relationships with Roman institutions, pagan worship, and the Jewish community. Thus, the distinctiveness of Christian social identity relative to these competing outgroup social identities is an important issue for the Ephesian Christ-following community.

Other issues in social identification that are familiar from the analysis of 1–2 Corinthians are visible in Ephesians as well, but in more general form. The superordinate nature of Christian social identity is defined in superlative terms: Christ is universal Lord over all (1:21-22) and God is the universal Patriarch (3:14-15). This provides a cosmic perspective on normal social identification issues. Nested identities remain visible in the unity between Jew and gentile (2:11-22). If, as Lincoln maintains, the letter is exclusively addressed to gentile believers (cf. 2:11, 3:1),[38] this unity would merely be a theoretical possibility, reflecting Paul's earlier difficulties on this count and perhaps reminding gentile believers of the Jewish roots of their faith community. However, Paul, as Jewish Christ-believer,[39] wrote of "we" by contrast to "you" gentiles, and it is quite conceivable that a small portion of his addressees counted themselves part of "we" instead of "you."[40] Moreover, the author's intensive use of Jewish concepts and traditions[41] seems odd when addressed to an exclusively gentile audience that already held to such beliefs (as suggested by the role of

---

36. Murphy-O'Connor, *Ephesus*, 34, 200, suggests that the dominance of Artemis was the occasion for Paul's portrayal of Christ's lordship in universal terms. However, Strelan argues that Paul's concern in Ephesians was not so much to resist Artemis worship per se, but to refute all idolatry and to present the real struggle of believers as against supernatural powers (Strelan, *Paul, Artemis, and the Jews in Ephesus*, 155-62).

37. Trebilco, *Jewish Communities in Asia Minor*, 186-88.

38. Lincoln, *Ephesians*, lxxvi, who also refers to 2:1-3, 11-13, 3:2-13 and 4:17-19 in support of his position.

39. As generally acknowledged by all scholars.

40. See for instance the argument by MacDonald, *Colossians and Ephesians*, 17-18, 203-4. Strelan pushes this argument too far, suggesting that for instance diaspora Jews who had abandoned a Torah-abiding lifestyle could also identify with those who "were far off" but had now become near (2:13). Thus, he proposes that a significant proportion of the addressees could have been Jewish (*Paul and Artemis*, 292-93).

41. Yee, *Jews, Gentiles, and Ethnic Reconciliation*, 35-45, 72-87.

Ephesians as leadership maintenance document). Thus, the presence of at least a minority of Jewish Christ-believers is likely, so that the letter's rhetoric reflects actual and mostly successful negotiations of ethnic unity ongoing in Ephesus.[42] Jewish and gentile Christ-believers as ethnic subgroups are conceived of as nested identities within the superordinate, universal vision of Christian social identity.

The superordinate nature of Christian social identity also provides the cosmic perspective for downgrading the interests from cross-cutting identities. The giving of gifts, including the giving of people in certain leadership positions (4:7, 11) is portrayed as flowing from the Spirit, the Father, and Christ (4:4–6) for the purpose of attaining the unity and stability of the faith community (4:13–16).[43] Certain behaviors are stereotyped as outgroup behavior, and are contrasted with stereotyped ingroup behaviors (4:17—5:1), clarifying group norms and boundaries since members continue in social relationships with outsiders. The various members of ancient households are instructed about how to prioritize their Christian social identity as they function in their subordinate household identities (5:21—6:9). Although these passages employ rather generic language about community participation, behavioral norms, and household roles, the reality of conflicting interests from cross-cutting identities remains visible as the concrete, albeit it remote, socio-cultural background.

Community activities and rituals, such as in 1 Cor 11–14, are not treated as separate topics but are embedded in broader identification issues. The topics of giftedness and leadership are briefly and formally embedded in a section that highlights the divine call and intention in community formation (2:20; 4:11). Participation in worship (5:19–20) becomes part of a section on group norms, which require the filling with the Spirit. Male and female roles are generically addressed in the household code (5:21–33). Discussion about the eating of sacrificial meat is no longer necessary, since the addressees are warned more generally to leave behind their former lifestyle (4:17–19) and to engage in spiritual conflict (6:10–20). In addition, various allusions to

---

42. Roitto argues rather minimally that gentile and Jewish Christ-believers "perhaps . . . even participated in the same commuities" (Roitto, *Behaving*, 129). This would leave the language of unification without any realistic referent in Ephesians, which is unlikely and unnecessarily minimal.

43. For more detailed argumentation about these and the following passages, see the discussion below about Paul's identity management.

baptism and the eucharist have been proposed in this letter.[44] Yet, in spite of the riches of Ephesians with regard to community activities, these are not discussed as a topic in themselves, but are embedded in Paul's presentation of a universal vision of Christian social identity.

It thus appears that Ephesians relates to issues in social identification that were familiar from other locations like Corinth, but treats them as it were from a distance. The concreteness of the issues is less evident. Instead, these issues are now situated in a portrayal of Christian social identity as superordinate, or in theological terms, as universal. This could be the work of a later author, but it may just as well be assumed that Paul was vitally interested in generalizing his teaching to apply more broadly to community development in an expanding network of communities, as is evident from a comparison of Galatians and Romans. Moreover, Paul's earlier teaching, available through the group's social memory, as well as through copies of his earlier letters (as argued above), would have been sufficient to resolve concrete issues. Paul's social distance from Ephesus, and his awareness of ongoing community development in Asia Minor likely prompted him to generalize his earlier teaching. It is not so much that the basic issues of social identification in Ephesus are different from those in Corinth, but rather that Paul recasts these issues in a more comprehensive vision of Christian social identity, which defines its distinctiveness over against the major competing identities of his time: Roman ideology, pagan worship and Jewish tradition.

The Ephesian Leaders as Managers of Christian Social Identity

Within this more generic vision of Christian social identity, the Ephesian leaders appear as an extension of the apostolic leadership team, instead of as competitors of Paul as in Corinth. Thus, chapters 4 and 5 on 1–2 Corinthians included extended sections on the

---

44. See Barth, *Ephesians 1–3*, 135ff, who mentions 1:18, 20–23; 4:5, 22–24, 30; 5:8–13, 14 and 16 as possible allusions to baptism (p. 137), and Schlier, *Der Brief an die Epheser*, 249–50, who mentions 5:20, 22–23 and 29 as allusions to the eucharist. Barth does not think that the reference to Christ's blood in 2:13 refers to the eucharist, although the eucharist may have been the occasion when the unity realized by Christ's death was actively remembered (Barth, *Ephesians 1–3*, 83). See also the chapter on "The Concept of Baptism in Ephesians" by Dahl et al., *Studies in Ephesians*, 413–40.

identity management of the Corinthian leaders, which differed on several counts from Paul's leadership. These leaders competed with Paul over how Christian social identity was relevant in their local Corinthian context. Such tension is not evident in Ephesians. Evangelists, pastors, and teachers are portrayed as divinely legitimated leaders, maintaining the unity of the community amidst social change. They are portrayed as a leadership subgroup functioning on a collegial level next to apostles and prophets. The lack of social tension in how these leaders are presented may partially reflect Paul's distance from the church, not being fully up to date about the current situation; more importantly, it probably reflects the shared perception by Paul and his audience that the local Ephesian leaders were essentially in harmony with Paul.

These leaders, then, are presented as an independently functioning leadership subgroup, in harmony with Paul and his vision of Christian social identity. Later in this chapter, as the analysis progresses and Paul's leadership becomes clearer, the place and function of the local leaders will be further defined.

Paul's Leadership as Identity Management

Lincoln has aptly observed

> that the mixture of rhetorical genres [in Ephesians]—epideictic in the first half of the letter and deliberative in the second half—reflects the writer's twofold strategy. He wishes both to intensify the readers' adherence to the Christian convictions, values, and concepts that he and they have in common and to persuade them to take action that will bring their lives into greater conformity to what he deems to be appropriate to their shared perspective.[45]

This observation accords with the above arguments that the author accentuated or intensified his vision of Christian social identity that he shared with his addressees. Paul's identity management in Ephesians is thus quite different from 1–2 Corinthians, since he does not have to compete with or even defend himself against local leadership, nor does he have to engage with concrete issues in Ephesus which local

---

45. Lincoln, *Ephesians*, lxxv, who speaks of a sense of "Christian identity" in his explanations.

leaders can be assumed to handle adequately. Instead, Paul can focus on developing his perspective on the foundations and implications of his vision of Christian social identity.

Celebrating the Universal Nature of Christian Social Identity

The letter opens with a celebration of the universal nature of Christian social identity. God is portrayed as the heavenly benefactor who bestows the richest of benefactions on his clients, portrayed as children who depend upon and honor him (1:3–14). God's benefactions through Christ and our response in praise initiate a relationship between benefactor and client, which forms the basis of the community of all who receive God's benefactions with praise.[46] By celebrating these benefactions, the recipients publicly demonstrate their social identification with the benefactor's community. The origin of their social identity not only lies in recent evangelism in Ephesus and elsewhere (1:12–13), but more importantly in the divine plan unfolding from "before the foundation of the world" (1:9). These initial statements about Christian social identity situate the foundational beliefs in a cosmic, universal setting, and provide a basis for social comparison, not from the realistic position of a minority social group of largely lower status people, but from the idealized position of a universal community, which outranks any other competing social identity because of its divine origin and destiny.[47]

The subsequent prayers impress upon the audience the supreme value of their new social identity as believers (1:15–23). The "Father of glory" is called upon to enlighten group members through his Spirit about his rich benefactions (1:17–19), of which Christ is his cosmic broker, "far above all rule and authority . . . and above every name that is named" (1:21). Moreover, Christ is given "as head over all things to the church, which is his body" (1:22–23). Thus, Christ is positioned as head both over his community and over all (Roman) institutions of power, implying that Christian social identity outranks any other

---

46. Gosnell, "Honor and Shame in Ephesians," 112 ff.

47. Interestingly, Eph 1:3–14 contains some significant parallels with an ancient honorary decree (Hendrix, "On the Form and Ethos of Ephesians," 5–8). Although some suggest that all of Ephesians can be understood as honorary decree (Mouton, "The Communicative Power of Ephesians," 284–90), it is best to suggest that the Ephesians has some affinities with this genre (Best, *Ephesians*, 62).

social identity that competes for allegiance in the complex social world of a Roman society. Paul celebrates the universal nature of Christian social identity in order to encourage social identification with the Christ-following community.[48]

This celebration comes to a climax as Paul expresses his ultimate devotion to the heavenly benefactor by describing him as the Father "from whom every family in heaven and on earth is named" (3:14), in direct competition with Roman ideology. Cicero admitted that a man may acknowledge his own town as homeland or *patria*, "but ultimately, the *patria* of Rome trumps all others" (*De legibus 2.2.5*).[49] Instead, Paul argues, God is the *pater patriae* of all earthly and heavenly *patriae*, and members of his communities need not be intimidated by Rome's power and glory, for God's power and glory will strengthen us with his Spirit (3:16). Christ's love, which "surpasses knowledge" (3:19), is far superior to Rome's "love," which provides *some* benefactions to citizens, and mostly those of higher status.

Paul presents a strong counterpoint to Roman ideology, which has significant social implications. Through a strategy of social creativity, Paul compensates for the social marginalization of the Christian community by attributing to Christian identity the value and honor usually attributed to Rome and its institutions. Paul's ideological portrayal of the Christ-following communities makes the social point that no social network or group is independent of God the Father. In cosmic language, inspired by Roman ideology, Paul ranks all social identities as subordinate relative to Christian social identity. As artist of social identity, he settles the conflicts he experienced in Corinth with nested and cross-cutting identities once and for all by celebrating the universal nature of Christian social identity.

Celebrating the Distinctiveness of Christian Social Identity

Next, Paul celebrates the distinctiveness of Christian social identity by maximizing its differences with the Roman outgroup, and minimizing internal differences between subgroups. First, Paul sharpens intergroup comparison by contrasting outgroup and ingroup members

---

48. Mouton, "The Communicative Power of Ephesians," 293 ff.

49. Cited in Dunning, "Strangers and Aliens," 6. For a similar analysis of the father metaphor, see Eva Marie Lassen, "The Roman Family," 112–13.

using familiar Jewish language (2:1-10). Outgroup members are "dead in the trespasses and sins" (2:1), being "sons of disobedience" (2:2),[50] while ingroup members are "made alive" through God's rich mercy and love (2:4-6).[51] Roman language of authority and enthronement (2:2, 6) portrays their former status as dominated by evil powers, and their current status as participating in God's reign.[52] Membership in Roman social identity is stereotyped in starkly negative terms and compared with the equally stereotyped exalted nature of Christian social identity. These contrasts maximize the differences between ingroup and outgroup members to emphasize the intergroup boundary as well as the need to remain distinct.[53] They also maximize the similarity of ingroup members to one another, which encourages deepening social identification with and social mobility towards Christian social identity, since the usual differentiation based on social status, reputation, and power is irrelevant.

Second, Paul minimizes intragroup differences by redefining typical identity language to harmonize with Christian social identity (2:11-22). Jewish identity categories predominate in the references to insiders who label themselves as "circumcision" and derogate outsiders as "uncircumcision" (2:11), separated from Christ, alienated from Israel, strangers to the covenants, and without hope (2:12). Moreover, gentiles joining the believing community were "far" but are brought "near" (2:13, 17), reflecting Jewish proselytism terminology.[54] These

50. MacDonald compares these expressions "sons of . . ." and "children of . . ." with Qumran texts. See MacDonald, "The Politics of Identity," 422-23.

51. For an overview of Jewish terminology in Eph 2, see Yee, *Jews, Gentiles, and Ethnic Reconciliation*, 34-212. This indicates that the author often operates from within a Jewish symbolic universe.

52. See also Dunning about pairs of identity markers in Ephesians: saints vs. sinners, adopted children vs. children of wrath, Jew/gentile vs. one new man, alien/stranger vs. citizens ("Strangers and Aliens," 8).

53. MacDonald interprets these contrasts as strong language of dissociation from the world, and argues that this is significantly different from the way the (undisputed) Paul advised about "accepting dinner invitations to the homes of unbelievers in 1 Cor 10.23-33!" ("The Politics of Identity," 422-23). However, 1 Cor 10 also contains strong language of dissociation (10:14-22), so that a contrast between Ephesians and 1 Corinthians as one of dissociating and associating with the world is too simplistic. More importantly, MacDonald fails to consider how the different social settings of these letters account (at least partly) for the different rhetorical presentations of intragroup distinctiveness and intergroup boundaries.

54. Lincoln, *Ephesians*, 138. Suh provides evidence of other Jewish traditions in

Jewish boundary markers are transformed with respect to Christian social identity, for in Christ circumcision and the law no longer serve as boundary markers. Instead, Christ bridged this boundary, not by making the gentiles one with the Jews, but by uniting both of them into one new man (2:14–15). Thus, Paul adjusts the Jewish definition of group boundaries to include both groups into a higher level social identity.[55] Roman identity categories are also evident. Christ, not the Roman emperor, bestows peace on all peoples in his kingdom.[56] The language of Roman citizenship is transformed to mark the boundaries between the despised outgroup ("strangers and aliens") and the privileged ingroup ("fellow citizens," "members," 2:19).[57] The language of Roman architecture ("household ... foundation ... cornerstone ... building ... temple ... dwelling place," 2:19–22) reminds the addressees of the Roman world of patronage and benefaction.[58] In a strategy of social creativity, Paul reinterprets this Roman imperial imagery to ascribe value and honor to all members of Christian social identity, regardless of their social status in other contexts. Thus, the usual social and ethnic differences between members of the Christ-believing communities are minimized to celebrate their common ingroup identity.

MacDonald interprets this use of Roman, Jewish, and Christian identity categories as an indication of identity confusion, as if the

---

his analysis of the structure of Eph 2 which indicates significant parallels to Ez. 37 about how Israel and Judah come to life in one new nation ("The Use of Ezekiel 37 in Ephesians 2," 732–33).

55. The relationship between Israel and the church is a strongly debated issue. Merklein and Hoehner support the above analysis that both ethnic groups form one new group (Merklein, *Das kirchliche Amt*, 72–76; Hoehner, *Ephesians*, 395–96). Barth holds that believing gentiles are incorporated in (believing) Israel (*Ephesians 1–3*, 269–70), while MacDonald believes that for the author the boundary between Israel and the church is ambiguous ("The Politics of Identity," 432–33). Roitto proposes that the covenant with Israel represents the highest level superordinate ingroup, within which Christian social identity is a medium level ingroup, which in turn includes the two lower level subgroups of believing Jews and believing gentiles (Roitto, *Behaving*, 191–93). The important point for this study is to recognize that Paul redefined Jewish boundary markers to attribute distinctiveness to his vision Christian social identity in order to legitimate it.

56. MacDonald, "The Politics of Identity," 439.

57. Identifying others as strangers was typically "a powerful language of reproach" (Dunning, "Strangers and Aliens," 6 and Ubieta, "'Neither *xenoi* nor *paroikoi*,'" 268ff).

58. MacDonald, "The Politics of Identity," 438ff. The reference to God's household foreshadows the household code of 5:21ff.

author borrowed honor from other social identities without awareness of the now familiar distinctions.[59] Admittedly, the author may appear to be ambiguous in his use of Jewish tradition, for instance to praise the divine benefactor (1:3–14), while he transforms Jewish identity categories to emphasize the difference between Jewish and Christian identity (2:11–22). This enables him to respect the chronological priority of Jews in God's cosmic plan, without favoring them as members of Christian social identity. However, the variation in his use of these Jewish traditions and identity categories represents a strategy of social creativity, which adopts and reinterprets significant comparison dimensions from a dominant, competing social identity and transforms them to ascribe value to Christian social identity. Instead of signaling identity confusion, this usage signals skillful boundary marking and contextualized social identification strategies on behalf on the Christian community. It enhances the distinctiveness of Christian social identity in the perception of the hearers, and evokes responses of praise, commitment, and obedience for the privilege of belonging to it. These passages demonstrate Paul's skill as artist of social identity to formulate a distinctive, socially relevant and compelling vision of Christian social identity.

Structuring the Identity Performance of Ingroup Members

Paul's celebration of Christian social identity heightens its value in the eyes of the ingroup members, and may draw the attention of outgroup members. However, the credibility of such a celebration hinges on the leader's ability to translate this vision of social identity into common social action. This is what Paul sets out to do from 4:1ff. The first section contains substantial information about leadership and will be discussed below; the current focus is on the extended paraenesis of 4:17—6:9, which contains two sections that are often considered quite distinct, if not contrary. However, a social identity perspective resolves this tension.[60]

The first passage (4:17—5:21) focuses on group norms, and uses bold, contrasting stereotypes to picture the two ways of life: falsehood

---

59. Ibid., 432–33.

60. Darko's study is dedicated to investigating this tension (Darko, *No Longer Living as the Gentiles*, 2).

versus truth, darkness versus light, immorality versus love, and foolishness versus wisdom. Such ethical teaching is familiar from Roman and Jewish traditions. MacDonald points to Qumran parallels in particular to argue that the ethical dualism of this passage is intended to encourage social withdrawal from the outgroup, which she interprets as a significant increase in introversion as compared with the early Pauline letters.[61] However, as Perkins had already observed, signs of physical structures for such social withdrawal are not found in Ephesians as they are in Qumran literature.[62] O'Brien and Hoehner read this passage as a straightforward exhortation to proper conduct, as if Paul realistically described gentile and Christ-believing behavior.[63] However, in reality not all unbelievers live in such immorality, nor do all believers live in such purity; stereotyping is a rhetorical strategy to strengthen social identification with the ingroup so that group members will be highly motivated to appropriate identity performance that affirms strong community ties and mutual concern.[64] Since Ephesians most likely addresses an expanding community, this is not an isolationist strategy, but a way to orient new group members towards the norms of their new social identity, and to encourage long-term members to continue and deepen their social identification.[65] That is to say, these group norms provide general instruction to assist ingroup members in resolving conflicts of interest between their Christian social identity and other cross-cutting social identities that were part of their daily social functions.

The motivation for ethical conduct does not come from novel ethical instruction, since its content is typical of ancient ethical discourses that were moreover often critical of their society.[66] This motivation is rooted in a new identity in Christ, in whom ingroup members are created a new man (4:22–24), highlighting the intergroup boundary

61. MacDonald, *Colossians and Ephesians*, 321–22.

62. Perkins, *Ephesians*, 117–18. MacDonald quotes Perkins but disagrees with her.

63. O'Brien, *Ephesians*, 318; Hoehner, *Ephesians*, 582–89.

64. Darko arrives at the same conclusions (Darko, *No Longer Living as the Gentiles*, 129).

65. This accords with the observation that this section does not introduce new material, but reinforces values and norms already held. Paul could thus expect his addressees to readily assent to his ethical instruction (Witherington, *Letters to Philemon, Colossians and Ephesians*, 293–94; Darko, *No Longer Living as the Gentiles*, 109).

66. Darko, *No Longer Living as the Gentiles*, 68.

they crossed to join a new social identity. The model for their identity performance is God himself, who in Christ demonstrated sacrificial behavior as benefaction for the community (5:1–2).[67] The goal of their identity performance is to maintain the unity and cohesion of the community (4:25–32), and to maintain moral purity in full view of the outgroup (5:3–14). The "Christological and ecclesiological framework" provides the ideological shaping that identifies Paul's ethical discourse as distinctive for the Christ-believing community.[68] Thus, Paul integrated general ethical instructions into the Christian identity narrative to structure the identity performance of ingroup members.

The second passage (5:21—6:9) focuses on the household relationships of community members. While the stark ethical dualism of the previous passage has often been read as a strategy of isolation, the current passage has often been read as a strategy of accommodation.[69] Like the ethical discourse, it runs parallel with Greco-Roman household codes that were intended to reinforce the traditional household hierarchy as the basis for a stable society.[70] Against this background, Balch proposed that the household code defended the church against accusations that it undermined the stability of society.[71] MacDonald and Carter argued that as second generation Christians coped with the delay of the return of the Lord, they accommodated the original vision of equality to the usual household structures to reduce tension with the outside world.[72] Williams even suggested that such accommodation was necessary to secure the survival of the community.[73] Thus, the household code is often read as accommodation to societal pressures.

---

67. Questions about the imitation of God versus the imitation of Paul are discussed below.

68. Darko, *No Longer Living as the Gentiles*, 130.

69. For instance, Shkul most recently wrote that "although Ephesians is culturally radical when it comes to legitimating the community, and the writer is happy to renegotiate Jewish identity and cultural boundaries when it comes to the Law obedience, similar radicalism is not manifest in the positioning of the members in social relations" (Shkul, *Reading Ephesians*, 206).

70. Gombis, "A Radically New Humanity," 320–22.

71. Balch, *Let Wives Be Submissive*, 54ff.

72. MacDonald, *The Pauline Churches*, 109. See also Carter, *The Roman Empire and the New Testament*, 22.

73. Williams, *Stewards, Prophets*, 34–39.

It is unlikely, though, that this passage is an accommodation to society, considering the strong contrasts to emphasize group boundaries between the Christ-following communities and all other social identities.[74] Instead, a better option is to interpret this passage as a realistic assessment of appropriate identity performance within the existing social constraints. Household roles are determined by social station and social identification with a particular voluntary group does not change that: one cannot simply choose another role. How one performs that role, however, is a matter of choice. Thus, Paul assists Christ-believing household members to learn new ways in which to perform their individual roles in accord with their Christian social identity. Traditional roles of dominance and submission are recast as imitation of Christ, so that all can value their behavior as enhancing their positive distinctiveness as Christ-believers. Paul does not so much reinforce traditional societal roles, but rather transforms these roles by the distinct norms that characterize the interpersonal relationships of Christians with ingroup and outgroup members.[75] As with the ethical discourse, Paul anchors his instructions in christological and ecclesiogical themes, which provides the ideological shape of the household code that marks it out as distinctive for Christian social identity.[76]

Interpreted in this way, both the two-ways ethical discourse and the household code serve to heighten social identification with the ingroup.[77] The goal is neither social withdrawal nor social integration but appropriate identity performance before an audience of both ingroup and outgroup members. By way of social creativity, Paul reinterprets familiar Greco-Roman paraenetic discourses to fit with Christian social identity, with the likely goal of improving the ability of believers to memorize and apply his ethical instructions. In other words, Paul casts his unique Christian content into a culturally familiar rhetorical

---

74. See also Gombis, "A Radically New Humanity," 318.

75. Cf. Gorman: "the household code in Ephesians is not an attempt to impose pagan, patriarchal values on the church but to impose spiritually empowered, mutual submission on a pagan, patriarchal structure" (*Apostle of the Crucified Lord*, 524). Similarly, Bartchy, "Who Should Be Called Father," 145 and Dudrey, "A Sociohistorical Look at the Household Code of Ephesians 5:15—6:9," 40.

76. For in-depth treatment of the theological context of the Ephesian household code, see Hering, *The Colossian and Ephesian Haustafeln in Theological Context*, 165–202.

77. Darko, *No Longer Living as the Gentiles*, 130–31.

pattern for ethical instruction, in order to provide believers a moral framework that is workable and memorable in their social and cultural context. By reshaping their ethical framework this way, Paul improves category fit and category accessibility, since this provides an easy way to remember one's Christian duty in identity performance. Thus, Paul empowers the Ephesians to perform their Christian identity consistently with less cognitive effort so that even new community members quickly adopt his instructions and the expansion of the church is facilitated. As engineer of social identity, Paul must have reflected on the earlier problems with social identification in Corinth (and elsewhere), so that upon further reflection, teaching, and interaction he used a more generic model to empower ingroup members to fulfill various social roles in accord with their Christian social identity. As a missionary, speaker, and writer who is familiar with Greco-Roman rhetorical traditions and who has already demonstrated sensitivity to issues of social identification in specific local contexts, Paul can easily be envisioned as author of this tradition within just a few years after his departure from Ephesus.[78]

Legitimating Christ and Paul as Brokers of Christian Social Identity

In Paul's celebration and structuring of Christian social identity, Christ plays the key role. It is almost too obvious to bear repeating, but ingroup members receive God's benefactions "in Christ" (1:3)[79] who is head over all things (1:22). Members are made alive with Christ (2:5–6), who embodies our peace (2:14)[80] and is our cornerstone (1:20) so that the whole community depends on him (2:21). The gospel concerns the mystery and riches of Christ (3:4, 8), whose love can only be fathomed by all ingroup members together (3:18–19). This listing could be multiplied, but the point is clear. Christian social identity in Paul's view revolves around the death and resurrection, past and

---

78. This is quite the contrary of the often heard proposal that the use of household language in Ephesians is reason to doubt Pauline authorship (Horrell, "Social Transformation in Pauline Christianity," 304–6; Roitto, *Behaving*, 193–200).

79. O'Brien mentions that just in 1:1–14, "Christ" or an equivalent occurs fifteen times, while "in Christ" or an equivalent occurs appears eleven times (O'Brien, *Ephesians*, 91).

80. Lincoln, *Ephesians*, 140.

current ministry of Christ, who is in one respect the divinely authorized broker of heavenly benefits.[81] As Paul accentuates his vision of Christian social identity, and as he engages in social structuring, he celebrates Christ as the only legitimate Lord and Savior in whom and through whom the whole community exists.

Within this framework, Paul legitimates himself as the lesser broker of Christian social identity. Paul refers to his commission to make known "the mystery of Christ" (3:5),[82] which not only reminds his addressees of his apostolate,[83] but also portrays it as divinely authorized and legitimated. Moreover, assuming the Ephesian community had expanded, this legitimation allowed Paul to extend his apostolic authority to new Christ-believing communities in the area. Paul acknowledges his place among the other holy apostles and prophets (3:5), but highlights his unique role in God's plan by frequently speaking in the first person singular (3:1-8). In the imagery of the Roman envoy, Paul brings to light the "unsearchable riches" of God's mysterious plans (3:9), to display the "manifold wisdom" of the heavenly benefactor before all "rulers and authorities" (3:10). Such a commission normally results in great honor and status for the broker, but Paul deflects this honor by picturing himself as least of all the saints (3:8) and highlighting his own suffering (unlike Roman envoys) as an honor to his addressees (3:13). These parallels with Roman ideology legitimate Paul's status as privileged broker of God's honor and glory,

---

81. Neyrey, "God, Benefactor and Patron," 475–76, who emphasizes that not all of God's names or Christ's functions can be subsumed under patronage.

82. Merklein argues that this revelation in 3:5 indicates the historical reality of the church through the agency of apostles and prophets. Through them, the church became a historical reality, it was fleshed out and 'experiencable' (*Das kirchliche Amt*, 187).

83. Paul assumes that the addressees "surely have heard" of his commission (3:2), which is Hoehner's translation to indicate the certainty he sees in this assertion, which he interprets as a sign that Paul is familiar with his addressees (Hoehner, *Ephesians*, 421). MacDonald, who also acknowledges the element of uncertainty in this passage, suggests that this expression fits best if addressed to communities that did not know Paul personally. Thus, they agree on the grammatical implications of the phrase but differ in their socio-historical reconstruction, which differs because their views on authorship and context differ. The preferred option in this study is that Paul addresses Ephesian communities that have grown substantially since Paul's departure about 5 years earlier, so that they contain numerous members with whom Paul is not personally acquainted. This interpretation, too, derives more from the preferred socio-historical reconstruction than the wording of the text by itself.

and thus as impresario of Christian social identity, on behalf of his network of Christ-believing communities.

Paul's Social Power and the Agency of the Ephesian Believers

The last section of the letter (6:10–20) may be characterized best as Paul's closing arguments[84] to mobilize the Ephesian community in Christian identity performance, in spite of social pressures from all sides. For this purpose, Paul, who is held captive by Roman soldiers, presents his oppressive captors as symbol for the battle of the Christian community. The Roman soldier, a preeminent Roman symbol of strength, had become a source of oppression for Paul and most likely for other Christ-believers. Now Paul reinterprets this source of oppression as a symbol of strength for Christ-believers to motivate them towards robust identity performance against all opposition. Paul's transformation of Roman military imagery is not merely a convenient object lesson, but a strategy of social creativity, whereby Paul transforms a Roman symbol of domination into a metaphor of resistance and perseverance for Christ-believers who face the pressure from Rome's imperial ideology everywhere around them.[85] Thus, Paul's social agenda climaxes in the closing argument of the letter: to motivate believers to strengthen their identification with the Christ-following community and to mobilize them in faithful identity performance over against all other competing social identities and their influence. Paul claimed significant privileges and powers in leadership for his churches, but only in order to motivate and mobilize ingroup members, thus enhancing instead of restraining their agency.

Summary and Discussion

Paul's leadership, as practiced in Ephesians, clearly has important social implications, which receive sharp focus in chapters 3 and 6. Ephesians 3 advocates that every group, network or social identity finds its origin and legitimacy in God the Father, implying that any conflict between

---

84. So for instance Arnold, *Power and Magic*, 103–5 who comments that few commentators take this passage seriously in considering the theology of Ephesians.

85. See MacDonald's comments on the use of militaristic language in Ephesians, especially in chapter 6 ("The Politics of Identity," 425–26).

various levels of social identities is principally resolved in favor of the superordinate Christian social identity. Ch. 6 exhorts believers to maintain a firm commitment to their Christian social identity, so that it will be safeguarded from the pressures of outgroup Roman propaganda and ideology. This mobilizes the addressees to conform to Paul's portrayal of them as saints who "are *faithful* in Christ Jesus" (1:1), in spite of the social reality that Christ-following communities were of relatively low status, subordinate to Roman powers.

Paul's identity management leads to several observations. First, Paul frequently used readily available symbols and literary schemes in his writing. The above analysis observed how Paul used and reinterpreted Roman propaganda of peace and harmony, Roman architecture, Greco-Roman household codes, and the metaphor of the Roman soldier. Often, Paul's reinterpretation contained elements of Jewish traditions about the temple and from the prophets (Isaiah and Ezekiel were noted). Frequently the debate over such parallels centers on Paul's hermeneutical principles or the extent of his borrowing from Greco-Roman culture. However, in the context of Paul's leadership as identity management, such use of familiar symbols and literary schemes can be seen as social creativity to enhance category accessibility and normative fit. In other words, Paul used familiar cultural categories as framework for his own teaching tradition to make his instructions easier to comprehend, memorize, and perform. Besides all the other questions rightfully asked about ancient parallels, their function as teaching templates for Paul's ministry, adopted by later generations of churches, deserves greater priority in scholarly analysis.

Second, in Ephesians Paul generalizes his strategies of identity management, compared to the case-by-case approach of 1 Corinthians. Instead of demonstrating how in a variety of concrete situations believers are to give priority to their Christian social identity, Paul now presents this priority in almost cosmic language. While in a Roman prison, Paul undoubtedly reflected on the expanding church and its growing complexities, and found the universalist language of Roman ideology suitable to generalize his own vision of Christian social identity. The cosmic claims of the Ephesian Artemis and her powers offered another source for generalization.[86] Paul thus contextualized his

---

86. Although this was not expanded in detail in the current study, see Murphy-O'Connor, *Ephesus*, 34, 200; Strelan, *Paul and Artemis*, 24–93; and Arnold, *Power and Magic*, 20–28.

gospel to enhance its value and fit in the Roman world of Ephesus. He converted Roman (and Ephesian Artemis) ideology into a universalizing Christian ideology that shows not the Roman emperor but the Lord Jesus Christ to be supreme, which in principle settles all questions about the relative value of Christian social identity in the daily social affairs of the community. This offers the Ephesian church the platform from which they can address concrete and varying situations in a practical and contextually relevant manner. Therefore, the more generic character of Ephesians does not indicate a change in theology or ecclesiology, but rather Paul's reflection at a greater social distance on the social development of his churches, with as a result new rhetorical strategies to contextualize and generalize his message.[87]

Third, it is doubtful that Paul, as engineer of social identity, aimed to subvert or even overturn Roman social structures.[88] Clearly, Paul redefines Roman symbols of strength and status in a way that converts their meaning almost into their opposite. The value of these redefinitions depends on one's group membership. The emperor's gospel of peace is valued by ingroup members (i.e., Roman citizens), but it is bad news for outgroup members (i.e., minority groups that appear to Roman authorities as a threat to social order). The Roman army is perceived by the ingroup as creating a just system of righteousness and peace, while various outgroups regularly experience Rome's protective forces as oppressive and destructive. Since Christ-following communities could not engage in actual social competition with the Roman empire due to their low, minority status, these redefinitions are intended for ingroup consumption to bolster the morale of the Christian communities without endangering the Roman social order. Thus, Paul does not so much *subvert* Roman values, as he *adopts* them as a symbol of status and strength even while *reinterpreting* them for his own ingroup.[89] And yet, another political order is proposed, which is

---

87. If this proposal correctly reflects Paul's theological engagement with the social realities, this has important ramifications for our understanding of the concept of "universal church," which may be more a contextualized picture of expanding inter-church relationships than a theological ideal by which every local church must be measured.

88. As advocated, for instance by Crossan and Reed, *In Search of Paul*; and Horsley, *Paul and Empire*.

89. See the studies by Carter, *The Roman Empire* and Kim, *Christ and Caesar* for a similar moderate perspective.

expected to replace the existing order at some future time and which is already now exercising its influence through individual believers. If in later centuries Christian communities gain social ascendency in some regions, Paul's reinterpretation of Roman ideology easily becomes a new imperial ideology, but now in service of the church instead of the empire.[90] History witnesses to this on various occasions. It is doubtful, however, that Paul intended such use of his vision of Christian social identity, and we should not project onto Paul the subversive tendencies that his rhetoric achieved in later social contexts when Christian social identity became dominant.

Finally, lines of social development surface in this analysis. Social identification went through testy periods in Corinth when internal conflicts with nested and cross-cutting identities needed to be addressed. Ephesus benefited from these insights and developed beyond the stage visible in 1–2 Corinthians. Ephesians thus addresses a slightly further stage of Christian community formation, which prompted Paul to generalize his vision of Christian social identity.[91] Paul's own development keeps pace with these community developments. Paul proves himself a skilled entrepreneur of identity, adapting his rhetoric of identity to the changing context. Pauline authorship and Ephesian community development fit hand in glove.

The Development of Local Leadership Patterns at Ephesus in 61 CE

From the distance of a Roman prison, Paul wrote to the Ephesian community in a more generic fashion than thus far in his letters. Although this makes it more difficult to analyze the underlying social situation, quite a few links with social reality were pointed out in the analysis above. This is no less true for the information on leadership in the letter. Ephesians is rich in its leadership language and concepts. It does not contain the kind of historical details about Paul's ministry that

---

90. Ubieta traces later imperialist tendencies of the church to sections of Ephesians: "The adoption of the way of thinking and acting peculiar to Roman imperial leaders with whom the church leaders increasingly identified once it was considered the official religion was one of the reasons for this type of imperialist development" (Ubieta, "Neither *xenoi* nor *paroikoi*," 279ff).

91. This aligns with Malina's application of small group formation theory early Christianity (Malina, "Early Christian Groups," 96–113).

we find in 1–2 Corinthians, but it provides an ideological legitimation for leadership in Paul's vision of Christian social identity. Paul's universalizing narrative of Christian social identity is not only a help for Ephesian community members in their social identification, but especially so for its local leaders who were responsible to guide their community in social identification.

Leadership Emergence. The apostles and prophets are presented as the foundation of the church (2:19–21). The genitive τῶν ἀποστόλων καὶ προφητῶν (2:20) can be taken as subjective, meaning "the foundation laid by the apostles and prophets," but this does not accord with the imagery of Christ as cornerstone. It is best to take this genitive as appositional, meaning that the apostles and prophets are the foundation.[92] Their foundational role is intimately connected with the revelation they received (3:5), which indicates that they were uniquely privileged speakers in the Christ-movement.[93] Paul does not speak here about the foundation of the Ephesian community only, even though he singles out his own apostolic role (3:1–7), but he has in view the entire Christ-movement.[94] Thus, the origin of the church is ascribed to the apostles and prophets, who emerged as leaders because they were divinely commissioned and legitimated in their foundational role.

While thus highlighting the ideological underpinning for the emergence of apostles and prophets, the social processes of leadership emergence remain underspecified. Although these passages undoubtedly reminded the addressees of Paul's foundational work, the foundation discussed lay further back. From a social point of view, the first communities in Israel and elsewhere formed around those who first proclaimed the gospel, and who embodied this foundational message in their own self-sacrificial behavior. From a social identity perspective, it was not just their witness and proclamation that provided the foundation, as Barth argued[95]; rather, people gathering in response

---

92. Wallace argues that this noun + noun construction indicates either two distinct concepts or an overlap, suggesting that apostles and prophets are two separate categories, or that the apostles are possibly a subcategory of the larger group of prophets (*Greek Grammar beyond the Basics*, 284–86, 735). Thus, Grudem's position that the groups are identical, meaning that "apostles who prophesy" is the foundational group, lacks syntactical basis (*The Gift of Prophecy in 1 Corinthians*, 82–105).

93. O'Brien, *Ephesians*, 216.

94. Hoehner, *Ephesians*, 398.

95. Barth, *Ephesians 1–3*, 316.

to the proclamation of the apostles and prophets accepted them as prototypical for the new ingroup, so that from the very start they emerged as generally uncontested leaders.[96] In this sense, they were simply the first and foremost leaders of the Christ-movement. As the movement expanded, the historical and social priority of the apostles and prophets became a theological priority as well. Thus, historically and ideologically, the apostles and prophets formed the foundation of the church and provided its first leaders.

Since Ephesians looks towards the past in discussing the foundation of the church, a key question is how far back this past lay behind the author and his addressees. Merklein remarks that the apostles and prophets function like a "traditional norm" and that they belong to the "great leaders of times past."[97] Both Merklein and Lincoln argue that this perspective on the past would be most appropriate when apostles and prophets were no longer functioning or at least when they were marginalized "as their leadership role was taken over by the more stable teaching and ruling ministries."[98] Although this is possible for just these two passages, this is contradicted by a third passage, where these foundational leaders are simply juxtaposed to evangelists, pastors, and (other) teachers (4:11). Barth argues that this listing presupposes that the apostles and prophets were alive and well, functioning in the church at the time when this passage was written.[99] Thus, it is very likely that the foundational ministry of the apostles and teachers was still part of the living memory of some of the believers in Ephesus, while many more would have remembered Paul's foundational ministry in their own city. It was still during this time that other local leaders had emerged next to this foundational leadership.

The relationship between apostles and prophets, and the three additional leaders of evangelists, pastors, and teachers is not clearly

---

96. Merklein argues that these passages show the historical reality of the agency of the apostles and prophets in founding the church (Merklein, *Das kirchliche Amt*, 201–2).

97. "Traditionsnorm" and "Größen der Vergangenheit" (Ibid., 156). See also Lincoln, *Ephesians*, 249.

98. Lincoln, *Ephesians*, 249.

99. Barth, *Ephesians 1–3*, 316–17. He adds that the reference to apostles in Eph 4:11 is in harmony with Rom 16:7 and 1 Cor 12:28, and that in the post-apostolic age, "the twelve apostles" instead of "apostles and prophets" would have been the church's greatest authorities.

indicated. Since Ephesians connects the first two with foundational ministries beyond the scope of Asia Minor, they represent non-local leaders, suggesting that the latter three are local.[100] Lincoln suggests that the three local leaders mirror the ministry of apostles and prophets with the exception of their foundational and revelatory functions. Thus, evangelists fulfill a function similar to the apostle, and the pastor and teachers exercise the leadership role previously carried by the prophets.[101] This seems reasonable, but the text itself does not provide enough indications to be conclusive. Instead, the burden of the author seems to be to portray the local leaders as prototypical and self-sacrificial, similar to the apostles and prophets. In addition, they are divinely commissioned, although they do not receive revelation but only hand down the revelations already transmitted by the foundational leaders. Thus, just as the foundational leadership, they provided the essential social structures necessary for maintaining the original vision of Christian social identity. MacDonald comes close to this with her suggestion that the listing of 4:11 serves to legitimate the authority of the local leaders,[102] while Merklein argues perceptively that these leaders as gifts for proclamation are constitutive for the church.[103] Thus, the exact functions in the community and the relationships to one another remain unclear, but the main point is that such local leadership provides the necessary social structures to build long-term coherence and stability for the vision of Christian social identity as originally proclaimed by the apostles and prophets.

As before, this highlights the ideological underpinning for the emergence of local leadership, but the social processes remain under-specified. Ephesians 4:11 assumes an already functioning leadership group, next to still available apostles and prophets. Note first, that local

100. Westcott had observed much earlier that the evangelist was also not locally bound (*Ephesians*, 62), but the exhortation to Timothy to do the work of an evangelist makes it doubtful that an evangelist had no local basis of operation (see 2 Tim 4:5).

101. So for instance Lincoln, *Ephesians*, 250 and Merklein, *Das kirchliche Amt*, 345. Merklein also suggests that the ποιμήν of Eph 4:11 may well be the summary term that captures the earlier references to κυβέρνησις (1 Cor 12:28), προϊστάμενος (Rom 12:8; 1 Thess 5:12) and ἐπίσκοποι (Phil 1:1) (Ibid., 363).

102. MacDonald, *Colossians and Ephesians*, 299.

103. Merklein, *Das kirchliche Amt*, 80–81. Merklein explains that they were exercised in a durable manner, and that the tendency towards a church canonical institution is evident. He believes that this is probably the complete list of charismas that could be interpreted as office around 90 AD, which is his preferred date for Ephesians.

leaders likely emerged within a relatively short period. Several passages refer to living memory of the founding of the church in Ephesus among the addressees (1:12–13; 2:11),[104] indicating that local leadership structures had stabilized before first-hand memory of Paul's evangelistic efforts had faded. It was already observed in 1 Cor 16:15–16 that local leaders were commended within 5 years from their church's foundation, although still under the shadow of the apostle. Since Paul and his missionary team were no longer readily accessible for Ephesus as they had been earlier for Corinth, the shift from a plurality of recommended leaders to an independently functioning leadership group must have taken place within just a few years. Thus, it is not surprising that Ephesians refers to an established local leadership group within ten years after its founding.

Second, Paul charges the local leadership to join apostles and prophets in doing the work of the ministry and building up the body (4:12).[105] Their joint leadership empowers all group members (4:13) to guard the stability (maturity) and cohesion (unity) of the community in defense against deviant influences (4:14–16). This portrays local leaders as loyal to apostolic teaching, especially Paul's, and as prototypical in the community since they embody unity and love in their collegial functioning. Thus, it may be assumed that local leaders emerged from the ranks of prototypical members who were loyal to Paul.

Third, the household table reflects the centrality of household relationships in the Ephesian church, as was the case in Corinth. Local leadership likely came from the ranks of householders of higher social status, since they provided facilities and benefits for groups meeting in their house and for the overall community. Thus, the local leadership

---

104. MacDonald sees the word προηλπικότας and the switch from "we" to "us" in 1:12–13 as most likely an contrast between Jewish Christians, with 2:11ff. reminding the congregation of its Jewish origins (*Colossians and Ephesians*, 203). Hoehner argues instead that the "we" refers to Paul and his coworkers and "you" to the addressees. Although the first option seems the more likely one, the key thought for the argument above is that the letter refers to evangelism and conversion in Ephesus as something that the addressees remembered (ἀκούσαντες, "when you heard," 1:13; μνημονεύετε, "remember," 2:11).

105. Page argues that the phrases of 4:12 are to be interpreted not as a logical sequence, where leaders (a) equip the body (b) to minister, so that (3) all are build up, but as coordinate, indicating three tasks of the leaders. 4:13 then identifies three community-wide tasks or results ("Whose Ministry," 26–46).

group in Ephesus most likely arose from among the householders with exemplary behavior who were loyal to Paul's teaching. This occurred at the latest within a few years after Paul's departure from Ephesus so that Ephesians could acknowledge an existing leadership group without concern to explain or legitimate its origin.

What can explain the difference in leadership development in Corinth and Ephesus? In Corinth, Paul corrected skewed leadership models to stabilize the church as well as its local leadership, while he simply assumes a functioning leadership group in Ephesus only 4–5 years later. Paul's ministry developed differently in these cities, since he spent about twice as long in Ephesus as in Corinth in the initial founding phase. In Corinth, his ministry took place mostly in households (Acts 18:7–8), while in Ephesus he also used semi-public venues such as the hall of Tyrannus from the very start (Acts 19:9). In addition, the Ephesian church is about 8–9 years old when Paul writes them (founded around 52–53 CE), while the Corinthian church is only 5–6 years old when Paul writes them (founded in 50 CE). If the Corinthian church made the switch to collegial leadership with many difficulties after only 6 years, the Ephesian church could have made this switch earlier in its life with the benefit of lessons Paul learned in Corinth, making an established collegial leadership team at an age of 9 years quite likely. Finally, even though both churches developed independently for about 5–6 years after Paul's departure,[106] Corinth had the benefit of Paul's continued accessibility from Ephesus, while Ephesus was forced to operate more independently because Paul was relatively inaccessible, imprisoned first in Caesarea and then in Rome. These differences in leadership development, then, can be explained by the different trajectories along which Paul's ministry in these locations developed. However, these different trajectories can be read as complementary. 1–2 Corinthians portray leadership development up to the likely emergence of collegial leadership, while Ephesians portrays a stage of leadership development where such collegial leadership has recently emerged. At least, these differences arguably do not present developing leadership patterns that are inconsistent with one another. Considering the network of churches that Paul and his team built, and the availability of Paul's letters in his Aegean network, the

---

106. Paul departed from Corinth around 51 and wrote 1 Corinthians around 56, while he departed from Ephesus around 56 and wrote Ephesians around 61.

argument can be pushed further. It is likely that—aside from the initial 'start-up' problems with emergence—leadership patterns in Corinth and Ephesus continued to develop in tandem.

Leadership Maintenance. While leadership emergence was mostly implicit in Ephesians, leadership maintenance is an explicit theme. It focuses in part on affirming the enduring value of the foundational ministry of apostles and prophets. Paul portrays the founding (2:20) and revelatory (3:1–7) activities of these leaders not simply as an historical record but he activates the social memory of the community in memorializing these foundational roles and thereby permanently embeds them in their identity narrative. This affirms their continuing normative value, for although their historical role will soon finish, ideologically their role continues to shape the identity narrative and thus the social identity of the community far beyond their own lifetime.

Curiously, Paul's self-presentation figures largely in this ideological legitimation of foundational leadership, but it differs significantly from his self-presentation in earlier letters. References to his self-sacrifice and extensive suffering are absent, except for the mere mention of his imprisonment (6:20) and his emphatic self-reference as "I Paul, the prisoner of Christ Jesus" (3:1; 4:1). Esler suggests that the memory of Paul as "the prisoner" is more plausible after his death,[107] but it is equally plausible that Paul's status rose already during his lifetime to become a paradigmatic model of ministry.[108] Indeed, this is highly likely, since the Ephesian community had observed Paul's effective resolution of the Corinthian crisis, which generally would lead to charismatic leadership attribution. Such an attribution process would have created the image of Paul as uncontested and unparalleled apostolic leader of his communities, probably both in Corinth and in Ephesus. However, it is curious that Paul refers to himself in this way, considering how he consistently emphasized suffering and self-sacrifice as key

---

107. Esler, "Remember My Fetters," 233. Lincoln only remarks that "the definite article . . . heightens the distinctiveness of Paul's apostolic imprisonment," and does not associate it with dating or authorship (*Ephesians*, 173). Note, that the expression ἐγὼ Παῦλος, "I, Paul," occurs in Paul's earlier letters (2 Cor 10:1, Gal, 5:2) as well as in the prison epistles (Eph 3:1, Col 1:23, Phlm 19).

108. A modern example would be Nelson Mandela, everywhere remembered for his imprisonment for the sake of apartheid, and paradigmatic for a peaceful rise to power in a new South Africa, already long before his retirement from politics.

to his leadership in 1–2 Corinthians. It was suggested above that Paul, by way of social creativity, reinterpreted his weakness and suffering as signs of honor with God and faithfulness to the community, instead of as signs of shame and ineffectiveness as his critics in Corinth appear to have presented them. In Ephesus, however, Paul's career of suffering was no longer considered problematic, so that there was no need for an apology. Yet, suffering as well as revelatory claims strengthen social identification processes,[109] which is an important purpose in Ephesians. Thus, Paul mentioned his own experiences of suffering and revelation, and appealed to his image as uncontested apostolic leader, which undoubtedly he knew to be current in Ephesus, in order to raise the status of his vision of Christian social identity and strengthen social identification processes. Paul reinterpreted the past, including the community's memory of himself as apostle, in order to provide an identity narrative as foundation for the community's vision of social identity, in which Paul figured as key exemplar and prototype.[110]

Leadership maintenance in Ephesians also addresses local leadership. The letter not only registers an existing local leadership group, but also attributes its presence to institution by Christ with a Christ-ordained function. Paul orchestrated the reception of local leaders as a divine benefaction for the community and not as a social contest for influence and honor. These leaders were called to transmit divine mysteries so that the whole community would demonstrate mature behavior towards their divine benefactor (4:12–16).[111] Paul transforms

---

109. Esler refers to social science research which indicates that suffering heightens social identification ("Remember My Fetters," 236–37). It might be added that early Christian traditions of martyrdom testify to this process. See, for instance, Brent's study of martyrdom and leadership in the person of Ignatius (Brent, *Ignatius of Antioch*).

110. See also Esler's arguments, drawing not only on social identity theory, but also on cognitive theories of narrative, memory and autobiography ("Remember My Fetters," 241–55). Barton also remarks that Paul's letters "are pervaded by remembrance and commemoration" ("Memory and Remembrance in Paul," 329). Thus, Campenhausen's observation that the emphasis on Paul's apostolic office "for its own sake" is completely post-Pauline (*Ecclesiastical Authority*, 53), is partially correct in that Paul's self-reference is not 'for its own sake' but for the sake of the long-term cohesion of the community; however, the above presentation shows that such a self-reference is not necessarily post-Pauline.

111. Harland cites several Ephesian inscriptions that "emperors were viewed as patrons on a level with other patron deities and were sometimes equated with these gods." It would not, then, be surprising for an Ephesian audience to understand Paul's

these cultural factors to place the local leaders within an ideological framework; thus, the theological legitimation of church leadership appears to follow the social development of leadership patterns.[112] Such ideological grounding in turn encourages further social development of these leadership patterns, in an ongoing cycle of interaction between social and ideological factors.

Even though unity is emphasized as a primary value for the community (4:3–6, 13–16), Paul's presentation of the local leaders encourages intragroup differentiation. The role of the leaders aligns with Jewish traditions about revelation and teaching, but also with the Ephesian image of teachers as a moral example in their social environment, which earned them honorable status within the community.[113] They figure prominently within the community to provide ongoing leadership in conjunction with the foundational leadership group. It is a picture of joint leadership rather than of succession. This picture expands Paul's earlier presentation of the apostle, prophet, and teacher as primary gifts to the church (1 Cor 12:28) by including the evangelist and the shepherd, while narrowing this presentation by not including any other gifts. This indicates more clearly the priority of leadership, which effectively enhances the social status of local leaders within the community.[114]

This raises the question to what extent Ephesians reflects a movement towards the formal institution of church office. In summarizing his findings on Eph 4:11, Merklein concludes that the charismatic proclaiming gifts are theologically postured as offices, and that this gift list probably represents the complete list of charismas that could be interpreted as office.[115] Does this fit with the analysis above? A posi-

---

reference to God as a divine patron or benefactor, especially in light of Paul's strategy to reinterpret Roman symbols of honor to ascribe honor to the Christ-believing community ("Honours and Worship," 329).

112. Cf. Martin, *Der priesterliche Dienst*, 19, who wrote, "Die theologische Begründung der kirchlichen Ämter der konkreten Institutionalisierung folgt. Sie wird durch die konkreten Umstände ausgelöst und ist Reaktion darauf. Je mehr Rechte die kirchlichen Ämter . . . erlangen, desto stärker wird das Bedürfnis, sie theologisch zu legitimieren."

113. Judge found four inscriptions related to teachers, out of a total of 3000 available Ephesian inscriptions ("The Teacher as Moral Exemplar," 175–88).

114. Lincoln explains that "to assert that the ministers are gifts of the exalted Christ, rather than merely officers created by the Church, is clearly meant to enhance their significance in the eyes of the readers" (*Ephesians*, 248–49).

115. Merklein, *Das kirchliche Amt*, 80–81. He dates the letter around 90 CE, and

tion of leadership as organizational office is a structurally and legally defined position of authority as recognized by the group with due procedures for maintenance and succession. This can be analyzed into various components:

Table 6.1: Components of Church Office[A]

(a) duration, since it is a structural and not incidental group role; an office exists independently of the one who fills it
(b) recognition by the community
(c) authority or a special status of the officeholder as distinct from other group members
(d) legitimation through a commission or ordination
(e) legal arrangements to secure the position
(f) provisions for maintenance and/or succession, including possible financial provision

A. Brockhaus lists the (a) through (e), but also mentions payment later (*Charisma und Amt*, 24, n. 106 and 123). Clausen partially adds (f) as the ability to move an office from one person to another ("The Structure of Pauline Churches," cited in Dunn, *The Theology of Paul the Apostle*, 566, n. 3). Merklein provides a different list of 5 key concepts that are part of church office (*Das kirchliche Amt*, 280).

Duration (a) evidently applies to the local leaders in Ephesus, since their function is registered and legitimated, but the text contains no suggestion that their leadership role is abstracted as an office independently of the person. Recognition (b) and authority or status (c) are also already part of the Ephesian structure. Legitimation (d) is provided ideologically, but the text does not indicate procedures for ordination such as the laying on of hands; instead, the legitimation provided rests on the identity narrative in the letter, and they may or may not affirm particular Ephesian practices of commission or ordination. The letter provides no evidence of any legal arrangements (e), even though the institution of this leadership group by Christ likely functioned as basis for later ecclesiastical legal developments.[116] No

---

thus looks for offices around that time.

116. Merklein indeed argues that the selection of such leaders created a model, which became the precursor to the ecclesial institution of office, but there was no conscious effort to mover towards a formal institution of office (in the uncontested Paulines) (Ibid., 330–31).

financial provisions for leadership are indicated in the letter, while future provisions of leadership are not specified (f). This evidence is not sufficient to speak of local leadership in terms of a full-fledged institutionalized office. Local leadership is simply addressed as it currently functioned, which highlights the social authority of the local leaders as prototypical members and exemplars of the community.[117] However, the already developed intragroup differentiation is recognized as a legitimate leadership status, so that the authority of teaching leadership is inscribed into the essence of the community's identity. Considering the cultural context of a well-structured and hierarchical Roman society, with abundant experience in community formation and leadership at all social levels, it is likely that the above evidence signals the emerging contours of organizational office, even as early as 61 CE.

In order to maintain vital leadership for the Ephesian community, Paul presented both apostolic and local leadership as a divine grant to the community. Although earlier in 1–2 Corinthians, Paul had clearly affirmed the primacy of his apostolic leadership and teaching, those were occasional documents, and it could be argued that their arguments were mostly ad hoc. However, Ephesians presents itself not as an ad hoc resolution of local difficulties, but as a universalizing vision of Christian social identity, in which both apostolic and local leadership receive ideological legitimation for current and future generations. Ephesians embeds this ideological legitimation in the identity narrative of the community's foundations to present a comprehensive, universal vision of Christian identity.[118] Ephesians hereby presents a deeper reflection on earlier issues in social identification and leadership practice in order to assist community members to negotiate these and similar difficulties independently of apostolic direction. Ephesians is thus future oriented, not anticipating a visit from Paul but providing for continuity of social identification and leadership processes in the

---

117. White, "Social Authority," 225–26. Much earlier, Westcott had already argued that "there was not as yet a recognised ecclesiastical hierarchy; while there is a tendency to the specialisation of functions required for the permanent well-being of the Church" (*Ephesians*, 62).

118. Merklein points out that Ephesians is the first document in the Pauline corpus and in the whole NT that contains theological reflection for the grounding of the offices (*Das kirchliche Amt*, 224).

absence of apostolic leadership. In this way, Paul engineers the maintenance not only of his own leadership but also of local leadership.

Leadership Succession. Even though Ephesians does not mention succession explicitly, Paul wrote after an absence of 5 years without immediate prospect for a visit. Thus, Ephesians addressed a situation where succession had de facto begun, and it appears to affirm and legitimate this process.

A leader is dependent on his intragroup status and social power to institute succession (leader as artist). Paul's leadership status as privileged apostle was without doubt in Ephesians. Normal leadership attribution processes in Ephesus intensified as the community learned of Paul's effective resolution of the Corinthian crisis. This fostered confidence that Paul was the prototypical and self-sacrificial leader he claimed to be, with privileged access to key resources. The community attributed charismatic leadership to Paul, which in essence was a vote of confidence that they trusted his leadership even in turbulent times. As argued above, Ephesians reflects Paul's awareness of this attribution process, which gave him the social power to structure local leadership and to provide for succession in a way that could not yet be envisioned in the Corinthian correspondence. Thus, Paul's leadership status allowed him to affirm and legitimate the leadership succession that had already taken place in Ephesus.

Paul presented local leaders as Christ's gifts, loyal to his own teaching and closely associated with apostolic leadership (leader as impresario). He attributed to them the same leadership abilities that he himself had demonstrated, and thus presented them as similar to himself. He charged these leaders to be dedicated to the unity and the maturity of the community, portraying them as prototypical ingroup members. Since these leaders served as Christ's gift to the community, Paul encouraged the community to attribute charismatic leadership to them; in other words, he "charismatized" the local leaders in order to enhance the community's acceptance of their leadership.[119] The theoretical account of succession predicts that effective predecessors are most likely succeeded by similar new leaders; thus, Paul's presentation of local leadership confirms that he expected the Ephesian community

---

119. This presentation generalized Paul's earlier argument (1 Cor 3:22-23) that members do not belong to the leaders as their followers, but that leaders belong to the community as God's servants.

to consider him an effective leader. Even though further succession is not explicitly addressed, Paul's presentation of local leaders already provides the legitimation for this process in the future.

Paul also embedded local leadership in the long-term structures of the community (leader as engineer). The local leaders were more than only the leaders of the moment; they are portrayed as essential to maintain the unity of the congregation and the clarity of Christian social identity faithfully. As Merklein puts it, such leadership is not only derived from Christ and instituted by him, it is constitutive for the church.[120] These local leaders became the guardians of faithful teaching,[121] committed to pass the apostolic teaching tradition on to each next generation. This allowed Christian social identity to remain connected with its authoritative source of revelation as proclaimed by the apostles. Ephesians likely did not initiate these structures, but it affirms and legitimates them, because of its concern for the future development and stability of the community.

Conclusions

Ephesians presents the apostles and prophets as foundational leaders, historically and socially as the very foundation of the church (2:20), and theologically as divinely privileged speakers in the community (3:1–7). These foundational leaders shaped and embodied the ingroup prototype by their proclamation and behavior. In spite of initial disputes about his leadership elsewhere, Paul was perceived in Ephesus as a charismatic and foundational leader based on his effective leadership in Corinth.

Local leadership emerged within the church before first-hand memories of Paul's evangelism in Ephesus had faded. They had a higher profile and functioned more independently in the Ephesian community than earlier in Corinth, because Paul was no longer available to Ephesus a he had been to Corinth, while the Ephesian believers benefited from lessons Paul learned in his teaching in and negotiations with Corinth. The local leadership group in Ephesus is portrayed as loyal to apostolic teaching and probably emerged from among householders with already existing social influence.

---

120. Merklein, *Das kirchliche Amt*, 80–81.
121. Malina, *Timothy: Paul's Closest Associate*, 69.

Apostolic and local leaders are legitimated as given by Christ to maintain the cohesion of the community (4:11–12), which enhanced the attribution of charismatic leadership even to the local leaders. Ephesians represents the furthest stage of leadership development analyzed so far. First and second Corinthians devote much attention to stabilizing and legitimating apostolic as well as local leadership. Ephesians reveals the structuring of leadership in terms of role and status differentiation for the apostles and prophets, and to a lesser extent for the local leadership team, but it has not yet been shaped into the full-fledged form of church office.

Apostolic and prophetic leadership had been joined by local leaders, who effectively led the church. Ephesians inscribed the authority of teaching leadership into the very essence of the community's social identity and empowered the local leaders to maintain their vision of Christian social identity, to oversee community rituals, which would assist members to deepen their social identification, and to initiate identity-embedding structures that would build up the body.

In this way, Ephesians began to function as a succession or mentorship text, presenting the Christian identity narrative and the identity management strategies that are needed in leading an expanding church in a Greco-Roman context. Paul legitimated these local leaders ideologically, which enables them to emerge from the long shadows cast by the foundational leadership. Thus, Ephesians prepares for and enables future succession, even if this intention was not stated explicitly in the letter. Clearly, Ephesians plays a crucial role in leadership development in Paul's ministry, both socially and ideologically.

Ephesians as Paul's Intentional Model for Empowering Local Leadership

These results shed new light on some introductory issues of Ephesians. One question relates to the impersonal nature of a letter to a church where Paul had served the longest period in his missionary career (according to Acts). What can account for this lack of personal information? It is unimaginable that Paul would know details about the Colossian situation where he had not been before (Onesimus probably informed him), while he would not know details about the situation in Ephesus which he had left only about five years prior to writing

Ephesians. Given the level of contact Christian communities maintained with one another, news from that city must have reached Paul in Rome, just as news from the church in Rome had reached Paul when he worked in Ephesus and Corinth. Thus, even if the Ephesian church had expanded significantly since Paul's ministry there, and even if Paul or the church had recovered from serious conflict,[122] the generic and impersonal nature of the letter is probably not due to a lack of knowledge, and certainly not a lack of interest, but must have a different cause.

The above analysis suggests that Ephesians is Paul's intentional supplement to his earlier letters to empower local leaders in their identity management. During Paul's ministry in Ephesus, he dealt with conflicts in Corinth which naturally he would have discussed with his coworkers and the Ephesian leadership (cf. Acts 20:28–31). Moreover, Paul probably shared copies of his letters to Thessalonica and Corinth with believers in Ephesus. This entails that Paul had provided the Ephesian believers with the basic conceptual tools to handle conflicts with social identification and authority in Ephesus. In such a setting, a more 'generic' letter like Ephesians functions as additional legitimation for the already active leaders, and offers additional perspectives on the church to support the social and ideological principles that they had already learned; a more ad hoc letter similar to 1–2 Corinthians would only duplicate information already available. Thus, Ephesians presents a universal portrait of Christian social identity, which empowers local leaders to direct the Ephesian community as their particular circumstances required. The letter was probably integrated into the community's teaching quickly and became part of their identity narrative, almost from its first reading. Moreover, its generic nature made it very suitable for distribution, and if the absence of "in Ephesus" (1:1) in some early manuscripts is any indication, this must have occurred almost immediately with one or more copies sent to Syria and Egypt.

122. Based partly on the interpretation of passages like 1 Cor 15:32, 2 Cor 1:8 and Acts 20:29–30. Barth summarizes a number of such conflict theories, ranging from conflict between Jewish and gentile Christians, influx of Gnosticism, or even conflict with Johannine influences in Asia Minor (Barth, *Ephesians 1–3*, 57–58). The current social identity analysis suggested that the lofty portrayal of Paul's apostleship was not due to major internal conflicts nor to a desire to rehabilitate Paul as apostle by a later generation, but that it reflects the normal processes of charismatic leadership attribution based on the Ephesians perception of Paul's leadership in Corinth. Thus, external conflicts are more likely indicated by the above cited passages.

Hence, this study proposes that Ephesians is impersonal and generic because it reflects a situation where local leaders are functioning effectively, with sufficient training in leadership and conflict management based on Paul's personal ministry and early letters. Ephesians then serves to further empower these local leaders by a strengthened ideology of leadership in the context of a more universal vision of Christian social identity that is ideally suited to a setting of Jewish and gentile Christians in the Roman world.

The Roman Origin of the Leadership Model of Ephesians

A second question relates to the location from which Ephesians was written. Does the traditional setting of composition from a Roman prison contribute to a further understanding of the leadership structures in the letter? First, when Paul wrote Ephesians, the network of his Aegean ministry had expanded to include Rome: Paul wrote Romans from Corinth (1 Cor 16:23), mentioned numerous people from the East that he knew in Rome (Rom 16:3 ff.), and enlisted Roman prayers for his trip to Jerusalem (Rom 15:30–32). The church in Corinth supported Paul's ministry to Rome by providing facilities for the composition of the letter (Rom 16:22–23), by sending Phoebe to Rome along with Romans (Rom 16:1), and by supporting his travel to Judea as the first part of the trip to Rome (1 Cor 16:6, 2 Cor 1:16). While in Rome, Paul is in contact with believers from Philippi, from Colossae, and Ephesus. This expanding network suggests not only that lessons learned in Corinth were applied in Ephesus, but also that these lessons could be applied in Rome, while lessons learned in Rome could be incorporated in letters sent back to the Aegean region. This opens up the possibility that a more generic letter like Ephesians may contain elements that reflect Paul's experience in Rome.

Second, Rome and Ephesus share a number of aspects. Ephesus ranked with Rome (as well as Alexandria and Antioch) as "world class" city.[123] Rome claimed political and religious world dominance through its emperor worship, while Ephesus—to a lesser extent—claimed worldwide influence through its dominant Artemis worship.[124] Paul's experience of Rome's political and religious dominance

---

123. Arnold, "Ephesus," 249.
124. Murphy-O'Connor, *Ephesus*, 199–200.

thus had relevance for the politico-religious situation in Ephesus, so that the universalist and cosmic language of Ephesians resonates with both Rome and Ephesus.

Third, it can hardly be accidental that Paul writes a letter, in which he engages as nowhere else with the pressures and influences of Roman imperial ideology, from a Roman prison. Concepts like victory over rulers and authorities, the gospel of peace, unity of the empire for all people, orderly Roman homes and the lively picture of the Roman soldier are rooted in the daily pressure of Roman propaganda that Paul faced while chained to Roman soldiers for two years. Within this "peaceful" and "unified" Roman empire, Christians had no legal or social status; they were marginalized. Paul has ample time to think through the Roman symbols of status and power, and to learn how to reinterpret them to reverse the marginalization of Christian social identity, at least in the perception of the community members. Paul contextualized his belief in the superior value and strength of God's kingdom in the language of imperial ideology.

Fourth, the church situations in Rome and Ephesus contain similarities. An analysis of the names listed in Rom 16:3–15 suggests that at least five, perhaps as many as seven house churches were functioning in a loose network in Rome.[125] It is likely that, due to distance and perhaps group size, these house churches in Rome were unable to meet together in one city-wide assembly, necessitating new structures to maintain the unity of the expanding Roman network of Christ-believing communities. It appears that the Ephesian church had developed into a multi-site network around the same time, meeting in a number of house churches and no longer able to hold assemblies, which included everyone. Since the city of Rome was larger in population and acreage than Ephesus,[126] the Roman church had likely developed further in this direction than the Ephesian church, especially since the gospel appears to have reached Rome several years before Paul reached Corinth and Ephesus (cf. Acts 18:1–2). This suggests the likelihood that when Paul wrote Ephesians about the universal church and its leadership, he was not contemplating a theological ideal about

---

125. Barentsen, "Pre-Pauline Leadership in the Roman Church," 594–97. For a slightly different count, see Lampe, *From Paul to Valentinus*, 359–60.

126. Rome had an estimated 1 million inhabitants in the first century, Ephesus 250,000. See Reasoner, "Rome and Roman Christianity," 850; and Arnold, "Ephesus," 249.

the universal church, but he was describing organizational structures for a city-wide church that had outgrown the small network of house churches with regular common meetings in one location. Paul used the cosmic and universalist language of reinterpreted imperial ideology to do so, knowing that the Ephesians would be able to contextualize the jargon for their own situation with similar levels of social development.

The following scenario results. While imprisoned, Paul served the churches in Rome in a complex situation that called for additional structures of leadership in order to maintain the desired unity. At the same time, Paul was aware of a similar complex situation developing in and around Ephesus, where already during Paul's presence his disciples had spread the gospel to outlying areas. Paul then supplied the leadership lessons he learned in Rome to Ephesus. Thus, the theological foundation for leadership in Ephesus most likely reflects his practice in Rome. Just as Paul reinterpreted Roman status symbols to fit Christian identity, he reinterpreted Roman leadership hierarchies to fit Christian identity, with apostles and prophets as divinely legitimated envoys of their emperor-God to found local communities, and with local leaders as divinely commissioned local agents to watch over these communities. Earlier, Paul had proven willing to work within patronage structures to provide leadership in his churches, but not without first transforming cultural leadership patterns to fit with Christian social identity. So now, he adopted and reshaped Roman leadership structures, providing for leadership structures that enabled regional churches to maintain their unity, even with growing numbers and increasing geographical separation.

These suggestions amount to a reading of Ephesians as a legitimating document for new levels of leadership to carry forward Paul's vision of Christian social identity in expanding local and regional networks of Christ-believing communities. This makes Ephesians a key leadership succession document, even if only implicitly and in the very early stages of succession. Leadership succession becomes an explicit theme in 1 and 2 Timothy, to which we now turn.

7

Structuring Leadership and Group Participation in 1 Timothy

CHURCH LEADERSHIP STRUCTURES ARE SO PREVALENT IN 1 TIMOTHY that Dibelius and Conzelmann characterize the letter as a document regulating church order.[1] A number of studies point out textual parallels that link the leadership instructions of 1 Timothy with its Greco-Roman environment. Harrison and Paschke compare the character ists to other ancient lists to suggest that selection and approval of leadership by character is not unique to the Pauline corpus.[2] Fiore portrays 1 Timothy as a typical letter of instruction to junior leaders, while Stepp has found several ancient patterns of succession in the letter.[3] In discussions on church office, the structures in 1 Timothy are positioned in various ways in early Christianity. Some see a movement in the direction of the monepiscopacy,[4] sometimes with conflicting definitions of leadership competing for dominance,[5] while others see at the most a beginning differentiation in local leadership functions.[6] Difficulty in determining the genre, date, and social setting contribute to the bewildering variety of proposals.

First and Second Timothy differ in genre from the letters analyzed thus far. First and second Corinthians were ad hoc letters to address issues that had arisen in Corinth during the early years of community formation. Ephesians presented a generic picture of Christian social

1. Dibelius and Conzelmann, *Pastoral Epistles*, 5–7.
2. Harrison, "Paul and the Gymnasiarchs"; and Paschke, "The *cura morum*."
3. Fiore, *Personal Example*; Stepp, *Leadership Succession*.
4. Campbell, *The Elders*; Söding, "1 Timotheus 3."
5. Polaski, "Let No One Despise Your Youth"; Horrell, "Leadership Patterns and the Development of Ideology in Early Christianity."
6. Sullivan, *From Apostles to Bishops*, 73.

identity to assist the Ephesian community in ongoing community formation and to empower their independently functioning local leaders in this process. First and Second Timothy are again ad hoc, addressing not the community but Timothy as Paul's delegate in Ephesus to instruct him, and through him the community, in leadership tasks. Social issues are once again prominent, some in stereotyped form and others relating to various subgroups in the congregation.

If the differences between Ephesians and the early Paulines already led many scholars to propose pseudonymous authorship, this is even more the case with the Pastoral Epistles. As Ephesians is often labeled deutero-pauline, so the Pastorals are often labeled trito-pauline. Authorship and date are significant elements of a socio-historical reconstruction of leadership patterns, so that the proposed social identity analysis requires a brief overview of the relevant arguments concerning authorship and date before proceding.

Excursus: The Authorship and Social Context of 1–2 Timothy

One of the challenges in the debate on early church leadership structures is the dating and authorship of the Pauline corpus. The rise and dominance of the Holtzmann-Sohm hypothesis is dependent on the pseudonymous authorship of the Pastorals. Often, pseudonymous authorship is assumed in scholarly work on the Pastorals on the supposition that this issue matters little for the discussion at hand. However, this excursus first explores reasons why the authorship question should not be avoided, and then provides an overview of the main arguments in the authorship debate. The purpose is to present a credible defense of the position on which the next two chapters of this study will be based, without attempting to answer the question exhaustively. Although the arguments are somewhat of a detour from the main research question of the study, their absence would leave basic presuppositions unexamined, which would undermine any results obtained.

Can the Authorship Question Be Avoided?

A few recent studies advocate Pauline authorship for the Pastoral Epistles,[7] which is a minority position within biblical studies. The majority of scholars considers them pseudonymous and dates them in the third generation after Paul towards the end of the first or beginning of the second century. The pseudonymity of the Pastorals has become paradigmatic for ongoing research on the letters,[8] so that many monographs on the Pastorals simply assume pseudonymity or sidestep the discussion altogether in the main body of their analysis. Only in their conclusions, these studies provide suggestions for how their results affect the authorship debate.[9] Such a procedure is often necessary, since the literature on the debate is extensive and cannot be easily summarized within the confines of most monographs. Yet, this procedure has its difficulties.

First, it is often assumed that one can situate the Pastorals in their social and religious environment by comparison with other documents. Thus, Fiore compares hortatory epistles with the Pastorals, and takes the pseudonymous authorship of the Socratic letters as support for the pseudonymous character of the Pastorals. Richards finds in epistolary parallels from the late first to the middle of the second century support for a late date of the Pastorals. Merz and Aageson follow similar approaches in locating the intertextuality and the theology of the Pastorals in the literary and theological context of the first and second centuries. These studies provide important windows on the exegesis of the Pastorals but are limited in their ability to interact with the authorship debate. A comparison of epistolary, literary or theological features draws on broadly circulating written traditions in the Hellenistic world. By their very nature, such comparisons can only result in general correlations with the social and historical context of the Pastorals, allowing a range of 50 years or

---

7. See the overview article Herzer, "Abschied vom Konsens?" on the issue, as well as such commentaries as Mounce, *Pastoral Epistles,* Quinn and Wacker, *First and Second Timothy,* and Johnson, *First and Second Timothy.*

8. Merz, "Amore Pauli," 274–77; Johnson, *First and Second Timothy,* 55; Fuchs, *Unerwartete Unterschiede,* 1–2.

9. Following this strategy, Fiore, Richards, Merz and Aageson interpret their findings as support for pseudonymous authorship, while Towner and Kidd take their study as support for authentic Pauline authorship. Stepp hedges and finally suggests Timothy as author, following Marshall. See Fiore, *Personal Example*; Richards, *Difference and Distance in Post-Pauline Christianity*; Merz, *Selbstauslegung*; Aageson, *Paul, the Pastoral Epistles, and the Early Church*; Towner, *The Goal of Our Instruction*; Kidd, *Wealth and Beneficence in the Pastoral Epistles*; Stepp, *Leadership Succession.*

more as possible date of composition. To gain further precision, these studies draw information for situating the Pastorals from the scholarly consensus on authorship and date. This helpfully indicates how their findings can be related to the scholarly consensus, which is simply assumed as historical background, but it would be circular reasoning to suppose that this offers new support for the consensus. Thus, the range of 50 years or more is not narrowed down any further, which implies that the Pastorals may be situated as late as at the beginning of the second century or as early as the 60's of the first century. Such studies are therefore compatible with both pseudonymous and orthonymous authorship, even if these scholars only support one side of the debate.

Second, sidestepping the question about authorship suggests that one's position does not significantly influence one's exegesis. Granted, in considering various literary or theological parallels, one's position may not be greatly influential, but it is of great consequence in the social reconstruction of the letters. For instance, if the Pastorals are pseudonymous, they may have originated from a small group of Paul's disciples with a distinct perspective on the Pauline tradition. The Pastorals could then be read as an attempt to legitimate one of several competing perspectives on Pauline theology by the writing of a corpus of fictional letters in Paul's name. The author(s) would in effect try to sway the reception of Paul's heritage into a particular direction, which is exactly what the letters warn against. This warning, however, is to be interpreted as a rhetorical technique to achieve a dominant position for the pseudonymous author's distinct perspective on Paul.[10] If, however, these letters are orthonymous, then their presentation of Paul's heritage comes from Paul's own pen. They would be interpreted in a manner consistent with Paul's earlier letters and be perceived as bringing the Pauline tradition to a close on Paul's own authority.[11] These two perspectives (and other variations besides) differ significantly, for instance in their interpretation of the self-presentation of Paul and his example, in their identification of the opponents or in their evaluation of the leadership structures. Thus, one's position on authorship is of great consequence when literary analysis is connected with social and historical reconstruction.[12]

10. Merz, for instance, argues that "the fictitious authorial situation" intends to ensure "that the Pastorals will have *supreme interpretative authority* should there be any conflict between statements in other Pauline letters and statements in the Pastorals" (Merz, "The Fictitious Self-Exposition of Paul," 127. See also Merz, "Amore Pauli," 286–94.

11. See for instance Johnson, "First Timothy 1,1–20," 20–21.

12. Moreover, significant value judgments are attached to these positions. For

Third, the present study engages expressly in a reconstruction of the social setting of the documents since patterns of leadership are embedded in the social reality of particular communities. One of the strengths of a social identity approach is its ability to integrate social and psychological aspects of group dynamics, which requires that these letters can be located with some confidence in a particular social setting. Clearly, this approach is limited in its analytical potential when the social setting cannot be determined. This limitation is to some extent inevitable, since the historical details of the Pastorals do not easily fit with other NT sources. However, in case of pseudonymity, the social context which the letters themselves present would be fictional, so that any indications of the real social setting are at best 'hidden' in the document. Social reconstruction with the help of social identity theory, or for that matter with any other socio-historical method, then becomes a precarious exercise, often left to "the creative imagination of the author."[13] Thus, the issue of authorship cannot be avoided or deferred until the conclusion,[14] even if a full-fledged defense remains beyond the scope of this study.

The Contours of the Authorship Debate

A position on authorship is based principally on an evaluation of differences between the Pastorals and other Pauline epistles in relation to the self-testimony of the Pastorals and their early attestation. The differences are generally categorized as issues concerning language and style, literary dependence, theology, opponents, historical setting, and ecclesiastical organization.[15] The clear self-testimony of the letters and their unanimous external attestation

---

instance, Martin who favors pseudonymous authorship, believes it is "misleading ... to attribute positions advanced in the Pastoral Epistles to Paul" (*Pauli Testamentum*, 9, n. 3). The opposite may, of course, be argued by those who favor authenticity. The debate needs to be carried with respect for these and other sensitivities.

13. Donfried, "Rethinking Scholarly Approaches to 1 Timothy," 155, citing Childs, *The New Testament as Canon*, 383.

14. It is noteworthy that L.T. Johnson, M.M. Mitchell, T. Söding and D. Horrell, contributing to the 2006 Colloquium Oecumenicum Paulinum, spent considerable time engaging with their various perspectives on authorship before turning towards the exegesis of 1 Timothy. Evidently, they too felt that the question of authorship cannot be avoided or deferred. See their contributions in Donfried, *1 Timothy Reconsidered*.

15. For representative discussions of these issues, see Dibelius and Conzelmann, *Pastoral Epistles*, 1–5; Oberlinner, *Der erste, zweite Timotheusbrief*, 1:xxxiv–xl; Fiore, *Pastoral Epistles*, 5–8, 14–18; Johnson, *First and Second Timothy*, 56–77; and Towner, *Timothy and Titus*, 9–93.

as authentic are then evaluated in light of the conclusions drawn from the observed differences. Most agree that no single argument is decisive, and that the accumulated weight of several lines of argument is needed to reach a conclusion. More precisely, the conclusion depends on the relative weight attached to the observed differences on the one hand and the self-testimony and external attestation of the Pastorals on the other hand. A survey of the literature shows that pseudepigraphy proponents usually start their argumentation by highlighting the differences in order to show that the internal and external testimony do not weigh up against them; once this is argued, considerations about the nature, frequency, and acceptability of pseudepigraphy in antiquity become relevant to offer an alternative to Pauline authorship. Authenticity proponents are less united in the starting point of their argumentation. Some start by reviewing the phenomenon of pseudepigraphy in antiquity,[16] some by reviewing the internal and external testimony[17] and some by evaluating the differences with the other Paulines.[18]

This excursus begins with a consideration of the internal and external testimony. It expands the discussion with a review of scribal practices and literary criticism in antiquity as background for a consideration of ancient pseudepigraphy. Finally, the differences between the Pastorals and the other Paulines will be considered, focusing on those usually considered most challenging for orthonymous authorship: differences in language and style, in theology, and in historical details.

The Pastoral Epistles and Their Early Reception

The Self-Testimony of the Pastoral Epistles. First and second Timothy present themselves as written by Paul and addressed to Timothy. The letters contain numerous details that relate specifically to the personal relationship between Paul and Timothy and, in the case of 2 Timothy, to numerous coworkers (1 Tim 1:3, 18, 20; 2 Tim 1:15–18; 2:17; 3:15; 4:9–13, 19–21). Not all of these details fit well into the known traditions about Paul from his earlier letters and Acts, but they are listed unapologetically as factual. In addition, Titus mentions an otherwise unknown visit of Paul to Crete (1:5), lists two well known coworkers of Paul (Tychicus, Apollos) and two otherwise unknown people (Artemas, Zena, 3:12–13), while the leadership instructions omit

---

16. Witherington, *Letters and Homilies for Hellenized Christians*, 23–38.
17. Knight, *Pastoral Epistles*, 4–14 and Towner, *Timothy and Titus*, 3–8.
18. Mounce, *Pastoral Epistles*, xlviii–lxxxiii.

a reference to deacons (1:5–9). These difficult to harmonize details would undermine a pseudonymous author's intent to imitate Paul, especially if he had already written (or was planning to write) 1 Timothy. On the other hand, these seemingly irrelevant details suggest an eyewitness account, much like the so-called lively details in the gospel of Mark argue for its eyewitness character. If from Paul's hand, these details therefore represent the unconcerned and unapologetic narration of known historical facts. Thus, internal evidence points to Paul as author and to Timothy and Titus as recipients, while the historical details provide eyewitness testimony about the ministry setting of Paul's latter days.[19]

External Attestation. From the earliest post-NT witnesses until the 19th century, the Pastorals were unanimously considered to be authentically Pauline. All ancient versions and virtually all major manuscript traditions contain the Pastorals, with the exception of the incomplete papyrus P46 and the collections of a few deviant teachers (Tatian, Basilides, and Marcion).[20] Late in the second century, Irenaeus, Clement of Alexandria, and Tertullian refer frequently to the Pastorals. However, already the Apostolic Fathers appear to have used the Pastorals at the beginning of the second century. References to the Pastorals in Polycarp are usually considered highly likely,[21] in Ignatius somewhat likely, and rather uncertain in 1 Clement and Barnabas.[22] Recently Merz demonstrated that Polycarp as well as Ignatius make use of the Pastorals, not only by deliberate citation (1 Tim 6:7 in *Ign. Pol.* 4) but also by parallel wording and argumentation. Merz interprets Ignatius' personal letter to Polycarp as an effort by Ignatius to imitate the Pauline corpus with its twofold division into congregational and personal letters.[23] This suggests that around 110 CE Ignatius treated the Pastorals as an uncontested part of the Pauline corpus. No debate on Pauline authorship is known at this date from Antioch, where Ignatius was a senior bishop, nor from Asia Minor and Rome

---

19. Further discussion of the historical difficulties follows below.

20. Ellis, "Pastoral Letters," 659. Dibelius interpreted the evidence from P46 and Marcion as a sign that the external attestation of the Pastorals as Pauline was weak (Dibelius and Conzelmann, *Pastoral Epistles*, 1–3). However, the evidence from one (possibly incomplete) papyrus and one heretical author (at least by 2nd century standards) is hardly sufficient to bear the weight of this conclusion.

21. Berding, *Polycarp and Paul*, 143ff.; Hartog, *Polycarp and the New Testament*, 177–79, 228–36.

22. Marshall, *Pastoral Epistles*, 3–5.

23. Merz, *Selbstauslegung*, section II. Merz does not push the date this far back, but remains firmly convinced of pseudonymous authorship.

to which he addressed his letters. This probably indicates that the Pastorals were accepted as Pauline by senior church leaders in these areas at this date, which dates their initial acceptance as Pauline significantly earlier, perhaps as early as the 70s or 80s during the formative stages of these senior church leaders when they would have still been open to the reception of such letters. Such broader acceptance in the early 70's or 80's is precisely what would be expected if Paul himself penned these letters in the turbulent days of the mid to late 60's. Thus, external attestation strongly favors Pauline authorship.

The Pastoral Epistles and Ancient Literary Practices

Ancient Scribal Practice. Research on scribal practice affects the authorship debate in two ways. First and most familiar, the role of secretaries in letter writing varied from recorder to editor to co-author.[24] It is clear from Paul's letters that he used secretaries (Rom 16:22, Gal 6:11), while often people are listed as co-author in many of Paul's letter openings. First and second Timothy contain no explicit indication of the use of a secretary or co-author (unless 1 Tim 6:20–21 is a closing summary in Paul's own hand[25]), but some secretarial involvement is likely, which may well account for at least some of the observed differences in style and expression between the Pastorals and other Pauline letters. Second, classical scholars have long recognized that ancient authors kept copies of their letters.[26] Richards argued extensively that Paul would have done likewise, so that from the time of its composition two or more copies of any letter were made, one for Paul's own use, one to dispatch, and probably others as they were read and copied at the destination.[27] This probably accounts for the rise of text traditions already during Paul's lifetime, as well as for the start of the Pauline letter collection.[28] It would be extremely difficult to include a pseudonymous letter thirty years after Paul's death in such a collection, without any prior trace of it in the already existing

---

24. Richards, *Secretary*, 23–52.
25. See Marshall, *Pastoral Epistles*, 674.
26. Richards, *Secretary*, 3–7; Gamble, *New Testament Canon*, 34–43.
27. Richards, *Paul and First-Century Letter Writing*, 156–60. See also Ellis ("Pastoral Letters," 660) who quotes Cicero (*To Friends* 7.25.1 and 16.18) and several Pauline passages to show that authors usually kept a copy of the letters they sent.
28. Ellis, "Pastoral Letters," 660.

manuscripts available from various locations, even if broader acceptance of a Pauline canon may have taken additional time.[29]

Ancient Literary Criticism and Pseudepigraphy. Pseudepigraphy was well known in the ancient world, nearly unanimously considered a serious encroachment upon the work of others.[30] For at least a millennium after Aristotle, ancient literary criticism consisted of careful scribal training in attribution analysis to distinguish authentic from inauthentic works, to avoid confusion for authors with popular names, and to detect plagiarism and unintentional errors in textual transmission.[31] Moreover, in the largely illiterate world of the first century, written documents were performed orally with accompanying oral traditions to regulate the transmission and performance of these texts.[32] Both aspects of ancient literary criticism are found in early church literature. A concern for authorial attribution is evident in the case of the deposed author of 3 Corinthians, and a concern for accompanying oral traditions is frequently found in early church fathers to confirm or deny the authenticity of a particular document.[33] This functioned primarily as an historical criterion; it reflected the accepted custom that an author and other contemporary eyewitnesses provided oral testimony to the authenticity of a document, which formed the basis of an oral tradition that would last generations.[34] In the case of the NT, our first written evidence for the existence of these oral traditions is both early and reliable, since it dates from the generation who themselves heard the apostles teach. The fact that the Pastorals are almost universally known in early traditions as Pauline is thus significant evidence in favor of authenticity; conversely, it is highly unlikely that a fictional letter gained acceptance within the Pauline letter collection thirty or more years after Paul's death without an oral eyewitness testimony about its authenticity that was traceable back to Paul's days. Thus, the early Christian reception of the Pastorals parallels the general practices of ancient literary criticism, making it extremely difficult, though not impossible, for any pseudonymous document to infiltrate the Pauline corpus.

29. Capes et al., *Rediscovering Paul*, 273–94.

30. Baum, *Pseudepigraphie im frühen Christentum*, 7–31; McDonald and Porter, *Early Christianity*, 388–90.

31. Wyrick, *The Ascension of Authorship*, 222, 283–84.

32. Ibid., 184–85.

33. Such references are found by Papias (Pap. *Fragm.* 3:4 or Eusebius, *EH*, 3.39.4), the bishop of Serapion (Eusebius, *EH*, 6.12.3), Irenaeus (*AH* 3.3.4; 3.4.1) and Augustine (*Contra Faustus Manichaeum* 33.6).

34. Baum, *Pseudepigraphie*, 28–30.

Contrary to this scenario, it is often suggested that pseudepigraphy was acceptable in the ancient world.[35] Examples are cited of disciples who wrote in the name of their masters out of love and reverence for their heritage, such as the writings of the Neo-Pythagoreans, the writings attributed to Enoch, the Testaments attributed to the twelve patriarchs and the works ascribed to Dionysius the Areopagite. These works can be interpreted as honoring 'masters,' even if they lived many centuries earlier.[36] Perhaps apocryphal gospels like the Gospel of Thomas can be similarly interpreted, and it is much closer chronologically to its "master."[37] Could the Pastorals likewise be interpreted as an acceptable attempt to honor their master Paul? Note that the Pastorals not only honor Paul but also extend his concepts significantly. Their strong emphasis on Paul's inviolate authority as well as on his established teaching tradition affirm and extend Paul's earlier teaching, while their proposals for church order have developed beyond Paul's earlier ecclesiological structures. For this novelty, these letters claim Paul's authority as their own. Moreover, the author—if pseudonymous—added numerous fictional details about Paul's ministry to create the impression of authenticity. Clearly, the author wants the Pastorals to be read and accepted as Pauline, and is intent on hiding his own identity. It is unavoidable to conclude that the author intended to deceive his recipients about his real identity.[38] This intent to deceive not only concerns authorship, but also the content, which the author knows to be non-Pauline but which he nevertheless wants to pass off as Pauline. If the Pastorals are indeed fictional documents, then they were written with an intent to deceive and they could be appropriately labeled as literary forgeries, which hardly counts as a benign attempt at imitation.

Moreover, pseudonymous works were often recognized to be of sectarian origin. Thus, it is often supposed that the Pastorals as fictional documents represent a particular faction of Pauline Christianity, which competed with

---

35. For a representative source, see Burkett, *Introduction to the New Testament*, 438.

36. Dunn, "Pseudepigraphy," 978.

37. Ehrman dates it quite early, 110–120 (*The New Testament*, xxxiii, 205–6), while Perrin dates Thomas towards the end of the second century (*Thomas and Tatian*, 27).

38. As recognized by proponents on both sides of the debate, Donelson and Merz advocating pseudepigraphy, Baum and Wilder orthonymy (Donelson, *Pseudepigraphy and Ethical Argument*, 24; Merz, "Amore Pauli," 275–78, and "The Fictitious Self-Exposition of Paul," 115; Baum, *Pseudepigraphie*, 7–31; Wilder, *Pseudonymity and Deception*, 125.

other factions over the 'right' interpretation of the Pauline heritage.[39] If the Pastorals indeed originated in such a conflictual environment, the suspicion and subsequent scrutiny of documents arising from this conflict would have been substantial, especially for documents produced by other factions. The above processes of authorial attribution and oral attestation would have received more attention than usual. It would have been virtually impossible under these conditions for a factional (and fictional) document to break through to general acceptance by all parties, or—yet more unlikely—for these documents to achieve general acceptance without any traces of the conflict in later oral traditions. At best, the Pastorals would have remained isolated in particular pockets of Christianity, whether regional or ideological, and they would have taken their place besides such documents as the *Acts of Paul and Thecla* as documents with contested authorship current in some early Christian traditions.

A pseudonymous scenario would have presented an acute psychological dilemma for early Christian authors, since most sources show a deep reverence for the unique role of apostles.[40] The Apostolic Fathers wrote in their own name (orthonymy: Ignatius, Polycarp, Hermas, and probably Papias), anonymously (*2 Clem., Did., Barn., Diogn.*) or collectively (*1 Clem., Mart. Pol.*), but none wrote pseudonymously in the name of an apostle. These authors often addressed conflict or circumstances that they perceived as a threat to the church, and some claimed significant authority for their writings. Yet, none of them chose pseudonymity as a way to buttress their own claims, but instead clearly differentiated their own claims from those of the apostles. For instance, 1 Clement, Papias, and Ignatius all explicitly portray their own writings as secondary relative to the apostles. There is thus no evidence of a generally felt need to resolve church conflict, however great the stakes, by resorting to a deceptive literary technique such as pseudepigraphy. It is thus highly unlikely that an author would express his devotion to Paul by deceiving his audience in their estimate of Paul through a technique that the ancient world would have labeled as deceptive. Other means were readily available and acceptable.

---

39. So Merz, "Amore Pauli," 286–94.
40. See Wilder, *Pseudonymity and Deception*, 172–73.

Differences Between the Pastorals and the Early Pauline Epistles

The review of internal evidence and external attestation thus unanimously supports Pauline authorship. The review of ancient literary practices, including the occurrence of and attitude towards pseudepigraphy, also indicated that orthonymy is a much more likely hypothesis than pseudepigraphy. Even so, the majority of biblical scholars subscribe to the pseudepigraphy hypothesis,[41] primarily because various observed differences between the Pastorals and the other Paulines are difficult to explain on the hypothesis of Pauline authorship. This section discusses three such differences: literary differences in language and style, theological differences, and historical differences. That leaves differences in handling Paul's opponents and in ecclesiastical organization for later comment, as the proposed social identity approach will analyze these features in the main body of this chapter and the next.

Literary Differences. The Pastorals contain many literary differences compared to the earlier Pauline epistles, which led Holtzmann and Harrison to conclude long ago that another author than Paul must have written them.[42] More recent studies have refined these arguments.[43] Baum corroborates many results in a fresh statistical analysis, and comes to a different conclusion about authorship. All agree that the Pastorals contain a higher proportion of distinctive words as compared to the other Paulines. Baum demonstrates that 37% of the total vocabulary of the Pastorals is unique in the Pauline corpus, compared with 25% unique vocabulary in Romans and 1–2 Corinthians, and only 17% in Galatians, Ephesians, Colossians, and Philippians. Generally, the shorter letters have less distinctive vocabulary, with exception of the Pastorals that have 20% more distinct words than one should expect based on their length. Baum concludes, "the vocabulary of the three Pastoral Epistles is therefore considerably richer than the vocabulary of the other ten Paulines."[44] Moreover, it has been observed that the syntax of the Pastorals is grammatically more consistent than in the other ten Paulines, which contain many broken or unfinished sentences (i.e. parentheses and *anacolouthon*). Holtzmann interpreted this contrast as an artificial attempt

---

41. See the studies by Herzer who advocates a new orientation in favoring pseudepigraphy in the face of several major commentaries advocating authenticity ("Abschied vom Konsens," 1267–82, and "Rearranging the 'House of God,'" 547–66).

42. Holtzmann, *Die Pastoralbriefe*; Harrison, *The Problem of the Pastoral Epistles*.

43 Morgenthaler, *Statistik des neutestamentlichen Wortschatzes*; Neumann, *The Authenticity of the Pauline Epistles*.

44. Baum, "Semantic Variation within the Corpus Paulinum," 273–77.

at clarity on the part of the Pastorals, but a strictly linguistic perspective leads to the more modest conclusion "that the correct sentence structure of the Pastoral Epistles is not as close to spoken language as the less regimented structure of the other ten Paulines."[45] Finally, it has been observed that the Pastorals contain none of the particles that sometimes occur 30 times or more in the other ten Paulines. The number of particles thus identified varies from about 20 (Holtzmann) to 112 (Harrison).[46] Thus, the Pastorals are significantly different in their richer vocabulary, in their more consistent grammar, and in the absence of non-inflected particles.

It is doubtful that any conclusions about authorship can be based on these or similar observations. Baum has demonstrated that the distinctive words of the Pastorals often have synonyms or other close semantic neighbors in the other ten Paulines, so that the linguistic distance is less than an unweighted counting of words at first suggests.[47] Linguistic research shows that features like a richer vocabulary and better syntax usually require more time and reflection in composition, as is typical for written instead of spoken language. This suggests that the Pastorals are closer to formal written language, while the other Paulines are closer to oral expression.[48] Research on the use of particles in varying linguistic contexts needs further work before conclusions can be drawn, but in light of the foregoing linguistic argumentation, the option needs to be kept open that the abundance of particles in oral contexts functions similarly to an increased inflected vocabulary in the more complete syntax of written language. Thus, modern linguistic theories account adequately for the observed literary differences, independent of

---

45. Ibid., 288–89, citing Marius Reiser, "Paulus als Stilist," *Svensk Exegetisk Årsbok* 66 (2001): 157.

46. The term particles here refers loosely to the collection of non-inflected words, such as "adverbs, conjunctions, model particles and prepositions." Baum also notes that almost 85% of Harrison's 112 particles occur in five Paulines or less, so that they are less unique than at first appears (Baum, "Semantic Variation," 290–91, citing Holtzmann, *Die Pastoralbriefe*, 100–1 and Harrison, *The Problem of the Pastoral Epistles*, 36–37).

47. Baum, "Semantic Variation," 278–85.

48. Ibid., 291–92. Surprisingly, Richards comes to an opposite conclusion in his studies on the use of secretaries in ancient letter writing. He reconstructs the composition of the Pastorals as either while travelling (1 Timothy and Titus) or in prison (2 Timothy), and concludes that they must have been written hastily or under adverse conditions (Richards, *Paul and First-Century Letter Writing*, 46). These conclusions, however, are based only on some sketchy considerations of historical context without any linguistic analysis. Thus, they are less convincing than the analysis and argumentation proposed by Baum.

considerations of authorship. Therefore, however significant these literary differences may be, their presence has no necessary correlation with authorship and the discussion about authenticity is not advanced one way or the other by their analysis.

Theological Differences. The Pastorals also contain significant theological differences from the earlier Paulines in their perspective on eschatology, soteriology, godliness, and heresy. Dibelius and Conzelmann popularized a reading of the Pastorals as a thoroughgoing accommodation to the civil world, motivated by disappointment over the delay of Christ's parousia (now described as ἐπιφάνεια). Thus, the letters redefine salvation as a past event instead of as an immanent future, they adopt a Hellenistic perspective on godliness (εὐσέβεια) and they address heresy as a generalized concern over gnosticizing asceticism in the second century instead of as actual opposition.[49] However, Towner has demonstrated that the Pastorals employ ἐπιφάνεια as well as the σῴζω word group in a manner consistent with the 'already-not yet' schema familiar from the earlier Paulines.[50] The terms εὐσέβεια and ἐπιφάνεια seem to reflect usage in the Ephesian worship of Artemis,[51] which may well provide the contextual occasion for their use in the polemical setting of 1–2 Timothy. In addition, the opponents in the Pastorals can be sufficiently understood with reference to Jewish and ascetic tendencies, and without recourse to gnosticism of some sort.[52] Thus, as important as these theological differences are, they may well represent an Ephesian contextualization of concepts familiar from other Pauline contexts and should probably be interpreted as compatible with the theology of the earlier Pauline epistles. Again, these differences do not significantly affect the discussion about authenticity.[53]

Historical Differences. The third set of differences relates to the historical details in the Pauline corpus and Acts. The historical setting of the author as presented in the Pastorals does not appear to match the information available from earlier Pauline letters and Acts. Paul is reported to be a free man in 1 Timothy and Titus, having visited Crete (Titus 1:5), spending a winter in Nicopolis (3:12), and desiring to return to Ephesus (1 Tim

---

49. Dibelius and Conzelmann, *Pastoral Epistles*, 39–41. For a helpful overview of terms, see Burkett, *Introduction to the NT*, 437.

50. Towner, *The Goal of Our Instruction*, chapters 4 and 5.

51. Towner, *Timothy and Titus*, 171–73.

52. Marshall, *Pastoral Epistles*, 46–51.

53. See also the extensive discussion of vocabulary and its impact on the theology of the Pastorals by Mounce, *Pastoral Epistles*, xcix–cxvii.

3:14). Second Timothy reports a second defense and imprisonment in Rome (1:16–17, 4:16–17) while Titus has gone to Dalmatia (4:10). None of this is known from other NT documents, while any report of Paul's planned visit to Spain (Rom 15:24–28) is missing from the Pastorals. It is suggested that a lack of historical fit points to a later author who was insufficiently aware of the actual historical details of Paul's later ministry.[54] However, Acts offers a very selective history of the Pauline mission, and Paul's earlier letters only add biographical information as the occasion for the letter requires, leaving many white spots on the map of Paul's life. Information from the Pastorals does not necessarily conflict with other known data, but may simply provide additional but unrelated bits of historical information about these 'white spots,' supplementing what was already known from other sources.[55] One's position on authorship does little to help integrate this information into a coherent historical reconstruction.

Furthermore, rather than supporting the pseudonymity hypothesis, the historical argument seems to undermine it. The invention of additional travels, unknown coworkers, and growing Christian networks in the supposedly later years of Paul's ministry in effect invents a completely new scenario for the end of Paul's ministry and life. With many independent eyewitnesses about Paul's life available across the Mediterranean basin until at least the 90s, this invention exposes a pseudonymous author unnecessarily to discovery. It also undermines the attempt to imitate Paul closely in order to claim Paul's authority for this fictional writing. If these details were indeed fictional—for instance in imitation of Rom 16:3–16, 21–23 and Col 4:7–17—then this presupposes an early second century date for the composition of the Pastorals, beyond the lifetime of most eyewitnesses to avoid detection. However, as argued above, the use of the Pastorals in Ignatius and Polycarp prevents such a late date. Alternatively, these historical details were incorporated because the author knew them to be factual. This presupposes that the author had access to eyewitness testimony of Paul's last days and that he wrote in the company of such eyewitnesses. But this alternative considers the observed historical differences as factual details of Paul's life and removes them as objection against Pauline authorship. Moreover, if the pseudonymous author wrote in the company of eyewitnesses, his forgery would certainly have been detected,

---

54. Brown aptly summarizes that the pseudepigraphal nature of the Pastorals (if correct) leads to serious questions about the historical value of most of these references (Brown, *Introduction to the NT*, 669–70).

55. Marshall, *Pastoral Epistles*, 67–72.

again ruling out pseudonymous authorship. Thus, consideration of the historical differences advances the authorship discussion only in the direction of authenticity.[56]

Further Areas of Difference. Not all relevant issues have been discussed. One of the principal objections against Pauline authorship is the difference in the organization of the church's leadership. Since this study focuses on analyzing local leadership patterns, specific discussion is deferred. For now, it can be noted that both the church structures as derived from a close reading of the Pastorals as well as the developing church structures over the course of the first century are hotly debated issues with little scholarly consensus. Reconstructions remain dependent on one's position on the authorship and date of the relevant documents, rather than vice versa. Second, the polemical argumentation and rhetorical style in the Pastorals differs from earlier Pauline letters, so that it appears that the Pastorals handle the opponents quite differently from the ten Paulines.[57] Third, the Pastorals contain instructions that Timothy and Titus as Paul's close long-term coworkers probably knew and did not need, including the use of pre-existing traditions.[58] Also, the genre of the Pastorals is quite unlike any other NT document.[59] These issues will receive due attention in the main body of these chapters on 1–2 Timothy, but in line with the foregoing review, it can be observed that at best these differences play an ambiguous role in discussions about authorship. On the one hand, differences are emphasized as an indication of distance from the earlier Paulines and are frequently interpreted as an indication of pseudonymous authorship. On the other hand, similarities are interpreted as an attempt at faithful imitation of the earlier Paulines in order to explain the early and universal acceptance of the Pastorals as canonical. However, based on the unanimous internal and external testimonies as reviewed above, a more consistent approach would be to interpret the similarities as indications of Pauline authorship and the differences as due to geographical, social, and literary context.

---

56. For a more extensive reconstruction, see Mounce, *Pastoral Epistles*, xlviii–cxxix, who situates the Pastorals after the close of Acts, or the reconstructions by Houwelingen, *Timoteüs en Titus*, 20–23 and Reicke, *Re-Examining Paul's Letters*, 51–59 who situate the Pastorals after Paul's departure from Ephesus in 56 C.E. and thus within the chronology of Acts.

57. For these and other objections, see Towner, *Timothy and Titus*, 15–16.

58. On this particular point, see Marshall, *Pastoral Epistles*, 75.

59. For detailed studies, see Fiore, *Personal Example*; Martin, *Pauli Testamentum*; and Wolter, *Die Pastoralbriefe als Paulustradition*.

To take the argument from observed differences one step further, a pseudonymous author is presumably motivated to reduce differences between himself and his model in order to successfully pass off his writing as penned by his model. Therefore, the greater the differences between the Pastorals and the other Paulines, the less likely pseudonymous authorship becomes, which seems to be quite the reverse of the usual argument that greater differences increase the likelihood of pseudepigraphy. Instead, a consistent line of argument would be: in the absence of any oral or written testimony in the early church about the pseudonymous authorship of the Pastorals, the observed differences between the Pastorals and the other Paulines actually increase the likelihood that the stated author, Paul, wrote it.

Conclusion

The literary, theological, and historical differences of the Pastorals as compared to the other ten Paulines do not require pseudonymous authorship, but can be resolved by an application of linguistic theory, by considering Paul's local contextualization and by allowing for the fragmented nature of historical evidence. Even though these differences are significant and provide important windows on the exegesis of the Pastorals and the setting of Paul's later ministry, they do not overwhelm the internal and external testimony about the authenticity of the Pastorals. This testimony was supplemented with insights from ancient scribal practice and ancient literary criticism, demonstrating the near certainty that a pseudonymous document would have been detected and unmasked as forgery, whether written shortly after Paul's death or even two generations later. It is concluded that these testimonies to Pauline authorship still stand, and that their value as evidence outweighs the significance of the discussed differences. The case for pseudepigraphy is not as convincing as is often assumed and cannot be considered successful. Consequently, the case for authentic authorship is sufficiently warranted to take it as point of departure for situating 1–2 Timothy.

Situating 1 Timothy in Paul's Ministry

First Timothy indicates that Paul traveled freely, visited Ephesus with Timothy, and then left him in Ephesus to go to Macedonia. From there he wrote back to Timothy in Ephesus (1:3), indicating that he intended to return soon (3:14). Van Bruggen and Reicke combine these details with historical indications from Acts and 1–2 Corinthians and propose that Paul had left Timothy in Ephesus when he departed for Corinth in 56 CE. Delay in Troas and Macedonia over the collection project is reflected in Paul's apologies for his cancelled and delayed visits (2 Cor 1:15–24), as well as in more extended instructions for Timothy in Ephesus (1 Tim 1:3).[60] A more familiar proposal is that 1 Timothy and Titus were written after Paul's release from a Roman prison and before the Neronean persecutions, dating between 61 and 65 CE.[61]

The balance of argument leans towards the later date. If Timothy had just returned from Corinth (cf. 1 Cor 4:17; 16:10) where, as argued above, he was not succesful in implementing Paul's instructions in 1 Corinthians, would Paul have left him in charge of the Ephesian community in 56 CE. with the very similar charge of dealing with opposition? This seems unlikely, although it may indicate why Paul needed to write Timothy so soon: Timothy's leadership was criticized in Ephesus as it had been in Corinth, and the letter serves to legitimate his leadership role, just as 2 Corinthians legitimates Paul's leadership role. Further, the similarities between 1 Timothy and Titus suggest that both letters reflect similar ministry situations, indicating a date after Paul's Roman imprisonment. However, the travel data of both letters are difficult to correlate[62] and they do not necessarily

---

60. Bruggen, *Paulus: Pionier*, 251–53; Reicke, *Re-Examining Paul's Letters*, 51–59. See also Houwelingen, *Timoteüs en Titus*, 20–23. DeSilva, *Introduction to the NT*, 734 also suggests this historical connection as a possibility, although he is less firm on Pauline authorship.

61. Kelly, *Pastoral Epistles*, 34–36; Witherington, *Letters and Homilies*, 65–68; Lea and Griffin, *1, 2 Timothy, Titus*, 40–41. All commentators admit that this is a 'shadowy' period of Paul's life about which little information is available, but this merely reflects that fact that Acts provides no historical outline within which these letters can be situated. Yet, the Pastoral Epistles provide significantly more historical information than the general epistles, so that the 'darkness' of this later period in Paul's life is only relative to the wealth of information available for the middle part of his life.

62. Knight observes, "the evidence is not sufficiently interlocked that an itinerary emerges" (*Pastoral Epistles*, 9).

cover the same period. Moreover, although these similarities may indicate that the letters were written at about the same time at a later date,[63] they may also indicate that Paul used his own copy of one letter to compose the other some years later. Perhaps the most significant information comes from 1 Timothy about the increased social complexity of the community, suggesting some years of further development after Paul's writing of Ephesians. In addition, Titus and 2 Timothy contain historical information about Paul's expanding Aegean network. This requires a later date for these two epistles, but does not necessarily require the same date for 1 Timothy. Finally, the excursus above showed that the Pastorals contain more consistent grammar and a richer vocabulary than Paul's other letters, requiring reflection and time for composition. On that count, it seems unlikely that Paul composed 1 Timothy during a journey, which was marked by anxiety over the Corinthian troubles, as 2 Corinthians testifies.[64] On the balance, then, it seems a date for 1 Timothy around 63 CE after Paul's imprisonment is the more likely option.

Social Identification in the Ephesian Community in 63 CE

First and Second Timothy present themselves as personal letters from Paul to his close associate Timothy, which raises a methodological issue for a social identity analysis of this letter. The letters aware of a wider audience, reading over Timothy's shoulders, so that they consist of a communication from one leader to another in the presence of the group. Thus, the instructions to Timothy, such as those about sound doctrine and leadership succession, have both a personal dimension—to instruct Timothy as junior leader—and a community dimension—to encourage the community's loyalty to Timothy in carrying out Paul's instructions. This raises the question whether it is legitimate to speak of social identification in a personal letter. That is, do these letters reveal the kind of the intergroup and intragroup features, which make a social identity analysis possible?

---

63. Ibid., 36.

64. Reicke dates 1 Timothy in the summer or fall of 56, 2 Cor in the summer of 57, Titus in the spring or summer of 58, and 2 Timothy in 60 CE (*Re-Examining Paul's Letters*, overview on p. 141).

A quick glance suggests that such an analysis is feasible. In 1 Timothy, Paul instructs Timothy about the leadership of Christian communities, so that the group context is part of the perspective of the letter. The letter addresses both intragroup dynamics—such as deviant teaching, orderly behavior, and care for different social groups—and intergroup dynamics—such as warnings against opponents and the community's testimony before outsiders. The community is never directly addressed (note the absence of second person plural verbs), but several sections instruct the community indirectly, such as the instructions about prayer and dress (2:8–15), about elders and deacons (3:1–13), and about widows and elders (5:3–25). Thus, even though the community is not directly addressed in the letter, it is indirectly included, which warrants a study of group dynamics in this personal letter.

As Paul's Aegean network had grown, so had the church in Ephesus. The community developed to a size and complexity that reached beyond a few households. Indications of this complexity are the references to social groupings by age, gender, and marital status (5:1–3), indicating the presence of at least two generations in the church and the presence of widows as a significant subgroup. The references to elders and deacons, with further instructions about leadership payment and accountability, indicate the presence of a complex leadership subgroup. Further references to slaves as well as riches indicate that group members come from the full urban spectrum, that the church had "substantial personal and financial resources," and that its leaders "consisted in large part of prosperous householders."[65]

Social identification seems to be under pressure from both Jewish and Greco-Roman sides. Although the community is not directly addressed, their processes of social identification are indirectly visible. The influence of Jewish social identity is felt from some who "desired to be teachers of the law" (1:7), but applied the law to "the just" instead of to the "lawless and disobedient" (1:8–9. These same people are characterized as devoted to "myths and endless genealogies" (1:4). The references to the law suggest the tendency to apply principles of the OT law to members of the Christ-believing communities; in this context, "myths

---

65. Verner, *The Household of God*, 180–82. See also Marshall's description of the amazingly rich congregational life in the Pastorals ("Congregation and Ministry in the Pastoral Epistles," 107–15).

and genealogies" are often understood as the fallacious and speculative use of OT narratives, biblical characters, and OT family trees.[66] This passage often fuels the debate about the identity of the opponents,[67] but it is doubtful that the passage is very concerned to specify the identity of the opponents (which would be obvious to the addressees) or the content of their teaching.[68] Although references to the law indicate Jewish influence, their "law-teaching" (νομοδιδάσκαλοι, 1:7) is defined not so much as "false" but literally as 'other' (ἑτεροδιδασκαλεῖν, 1:4). The "otherness" is defined in comparison with "sound teaching" (εἴ τι ἕτερον τῇ ὑγιαινούσῃ διδασκαλίᾳ, 1:10).[69] Within this context, "myths and genealogies" most likely refer to Jewish narratives that highlighted the value of Jewish or Jewish-Christian social identity, and to genealogies that indicated one's inclusion in this "privileged" ingroup or subgroup. However, using the language of deviance labeling, the value of these narratives and genealogies is downgraded while the value of Paul's and Timothy's teaching is commended.[70] Such labeling challenges ingroup members to dissociate from the "others" and to maintain loyalty to "sound teaching"; the passage functions as an exhortation to abide by the "sound teaching" that will be offered in the next section of the letter.[71] Thus, this passage focuses on clarifying the boundaries of the social identity of the group with a view to aligning the social identification of its members, and offers little information about the identity and teaching of the opponents, or about their number and influence.[72] Moreover, these "other" teachers are still within Timothy's audience so he can restrict their teaching, which suggests that this teaching comes from ingroup members. Mostly likely then, this indicates that some of the Christ-believing members

66. So for instance Marshall, *Pastoral Epistles*, 365–66.

67. See the discussions in Towner, *The Goal of Our Instruction*, 21–46; Marshall, *Pastoral Epistles*, 40–51.

68. Kelly recognizes that these terms come close to disclosing the content of the heresy, without giving clarity (*Pastoral Epistles*, 44).

69. Weiss, "Didaskalia," 137.

70. Pietersen indicates parallels with the use of these terms in Polybius, who uses them to devalue histories that are more fiction and entertainment than fact, in order to promote his own historiography as trustworthy (Pietersen, *The Polemic of the Pastorals*, 121–22).

71. Witherington, *Letters and Homilies*, 190.

72. Although it is often interpreted as such. For instance, Marshall interprets the evidence as an indication that the opposition "is . . . sizable, is winning support and is dangerous" (Marshall, *Pastoral Epistles*, 42).

accommodated their Christian social identity to the foundational beliefs and values of their Jewish identity; such members could be converted God-fearers, proselytes or ethnic Jews.

The influence of Roman identity is felt more from pervasive values than from particular teachers. Men are warned against praying with "anger or quarreling," while women should not dress to flaunt their riches (2:8–9). The setting suggests competition for honor and status, for the men through quarreling, for the women through their dress.[73] Community oversight is qualified as a "noble task" (3:1), which suggests that the work of leading is a sign of honorable service, as a patron might provide for a community. The following virtue list (3:2–7) casually refers to wine, money, and the household, assuming that the leader addressed is one of significant social standing.[74] Moreover, the letter warns against those who are greedy (6:5–10), probably referring to some of the wealthier believing householder-leaders who mistakenly thought that this function would bring them increasing honor and financial gain.[75] These references reflect the patronage structures of leadership, as they were also visible in Corinth. Christ-believing group norms appear to be in conflict with cultural values, so that some members, especially some of the higher status members, had difficulty with comparative fit ("I fit best with social peers, much less with other Christ-believers") and category accessibility (the relative unfamiliarity of their new group norms). This may be surprising in a well established community like in Ephesus, but it may very well indicate the influx of new members who needed to be immersed more fully into group beliefs and norms.

Thus, the influence of Jewish identity was felt mostly as pressure to adjust the foundational beliefs of the community from a few ingroup members with connections to Jewish identity. The resolution was to call for dissociation from those who attempted to redefine Christian social identity in this way. The influence of Roman identity was felt as pressure to conform to cultural norms from the membership at large, but especially from some higher status members. The resolution was a call to reorient one's values and to increase (or renew)

---

73. Witherington, *Letters and Homilies*, 223, sees both male and female behaviors as an expression of high status and honor competition.

74. Verner, *The Household of God*, 132–34.

75. Kidd, *Wealth and Beneficence*, 96–100.

one's socialization as community member, to prevent a weakening of commitment to group norms. Thus, these influences diluted the clarity of Paul's vision of Christian identity, and weakened its cohesion and stability in its social environment. Both cases of influence can be described as the negative influence of cross-cutting social identities.

The handling of nested identities in 1 Timothy is somewhat ambiguous. On the one hand, some teachers appear to have been intent on gathering a following for their more Jewish conception of Christian identity, as outlined above. There was a danger of intragroup competition, instead of recognizing subgroups as nested identities within the larger whole. On the other hand, the increasing complexity and subgroup formation (5:1—6:4) solicits further instructions about how to shape these subgroups as part of the overall community, which shows an understanding of subgroups as nested social identities within a superordinate Christian social identity.

The Ephesian Leaders as Managers of Christian Social Identity

The only Ephesian leaders named in 1 Timothy are Hymenaeus and Alexander (1:20), deviant leaders who were exposed and excommunicated from the church. One or more other leaders were marked as deviant in their teaching of the Jewish law (1:7–11) and possibly in using strategies of honor competition and financial gain as leadership style (2:8; 6:4–5). Marshall presents these deviant teachers as leaders of an opposing group,[76] as suggested by the sheer number of references to deviant teachers. Timothy was instructed to charge "certain persons" (τισίν, 1:3) to stop various teaching practices, which had resulted in "certain persons" (τινες) getting into "vain discussions" (1:6), while some (τινες) actually made shipwreck of their faith (1:19). Similar references to errant teachers with plural forms of τις punctuate the letter (4:1, 5:15, 24, 6:10, 21), usually indicating that "some" have deviated from the main group.[77] A number of these are described as having wandered away from the faith, suggesting that they are now outsiders to the community (1:19–20, 4:1, 5:15, 6:10, 21), while other deviant teachers may still have functioned within

---

76. Marshall, *Pastoral Epistles*, 40.
77. Ibid., 574–81.

the church (1:3, 6, 5:15?, 5:24, 6:3). Since Paul directed Timothy's intervention from the outside, it is likely that at least some deviant teachers were elders; otherwise, the elders could have provided the correction themselves. Thus, deviant teachers are not represented as an opposing subgroup nor as leaders of significant subgroups within the community, but as individual deviant group members, some of whom had already left the group. The function of these many references to deviant teachers is not to provide an indication about their number or influence, but rather to "serve as negative foil to the positive examples in the letters . . . to promote fidelity to tradition through correct knowledge and action."[78] They are portrayed as out-group prototype to enhance the comparative fit of group members with teachers who remained faithful to Paul and Timothy.

The majority of the local leadership remains unnamed and are thus assumed to be loyal. These leaders came most likely from the ranks of higher status believers, who functioned as patrons or benefactors to the community. The frequent warnings against strife (2:8; 3:3; 6:4), pride (3:6; 6:4, 17), and greed (3:3, 8; 6:17–19) indicate the dangers of leadership based of patronage and honor competition. It appears that these leaders did not consistently succeed in shaping their leadership according to Christ-believing instead of Roman values.

Paul first empowers them to relate their vision of social identity to their leadership. He reminds the local leadership through Timothy of God's mission in the world as a distinctive aspect of monotheistic belief (1:17; 2:1–7). These passage emphasize that all honor is God's, and that He desires prayer for *all* people and for *all* to be saved. Towner observes that this reference to monotheism ascribes all honor and glory to God, implying that "all other claimants to such things are subordinate or false,"[79] but he fails to indicate the social dimension of Paul's monotheism, namely that all intragroup competition undermines the social identity of the group, and that ethnic or social privilege is no basis for ministry.[80] Moreover, Paul relates their leadership roles to the

---

78. Fiore, *Pastoral Epistles*, 15.

79. Towner, *Timothy and Titus*, 420.

80. Couser also overlooks the social implications of Paul's christology in 1 Tim 1:15–17: "for whatever reason Paul senses the need to nail down the real humanity of Jesus within the context of of Christian monotheism" (Couser, "The Mystery of Godliness is Great," 141). Paul's christology in the context of his monotheism offers important theological insights, but they are voiced to serve his vision of a universal

church's mission as "household of God" and "a pillar and buttress of the truth," to uphold the proclamation of the mystery of Christ (3:14–16). Oberlinner and Verner argue that οἶκος θεοῦ refers to the community as God's household, which is interpreted as an indication of increased household ideology in the Pastorals.[81] Herzer counters that this verse would be the only one in 1 Timothy that refers explicitly to household, and that the phrase rather portrays the community as the "House of God," which fits better with the temple imagery of the passage and with OT conceptions about the temple.[82] However, in the leadership context of 1 Tim 2–3, it is likely that Paul plays on both meanings in order to portray household subgroups as God's house or temple. Paul's references to monotheism and the community as God's house, based in part on OT roots, would not have been new to the Ephesian community. It is thus not an open rebuke or criticism, but rather a reminder of core elements of their identity narrative as framework for how they are to exercise their leadership. Paul affirms and clarifies their vision of Christian social identity as basis for their leadership (the leader as artist).

After realigning their social identification, Paul directed local leaders to participate appropriately in the ministries of prayer, evangelism, and teaching (2:1–15). Apparently, these ministries had been hindered by a spirit of interpersonal competition, expressed differently for men ("anger" and "quarreling," 2:8) and for women (emphasizing their riches and status, 2:9–10). Such competition eroded the unity of the community and its mission, so Paul corrected their ministry style (leader as impresario) based on a renewed understanding the divine mission. Thus, in these ministries, their proper social identification would lead to a decrease in honor-oriented leadership strategies. In the process, Paul presents several exemplars. First, God's desire for salvation for all becomes model for leadership concerned with the whole church. Second, Paul is a model as spokesman for divine intentions, since he is explicitly authorized to do so. Third, the narratives of creation and fall are employed to encourage particular leadership

---

Christian social identity, where leaders and members rise above their ethnic and social preferences.

81. Oberlinner, *Timotheusbrief*, 1:151–55; Verner, *The Household of God*, 186. See also Horrell, "Social Transformation," 294ff.

82. Herzer, "Rearranging the 'House of God,'" 558–61.

performances. Again, these models would have been mostly familiar, but they serve to underline Paul's directions for leadership in core community activities.

Although Paul often downplays honor as motivation for leadership, he strangely seems to heighten their sense of honor in encouraging group members to aspire to the office of oversight (ἐπισκοπῆς ὀρέγεται, 3:1). Tamez suggests that this indicates a situation of conflict and strife for the position of oversight,[83] but then ambition would need to be restrained rather than encouraged. Fiore points out the positive connotation of desire in this passage, but says little to explain the need to portray the task as desirable.[84] Oberlinner suggests that next to the highly esteemed roles of apostle, prophet, and teacher, oversight must have appeared as a more mundane and less desirable function.[85] However, 1 Timothy does not suggest competition between overseers and apostles or prophets.

A more satisfactory explanation for Paul's recommendation of the task of oversight is as follows. In a competitive environment, patrons would not usually feel restrained to step forward in support of their favored leader, which earlier developments in Corinth had amply demonstrated. Paul had become embroiled in difficult conflict, which led to reconciliation with local Corinthian leaders who learned through this painful process to restrain their ambitions; but for the visiting Jewish-Christian teachers this process led to disgrace and isolation if they refused to accept Paul and his teaching. Furthermore, in Ephesus Paul had excommunicated Hymenaeus and Alexander (1:20),[86] left instructions for Timothy to restrict deviant teachers (1:3), and initiated procedures for public censure of deviant elders (5:20, 22). Paul's reversal of honor values and his actions in censuring deviant leaders must have created uncertainty about his countercultural leadership model. Not surprisingly, potential Ephesian candidates for leadership had grown reluctant to lead and needed to have their leadership ambition rekindled by having Paul portray it as a good work of benefaction, directing their competitive urge in the right direction.

---

83. Tamez, *Struggles for Power*, 93.

84. Fiore, *Pastoral Epistles*, 73.

85. Oberlinner, *Timotheusbrief*, 1:115.

86. Oberlinner also commented that the appeal of the function of oversight could also have suffered from some who fulfilled it unworthily (Ibid).

The qualifications for leadership motivate the householder to identify themselves and their *own* house (3:4–5, 12) with *God's* house (3:15), so that their leadership service is seen in light of serving the divine mission. As a result, any aspirations towards leadership contribute to God's honor (cf. 1:17; 3:16). Thus, Paul responds to social factors that create a certain reluctance to lead by reframing their leadership ambition within the framework of his vision of Christian social identity.

On a more positive note, local leaders had succeeded in organizing themselves on a level of collegial coordination for the whole community, rising above the level of household supervision only (4:14). Some leaders were able to devote themselves more than others to the ministry of "preaching and teaching" (5:17), while certain procedures such as the laying on of hands in initiating a new elder (5:22) were in place. Local leaders had made some gains in structuring the community (the leader as engineer), but they still needed assistance to make their understanding of Christian identity relevant for these and other structures. The letter provides this assistance by affirming their foundational beliefs and values, and connecting them with community practices as well as with how to handle various other subgroups in the church, notably the widows. Moreover, the handling deviance is an exercise par excellence in creating identity-embedding structures. Timothy's charge to provide this service to the community suggests that local leaders had great difficulty with this task, especially since some of the deviants were part of the local leadership. Thus, Paul empowered local leaders to bring their social structures in line with their vision of Christian social identity.

Johnson summarized the situation in Ephesus as "a crisis in local leadership." He refers to competition for leadership among those not worthy, to charges may have been brought against a leader (cf. 5:19), and to the danger of deviant teachers.[87] "Crisis," though, is too strong a label. Admittedly, the Ephesian Christ-believing community has its leadership challenges, but they fit well in a social setting of an expanding community whose social identity is still unsettled in the minds and lives of the group members. The Ephesian leaders were coping with the growing complexity of the church with moderate success. A variety of ministries was maintained with new levels of leadership developing, without the kinds of divisions that took place earlier

---

87. Johnson, *First and Second Timothy*, 235–36.

in Corinth. Yet, uncertainty remained over how to implement their vision of Christian social identity in their community activities and in various organizational aspects. They were familiar with Paul's perspective on God's mission in the world and his purpose for the church, but they had not fully succeeded in making this relevant (a) for the way men and women functioned in the ministries of prayer and teaching, (b) for which group members to select for leadership, and (c) for how to create structure that reflected their social identity. Consequently, certain practices had entered the community that reflect their social identification with different groups, some with Jewish identity (the deviant teachers in their "law-teaching") and others with the Roman identity of the city's elite. Paul reaffirmed their common vision of Christian social identity, and argued that "law-teaching" was an illegitimate content for the group's beliefs. Moreover, Paul reoriented group members to appropriate group norms to reprioritize Christian identity performance. In the terminology of SIMOL, their leadership as artist of social identity was not yet fully integrated with their leadership as impresario and as engineer.

Paul's Leadership as Identity Management

Paul's leadership focuses partly on his relationship with Timothy, partly on his relationship with the community through Timothy's mediation. The relationship between Paul and Timothy frames the major sections of the letter in the form of three personal exhortations to Timothy[88]:

Table 7.1: Paul's Personal Exhortations as Frame for 1 Timothy

	1 Tim 1	1 Tim 4	1 Tim 6
Stereotypical portraits of the opponents	1:3–7	4:1–3, 7–8	6:3–10
Charge to Timothy	1:3	4:6–7, 11–16	6:3, 11–14
Timothy's commission	1:18 Prophecy	4:14 Gift; Elders	6:12 Confession

---

88. See Redalié, "Sois un modèle pour les croyants," 87–88. See also Marshall, *Pastoral Epistles*, 25 for a similar discussion, although he follows a different outline.

	1 Tim 1	1 Tim 4	1 Tim 6
Timothy's models	Paul (his commission) 1:12–15	(the church observes) 4:15–16	Christ (his testimony) 6:13
Closing doxology	1:16–17	—	6:15–16
A final charge	1:18–20	—	6:17–21[A]

A. 6:20–21 may well be the closing lines in Paul's own handwriting, repeating the main themes in just a few words after the closing arguments of 6:3–19.

These personal exhortations to Timothy define and legitimate his task as leader. Two other sections that are enclosed between these personal exhortations provide Paul's instructions for the community, which Timothy is to pass on. The first set of community instructions (2:1—3:16) reflects Paul concerns for the Ephesian leadership and discusses gendered participation in the ministries of prayer and teaching, as well as the evaluation of leadership character. The second set of community instructions (5:1—6:2) structures various subgroups by age, gender, marital status, leadership role and social status as part of the larger community.

Constructing a Chain of Succession Through Stereotyping

Deviance labeling in 1 Timothy, as referred to above, involves the construction of social stereotypes. In the first set of personal exhortations (1:3–20), Paul draws a contrast between the deviants and himself plus Timothy, which focuses on content (foundational beliefs and values) and character (ingroup prototype). The content is "the gospel of the glory of the blessed God" (1:11), entrusted to Paul for special service (1:11–12) in spite of his track record as opponent of this teaching (1:13), as compared with the myths, vain discussions, and ignorance of the 'other' teachers (1:4–7). The character is visible in Paul as prime exemplar for the community (ὑποτύπωσις, 1:16), both before and after his conversion. Paul's ignorance before his conversion (1:13) associates his former character as blasphemer and persecutor with the 'other' teachers,[89] while the grace and commission received

---

89. Johnson observes, "Paul is deliberately identifying himself in his former life with those who, in their faithlessness and ignorance, now wish to be teachers of law" ("First Timothy 1,1–20," 30).

with his conversion (1:14–16) associates him with Timothy, who is also charged to "wage the good warfare" and resist the deviant teachers (1:18–19). Paul's charge to Timothy to continue this ministry extends a chain of succession from Paul through Timothy to those who will heed Timothy's instructions about the apostolic teaching tradition. By contrast, the false teachers are portrayed as outside the chain of truth and authority, which originated with Christ.

Beker finds that such stereotyping "does not take the theological claims of his opponents seriously" and grossly misrepresents the actual situation.[90] Beker is particularly sensitive to what he perceives as the authoritarian stance of the letter, since it tends to exclude these "other" teachers from the community.[91] Beker is correct that this differs notably from the earlier Pauline letters where Paul often engaged in extended argumentation about the content of the faith, but he misjudges the function of this rhetorical strategy.

First, this chapter is cast as a charge from Paul to Timothy, who would hardly have been surprised at Paul's stereotypical portrayal of the opponents and of himself. As long-term coworker of Paul, Timothy only needed half a word to be reminded of earlier discussions and contexts. Moreover, the wider audience is either familiar enough with Paul to fill in the blanks left by the stereotypical portrayals, or else Timothy would do this for them. In other words, 1 Timothy can be classified as a *high context* document, the type of communication that fits well within the collectivist culture of the first century Mediterranean world where social context and relationships are left implicit, to be filled in by the audience.[92] This *high context* effect would be heightened in a letter like 1 Timothy because of Timothy's long-term association with Paul. This explains the lower need for contextual background in the argument of 1 Timothy and the incompleteness of its stereotypical descriptions.

Second, such stereotypical language clarifies group boundaries for the purpose of maintaining or adjusting the social identification of the group. This is accomplished through a strategy of meta-contrast, which emphasizes the *difference* between Paul and the false teachers, and the *similarity* between Paul and Christ, with Timothy assumed to

---

90. Beker, *Heirs of Paul*, 40–41.
91. Ibid., 46–47.
92. Rohrbaugh, "Hermeneutics as Cross-Cultural Encounter," 567–69.

be on Paul's side. Thus, the letter defines the desirable alliances within the leadership subgroup and invites the wider audience to join this alliance and to stand unitedly against those who teach differently.[93] The portrayal of the false teachers as speculative and ignorant babblers is therefore an accusation meant to firm up Paul's (and Timothy's) constituency, not to provide an accurate and 'objective' description of these teachers.

Finally, stereotyping is a process that usually occurs in the context of stable group identity,[94] unlike the contexts of unstable group identity as was evident in Corinth. Thus, 1–2 Corinthians provided more contextual data in order to stabilize the community and prevent or correct misunderstandings. In spite of the focus on deviance in 1 Timothy, the extensive use of stereotypical language indicates that the situation in Ephesus is most likely relatively stable, diminishing the need for contextual explanations in the communication.

These considerations suggest that, if Paul's arguments are situated in their proper context, they will be seen not as a gross misrepresentation of the opponents, nor as an authoritarian power play against them, but as an affirmation of the alliance between Paul and Timothy, and a challenge to the Ephesian community to maintain their alliance with them over against the false teachers.

Christian social identity is here defined, not only with reference to foundational beliefs and values and ingroup prototype, but also with reference to particular authority structures (the leader as artist). Paul's construction of a chain of succession, with himself as God's key spokesman, and Timothy as his designated successor, has become part of Paul's overall vision of Christian social identity. It is not only the central beliefs but also the authority structure that gives stability and permanence to Christian social identity.[95] Deviant teaching is not only an incorrect belief about God or Christ, but always redefines the

---

93. Capes et. al. make the interesting observation that "when friends wrote each other, they customarily tightened the bonds of their alliance by reminding of their common enemies" (*Rediscovering Paul*, 208). They applied this only to their discussion of Philippians, but an application to 1 Timothy seems also possible.

94. Hogg et al., "Identification and Leadership in Small Groups," 1249; Hogg, "A Social Identity Theory of Leadership," 190.

95. "Authority makes possible the interchanges that bind a community together and enables the community to determine its identity" (Stagaman, *Authority in the Church*, 31).

ingroup prototype of Christian social identity, and inevitably involves a confrontation with the authority structure that holds this particular social identity together. Thus, the conflict of Paul and Timothy with the false teachers (and earlier with Hymenaeus and Alexander) is not merely an ideological debate, but a social struggle about who is most prototypical so as to provide the leading example for the community and a power struggle over who has the right to define Christian social identity. If Paul engages in a power play, it is not simply as a convenient way to outmaneuver his opponents, but because power and authority are an integral part of his vision of Christian social identity. Power, authority, and identity are here seen to cohere very closely, so that a contest in one area automatically involves the other areas.

Aligning Gender Roles with Prototypical Leadership

The first set of community instructions (2:1—3:16) focuses initially on gendered participation in ministry leadership. Instruction about the content of prayer (2:1-7) leads to a description of God's mission in this world, which is supported by the ministries of prayer (2:1, 8) and teaching (2:7, 11-12), in which Paul plays a unique role. Instruction about the manner of prayer details how men and women participate differently in the mission and its ministries. These later instructions especially seem aimed at leading men and women. The men are instructed specifically to pray "without anger or quarreling" (2:8). Such quarreling is typical for the agonistic honor competition in the ancient world, to which those of higher social status were more vulnerable, as was also evident in Corinth.[96] Timothy's task of restricting some teachers and empowering others may well have encouraged competition among some of the established household leaders.[97] The women engaged in a different kind honor competition by competitive display of gold, pearls, and costly clothing (2:9), for which only the few wealthier ones would have had such resources. Wives of key householder-leaders or wealthy widows appear to have flaunted their wealth and status in an effort to gain honor for themselves and their house.[98] The exhortation to excel instead in

---

96. See Malina, *The New Testament World*, 36ff. for the cultural anthropological background of this phenomenon.

97. See also Witherington, *Letters and Homilies*, 223.

98. Tamez, *Struggles for Power*, 4–6; Witherington, *Letters and Homilies*, 219-21.

good works probably refers to benefactions by wealthier members on behalf of the community.[99] Thus, ministry leadership seems to be the focus of this passage, although the principles apply to all. Quarreling leaders disrupt these and destabilize the community. As in 1–2 Corinthians, Paul corrects the honor orientation as an incorrect basis for leadership, and implies that all honor is due to the one God, our benefactor.

The passage shows distinct universalizing tendencies, with prayer for *all* people and God desiring *all* to be saved,[100] which seems to parallel the "mission" of Roman authorities to bring universal peace and salvation. This has been taken as a sign that the Pastorals advocate alignment with and even support of Roman society. MacDonald suggests, "for those who sought to win the whole world, accommodation to the standards of the world was to a certain extent inevitable and social respectability was crucial."[101] Beker interprets this as "cautious accommodation to the secular world of the Roman Empire."[102] Mitchell even concludes, "the Paulinist author wishes to present . . . Paul as having commanded his followers to place highest priority on standing in complete alignment with the forces of the *imperium*."[103] However, Paul's emphasis on monotheism suggests otherwise, since monotheistic belief formed a prime obstacle in the participation of Christ-believers in the customary rites of civic religion, emperor worship, and familial devotion. Rather, these universalizing tendencies may be interpreted as a strategy of social creativity. Paul addresses significant Roman dimensions of social identity: authorities that provide peace and prosperity for subjects that exercise proper piety and dignity (εὐσέβεια[104] and σεμνότης, 2:2) towards rulers and the gods. Yet, he clearly reinterprets these dimensions, for ultimately God provides the opportunity for a peaceful and quiet life, and true piety will honor

---

99. Tamez, *Struggles for Power*, 13.

100. Johnson lists these universalizing tendencies as follows: the prayer for *all* people (2:1), God's desires that *all* be saved (2:4), Christ as Mediator between God and *people* (2:5), Christ as a ransom for *all* (2:6), and Paul as apostle to the *nations* (2:7). See Johnson, *First and Second Timothy*, 189 and also the discussion in MacDonald, *The Pauline Churches*, 174ff.

101. MacDonald, *The Pauline Churches*, 224.

102. Beker, *Heirs of Paul*, 44.

103. Mitchell, "Corrective Composition, Corrective Exegesis," 49.

104. For a further discussion of εὐσέβεια in a Roman context, see below on 3:16.

the one God as divine benefactor who gave Christ as a ransom for all (2:3-6). God is more generous because his mission encompasses all people everywhere and Christ is more beneficent because He gave himself for our ransom. In a way that is reminiscent of Ephesians, Paul bends imperial ideology to universalize his vision of Christian social identity. This reminder of God's mission affirms and enriches the Christian identity narrative, and provides a focus for the leaders' ministries of prayer and teaching. Thus, the universalizing tendencies in the *Missio Dei* are not a sign of accommodation to the world, but of a strategy of social creativity to enhance the social identification of the leaders with Paul's vision of Christian social identity.

This section can best be described as instructions in how male and female leadership roles contribute to the fulfillment of the *Missio Dei* in the world. Paul's social identification strategies neutralize the influence of cross-cutting social identities. The identity narrative, based on the foundational stories of redemption and creation, stigmatizes honor competition as deviant and invites all members, especially the leaders, to maintain their previous allegiance to Paul and Timothy. Men and women are to identify themselves with more appropriate gender roles, the men not competing but praying in unity, the women not flaunting their status but doing good works while quietly and respectfully supporting the teaching of approved men.[105] Paul, then, corrects the way some exercised their leadership in their ministries of prayer and teaching, by stigmatizing honor competition and celebrating God's mission in the world; he corrected their identity performance as impresario of identity.

Maintaining Christian Social Identity Through (New) Leadership

Paul procedes to discuss recognized leadership roles as a function of Christian identity maintenance (3:1-16). The character lists for overseer and deacons provide an instrument with which to scrutinize

---

105. Female roles in leadership will be addressed further below. But the literature on this specific passage about the relationship of women to teaching and authority is voluminous. A few studies that are particularly relevant in considering leadership patterns are: Baugh, "A Foreign World; Capper, "Transition from Gathering in Private to Meeting in Public Space"; Winter, *Roman Wives*, 97–122; Witherington, *Women in the Earliest Churches*, 117–25.

potential candidates for leadership.[106] Such candidates were probably of higher social status, as indicated by the casual references to wine, money, and the household (3:3-4, 8),[107] and by the perspective on leadership as a work of beneficence (καλὸν ἔργον).[108] The word ἔργον also regularly referred to Paul's missionary work (cf. 1 Cor 9:1, 16:10; Phil 1:6, 22, 2:30) or to local leadership (cf. 1 Thess 5:12-13; 1 Cor 16:15-16; Eph 4:12),[109] which raised the status of those who did such 'work' as partners in the Pauline mission. Moreover, the leadership task was carried out within the community, but also before a watching world: the lists require a blameless (outsider) reputation (3:2, 7, 10) and exemplary conduct in one's household (3:3-4, 12). Thus, the characterization of community oversight as a "good work" commends oversight as a beneficent exercise of patronage for the community by which leaders participate in the Pauline mission on a local level with the outside world as a significant audience.[110]

Openness towards new leadership is implied in the stipulations that an overseer should not be "a recent convert" (νεόφυτος, 3:6) and that a deacon should "be tested first" (3:10), suggesting that a new convert might have the opportunity to move into leadership. Several developments could make this expedient. The church could be expanding so rapidly that the growth rate outstripped the social identification process of new converts moving into leadership; Timothy's restriction of false teachers could have led to some competition among established leaders, but may also have led to some gaps in the leadership ranks; or the reluctance to move into leadership described above created a shortage of new candidates. The social and missionary

---

106. Paschke suggests that Paul and Timothy served in the role of censor in examining potential candidates for the function of oversight ("The *cura morum*," 107-18). See Harrison, "Paul and the Gymnasiarchs," 152-63; and Fiore, *Personal Example*, 26-163 for further analysis of these virtue lists in the context of the ancient world.

107. Verner, *The Household of God*, 132-34.

108. Καλός also occurs in 3:7, 13 and likely has status indications: LN, 1:735, list the word under rubric 87.25 in a semantic field with other terms relating to social status.

109. The same is true in Acts 13:2; 14:26; 15:38, where the phrase εἰς ἔργον refers to the missionary task. See Heiligenthal, "*Ergon*," 49.

110. Unlike many commentators, Towner and Marshall each offer an excursus on "good works" in the Pastorals and the rest of the NT, but neither author connects it with leadership and patronage. See Marshall, *Pastoral Epistles*, 227-29 and Towner, *Timothy and Titus*, 210-12.

setting of 1 Tim 1–2 may well reflect all three factors and thus explains the need for new leaders, whom Paul may not have known previously. Thus, the letter envisions new ranks of leaders beyond Paul's direct, personal influence.

The key to understanding these leadership instructions is in the focus on social identity maintenance as a leader's task. The ability to teach (διδακτικός, 3:2) and to "hold the mystery of the faith with a clear conscience" (3:9) suggests that candidates had been instructed by Paul, Timothy or other teachers (cf. 1:3–5) to uphold "sound doctrine" (1:10) and to foster love from a "pure heart and a good conscience" (1:5), parallel to Timothy's own teaching ministry in Ephesus (4:11–16).[111] This emphasis comes to a climax in a description of the church's mission (3:14–16), which is to be a "a pillar and buttress of the truth," fulfilling the *Missio Dei* that "all people . . . come to the knowledge of the truth" (2:4).[112] Fulfillment of this mission was to lead to godliness (εὐσέβεια, 2:2, 3:16), the mystery of which is now explained in creedal or hymnic confession of 3:16.[113] Thus, Paul connects the roles of leaders to God's mission in the world and to His purpose for the church. In this way, leaders fulfill their charge to be faithful to Paul's gospel, which he received from Christ and committed to Timothy. This offers a foundational theological qualification of church leadership, but since God's mission with the church also defines the community, proper Christ-believing leadership involves the maintenance and enhancement of Christian social identity amidst a watching world.

Two features of Paul's leadership discourse highlight this public dimension of church leadership. First, Paul reinterpreted εὐσέβεια as a marker of Christian identity. Εὐσέβεια represented Roman piety with respect for the emperor and Roman family structures; such piety ensured the stability of the empire. D'Angelo and Standhartinger believe that the letter uses this term to accommodate to the oppressive

---

111. Cf. Verner's emphasis on the teaching role as key for the overseer (Verner, *The Household of God*, 152–56).

112. Towner summarizes, "in keeping with his [the author's] theme of salvation as a present reality and its dependent relation to the proclamation of the gospel, and in keeping with his concerns about heresy, he regards the Church as God's missionary vehicle, whose task is to proclaim and protect the message of the Christ-event" (Towner, *The Goal of Our Instruction*, 137).

113. For further details about the relationship between these verses and the rest of 1 Timothy, see Van Neste, *Cohesion and Structure in the Pastoral Epistles*, 45–46 and 87–89.

forces of the empire as a strategy of survival, similar to contemporary Jewish and Greek responses to Roman piety.[114] Yet, 1 Timothy clearly relates εὐσέβεια to the divine mission (2:2–5; 4:7–10) and to the central christological tradition (3:15–16), adapting "the meaning to reflect Christian experience, behavior, and doctrine."[115] The term does not simply indicate accommodation, but rather points to a mixture of accommodation and resistance.[116] 1 Timothy is aware of a watching world, realizing that identity performance occurred before both ingroup and outgroup audiences. This awareness of the outgroup as a significant audience probably led the author to identify the believing community in terms of a familiar Roman concept, while at the same time reinterpreting that valued term in a way that aligned it with Christian social identity. By way of social creativity, εὐσέβεια is adopted from Roman social identity and transformed into an identity marker for Christian social identity by associating it with the Christian mission and with foundational Christian beliefs.

Similarly, Paul adopts and transforms traditional household and temple language to harmonize with Christian identity. Söding points out that the household ("house," οἶκος, 3:15) provides only a partial analogy for the church, not a complete description of its identity. Concepts such as truth, glory, mystery, and confession point to other dimensions of identity, which complement the household metaphor.[117] Further, this house is qualified as "the church [assembly] of the living God" (ἐκκλησία θεοῦ ζῶντος), and its pillars and buttresses, as it were, are to uphold the confession of Christ (3:15–16). The household and temple imageries are fused to portray significant dimensions of Christian identity. First Corinthians redefines the temple as the Christian community founded by God (1 Cor 3:16–17), Ephesians adds to this the historical realization through apostles and prophets (Eph 2:20), while the Pastorals shift the imagery to consider the significance of the church for the world.[118] This is, again, a strategy of social creativity: Paul borrows strength and value for Christian social identity

---

114. D'Angelo, "Sexual Politics and True Piety," 156–62; Standhartinger, "*Eusebeia* in den Pastoralbriefen," 76–82.

115. Wainwright, "*Eusebeia*: Syncretism or Contextualization," 223.

116. D'Angelo, "Sexual Politics and True Piety," 164.

117. Söding, "1 Timotheus 3," 80–81.

118. Ibid., 82–83.

by fusing these Roman and Jewish images of gathering, proclamation, and worship. Thus, Paul defines Christian social identity in the public arena of Roman discourse in order to provide an understandable framework for the functioning of Christ-believing leaders. In other words, as impresario of identity, Paul used the familiar language of godliness, household, and temple to present the distinctive character of the ministry of leadership for their distinctive Christ-following communities.

The distinctiveness of this leadership does not necessarily arise from their character qualities. The need for high moral leadership standards was also voiced in other segments of Roman society.[119] Rather, distinctive leadership is based on the Christian identity narrative and on Christ-believing identity performance. The christological hymn (3:16) identifies the community's key beliefs and functions as a foundational identity narrative, while the community's mission (2:2–5) defines key dimensions for identity performance. Together, these beliefs and mission provide a literary but even more a social inclusio for defining the character of community leadership. In other words, the community's beliefs and mission provide the essential values and practices for describing the community's leadership. Leaders are selected partly on the basis of character, conform some of the better Roman standards, but mostly on the basis of their prototypicality (holding to and proclaiming the faith) and their identity performance (using the privileges of leadership and status on behalf of the community instead of for their own honor). This social identification of the leaders is essential, for their leadership performance consolidates Christian social identity and mobilizes the membership to similar Christian identity performance.

Exemplifying Prototypical Leadership

In the second set of personal exhortations (4:1–16), Paul presents Timothy as exemplary leader by contrasting him with the opposing teachers. Deviant teachers appear to focus on restrictions concerning food and marriage, and are demonized as begin devoted to "deceitful spirits and teachings of demons" (4:1–3). It has proven very difficult

---

119 See Paschke, "The *cura morum*," 107–18; Harrison, "Paul and the Gymnasiarchs," 152–63 and Fiore, *Personal Example*, 26–163.

to locate an historical source, which combines (Jewish?) food restrictions with an ascetic attitude towards marriage.[120] Instead, accusations about departing from the faith, and devotion to deceitful spirits are common stereotypes in polemical literature directed against opposing teachers; they are intended to marginalize them, not to engage their arguments.[121] Timothy, on the other hand, will be "a good servant of Christ Jesus" (4:6), faithful to Paul's teaching on faith and doctrine (4:7), an example to all believers (4:12), whose personal progress is visible to the whole community (4:15). This strategy of meta–contrast emphasizes Timothy's similarity to Paul in their faithful teaching and common opposition to deviant teaching. This presents Timothy as a model for the local community (τύπος, 4:12), just as Paul is model for all of his Christ–believing communities (ὑποτύπωσις, 1:16). Their exemplary function was future oriented, Paul being a model for those who were yet to believe the true gospel (1:16), and Timothy being a model of faithfulness to the gospel even when opposition would arise ("in later times," 4:1).[122] The point of including such stereotypes is therefore not to identify them or their teaching (which the readers would have known already), but to emphasize the contrast between false and true teaching,[123] and thereby to uphold Timothy as prototypical leader within the Ephesian community, capable of maintaining Paul's vision of Christian social identity even when challenged in the future.

Timothy's role is described specifically as example for local leaders. He is to resist "irreverent, silly myths" and be devoted to godliness, because his hope is in God "who is the Savior of all people" (4:6–10), demonstrating how to fulfill God's mission in the world (2:3–5). Timothy is to read Scripture and to teach (4:13), knowing that all things are made holy by "the word of God and prayer" (4:5), reflecting

---

120. Johnson, *First and Second Timothy*, 246.

121. Karris, "Polemic of the Pastoral Epistles," 551–55; Malina and Neyrey, "Conflict in Luke-Acts," 99–101.

122. Fiore argues that from the perspective of pseudepigraphy, this passage is an historical description projected back to Paul's days as prophetic (*Pastoral Epistles*, 89), but if identification of the opponents is not the intent of the passage, this is a moot point.

123. This is similar to Paul's use of Roman and Jewish paranaetic discourse, which overemphasizes the contrast between the two ways of life. See the discussion in chapter 6 on Eph 4:17ff.

the ministries of prayer and teaching that flow from God's mission in the world (2:1–7). Furthermore, this passage offers a detailed list of leadership functions. Some items relate to the leader's own life, such as training in godliness (4:6–7), hard work (4:10), and practicing what one teaches (4:15–16). Other items relate to community functions, such as avoiding silly myths (4:7), commanding, and teaching certain things (4:11), demonstrating exemplary conduct (4:12), and reading, exhorting, and teaching (4:13). The rhetoric of contrast in this passage suggests that its primary purpose is not so much to instruct Timothy, as to present Timothy as model for local leaders. Although Paul explicitly listed the character qualities for new leaders, he instructs local leaders indirectly through the instructions given to Timothy. No doubt, both aspiring and established leaders compared these instructions with their own leadership practice.

Paul's rhetorical strategy thus presents Timothy as a prototypical leader with whom local leaders could identify. Apparently, the earlier difficulties with leadership development in Corinth had not yet been fully resolved by the theological legitimation of local leadership that Ephesians had provided. The competitive spirit among the Ephesian leaders made it perhaps less desirable to instruct established leaders directly; Paul then circumvented this sensitivity by instructing them indirectly through Timothy. Thus, Paul enhanced category accessibility and clarified normative fit for both aspiring and established local leaders, empowering them to function more appropriately as impresarios of Christian social identity. This was crucial with regard to the future of Ephesian leadership, since without adequate normative fit and category accessibility, new generations of leaders would be more likely to repeat the errors that Paul had identified and corrected. Now, aspiring and established leaders are encouraged to identify in their leadership role with Timothy, and indirectly with Paul.

Disciplining the Identity Performance of the Community

In the previous sections, Paul embedded the style, character, and function of local leadership into his vision of Christian social identity. Paul next turns to the identity performance of several significant subgroups within the community. In a section that resembles a household code,[124]

---

124. So Quinn and Wacker, *First and Second Timothy*, 408ff. and Towner, *Timothy*

Paul encloses extended discussion on widows and elders between brief references to older and younger men and women (5:12), and to slaves (6:1–2). This passage has been noted for its lack of reciprocity and theological grounding, compared to the household code of Ephesians.[125] Others noted that it appears to reintroduce patriarchal structures into the community.[126] However, this passage seeks to bring the identity performance of widows and elders in line with their Christian identity. Caring for a widow in the family in "pleasing to God" (5:4), and refusal to do so stigmatizes someone as outgroup member ("unbeliever," 5:6). A "true widow" engages in prayer (5:5) and good works on behalf of the community (5:10), and thereby maintains the honor of the community before the outside world (5:7–8, 14–15). As to the elders, some "labor in preaching and teaching" (5:17), while the Scriptures are cited to support financial compensation as well as protection from false accusations (5:18–19). The public rebuke of an elder "that the rest may stand in fear" (5:20) has in view the prototypical role of leaders, even in their failures. Clearly, these instructions about social relationships, including various material provisions, are anchored in the Christian social identity of the community. Further motivations from an extended identity narrative about Christ's sacrifice (as in Eph 5:22–30) or about the gospel as entrusted to Paul are still fresh in the memory of the hearers from the previous sections. Horrell helpfully frames this passage by describing it a disciplining the performance of group members, which supposes that there are other ways to discipline their behavior.[127] It can be added that Paul's basis for this discipline is his vision of Christian social identity. That is, as engineer of social identity Paul infuses these roles with meaning from the foundational beliefs and values of Christian social identity.

Reinforcing the Leadership Exemplar

The last section contains Paul's closing charge to Timothy, which functions in the overall argument similarly to the closing section in

---

and Titus, 32ff.

125. See Marshall's excursus on the household code in the Pastorals, Marshall, *Pastoral Epistles*, 132–36.

126. Schüssler Fiorenza, *In Memory of Her*, 284–342.

127. Horrell, "Disciplining Performance," 112–13, 32.

Ephesians with the warfare metaphor (Eph 6:10–20). This third set of personal exhortations runs parallel with chapters 1 and 4, and connects the major themes of the letter together. Paul reviews the value of riches and patronage for Christian social identity. On the one hand, he warns against the desire for riches (6:9–10). The charge of being greedy is a standard charge in such a polemical exchange[128] and was undoubtedly directed towards the same individuals who were charged with false teaching (6:5).[129] Kelly argues that some teachers probably charged money for their teaching,[130] but in light of the polemical terminology, this is not certain. However, it is likely that Paul downgrades the importance of "a privileged educated group with time to discuss and speculate."[131] Moreover, Paul presents contentment with food and clothing (6:8) as normative fit, which must have appeared to most householders as very critical of basic patronage structures.[132] Paul defined Christian social identity on the social level of basic subsistence, so that the average community member is prototypical, and not the wealthier community patron. This benefits Timothy who could not compete with local leaders on the basis of wealth or status. On the other hand, Paul values the contributions of patronage to the community. He charges Timothy to instruct rich believers to "be rich in good works, to be generous and ready to share" (6:18). Instead of accumulating honor for themselves through patronage (6:17), they are to exercise general reciprocity without expectations of return, placing their hope in God's future compensation (6:19). Although applicable to the whole community, this would be especially applicable to the wealthier believers in their practice of leadership. Thus, Paul connects false teaching with a desire for honor and profit in a description of deviant leadership, while he connects general benefaction as community service with sound doctrine in a description of Christian leadership.

128. Karris lists greed as the first of 6 standard charges. The others are deception, not practicing what they preach, verbal quibbles, catalogue of vices, and success among women. See "Polemic of the Pastoral Epistles," 552–55.

129. So MacDonald, *The Pauline Churches*, 197–98.

130. Kelly, *Pastoral Epistles*, 135. Kidd suggests that this group represents some of the wealthier believing householders who served as house church leaders and who mistakenly thought that this function would bring them increasing honor and financial gain (Kidd, *Wealth and Beneficence*, 96–100).

131. Tamez, *Struggles for Power*, 62.

132. Ibid., 16 ff.

As climax of the letter, Timothy is charged, in the presence of God and by Christ's testimony before Pontius Pilate, to faithfully carry forward Paul's vision of Christian leadership.

Summary

Paul's leadership as identity management began with the construction of a chain of succession, from God to Christ to Paul to Timothy and beyond for the consistent maintenance of Christian social identity. Including Timothy in this line as prime exemplar for the Ephesian leaders empowered him to carry out his charge in Ephesus. Next, Paul reoriented the leadership styles as men and women participated in the ministries of prayer and teaching, and urged the community to monitor the character of those selected for leadership. These aspects of leadership were oriented towards God's mission in the world and His purpose for the church so that their leadership was framed as part of social identity enhancement. Finally, Paul turned to the significant subgroups in the community, notable widows and elders, to discipline their identity performance in line with the shared vision of Christian social identity. Paul's artistry as leader is evident in his creative adaptation of the foundational beliefs and values to create a chain of succession as well as an ideological framework within which local leadership could be embedded. Paul's impresarioship is evident in his presentation of Timothy as delegate and successor, and in his instructions for proper leadership style (1 Tim 2 and 4) which empowered Timothy and local leaders in their impresarioship. Paul's social engineering is evident in the way leadership and subgroup structures are addressed, that encourage various members to enact their Christian identity in appropriate ways.

How do the identity strategies of 1 Timothy compare with the earlier letters already analyzed? In Paul's earlier letters, the community as a whole is addressed in order to provide stability and cohesion for their Christian social identity. Such a sustained effort was needed to found and maintain new social groups in the Roman environment, in competition with Jewish identity. Paul serves as example, which positions him as ingroup prototype, and implicitly provides a leadership model. First Timothy departs from that pattern, since the social identity of the community is presented in more stereotyped fashion in order to shape and model leadership as the key to future identity maintenance. This change is occasioned by a change in addressee (from a community to a well known and trusted community leader) and a change in subject (from community formation to the structuring of leadership by a recognized ingroup prototype).

The Development of Local Leadership Patterns at Ephesus in 63 CE

Clearly, 1 Timothy is one of the key NT documents to study developing leadership. The letter seems to indicate that this development took place in a relatively stable Christ-believing community in Ephesus, but this is much debated. The focus of 1 Timothy on false teaching has been interpreted as an indication of serious deviance and instability in Ephesus. Several objections to his interpretation have been indicated. In general, ingroup deviance attracts a disproportionately larger share of the communication, so that its relative dominance in the letter signals the danger of deviance more so than its extent or strength.[133] Second, the rhetoric of contrast and deviance labeling functions as a foil for highlighting Timothy as model, without necessarily implying that the actual social situation was as black-and-white as the contrasts employed. Third, the references to common enemies as well as to common beliefs and values are typical of a friendship letter, with which 1 Timothy has some affinity.[134] Fourth, the use of stereotypes increases as the social stability of the group and its intergroup relations stabilize. Therefore, the dominance of communication about deviance in the letter cannot be straightforwardly interpreted as an indication that large numbers of Ephesian leaders and other believers had defected from Paul's gospel. Evidently, some leaders had defected (e.g., 1:3, 19–20), who undoubtedly influenced some other believers (e.g., 5:13–15), which created a need for new leadership (3:1ff.). But the rhetoric of deviance in 1 Timothy implies at the most a serious concern for discord on the part of a few leaders and a few of their followers, while the overall group, consisting of various house churches connected through a college of elders and through corporate teaching and worship events, is largely stable. Thus, Christian social identity

---

133. Brown, *Group Processes*, 141–42.
134. Fiore, *Personal Example*, 86–90.

appears stable in Ephesus and the community had sufficiently matured to conceive of its own identity performance as creating an attraction for outsiders.

This social setting, however, is interpreted quite differently if the rhetorical setting is interpreted as a pseudepigraphical device. In that case, the letter is addressed to a community where, in the author's view, leadership and community structures have become its dominant and defining features. Stereotyped traditional material is interpreted as a distant social memory of the historical Paul to claim his support for the current hierarchical authority structures. As well, the emphasis on deviance is often taken as an indication of serious divisions in the Pauline tradition.[135] Although this reading aims to take the letter's features straightforwardly as historical indicators, it is one-dimensional, extrapolating the rhetorical shift observed above only along a chronological axis of development. The conceptual tools of the social identity approach t ake into account the chronological, but also the social and the psychological axes. The letter is then read, not as an accommodation to existing Greco-Roman hierarchies, but as a correction of the excesses of the hierarchical patronage system, while carefully reinterpreting, adjusting, and refining household and leadership structures to align with Christian social identity. Thus, a social identity analysis concludes that the Ephesian church was largely stable and growing under Timothy's leadership, in spite of the danger of some deviant leaders and a handful of their followers, and that the church was in need of further developing its leadership structures.

Leadership Emergence. Although 1 Timothy discusses the rise of new leaders (3:1ff.), most of the letter is directed towards ordering already existing ministries and leadership roles.[136] Evidently, these roles needed to be clarified, consolidated, and kept in harmony with the founding leadership. First Timothy deals not so much with the emergence of a first generation of local leadership, but with the structuring of existing leadership and with securing local succession. However, local succession assumes the rise of new leadership, so some traces of leadership emergence processes can be expected in the virtue lists of 1 Tim 3:1ff.

---

135. See for instance Beker, *Heirs of Paul*, 36–47.
136. Herzer, "Rearranging the 'House of God,'" 558.

The character profile which Paul provides for aspiring leaders (3:1ff.) can be read as a model for gaining the social influence and trust necessary to grow into a leadership role. Characteristics such as being "above reproach . . . self-controlled . . . not a drunkard . . . not quarrelsome" (3:2–3) for the overseer are qualities that enhance a group member's social influence. Qualities like "respectable, hospitable . . . gentle" and a good reputation with outsiders (3:3, 7) point to group members who will likely be sought out for advice or direction. Those who are able to manage their own household well (3:4–5) are likely to be perceived as 'natural' leaders, especially if they desire to participate in the Pauline mission ("good work," 3:1). The characteristics for deacons run somewhat parallel, but contain some additional specifications. They are required to be tested before appointment (3:10),[137] affirming their trustworthiness, while their good service as deacon results in "good standing" (3:13), affirming that effective leadership enhances one's intragroup status. In other words, the virtue lists of 1 Tim 3 can be read through the lens of social identity theory as standard procedures for the emergence of new leadership in a stable community with existing leadership structures.

Based on this reading, these virtue lists encourage the rise of new believers into leadership roles to maintain or increase the ranks of leaders, rather than the 'promotion' of existing leaders to a new level of leadership. The major concerns of 1 Timothy align with this interpretation. The letter's concern about false teaching suggests that new leaders were likely needed as replacement for those who had fallen prey to heresy. The letter's clear missionary setting suggests that new leaders were needed as hosts for new house churches to facilitate the community's expansion. Since the letter aims to provide continuity of leadership in order to maintain Christian social identity, the goal of these virtue lists seems to be to maintain and possibly to increase the ranks of current leaders.

Alternatively, Campbell proposes that the overseer of 3:1 is a city overseer, supervising the city's house churches and their householder-leaders, which implies a new level of leadership. He argues that a

---

137. The phrase introducing the requirement for testing, καὶ οὗτοι δὲ seems to imply a comparison with the overseer, who also needed to be tested, but which was not listed in the overseer's virtue list. However, Paul returns to the testing of the overseer in 5:17ff. (if elder is taken as referring to the same position as overseer). See Knight, *Pastoral Epistles*, 169.

householder as de facto leader of the church in his house hardly needed to be encouraged to aspire to a role of oversight since he already exercised that function, unless this oversight had a broader range beyond his own household.[138] It is unlikely, however, that a standardized character list for the emergence of new leadership appears so long after leadership structures with elders, deacons, and a board (πρεσβυτέριον, 4:14, cf. 5:17ff) are effectively functioning, especially in such a highly structured society which was long familiar with such character lists. Campbell compensates for this difficulty by suggesting that an earlier version of the list used for house church leaders is now modified to apply to the city overseer.[139] Campbell offers no support for this suggestion, but this is in fact quite likely. Acts records that Paul's itinerant ministry was based out of households (16:15, 40; 17:5-7; 18:1-3, 7, 8; 18:19). These households were selected at least in part by the faithfulness of the householder to Christ, as Lydia expressly asks, "if you have judged me to be faithful to the Lord, come to my house and stay" (Acts 16:15), and as is narrated about Titius Justus ("a worshiper of God," Acts 18:7). This parallels the triple gospel tradition where Jesus sends out the Twelve with instructions to find a home as basis of operations (Matt. 10:11-14; Mark 6:10-11; Luke 9:4-5). Matthew elaborates that these homes are to be worthy (ἄξιός, 10:11, 13), deserving of peace (Matt. 10:13, cf. Luke 10:5-7). It is remarkable that several early Christian traditions run parallel in their esteem of worthy households as basis for evangelistic operations, which probably reflects a broad Christian practice in the mid to late first century. Thus, this triple gospel tradition, along with the Acts record, may well provide the background for the virtue lists of 1 Tim 3:2-13 with their prominent household language. That is, the virtue lists represent the mission instructions of Jesus, contextualized by Paul as Roman character lists, in order to facilitate the expansion of the church. Thus, it is likely that earlier virtue lists circulated, as Campbell suggested, but a 'new and improved' version in 1 Tim 3 does not support Campbell's proposal for a new level of leadership. Instead, it highlights the missionary dimension of the household motif, contextualized for a Roman world, which confirms the present analysis that 1 Tim 3 envisions the emergence

---

138. Campbell, *The Elders*, 197-98. Söding even suggests that the desire for oversight indicates the start of an ecclesial career ("1 Timotheus 3," 77).

139. Campbell, *The Elders*, 199.

of new leaders into existing leadership ranks as an effective way to combat the fall-out of heresy and to facilitate the church's missionary expansion.

Leadership Maintenance. First Timothy is mainly concerned with leadership maintenance. Paul described his own central role in proclaiming the gospel to maintain his own leadership. He presented Timothy as faithful follower, similar to himself and prototypical in his leadership, which legitimated and maintained Timothy's leadership. Paul also maintained local leadership by instructing Timothy to organize local leadership.

Paul claimed for himself a prominent place as ingroup prototype and founding member, since the message that defines Christian identity, the "gospel of the glory of the blessed God," had been entrusted to him (1:11). Paul turned the narrative about his conversion into a community archetype of the grace of God and salvation through Jesus Christ (1:14–16). Most of the community aligned with Paul and his message (1:8ff), but some did not. Paul stigmatized their teaching and behavior as deviant, because it would inevitably involve a redefinition of the ingroup prototype, which threatened the social cohesion of the group as centered in Paul's vision of Christian social identity. By accentuating his own vision of Christian social identity and stigmatizing these teachers' vision, Paul thus maintained his own leadership (as artist of social identity).

With the letter addressed to Timothy, and over his shoulders to the Ephesian community, the more important issue was to affirm and legitimate Timothy's leadership. Oddly enough, Timothy was urged to *conform* himself to Paul's prototype, fighting the same "good warfare" as Paul (1:18–19) while he was presented as a prototypical leader similar to Paul, who would faithfully maintain Paul's vision for Christian social identity. The question arises why Timothy needed to be urged to conform to the ingroup prototype, as if Paul doubted his ability or willingness to do so.

Kelly supposes that Timothy was unsure and timid and needed such encouragement.[140] Such encouragement would have been welcome, for Timothy faced a daunting task. Established Ephesian leaders may well have considered Timothy unsuitable for leadership, since he was not local, nor a householder, nor an apostle with revelatory claims

---

140. Kelly, *Pastoral Epistles*, 105–6, 42.

and relatively young besides (4:12).[141] Yet, Timothy had functioned alongside Paul as coworker, co-author, and delegate, presumably modeling the ingroup prototype, so that it appears inconsistent that he should now be urged to conform to this same ingroup prototype. Moreover, Paul himself appears confident of Timothy's prototypicality, since he had left him in Ephesus to deal with deviance, a task that by its very nature implies conformity to the prototype. If Timothy was not deficient in Paul's eyes, then Paul's exhortation of Timothy to conform to the prototype must have had some other reason.

Wolters found that the exhortation to "not neglect the gift" (4:14) comes from official letters to junior officers to carry out the charge of their office.[142] In this light, the reference to Timothy's "youth" suggests that Timothy is perceived as 'junior' by some of the senior leaders in Ephesus who resisted his leadership and "looked down" (καταφρονέω, 4:12) on him. In this case, Paul's charge that Timothy conform to the prototype is most likely intended to encourage other 'young' candidates for leadership (cf. 3:1) who may have faced a similar disrespect from senior leaders and to instruct these senior leaders with the community to welcome new leaders in the church.[143] Thus, the legitimation of Timothy's leadership serves to maintain and expand the community leadership. Paul's presentation of Timothy (as impresario of identity) does not suggest some deficiency on Timothy's part, but is rather intended to demonstrate his exemplary faithfulness to Paul's vision of Christian social identity, in order to encourage further leadership development in Ephesus as senior and junior leaders cooperate.

After securing his own central role as apostle and legitimating Timothy's leadership as exemplary, Paul provides structures for local leadership.[144] Paul affirms regulatory structures, which control the right and manner in which to speak to the community.[145] Such structures

---

141. Knight cites Polybius and Irenaeus to show that "youth" can refer to someone up to age forty (*Pastoral Epistles*, 205).

142. Wolter, *Paulustradition*, 186–88.

143. Marshall recognizes in these instructions both the personal dimension of encouragement for Timothy as well as the corporate dimension of reminding the church of Timothy's authority (*Pastoral Epistles*, 564).

144. Such structures are so prevalent in 1 Timothy that Dibelius and Conzelmann characterize the letter as a document regulating church order (*Pastoral Epistles*, 5–7).

145. For an anthropological model for classifying and controlling space, especially about who has the right top speak when, where, to whom and with what purpose, see

must already have been functioning in the Ephesian community, since speaking privileges in households and in private non-household space (such as the school of Tyrannus, Acts 19:9)[146] were controlled by the householder or by the owner or tenant of a building. Such control of access to public speech is probably part of the ministry of oversight (3:1): a householder-leader assisted Paul and Timothy by—among other things—faithfully exercising control of speech in his own household in line with apostolic tradition. Likewise, the dedication of some elders to preaching and teaching (5:17) suggests that local leadership exercised such control in the private non-household setting, a broader span of control that most likely required collegial coordination, with Timothy having the final say. These structures to control speaking privileges probably imply that the "overseer" of 3:1 is a generic, functional label for the honorary position of "elder" in 5:17-25, so that these terms refer to the same person but from different perspectives.[147] These elders are the householders who oversee a church in their own house.[148] Thus, elders exercise a ministry of oversight, which includes supervision of preaching and teaching, both in its content and in access to speaking opportunities.

By embedding control of speech in the ministry of oversight, Paul affirms the authority of local leaders as a way to maintain his vision of Christian social identity. It also allows Paul to distinguish between all elders who control access to speech and some elders who labor to provide the content of speech in their ministry of preaching and teaching. Van Houwelingen argues well that 5:17 is not intended to establish a two or even threefold classification of elders (general elders; those who

---

Neyrey, "'Teaching You in Public and from House to House,'" 72–85.

146. Was Tyrannus the hall's owner, the hall's patron or an orator? Was he a believer so that he cooperated with Paul in controlling access to speaking privilege, or did he rent it to Paul? And if rented, who would have sponsored it and thus secured the right to control such speaking privileges? For discussion, see ibid., 91; Fitzmyer, *Acts*, 648; and Witherington, *Acts*, 574–76.

147. Marshall, *Pastoral Epistles*, 177–80, lists five interpretations for the relationship between "overseer" and "elders" and indicates that the option above is the more common interpretation.

148. Conform Campbell, *The Elders*, 120 and 31, although he also believes that this overseer refers to a position of leadership among and over the collective elders (ibid., 194–96). While the current study the overseer of 3:1 as a householder moving into oversight of a church in his house, and thus joining other householder-elders, of which some might have a larger collective responsibility as well.

manage well; those who also teach),[149] but he overlooks the fact that depending on seniority, some elders might have more extensive ministries than others, which is behind the distinction that Kelly makes between "all elders" and "executive officials."[150] For instance, control of access could be exercised relatively easily by new leaders under supervision by Timothy or another senior leader, while preaching and teaching required the kind of labor for which financial compensation was needed.[151] Campbell argues that householder-leaders would hardly need financial support, since they supported the church in their house from their own resources. He concludes that this stipulation points in the direction of the single overseer over the city in an early move towards monepiscopacy.[152] Campbell's position is well taken but he overlooks the different forms of oversight that accompany the dual teaching venue of household and private non-household space. All householders who host a church in their house exercise oversight by virtue of their role as head of the household. Believers who aspire to such oversight submit themselves to a examination process under Timothy's supervision that determines their eligibility. These householder-overseers also function collectively as a group of elders in the private non-household space, where a more extensive preaching and teaching ministry takes place. In that context, some of the household-overseers devote additional effort to ruling well, i.e. to controlling the content of and access to this teaching platform. This extra effort appears to go substantially beyond the usual obligations of benefaction and stretches the resources of these householder-overseers, so that financial compensation is required.

These structures forge significant connections between Paul, Timothy, and local leadership. Paul is presented as authorized spokesman for the gospel, who faithfully teaches it and controls access to speech for others. Apparently, this control was not exercised well after Paul's departure, so that Timothy as Paul's authorized delegate has taken over this function; he faithfully preaches Paul's gospel and controls

149. Houwelingen, *Timoteüs en Titus*, 133.

150. Kelly, *Pastoral Epistles*, 125–26, although his terminology is somewhat anachronistic.

151. Houwelingen suggests that "double" honor refers to immaterial honor in the sense of respect and material honor in the form of a stipend (*Timoteüs en Titus*, 131–32).

152. Campbell, *The Elders*, 200.

speaking privileges by restricting some (1:3ff.) and mobilizing others (5:17ff). Only those who align themselves with Paul and Timothy in the prescribed authority structure will gain access to speech. It seems unlikely that any succession of Timothy in his supervisory role is in view, but these structures certainly serve to institute maintenance of Christian social identity by local leadership loyal to the Pauline tradition. Thus, the authority structure extends through Timothy to local leaders to provide cohesion and continuity for Christian social identity.

Although these instructions fall short of the type of church law that one finds in later church orders, it is the beginning thereof. Here, local leadership had moved beyond the oversight of single households and increased its span of coordination. With increasing influence comes increasing control over who gains access to such influence and how various subgroups are controlled. Paul initiates various identity-embedding structures (the leader as engineer) that secure faithful identity maintenance through Timothy's agency and those whom he approves.

Leadership Succession. Leadership maintenance is a dominant theme in 1 Timothy, but Timothy's role in Ephesus is temporary, so that the focus of the letter is on continuity of leadership from Paul and Timothy to local leadership. Evidently, succession is a major concern. Stepp identified four patterns of succession in 1 Timothy: from Christ to Paul, from Paul to Timothy, from the elders to Timothy, and somewhat less evident from Paul and Timothy to local leadership.[153] The first two patterns have already been discussed above. It was noted that Paul's self-presentation as well as his presentation of Timothy created an identity narrative that portrayed a particular structure of leadership and authority as starting point for legitimate local succession. The last two patterns need to be addressed now.

As *artist* of succession, a leader needs high intragroup status and adequate social power to initiate succession. This is clearly the case for Paul. As argued above, Paul was likely perceived as charismatic leader by the Ephesian community, since they had observed his difficult but successful conflict resolution in Corinth. They had also observed Paul's leadership in Ephesus. Paul formed a new community

---

153. See the introduction of Stepp's research in chapter 3, "The Leader as Engineer." For the references to these patterns of succession, see Stepp, *Leadership Succession*, 117ff., 135ff., 148–49, and 150, respectively.

with individuals who had previously identified with the synagogue and/or with other religious groups ("magic arts"), and who continued to interact with their kinship and other civic groups (Acts 19:8–14),[154] which required Paul to interact with various ethnic, religious, and civic identities.[155] The formation of the Ephesian community, including its role as center for further evangelistic activity (Acts 19:10), added to the perception of Paul as charismatic leader. Hence, Paul's status as apostle and teacher does not appear to have been questioned by the majority of the Ephesus community members, which implies that he had the status and social power to present Timothy as delegate and to institute further levels of succession.

However, Timothy's status and social power were ambiguous at best. New challenges in Ephesus required clear leadership, which Paul was unable to provide directly. While Timothy's status as coworker of Paul was likely unchallenged, this may not have been the case for his independent leadership. Since Timothy was not an apostle, nor of the local elite, he had few if any of the normal social resources to fall back on in time of conflict, unlike local householders.[156] Timothy's task to restrict certain false teachers often pitted him against such local householders, and these normal differences in social power could easily render Timothy's leadership ineffective. Polaski notes this discrepancy and argues that "Timothy" represents non-household leadership on the basis of prophecy over against the householder-leadership based on social status.[157] Horrell analyzes this discrepancy as a gradual development from itinerant to resident leaders, where 1 Timothy seeks to "legitimate the power and position of the resident male leaders and

---

154. The distinction between religious, civic and kinship groups is to some extent anachronistic, since in Paul's world almost any group had distinct religious components, as Harland ably demonstrated (Harland, *Associations, Synagogues, and Congregations*).

155. See Harland, *Dynamics of Identity in the World of the Early Christians*, which was published too late to be included in the research for this project.

156. Malina suggests that Timothy as change agent shared status and other characteristics with the main group of 'clients,' which may perhaps be taken as indication that Timothy has a social status in his native city comparable with the status of some of the Ephesian householder-overseers (*Timothy: Paul's Closest Associate*, 62). It is unclear, however, whether this would have automatically resulted in social status for Timoth in another city like Ephesus.

157. Polaski, "Let No One Despise Your Youth," 257–61.

the household structure upon which their leadership was based."[158] Polaski and Horell thus suggest a tension between two forms of leadership but disagree on the intention of the author: Polaski believes that 1 Timothy promotes non-household leadership to break the hold of householders on the leadership of the community, while Horrell reads 1 Timothy as accommodation and perhaps even a surrender to the existing power base of local householders. These contrary positions indicate that other presuppositions play a role in this construction beyond the immediate textual evidence, namely that 'Timothy' stands for a particular form of leadership late in the first century. A better proposal comes from Tamez who interprets this tension as an indication that "the wealthy are putting pressure on the young Timothy, because they think that since they are benefactors they have rights over the community and its leaders."[159] It might be added that along with benefaction, seniority is a likely concern. Thus, this tension does not necessarily indicate conflicting views of office late in the first century, but simply refers to the ambiguity of Timothy's intragroup status and social power as leader in Ephesus.

As *impresario* of succession, Paul had to resolve Timothy's ambiguous status in order to ensure that only loyal local leaders become eligible for succession. The theoretical account of succession suggests that Timothy should be presented as similar to Paul and as prototypical for the community. Paul presented Timothy as his "true child" (1:2, 18); that is, Timothy is uniquely similar to Paul, and can be expected to be a central model for the group.[160] Paul paralleled his own calling (1:11, 2:7) and example (1:16) with Timothy's calling (1:18; 4:14) and example (4:12, 15), which legitimated Timothy's leadership and pointed to his sacrificial service. Timothy's leadership commended him to the community as "a good servant of Christ" (4:6; cf. 6:11), whose progress should be publicly evident (4:15). Thus, Paul presented Timothy as prototypical leader, committed to the same vision, with the same willingness to sacrifice. By emphasizing Timothy's prophetic call, Paul attributed charisma to him, while the reference to his appointment by the elders reminded the community of Timothy's local recognition. Paul's rhetoric promoted recognition

158. Horrell, "Leadership Patterns," 338–39.
159. Tamez, *Struggles for Power*, 16.
160. Cf. similar comments by Polaski, "Let No One Despise Your Youth," 258–59.

of Timothy's leadership status and social power in Ephesus, and empowered him to lead the community through its next stages of development.

As *engineer* of succession, Paul provided structures for succession. Leaders are to be selected on the basis of their loyalty to God's mission (2:3-7) and the church's purpose in this world (3:14-16), remaining loyal to Paul's vision of Christian social identity. This constitutes part of Paul's heritage and his instructions ensure continued institutional vitality. Leaders are also to be selected on the basis of character (3:1-13), which marks them as prototypical members who live exemplary lives in the context of their homes, the Christian community and the broader environment. Moreover, Paul's instructions for Timothy's leadership (4:6-16) provide an accessible and effective leadership model to be emulated by local leadership. This leadership style is also part of Paul's heritage; since these instructions lead local leaders to adopt this leadership style, they ensure continuity of manner. These structures effectively connect local leaders with Timothy and Paul as loyal followers and prototypical for the community, which is precisely what Paul needed to accomplish in securing effective and appropriate succession.

How would the next generation of leaders, after those designated in 1 Timothy, negotiate social change or even conflict? Quite likely, they would have encountered situations where it was not immediately evident which side aligned with the Pauline tradition. Appeals to the Pauline tradition might not help, since both sides might claim it, and appeals to local bases of authority might make matters worse. It would be natural in such a situation to look for an outside authority to adjudicate the conflict. This was, after all, the role which Timothy and before him Paul had fulfilled. In a hierarchical, collectivist society, this would be perceived as a natural solution. It may well be that Paul's argument favoring Timothy's legitimate authority laid the foundation for the increasing prominence of the later bishops as local and even regional authorities, even if Paul did not have such a structure in mind at the time of writing.

Conclusions

The previous chapter on Ephesians showed the presence of groups of recognized leaders with significant status and authority in the community, but the description of these leaders fell short of indicating full-fledged institutionalized structures like church office. These leadership positions contained components such as duration, recognition, and authority, which indicates that their function was more than incidental or situational, while the position of apostles and prophets also contained the component of legitimation. The situation in 1 Timothy is more complex, and calls for a more extended discussion of church office before concluding with the usual summary on leadership patterns.

The Overseer and the Elders

An age-old question concerns the relationship between the overseer and the elders, and whether these labels in 1 Timothy refer to an organizational office. It will be helpful to first discuss the question whether "overseer" and "elder" refer to an office, which will then help to discern the relationship between these two terms.[161]

Oversight (ἐπισκοπή, 3:1) is (a) a function of some duration, which by its very nature requires (b) recognition by the community as well as (c) the ability to exercise authority. This is implied in the list of characteristics (3:2-7), which enlists people who are well respected in the community and outside, partly because of their ability to exercise their household authority in a fitting manner. For those who wish to enter into a position of oversight, this list functions as part of a selection process, which (d) provides legitimation as well as the beginning of (e) legal arrangements for the position. However, legitimacy and legality are not fully described in this character list, while (f) provisions for position maintenance are also missing. Only succession (f) is addressed by the opening statement (3:1) which encourages group members to aspire to the position of oversight.

The function of elders (πρεσβύτεροι, 5:17ff.) also contains the components of (a) duration, (b) community recognition, and (c) authority.

---

161. The letters (a) through (f) in the following analysis refer to the six components of an organizational office, as outlined mostly by Brockhaus, *Charisma und Amt*, 24 and 123. See pp. 174-76 for the initial discussion and the following table for an overview.

The function is (d) legitimated by an appointment procedure through the laying on of hands (5:22; cf. 4:14). At least some elders may deserve financial compensation for their leadership (5:17–18), which implies (d) further legitimation of their function, (e) possible legal arrangements on their behalf, and (f) provisions for their maintenance. Accountability procedures are operative to deal with accusations against an elder as well as with those found guilty (5:19–21), which implies (d) the possibility and risk of illegitimate authority, (e) legal arrangements to deal with illegitimacy, and (f) provisions for maintenance of legitimate leadership by the removal of illegitimate leadership. The element of succession (f) is addressed explicitly in the appointment procedure for elders, and implicitly in the recognition that some elders rule well and are devoted to a teaching ministry, suggesting that elders can grow from lesser to greater responsibilities.

Table 7.2: Components of Office in 1 Timothy

	ἐπισκοπή 1 Tim 3:1	πρεσβύτεροι 1 Tim 5:17
(a) Duration	Yes	Yes
(b) Community recognition	Yes	Yes
(c) Authority and Status	Yes	Yes
(d) Legitimation through commission or ordination	Partial	Yes
(e) Legal arrangements	Partial	Yes
(f) Provisions for maintenance and succession	No (succession only implied)	Yes

Thus, the description of the overseer contains many but not all components of office, while the description of elders contains them all. Campbell and Söding propose that the overseer is a new leader above the elders, representing a move towards monepiscopacy.[162] In that case, the relative incompleteness of the description of the overseer in terms of church office might be taken as a sign that this office was relatively new and still being developed. The overseer is pictured as arising from the elders, which fits the observation that some elders "rule well" (καλῶς προεστῶτες, 5:17) and thereby distinguish themselves

---

162. Söding, "1 Timotheus 3," 71; Campbell, *The Elders*, 194–96. For Campbell's further views on the relationships between the overseer and elder, see pp. 182–93.

from others. However, if the office of elder were already fully circumscribed in all its components, including financial compensation and regulations for maintenance and dismissal, why would the office of overseer as leader over the elders be left so ill defined? Why would the office of overseer be circumscribed with a listing of basic household characteristics (3:2-7), while the qualifications of ruling and teaching are attributed not to this one person but to a subgroup of elders (5:17)? And would not an elder functioning as single overseer deserve financial compensation, rather than several elders who rule and teach well? It seems, then, that in this case, the description of the overseer and the regulations for elders are mismatched so that the proposal of Campbell and Söding lacks support from the text.

The present study proposed above to see the one aspiring to oversight as a householder desiring to host a (new) house church, either to accommodate the church's expansion or to replace a leader lost through deviance (or both). This householder would naturally oversee the activities in his own house, even if various non-household members took part. Thus, a selection process was required, since not any householder would do. This is reflected in the list of basic household characteristics (3:2-7). Collectively, these householder-leaders are designated as elders, some of whom take upon themselves a broader ministry of oversight and teaching in the more public, non-household ministry (5:17ff.), as is reported in Acts (19:9-10). In this case, the qualifications of 3:2-7 and the regulations of 5:17-25 complement one another, applying to all overseer-elders equally. The only exception is financial compensation for only those elders who have distinguished themselves from other elders through their broader scope of ministry.

On this scenario, the office of oversight and the function of elder designate the same leadership position. Most leaders would be local householders, who would naturally oversee the church in their house. Their activity of leading or presiding is often indicated with προΐστημι (5:17; cf. 3:4-5, 12). Their activity of oversight is indicated with ἐπισκοπή (3:1), and their function as such with ἐπίσκοπος (3:2). In their role as respected and senior community leader, they bore the title πρεσβύτεροι (5:17ff). These titles refer to the same leader, viewed from the perspective of his social status (presiding householder), function (overseer) or community status (elder).[163]

---

163. Marshall comes to a very similar proposal, although he does not analyze each

Therefore, the function of overseer/elder contains all the components that according to Brockhaus make up a duly instituted church office. An interesting caveat is whether this office is considered to exist independently of the person fulfilling it, so that the office as such is passed on to the next office holder. For instance, the function of oversight (ἐπισκοπή, 3:1) is often translated as "the office of overseer" (ESV, NASB) or "the office of a bishop" (KJV, RSV). Together with the related word "overseer" or "bishop" (ἐπίσκοπος, 3:2), these terms clearly indicate a recognized community function in the Hellenistic world.[164] The choice of such a generic term enhances category accessibility for group members, since they have a basic understanding of such leadership, even if Paul subsequently redefines parts of it. It is not yet clear, however, if 1 Timothy refers to this function of oversight as an organizational slot independent of the person filling it. That is, there is no suggestion that a vacancy is created when an overseer or elder ceases to function as community leader, for which then another candidate must be sought. Even though the functions of overseer and elder denote a familiar leadership category, they continue to be related to certain people fulfilling particular functions. New overseers are sought, not because of organizational 'slots' to fill, but because the community is expanding and new hosts are necessary, or because some communities have suffered at the hands of a deviant leader so that they need new leadership. The community and its mission are primary, and those who hold a position of oversight do so only to the extent that they serve the community.[165]

The further development, where elder and bishop become distinct categories, essential in defining the essence of the church, is not yet in view in 1 Timothy. This further development can probably be explained as a shift in social identification. Paul defined the ingroup prototype with reference to the models provided by Christ and by his own ministry. He demonstrated that self-sacrifice on behalf of the community was the primary mode of leadership. Although organization and institutionalization were needed and indeed inevitable, this

---

function for its components of office. Also, he includes Titus in his analysis, while this chapter focuses exclusively on 1 Timothy. See Marshall, *Pastoral Epistles*, 180–81.

164. Rohde, "*Episkopos*," 36.

165. Which is, from a different perspective, the same point that Clarke makes (Clarke, *Serve the Community*, 233–47), although he does not include the Pastorals in his study.

focus on the centrality of Christ and Paul's gospel ministry as center of Christian social identity relativizes the concept of office as secondary to the person providing leadership. However, as Christ-believing communities developed further, the distinctive aspects of their organization and leadership likely rose in significance as visible markers for defining their distinctive Christian social identity in their social world in a way that differed from Paul's time. This allowed community members to identify with visible organizational and leadership structures, so that a particular form of hierarchy could become an additional identity marker for the true church. In such a context, "office" may loose its close connection to the person filling it, and can begin to function as an "organizational slot," which moreover may become a defining dimension for the social identity of the group. This appears to be the case in Ignatius' letters, but that would be the subject of another study.[166]

The Deacons

The term διάκονος ("servant, deacon," 3:8) has the basic meaning of service rendered on behalf of a significant other,[167] which is clearly evident in Paul's service of Christ (διακονία, 1:12) and Timothy's performance as servant of Christ (διάκονος, 4:6). However, διάκονος may also refer to an office, such as an "attendant or official in a temple or religious guild,"[168] which is in view in 3:8–13. Collins labels this use as "institutional language that has developed around this paring of bishop and deacon."[169] The position of the deacon after the overseer, as well as the shorter description, suggests that the office plays a subordinate role to the overseer. Since a further description of the deacon's function is lacking, the exact relationship between the deacons and the overseer remains uncertain.[170]

---

166. For a comparison of the leadership structure in the Pastoral Epistles and the post-apostolic age, see Mounce's insightful excursus on the topic (Mounce, *Pastoral Epistles*, 186–92).
167. Weiser, "*Diakoneo, Diakonia, Diakonos*," 1:302.
168. LSJ, s.v. διάκονος and DBAG, s.v. διάκονος.
169. Collins, *Deacons and the Church*, 99.
170. Marshall, *Pastoral Epistles*, 487–88.

Like the overseer, this is also (a) a function of some duration, for which respectable group members are enlisted as (b) recognized by the community. The function of a deacon as authorized servant of a significant other, as well as the requirement that he manages his own household well implies that (c) some kind of authority attaches to the office. Candidates must be tested beforehand, and subsequent good service leads to a rise in status, which implies that (c) the officeholder has a distinct status within the community. It also implies that his function in office has an identifiable beginning and end, which suggests procedures of appointment, which are not discussed in the text. The selection process combined with these procedures of appointment provides (d) the required legitimation for this office and indicates the beginnings of (e) legal arrangements to secure the position. Yet, such legal arrangements are not detailed any further. No explicit instructions deal with (f) financial compensation or succession. The lack of these components of office, as well as the absence of this office in the letter to Titus, suggests that this office has a more ad hoc character, with people being appointed as needs arise.

Collins suggests that serving as deacon may have functioned as an apprenticeship in anticipation of more responsible service in the church,[171] which he deduces from the test required for becoming a deacon, and from the good standing gained upon having served well in the office (3:13). Good standing likely refers to growing respect for the deacon in general, which parallels the processes of social influence and social attraction in leadership emergence. Great "confidence" (παρρησία) in the faith likely refers to boldness of expression, both before the church and the outside world.[172] Marshall interprets this word instead as "confidence" because of the prepositional phrase "in the faith that is in Christ Jesus," so that the boldness is directed towards Christ in faith.[173] However, serving as deacon (or overseer) has a non-household and thus more public dimension, not just for the believing community but also in the perception of the outside world. This public dimension is highlighted in the following verses (3:15–16) which tell of the public proclamation of the mystery of the faith which the church

---

171. Collins, *Deacons and the Church*, 99. Johnson suggests that deacons "served as a stage toward a still higher rank" (*First and Second Timothy*, 226).

172. Thus, Mounce, *Pastoral Epistles*, 206. See also DBAG, s.v. παρρησία.

173. Marshall, *Pastoral Epistles*, 496–97. So also the RSV, NASB, NIV and ESV.

is to uphold. Thus, it is not so much boldness towards Christ, but boldness in expressing the faith towards the church and the outside world that is in view. In all likelihood, this indicates a growing respect for the deacon's ability in communicating the gospel, both within and outside the Christian community. Of, in terms of social identity theory, serving as deacon provides the opportunity to grow in social influence and social attraction within the community; continued effective service leads to a greater intragroup status and to the attribution of leadership qualities to the person involved. This social process could over time lead to being perceived as senior leader within the community. Collins may well be right, then, that serving as deacon prepares for further responsibilities as overseer,[174] although the text itself is not explicit about this. Thus, the function of a deacon may be described as serving Christ and the community on behalf of the bishop, with the possibility of aspiring to the function of overseer upon the completion of the task.

Women in Office

First Timothy is notorious for the discussions it generates about the role of women in ministry, not least because it appears more restrictive than some of Paul's earlier letters, Acts, and the Gospels. There is no space to engage fully with this important debate, but a few comments from a social identity approach can be offered.

To begin with, it is unlikely that the enlisted widows (5:3–16) represent a leadership office. Although being a widow evidently involves (a) duration and (b) community recognition, which may well result in (c) a special intragroup status. In addition, (f) some widows are eligible for financial support (5:4, 8, 16), while the prescriptions of character can be taken as (e) legal arrangements. However, financial support for some widows is necessary because of their absolute lack of other sources of support and it is legitimated by the ingroup values of godliness (5:4) and community service (5:10–11). Godliness implies the obligation to provide for needy household members and the church functions as fictive household for widows without family. The community is motivated to provide for such widows as if they were members of their own household. A widow who had served the community has demonstrated that she practiced such godliness, and

---

174. Collins, *Deacons and the Church*, 99.

demonstrated by her prototypical behavior that she closely identifies with the group. Thus, she is eligible to receive support, unlike others who did not demonstrate similar commitment to social identification with the group. Thus, the 'regulations' of the passage serve to highlight the social identification of both the community in providing support and the widow in receiving it, but only with regard to how to assist poor ingroup members. By contrast, support for some elders is legitimated as financial compensation for their dedication to oversight and teaching, which maintains and enhances the social identity of the community. This, too, highlights social identification processes that motivate the group towards support, and the elders towards proper labors, but now with regard to social influence and leadership.[175]

Moreover, a distinction is made between older widows who deserve support as long as they have no other resources, and younger widows who should marry again (5:11–16). The character list (5:9–10) describes the older widow as a consistent model and prototypical community member with a proven tack record of group-oriented service. By contrast, the younger widow has no such track record and is in danger of abandoning group values by "going from house to house" and "saying what they should not" (5:11–13). Thus, a younger widow is a risk[176] for compromising community values and misrepresenting the ingroup prototype, so she should marry and manage her household (5:14). Schüssler Fiorenza believes that this testifies to the patriarchalization of the early church, where earlier freedom for female leadership was restricted by a renewed orientation towards patriarchal structures.[177] However, Paul's reference to "running the household" (οἰκοδεσποτεῖν)[178] focuses not so much on the woman's submission to a new husband, but on using her household as a basis for ministry, just like older widows had done in raising children, offering hospi-

---

175. For some brief overviews of the role of widows, see Johnson, *First and Second Timothy*, 271ff.; and Horrell, "Disciplining Performance," 117ff.

176. Osiek et al., *A Woman's Place*, 91–92.

177. Schüssler Fiorenza, *In Memory of Her*, 312. She interprets 1 Tim 5:14 as a contradiction of the authentic Paul who advocated abstention from marriage in 1 Cor 7:39ff.

178. A *hapax legomenon* in the NT, used sparingly elsewhere in astrological contexts (a zodiacal sign reigning over human life), but referring to rulling or running the household in this context. See DBAG, s.v. οἰκοδεσποτέω. LN even translate the word "to command and give leadership to a household" (1:250).

tality and caring for the afflicted. The reference to hospitality likely refers to hosting fellow believers in the house, whether for individual or community meetings, and this would give the hostess a measure of influence in a house church meeting under her roof.[179] Such activity would demonstrate godliness and reinforce Christian community values, while church support might tempt young widows to neglect their household and might even support false teaching, since it would tend to confirm celibacy in the eyes of some (cf. 4:3)[180] and it might provide these women the opportunity and social influence to teach the wrong things (5:13, 15). Thus, both older and younger widows are empowered to serve the community, the one while being supported by the community, the other by marrying and using her household as a basis for service.

A further discussion of women's roles relates to deacons. It is likely that "women" (γυναῖκας, 3:11)[181] in the middle of the character list for deacons refers to women who functioned as deacon, but it is often suggested that the term refers to a deacon's wife.[182] The introduction of these women by "likewise" (ὡσαύτως, 3:11) parallels the introduction of deacons (3:8) and may suggest that a third category is here in view. However, the discussion of "women" reverts to deacons in v. 12 so these "women" are likely part of the larger category of deacons. But then, the same word refers to the wife of the overseer or deacon (μιᾶς γυναικὸς ἄνδρα / ἄνδρες, 3:2, 12), while these "woman" are not called διάκονοι in 3:11. This leads Knight to suggest that the wife of the deacon is in view, to be examined before she served alongside her husband.[183] However, γυνή (3:2, 12) means "woman," even if in the context it refers to someone's wife; the structural and semantic parallels of 3:11 with 3:2 and 8 argue for a more official position of the women involved; and if a separate discussion of the deacon's wife is warranted, the absence

---

179. Osiek et al., *A Woman's Place*, 132.

180. Older widows over 60 were not expected to remarry in Roman times, but this was different for the younger ones (Witherington, *Letters and Homilies*, 270).

181. KJV, NKJV, NIV, ESV translate γυναῖκας with "wives," often inserting the pronoun "their" in order to contextualize the translation; NASB, RSV, TNIV and The Message have the literal rendering "women."

182. Knight, *Pastoral Epistles*, 170-71, who discusses for options for the interpretation of this verse.

183. This paragraph thus far follows the argument of Ibid., 170-73.

of a discussion of the elder's wife is inexplicable. Thus, it seems most likely that 3:11 indicates that women could also serve as deacon.[184]

This separate reference to women in 3:11 is necessary on several counts. First, the offices of elder and deacon were described in male categories, since they are both to be "the husband of one wife" (3:2, 12) and to manage (προΐστημι) their household well. Thus, if women could participate in these offices, it needed to be specifically addressed. Second, no separate feminine form of the word διάκονος exists, so that one can only specify female participation by circumscribing it. First Timothy 3:11 seems to do just that with the separate entry for γυναῖκας, while Rom 16:1 accomplishes the same by describing a female, Phoebe, with the term διάκονος. Third, the general prohibition against women teaching or having authority over men (2:11–12) rules out that women can be elder or deacon, unless explicitly balanced by adding a description of women in office to avoid the misperception that women would be barred from all such participation. It is likely, therefore, that the specification for women in 3:11 was intentionally added to indicate that the restriction on women did not apply to the office of deacon.

These observations resolve two further issues. First, the intertextual relationship between 2:11–12 and 3:11 suggests that whatever roles deacons were to play, female deacons were prohibited from fulfilling the kinds of teaching duties that are implied for the elders and male deacons. The analysis above pointed out that deacons who served well gained confidence in their communication of the gospel, both inside and outside the church. The limitation implied for female deacons is difficult to locate precisely, but it appears to apply to the setting within which they communicated, not so much to the content of their communication. The focus on household management, evident in both 2:11–15 and 3:11–16 suggests that female leadership may have related specifically to community functions taking place in and from her house.[185] Thus, while men and women could both serve as deacon, their sphere of influence is likely to differ.[186] Second, if this recon-

---

184. Marshall, *Pastoral Epistles*, 493–94. Fiori concludes similarly in just one brief paragraph, but believes that evidence is not conclusive (*Pastoral Epistles*, 81).

185. As Osiek et al. argue, the household was women's space, run by women (*A Woman's Place*, 152).

186. Marshall also argues that it is likely that the women did not do all that the men were permitted to do in that function (*Pastoral Epistles*, 494).

struction is correct and it was necessary to specify that women could participate in the office of deacon, the absence of specific instructions with regard to the overseer implies that women were not to participate in that particular office. Since elders or overseers were involved in oversight and teaching on both household and non-household levels, it is not surprising in the light of the prohibition for women to teach or have authority over men that women were not included in the exercise of this office.

Summary

In the increasing complexity of an expanding church, local leaders had succeeded in functioning at a collegial level of cooperation, maintaining the unity of the community and their loyalty to Paul. Yet, some persistent problems with deviance remained, Roman values of status and honor continued to influence local leadership, while the influence of some women needed direction. Paul left Timothy in Ephesus to assist the local leadership, but this placed Timothy in a difficult position, since he was not an apostle and had none of the usual resources that local householder-leaders had.

Paul engaged with these dynamics by writing to Timothy in the form of a *mandata principis* letter,[187] which instructed junior officials about their duties; this familiar format presented the church with a recognizable leadership document that could also be reapplied to new leaders in succeeding generations. Paul reminded the community of his primacy as apostle and archetypal exemplar for the Christian community, which allowed him to present Timothy as a leader similar to himself and prototypical for the community. Timothy was Paul's key delegate to communicate Paul's vision of Christian social identity and to direct the Christian identity performance of group members, especially of local leaders. Thus, Paul maintained his own leadership by boosting Timothy's leadership status and empowering him in his leadership.

But this was not, of course, enough. Paul also instructed Timothy about how to orchestrate the ministries of the church. Some men

---

187. On these letter forms, see not only Stepp's study, but also Fiore, *Personal Example*, especially 67–78; Richards, *Difference and Distance*, 27–66; and Johnson, *First and Second Timothy*, 137–42.

provided leadership by way of competition, so Paul instructed them to shape their leadership by a clear focus on God's mission. Some elite women and some young widows expected to exercise greater influence than Paul considered desirable,[188] so he focuses their influence on their role as manager of their household (in which case the younger widows should remarry), in effect directing them to focus their energy on household based ministries. If their household hosted a house church, for which the husband would presumably be the overseer, this focus would imply significant influence in this house church. More precise delineation of such a female role in leadership comes from the male-oriented description of the offices, which explicitly includes women as deacons. Likely, a female deacon's ministry was somewhat more limited than that of male deacons. Thus, men and women were to participate each in their own way in God's mission, and officers for the community were to be selected on the basis of their prototypicality and group-oriented service, so that they would uphold God's purpose with the church.

The letter envisions a stable Christ-believing community, with an already functioning group of differentiated local leaders. New local leaders were needed to facilitate the community's expansion and to compensate for leaders who had fallen prey to deviance. Paul's leadership expectations were not always clear, while senior leaders may have looked down upon junior leaders among their ranks, so that there seems to have been a reluctance of candidates to accept a position of leadership. Paul encourages Timothy and local leadership candidates with his frequent saying that oversight, as a good work of benefaction, is a desirable ministry. He establishes control, through Timothy and the elders, of access to teaching opportunities, and by scrutinizing new leadership candidates on character. Paul addressed some organizational and financial issues in the church with his instructions for widows, and also affirmed and enhanced the basic procedures and provisions for the local elders.

Even though deviance and control of access to speech were important concerns in the letter, Paul focused more on empowering Timothy and other loyal leaders than on restricting a few deviants.

188. Witherington adduces evidence from inscriptions to explain why women in Asia Minor might have expected to fulfill prominent leadership functions in Christ-believing groups, similar to what they had previously exercised in non-Christian religious groups. See Witherington, *Letters and Homilies*, 218–21.

Structures for organization and control were necessary for the expanding community, but they needed to remain connected with God's mission in the world and His purpose for the church. Organizational aspects as well as measures of control were designed to align with Paul's vision of Christian social identity. Those group members who were prototypical and who were aligned with Paul's teaching tradition would have sensed Paul's empowerment to implement Paul's instructions for their community life as they related to their shared vision of Christian identity. However, deviant members evidently would have experienced Paul as limiting and restrictive, since Paul's empowerment related to his own vision and teaching, not to any 'other' teaching that any particular leader might favor.

8

Correcting Leadership Misconceptions and Establishing Succession in 2 Timothy

SECOND TIMOTHY USUALLY DOES NOT FIGURE LARGELY IN THE LITerature on church leadership. It does not contain any leadership titles and its leadership dynamics seem limited to Timothy's interaction with some opponents. A number of studies treat general leadership themes in the Pastoral Epistles, and while 2 Timothy often remains in the shadow of 1 Timothy and Titus, it does receive some focused attention. Fiore analyzes some passages in 2 Timothy for its hortatory use of example and Wolter classifies the letter as a hortatory testament, highlighting aspects that are important for leadership but without drawing out the consequences.[1] Martin's study of 2 Timothy elaborates on its testamentary character, and emphasizes the role of several Moses narratives, while Prior's focus was more limited to Paul as letter-writer of 2 Timothy.[2] One of the few studies to devote significant attention to 2 Timothy from a leadership perspective is Stepp's monograph on succession in the Pauline world.[3] The meager literature on leadership in this letter may seem to suggest that it has little to offer for leadership studies, but this is not the case, as this chapter will demonstrate.

The matter of authorship has been dealt with in the excursus of chapter 7, which argued the credibility and likelihood of authentic authorship. The present chapter thus proceeds to the historical situation of the letter.

---

1. Fiore, *Personal Example*, 23–24, 201–9; Wolter, *Paulustradition*, 202–42.
2. Martin, *Pauli Testamentum*; Prior, *Paul the Letter-Writer*.
3. Stepp, *Leadership Succession*.

Situating 2 Timothy in Paul's Ministry

Second Timothy was written a few years after 1 Timothy. While in 1 Timothy Paul appeared to move freely, in 2 Timothy he is in a Roman prison for the second time.[4] References to being poured out as a drink offering (σπένδομαι), and to an imminent departure (ἀνάλυσις, 4:6) suggest that Paul does not expect to be released. Prior proposed that these words refer instead to being spent in active service and to Paul's hope to soon depart for Spain with Mark and Timothy as part of his missionary team (4:9, 11, 13), which would imply a date of composition towards the end of Paul's first imprisonment in Rome.[5] His arguments have not been found convincing.[6] Rather, the parallels with similar language in Phil 1:23 and 2:17 (co-authored with Timothy) indicate that the remote possibility of death at the end of Paul's first imprisonment now is about to become reality. Only an urgent occasion like Paul's impending death would allow Paul to extract Timothy from a situation where he was so direly needed. Thus, 2 Timothy is Paul's last letter, dating close to his execution in Rome.

The letter's destination is not clearly indicated, but in all likelihood, Timothy is still (or again) in Ephesus when Paul writes him this second letter. From Rome, Paul reminds Timothy of "all who are in Asia" who deserted him, while Onesiphorus—just now in Rome to refresh Paul—faithfully served in Ephesus (1:15–18). Paul urges Timothy to come to him soon, and Timothy's departure for Rome seems to be coordinated with the arrival of Tychicus whom Paul sent to Ephesus (4:9, 12–13). Hymenaeus and Alexander, who caused trouble in Ephesus (1 Tim 1:20) are mentioned again (2 Tim 2:17, 4:14). Finally, Timothy is to greet the household of Onesiphorus in Ephesus. These references to Ephesus suggest that Timothy as recipient is most likely located there.[7]

---

4. It is debated whether Paul's "first defense" (4:16) refers to the outcome of his first imprisonment as reported in Acts 28 or to the preliminary investigation of his second imprisonment, but on both views 2 Timothy originates during this second imprisonment. For an overview of the positions and arguments, see Knight, *Pastoral Epistles*, 468–69 and 17–20.

5. Prior, *Paul the Letter-Writer*, 92–112.

6. See for instance Johnson, *First and Second Timothy*, 431; Marshall, *Pastoral Epistles*, 805–6; and Oberlinner, *Timotheusbrief*, 2:160–61.

7. So Knight, *Pastoral Epistles*, 10. Mounce also considers the heresies of 2 Timothy to be Ephesian (*Pastoral Epistles*, lxix ff). However, deSilva and Johnson suggest that

While Titus was asked to join Paul in Nicopolis before his second Roman imprisonment, Timothy stayed in Ephesus where he remained after Paul's arrest and transport to Rome. Once imprisoned in Rome, Onesiphorus traveled from Ephesus to find Paul (probably with Timothy's knowledge) and Paul sent a good report about Onesiphorus back to Timothy. Tychicus, who may have served as courier of the letter, relieved Timothy as he had done earlier for Titus (Titus 3:12–13), upon which Timothy leaves for Rome to support Paul in his imprisonment.

One wonders if Paul's mission in Asia had fallen on hard times, since he complained that "all in Asia turned away" from him (ἀπεστράφησάν, 1:15). This might suggest that the situation of Paul's churches in Asia had seriously deteriorated since his visit and the writing of 1 Timothy.[8] However, even though ἀποστρέφω can refer to apostasy (cf. 4:4), it is rather unlikely that "all in Asia" would have apostatized from Paul's gospel. Not only are Timothy and Onesiphorus obvious exceptions,[9] but Paul also expected Timothy to correct deviant teachers and to find faithful men to carry forward the Pauline teaching tradition, which is patently impossible if all in Asia would have left the Pauline network of communities. In fact, such instructions, combined with the rhetoric of deviance, suggest a reasonably stable situation, as will be argued below, so that Paul's complaint is not about apostasy. Instead, the references to Onesiphorus who was not ashamed of Paul's status as prisoner (1:16) and to "all" who deserted Paul at his first defense (4:16) suggest that Paul complained that his Asian churches and their leaders had abandoned Paul in his defense. Perhaps they were ashamed of being associated with a 'federal' prisoner, or simply feared possible consequences. Thus, Paul's complaint says little about the health of his mission network in Asia, but reflects Paul's disappointment over the lack of support from his Asian converts, especially the Asian leadership.

This fits well with other indications about Paul's Aegean mission. Second Timothy supplies the names of no fewer than 25 contemporary

---

Timothy's whereabouts are uncertain (deSilva, *Introduction to the NT*, 734; Johnson, *First and Second Timothy*, 319).

8. See for instance Witherington, *Letters and Homilies*, 301ff.

9. Quinn and Wacker, *First and Second Timothy*, 612–14.

people[10]; besides the trio of Timothy, Titus, and Tychicus, the letter lists 13 people who are likely coworkers in various roles, three ex-coworkers and three opponents. These people are active in Galatia, Asia (Ephesus, Miletus, Troas), Macedonia (Thessalonica), Dalmatia, and Achaia (Corinth). Areas further south (like Crete) are absent, but Dalmatia is further to the north of Nicopolis. This testifies to continued networking and expansion in Paul's Aegean mission, now carried on in Paul's absence by his associates who face the same disappointments (deserting coworkers) and opposition as Paul himself had experienced.

Social Identification in the Ephesian Community in 66 CE

Second Timothy is a personal letter with a strong focus on Timothy's responsibilities and character as a leader, but it can still be analyzed with social identity theory. Relative to Paul and Timothy, most others are discussed as "they," sometimes referring to other believers (2:2, 10; 3:12), sometimes to unbelievers generally (3:1–2, 13; 4:17), and most often to deviant group members (1:15; 2:16–18, 23–26; 3:6–9; 4:3–4, 16). This last category is quite diverse and designates opponents to Timothy's ministry, earlier opponents to Paul's ministry or even in the more distant past, and wayward believers either current or in the future. References to deviant group members, therefore, do not represent any one historical group, while even current opposition (2:14, 25–26; 3:5; 4:2) is not presented as a deviant group or faction over against a Pauline faction. Paul's main charge is to Timothy to stabilize and expand the community, which includes correcting deviant group members but which focuses mostly on providing continuity of social identity from Paul to Timothy and beyond. Thus, the focus of 2 Timothy is more personal than 1 Timothy, but the community remains in view.

Second Timothy provides a few indications of the community's social identification processes. Paul emphasized Timothy's Jewish heritage (1:5–7; 3:14–15), which resonates with the report in Acts 16:3

---

10. Of the Pauline letters, only Romans names more people: 35. For a further description of these people, complete with a graph of relationships, see Richards, *Difference and Distance*, 103–8.

that Paul circumcised Timothy on account of the Jews when he first joined Paul's mission work. This emphasis suggests that Jewish identity was a important status indicator for Timothy's leadership, suggesting that ethnic Jewish background had become an important distinctive for leadership in Ephesus. Although the information is scarce, this may well parallel the earlier preference in the Corinthian community for Jewish leaders, if their mistaken divisions around Paul, Apollos, Peter, and Christ are any indication.

Several other themes indicate continuing difficulty over how Greco-Roman values relate to leadership. Paul encouraged Timothy not to be timid or cowardly (1:7), and to accept shame and suffering (2:3; 3:12). He depicts his leadership as honorable (2:20–21), but exercised in gentleness (2:25). It seems likely (see the analysis below) that some faulted Timothy's leadership for lack of competitive spirit and social status such as would customarily be expected. Moreover, the warnings against those who applaud teachers that suit their passions suggest a similar tendency towards valuing rhetorical display over Christian ingroup values.

Evidently, towards the end of Paul's life, cultural values concerning status and rhetoric affected the Ephesian community's social identification processes in ways very similar to what was observed in the earlier correspondence with the Corinthian community. This is to be expected since Ephesus and Corinth share the same Greco-Roman world, which continued to put stress on the social identification of Christ-believing communities. It is quite likely that the Ephesian community experienced similar identification difficulties with nested and cross-cutting identities as the Corinthian community. However, divisions in Ephesus are not reported and the nature of the evidence, drawn from the Ephesian correspondence which is either general (Ephesians) or personal (1–2 Timothy) in nature, does not permit the same evaluation of the actual extent of these difficulties as could be accomplished for Corinth. Nevertheless, it is possible to deduce the relative stability of the Ephesian community from some of the social identification processes indicated in these letters.

The Ephesian Leaders as Managers of Christian Social Identity

Since 2 Timothy is mostly about leadership issues, most of the above tensions in social identification reflected the social influence of leaders who were critical of Timothy. Paul branded them as deviant and portrayed them as being within reach of Timothy's control; apparently, the community had not divided and was not facing substantial opposition from the outside. Moreover, since deviance often attracts a disproportionate share of intragroup communication, it is likely that only a few leaders were affected. These critics were probably more open to honor-seeking leadership styles, and may have found a welcome hearing among some elite women (3:6), contributing to tension over gender roles. It may well be that these critics, although relatively marginal, contested Timothy's role as delegate and even as successor of Paul, considering how strongly Paul highlighted Timothy's status.

However, the majority of the local leaders were mostly supportive of Timothy and Paul. First, a succession letter presupposes at least a partially sympathetic audience if succession proposals are to be realized at all. Thus, enough local leaders must have remained loyal to Paul and Timothy to warrant sending such a letter. Second, Paul emphasized his own apostleship as well as Timothy's similarity to himself. This makes sense only in a setting where Paul's apostleship is appreciated so that similarity to Paul becomes a recommendation for other leaders; otherwise it would be a hindrance. Finally, the focus on Timothy's prototypicality, as Paul defined Christian social identity, presupposes a community that could largely identify with Timothy as ingroup prototype, so that they would be inclined to accept Paul's succession proposal. Thus, most local leaders can be assumed to have remained loyal.

The question then arises why Timothy needed Paul's recommendation and instructions for his function in Ephesus, if the community was relatively stable and most leaders remained loyal. One factor is Paul's sense that he is near death; he desires to transmit some particular concerns to a trusted coworkers who will succeed him. Another factor is that a vision of social identity needs to be continually contextualized within its social environment in order to maintain its distinctiveness, enhance its vitality, and resist deviant influence. Paul's communities were no exception to this. A proven strategy for maintaining distinctiveness in a competitive social environment is to accentuate the ingroup stereotype, preferably by pointing out exemplary group members, and to contrast it/them with the characteristics and leadership styles of deviant members or the outgroup. Both factors are operative in 2 Timothy, which suggests that in spite of the rhetoric of deviance, most of the ingroup and its leaders had remained loyal to Paul and Timothy.

Paul's Leadership as Identity Management

If 2 Timothy represents Paul's testament as Martin argued,[11] it seems the testament focuses not so much on the content of Paul's gospel, but on the way in which it should be transmitted to new generations. It involves not just the transmission of certain ideas, but it involves the transmission of Paul's group ideology along with strategies to maintain group cohesion and vitality. Of all of Paul's letters, this one comes closest to being a succession document,[12] so that Paul's identity management focuses mostly on that process.

Creating an Identity Narrative of Common Heritage, Belief, and Friendship

Paul embeds Timothy as successor into his vision of Christian social identity by composing an identity narrative that underlines their common heritage, their common foundational beliefs and their bond of friendship.

The first aspect of this identity narrative highlights a common heritage. Paul presented his own heritage as worshipping God "with a clear conscience," just like his forebears (1:3). Although this could refer to still living parents or grandparents,[13] it often refers to more

---

11. Martin, *Pauli Testamentum*, 43–52.

12. Stepp argues that "in 2 Timothy, the purpose is different—the concern is not with refuting false teaching [as in 1 Timothy] but with how Paul's gospel will continue with an authorized successor after Paul's death—a successor who will himself suffer for the gospel" (Stepp, *Leadership Succession*, 159).

13. As it does in 1 Tim 5:4, an option also suggested by EDNT, 3:154, s.v. πρόγονος.

distant ancestors, frequently referring to a Jewish way of life.[14] Thus, Paul extended his lineage of faith back to before the Christian faith was proclaimed. Timothy's heritage is also traced this far back, through his mother and grandmother. Acts 16:3 reports that Timothy's father was a Greek, so Paul points specifically to Timothy's Jewish heritage, highlighting what they have in common rather than where they differ. This common heritage is further emphasized by Paul's portrayal of Timothy as his "beloved child" (1:2), creating the image of a son following in his father's footsteps—a father without physical descendents, much like Jesus. In spite of his circumcision later in life, Timothy's heritage, too, could be perceived as built upon the ancient traditions of Paul's Jewish faith, conforming to Mediterranean custom which values ancient traditions more than novelty.[15]

While Timothy's Greek heritage might have enabled him to connect socially with Greek culture better than Paul,[16] his Jewish heritage connected him with Paul's faith and proclamation in a way that distinguished Timothy from gentile believers generally. This functioned most likely against a backdrop of largely gentile communities of faith, raising Timothy's leadership status since he was perceived as related to the Jewish roots of the Christ-movement, while against a backdrop of second temple Judaism, Timothy's heritage would most likely have been no match for Paul's Jerusalem education as a Pharisee under Gamaliel (cf. Acts 22:3). In other words, the similarities between Paul's and Timothy's heritages became significant from a gentile point of view, but the difference between their heritages would have been significant to the point of contention from some Jewish points of view. Thus, Paul narrated their individual heritages to create the perception that they were very similar in order to set both of them apart from gentile believers, while overlooking their intra-Jewish differences, which could create distinctions that were undesirable in the present social context.

The language of memory plays an important part in this description of their common heritage. Paul remembered Timothy consistently

---

14. Quinn and Wacker, *First and Second Timothy*, 573.

15. Witherington, *Letters and Homilies*, 310.

16. Malina describes Timothy as a change agent, able to bridge the gap between Jew and gentile because of his own mixed heritage in a Hellenistic environment (*Timothy: Paul's Closest Associate*, 53–65).

in his prayers, he remembered his tears and his sincere faith (1:3–5). Paul prompted Timothy to remember the gift of God he received through Paul's laying on of hands (1:6). Martin argues that this verse is an intentional parallel of Moses who laid hands on Joshua so that he was full of the "spirit of wisdom."[17] By itself this parallel is insignificant, but the later references to the Moses narrative (2:1, 19, 24; 3:8–9, 17, discussed below) suggest that Paul already began to weave the remembrance of Moses and Joshua into his identity narrative in support of Timothy's succession. Paul also exhorted Timothy to remember Jesus Christ and the salvation he brings (2:8ff.), while Timothy in turn was to remind his hearers of these memories (2:14ff.), continuing the exercise of memorializing Christ (as well as Paul and Moses) as central beliefs for Christian social identity. Finally, Timothy was exhorted to remain faithful to what he had learned from "the sacred writings" from childhood (3:14–15), another exhortation to remember even though no cognate of "memory" was used. These memories were no mere nostalgia on the part of a dying apostle, but presented Timothy's heritage with Paul, Moses and Christ as authoritative role models. Timothy is to keep these memories alive for himself as well as for his communities. In doing so, he constructs the social memory for his Christian communities in which he aligns himself with three key authority figures in the Christ-movement. Thus, memorializing past role models serves important social functions in maintaining the faithfulness of the community as well as in legitimating Timothy's leadership.[18]

The second aspect of Paul's identity narrative consists of the foundational beliefs he shared with Timothy. Timothy is exhorted not to be ashamed of Christ or Paul, but to share in suffering for the gospel (1:8, 12); only God brings life and immortality through the Savior Jesus Christ, as will become evident on "that day" (1:11–12). Lea and Griffin conclude that Timothy may have been embarrassed at how mockers

---

17. Martin discusses this passage as an allusion to Deut. 34:9 and concludes that "the image presented in 2 Tim 1:6 is of a latter-day Moses, Paul, authorizing his legitimate successor, Timothy, in a way which unmistakably assigns the latter a rôle in the community analogous to that of Joshua. Timothy is thereby endued with Pauline authority certainly, but also that of Moses and his successor" (*Pauli Testamentum*, 43–52).

18. Esler argues that reconstructing group memories is an important way to "propel a group in a particular direction" in a study of memory in relation to Paul's imprisonment as mentioned in Colossians, Ephesians and 2 Timothy ("Remember My Fetters," 244–54).

perceived Jesus, or that he felt humiliated that Paul was in prison,[19] but they fail to notice that shame and honor are core values in Paul's world. Paul focuses first on Christ and himself as two witnesses in suffering for the gospel,[20] two exemplars who demonstrate the value of true honor in a way that fits Christian social identity. Further, Redalié argued that the phrase "the appearing of our Savior" (τῆς ἐπιφανείας τοῦ σωτῆρος ἡμῶν, 1:10) showed influence of Greco-Roman savior cults in a post-Pauline development.[21] However, even if this phrase parallels cult terminology, it would simply demonstrate Paul's use of social creativity: he employed familiar Ephesian terminology to redefine true honor as conveyed by God and Christ on "that day," implicitly contrasting it with the life that the Roman savior gods or the emperor promise, which would actually prove to be shameful on "that day." The basis for Paul's redefinition of shame and honor is thus provided by core identity beliefs, which describe God's salvation and calling, manifested through the coming of "our Savior Jesus Christ" (1:9–10). Paul emphasized his appointment as "preacher and apostle and teacher" (1:11) and his conviction that God will guard him until "that day" (1:12), when both Christ and his messengers will be vindicated. Thus, Paul's apostleship is embedded in the kerygma, while Timothy's commission is also connected with this foundational identity narrative. This turns Timothy's response to shame into a matter of identity performance, strongly buttressing the motivation to stand up under pressure, which in turn will mobilize others in their Christian identity performance. Clearly, the insertion of basic Christian beliefs is not a mere formality, nor a stereotypical reminder of Pauline traditions, but provides a strong motivation for Timothy to persevere in his ministry by affirming a Christian perspective on suffering and shame.

Moreover, since honor is granted by a particular court of opinion, Paul essentially reorients Timothy's perception honor and shame towards an ingroup court of opinion. The first "court" is their common Jewish heritage; even if Timothy shrinks from the prospect of shame, it would be more shameful to abandon "one's ancestral traditions."[22] The

---

19. Lea and Griffin, *1, 2 Timothy, Titus*, 190.

20. Witherington, *Letters and Homilies*, 317.

21. Redalié, *Paul après Paul*, 157–74. See Johnson's interaction with him in *First and Second Timothy*, 355.

22. Johnson, *First and Second Timothy*, 358ff.

second "court" is God himself whose benefits of life and immortality are honorable beyond comparison, so that abandoning his commission is not only shameful but also foolish. The third "court" is personal friends, and abandoning them is as shameful as abandoning one's heritage. Thus, Timothy is reminded to shape his patterns of identification upon ingroup values rather than outgroup "courts of opinion."

This leads to the third aspect of Paul's identity narrative, which consists of negative and positive examples of friends and their loyalty to Paul. The negative example referred to significant numbers of people from the Roman province of Asia who "turned away" from Paul, of which Timothy is expected to be aware (1:15). This was explained above as an indication—perhaps hyperbolical—that most Christians in Asia had not supported Paul during his imprisonment, probably to escape the shame and suffering that such loyalty might bring. Phygelus and Hermogenes appear to be especially noteworthy for Paul and presumably also for Timothy, but nothing is known of them otherwise. They are not listed in other passages about deviant teaching, so they appear to be noteworthy believers, perhaps even coworkers or friends, whose lack of personal support for Paul during his Roman imprisonment was especially painful. The positive example describes Onesiphorus as an Ephesian householder (1:16–18; 4:18) who earnestly sought Paul out in a Roman prison without being ashamed for Paul's status as prisoner. These contrasting examples emphasize personal loyalty as a key value, and serve as both a warning and an encouragement to Timothy to remain loyal in spite of potential shame. Thus Paul, as artist of social identity, created an identity narrative of a common heritage, a common belief and shared bonds of friendship, in order to motivate Timothy to express his loyalty both in his teaching and in his leadership in Ephesus, as well as in coming to visit Paul in prison (4:9).

Orchestrating Succession in the Pauline Tradition

The identity narrative of a common heritage, common belief and common friends forms the basis for Paul's presentation of succession. From 2 Tim 2:1ff, Paul orchestrated the transmission process of his own teaching tradition through Timothy to other leaders.

Correcting Leadership Misconceptions and Establishing Succession in 2 Timothy 263

The model of transmission is indicated in the central charge to "be strengthened" and to "entrust to faithful men" (2:1–2). Martin argues that these words are reminiscent of the leadership transfer from Moses to Joshua (Deut. 31:6–8, 23; Josh. 1:6–9, 18), something that most commentators have overlooked. Both the Moses-Joshua as well as the Paul-Timothy stories are a central installation formula, comprised of (a) an encouragement of the person addressed, (b) a statement of the task or function, and (c) assurance of divine help.[23] Faithfulness to the Mosaic law and to the Pauline gospel respectively are central features in both succession stories. This parallel provided a familiar and treasured model for understanding the relationship between Paul and Timothy. It encouraged Timothy to see himself not just as Paul's delegate but also as Paul's successor, like Joshua and Moses. These parallels expand the Christian identity narrative to incorporate Paul as chosen apostle as well as Timothy as Paul's successor. Since the Moses-Joshua succession model is probably uncontested in Pauline communities, this model promoted Timothy's succession of Paul as likewise uncontested (which it was not, see below): Timothy was the authorized spokesmen for Paul's gospel, commissioned to maintain Paul's vision of social identity as the Pauline communities continued to expand.

The object of transmission is indicated in the phrase "what you heard from me" (ἃ ἤκουσας παρ' ἐμοῦ, 2 Tim 2:2), which repeats similar wording from 1:13, so that oral transmission is in view.[24] Paul speaks of the content to be transmitted as "a pattern of sound words" (ὑποτύπωσιν ἔχε ὑγιαινόντων λόγων, 1:13). Just as Paul had been a pattern or example for others in his salvation (ὑποτύπωσιν, 1 Tim 1:16), so now his teaching became an example or model for Timothy and others in their teaching. This does not refer to Paul's teaching in general, but to Paul's gospel, probably in a relatively standardized form.[25] Other transmission terminology points in this direction. The verb "entrust" (παρατίθημι, 2 Tim 2:2) links back to the "deposit" entrusted to Paul and passed on to Timothy (παραθήκη, 1:12, 14). Timothy is to guard the deposit, not only by not being ashamed—which merely deals with attendant circumstances—but by transmitting Paul's teaching to

---

23. Martin, *Pauli Testamentum*, 35.
24. See Marshall, *Pastoral Epistles*, 724–25.
25. Kelly, *Pastoral Epistles*, 172.

others who in turn will teach the next generation.²⁶ This content may not yet have the well-defined shape similar to the written creeds of the second century and beyond, but definite contours of faith can be expected.²⁷ Thus, a carefully delineated synopsis of Paul's gospel forms the object of transmission.

The authority in transmission is illustrated by three stock examples from popular diatribe that Paul had already used in 1 Cor 9:7, 24. Each illustrates a particular aspect of the leadership required of Timothy.²⁸ Timothy is to endure suffering like a soldier of Christ Jesus (2 Tim 2:3–4); he is to compete according to the rules as an athlete (2:5); and like the farmer, Timothy is entitled to receive benefits from his labors(2:6).²⁹ Note that reward only follows lawful competition (νομίμως, 2:5). Debates about which rules are intended focus mostly on ancient athletic contests,³⁰ but often the connection with the same word in 1 Tim 1:8 is missed. This suggests that only suffering that is experienced by remaining loyal to Paul's gospel leads to the expected reward and vindication. In other words, Timothy's authority is not merely derived from prophetic pronouncements or a commission from Paul, but from faithfulness to core identity beliefs. Turner's theory of power predicts that ingroup power arises through social identification,³¹ and this is what Paul instructs Timothy to do: articulate the gospel and embody through suffering the community's understanding of the gospel in order to earn the social power to define and maintain their Christian social identity and to initiate succession. Moreover, in these three stock examples, Christ is the one enlisting, rewarding and providing for Timothy. Paul's commission of Timothy recedes into the background, and Timothy's service is legitimated by

---

26. This also connects 2 Timothy with the same type of usage of these words in 1 Timothy: παρατίθημι in 1 Tim 1:18 and παραθήκη in 1 Tim 6:20.

27. Mounce, *Pastoral Epistles*, 489. Also, see Vleugels and Verhoeff, *De leer van de twaalf*, for arguments that early forms of the Nicene creed are already discernible in the Apostolic Fathers and in the NT itself.

28. See Kelly, *Pastoral Epistles*, 174.

29. Paul appears to suggest that Timothy could accept financial support from the Ephesians, although this seems at odds with his personal practice in Corinth. For a discussion, see Ibid., 176.

30. So, for instance Houwelingen, *Timoteüs en Titus*, 185, Kelly, *Pastoral Epistles*, 175–76 and Mounce, *Pastoral Epistles*, 510.

31. Turner, "Explaining the Nature of Power," 1–22.

its direct connection with Christ. Ideologically speaking, Timothy is dependent first on Christ, and only then on Paul, but socially speaking, Timothy is fully dependent on Paul's support for and commissioning of his ministry.

After thus orchestrating the model, object, and authority of transmission, Paul instructed Timothy about the manner of transmission. Timothy was to be guided by the remembrance of Christ (μνημόνευε, 2 Tim 2:8; cf. 1:3–5),[32] who also inspired Paul (2:8–10) to endure suffering.[33] The faithful saying (2:11b–13)[34] stirred Timothy to also accept suffering in transmitting Paul's gospel. With Christ as model, Paul instructed Timothy before a watching community. Timothy is charged to remind the community of Paul's gospel (ταῦτα, 2:14a), and to demonstrate himself an "approved" and "unashamed" worker (2:15). The key factor in this passage (2:14–26) is Timothy's intragroup status relative to opponents like Hymenaeus and Philetus, with whom he is extensively contrasted. Timothy's teaching took place in the presence of God (2:14) and with God's approval (2:15). As an honorable vessel and "the Lord's servant" (2:24) he interacted with opponents in hope that God might "grant them repentance" (2:25). Clearly, Timothy is on God's side in leading the community (2:19). The opponents, on the other hand, are portrayed with the typical repertoire of deviance labeling: they "ruin the hearers" (2:14), lead people into increasing ungodliness by their "irreverent babble" (2:16), and cause quarrels by their "ignorant controversies" (2:14, 23). Pietersen interprets these comments as a status degradation ceremony, which downgrades the status of an influential community member to outsider status; this may well imply that some of the opposing teachers "had previously been elders in Ephesus."[35] Thus, Paul's rhetorical strategy of demonizing some leaders as deviants may be interpreted as an attempt to curb the social influence of competing teachers and to enhance Timothy's

---

32. Cf. Johnson, *First and Second Timothy*, 373, who entitles verses 2:8–13, "Jesus as Exemplar."

33. This word is used elsewhere in the NT only in Luke to describe the criminals crucified with Christ (Luke 23:32, 33, 39). In this context about Christ's suffering and glory, Paul may well have this in mind, closely associating his suffering with Christ's.

34. See Knight, *The Faithful Sayings*, 112–15, who argues that this faithful saying does not refer back to the previous verses but instead introduces the teaching content in hymnic form.

35. Pietersen, *The Polemic of the Pastorals*, 139.

influence instead. Such teachers could return to the group by repentance (2:25–26), which implies an acknowledgement of Timothy as the legitimate leader of the community, and a willingness to conform to his prototypical leadership style.

Timothy's intragroup status is further heightened by two oblique references to the Moses narratives. The saying "the Lord knows who are his" (2:19) comes from the story of Korah (Num. 16:5), where the Lord judged the rebels and vindicated Moses and Aaron.[36] Moreover, the title "servant of the Lord" (δοῦλος κυρίου, 2:24) with which Paul designates Timothy, occurs only rarely in the LXX, and then only to designate Moses and his heir Joshua.[37] Even though Moses is not named explicitly until the next section, these allusions would hardly pass unnoticed. On the other hand, by naming his opponents, Hymenaeus (cf. 1 Tim 1:20) and Philetus become associated with the likes of Korah. These Moses narratives provide an evaluative framework upon which the leadership of Paul and Timothy, as well as of Hymenaeus and Philetus is projected, with predictable results. Community members who fail to acknowledge the parallels of Paul and Timothy with Moses, Aaron and Joshua categorize themselves as sympathizers with Korah, marginalizing themselves in the community. Thus, Timothy is here positioned in an unassailable position of authority, following closely in the footsteps of Paul, while the false teachers and those who side with them are stigmatized as deviants.

In summary, Paul orchestrated the process of transmission and succession, in which described the roles of himself and Timothy, but also of the community, its leaders, and those marked as deviant. Paul's description invites them to proper identify performance. As impresario of identity, he enlisted the congregation to approve of Timothy's manner of teaching, and thus to dissociate themselves from the opposing teachers. He enlisted local leaders to look towards Timothy as model for their own leadership. He enlisted the critics to change their mind and renew their loyalty towards himself and Timothy. He also enlisted the community to watch if their local leaders followed Paul's instructions. Thus, Paul does not just argue for a particular process of transmission, but he involves all parties of the process and encourages

---

36. Martin, *Pauli Testamentum*, 19–21.
37. Ibid., 29–32.

them to appropriate identity performance, i.e., in loyalty to Paul, at the risk of marginalizing themselves if they act otherwise.

Maximizing the Contrast Between the Deviants and the Faithful

After creating an identity narrative of common heritage, faith, and friends as basis for his proposal for succession (2 Tim 1–2), Paul revisited many of the earlier themes to reinforce his proposals. He sharpened the contrast between the heritages of opposition and loyalty (3:1–17; cf. 1:15–18). The demonization of false teachers and their followers was expanded in 3:1–9 by additional warnings about future and past opposition. Some currently influential people within the community were portrayed as part of the coming immorality, which stigmatized them and their followers as given to immorality, cut off from the power of God. These teachers were further downgraded by comparing them with Jannes and Jambres in their opposition to Moses and Aaron, continuing the parallel with the ancient Moses narratives evident above. Some of those reading over Timothy's shoulders would have found their perception of these teachers strongly challenged and reoriented from a perception as honored and influential leaders to a portrayal as deviant members. Thus, the influence of these teachers was curbed while Paul's confidence that such people "will not get very far" (3:9) expressed his hope and goal in mobilizing the community to dissociate from these teachers.

Timothy, by contrast, is faithful to his heritage. The emphatic "you, however" (σὺ δὲ, 3:10, 14) highlights Timothy's double heritage: Paul's personal example in suffering and dedication to Christ (3:10–13), and the heritage from his Jewish mother and grandmother (cf. 1:5). Timothy's Greek father and late circumcision are conveniently overlooked, since Paul's description of Timothy's heritage is not intended as a factual summary but as a persuasive appeal to mobilize Timothy (and others who read over his shoulder) to a robust leadership performance in Ephesus.[38] The reference to "man of God" (3:17),

---

38. Knight, *Pastoral Epistles*, 443. Fiore points to Timothy's lack of circumcision as an indication that his mother "was not a fully observant Jew" and suggests that this reference to childhood training "is not biographical but paradigmatic," as an exhortation to adopt this Jewish practice in the early church (*Pastoral Epistles*, 170). This reinterpretation of the reference to childhood fits well within a pseudepigraphal

a LXX phrase which often designates Moses,[39] reinforces the claims Paul makes about Timothy's heritage. Compared to the heritage of opposition, Timothy's heritage demonstrates that he occupies the moral high ground (3:10-11)[40] and is worthy of being followed.

In this strategy of meta-contrast, Paul maximizes the contrast between Timothy and his critics, and minimizes the differences between Timothy and himself, in order to present Timothy as ingroup prototype and leadership model to the community, and in order to mobilize the community to implement his succession proposal (the leader as impresario).

Empowering His Successor to Be Faithful

After constructing his succession proposals, and picturing the potential negative and positive results in a strategy of meta-contrast, Paul adds closing appeals to empower Timothy to comply (4:1-22). This section again reorients Timothy's conception of honor with respect to three courts of opinion (see pp. 258ff). The first court of opinion consists of God and Christ as witnesses (4:1-5). Christ's judgment and coming kingdom motivate Timothy to "preach the word," ready or not (4:1-2), in contrast to people who "will not endure sound teaching" (4:3-4). Ultimately, this court of opinion determines true honor. The second court of opinion is Paul himself (4:6-8). Even in his impending death (4:6), he presented himself as ingroup prototype to be imitated by Timothy. Paul was confident that he fought the good fight (4:7), and that he would receive his due reward from Christ (4:8). Paul's faithfulness unto death provided a powerful and urgent motivation for Timothy to seek the same honor and reward as Paul.

The third court of opinion consists of Paul's team of coworkers (4:9-22). Paul listed many loyal coworkers (Titus, Luke, Mark, Tychicus, Erastus, Trophimus, Prisca and Aquila, Onesiphorus, and

---

perspective, but needlessly ignores the possibility that a Jewish mother in a gentile household may well have the opportunity to teach her children the Torah privately, while similar opportunities for public expression, e.g. through a ritual like circumcision, are severely curtailed. Paul simply highlights only those parts of Timothy's heritage that clarify the connection with Paul himself and that also raise Timothy's leadership status within the Ephesian community.

39. Martin, *Pauli Testamentum*, 32-34.
40. Pietersen, "Despicable Deviants," 350.

Crescens, 4:10–13; 19–20), besides on defector (Demas, 4:10), and one notorious opponent (Alexander, 4:14–15). This list of coworkers (and their locations) did not merely inform Timothy about everyone's ministry. Witherington believes that this lists reveals much about Paul's character,[41] while Lea and Griffin see only a few requests and warnings in this list.[42] Johnson comes closer to identifying the purpose of this name list when he remarks that such name lists often reinforce "the networks of communication essential to the success of the mission" as well as Paul's "main argument."[43] However, this overlooks the strong motivational appeal that this list must have exerted on Timothy. From a social identity perspective, this list created an identity narrative of faithfulness, with Timothy pictured as one among many loyal friends of Paul (aside from the two negative examples). The portrayal of Paul as lonely and deserted aimed to increase Timothy's motivation to remain loyal to Paul, especially since so many coworkers and friends had remained loyal. Paul's network of coworkers in the Aegean mission had its own social identity, and Paul motivated Timothy to faithful identity performance by emphasizing his identification with that network of coworkers.

Summary

Paul presents Timothy as a leader very similar to himself, and he urges Timothy to complete leadership tasks, which will mark him as prototypical and willing to sacrifice for the community. Paul charged Timothy to transmit his gospel faithfully to those who would faithfully teach it to yet others. Paul strongly contrasted Timothy with deviant leaders and members in order to present him in the strongest possible way as the exemplary leader for the community. Moreover, he oriented Timothy's hopes and expectations to several courts of opinion (family, Paul himself, God and Christ, and the network of coworkers) to provide the strongest possible motivation. In this letter, Paul is not merely concerned about Timothy's personal loyalty as a personal encouragement for himself. Rather, Paul has the welfare and continuity of the Ephesian community in view. Timothy's faithfulness

---

41. Witherington, *Letters and Homilies*, 376.
42. Lea and Griffin, *1, 2 Timothy, Titus*, 251.
43. Johnson, *First and Second Timothy*, 446–50.

would subsequently mobilize the Ephesian believers in similar identity performance, which would guarantee the loyalty not just of Timothy, but also of the entire Ephesian church to Paul, successfully preserving Ephesus as hub in the Pauline mission for another generation.

The Development of Local Leadership Patterns at Ephesus in 66 CE

Leadership Emergence. Although leadership maintenance for Paul and Timothy features most prominently in 2 Timothy, leadership emergence plays a significant role. Timothy is to safeguard the deposit entrusted to him by entrusting it to other "faithful men who will be able to teach others also" (2:2). Paul develops his charge by instructing Timothy how to train these men. He is to "remind them of these things" (2:14); "them" is supplied from the context and refers to teachers, since they in turn have hearers (τῶν ἀκουόντων, 2:14) to whom their word spreads (2:16–17).[44] The emphasis falls on preventing the negative results of deviant teaching, which can ruin hearers (2:14), lead them to increasing ungodliness (2:16) and upset their faith (2:18). Thus, the maintenance of Timothy's leadership served to guide emerging leaders in faithfully teaching the Pauline gospel and avoiding their derailment, which had happened in some cases.

This emerging leadership was still strongly influenced toward honor-seeking leadership strategies. They are strongly warned about quarreling, irreverent babble, and generally about dishonorable behavior. It appears that the warnings and instructions of 2:14–26 reflect the kind of behavior that may come from leaders seeking honor in return for their leadership and benefaction. When a leader was challenged, it would normally be taken as a challenge to one's honor, and a strong riposte was the expected cultural answer.[45] Timothy would have certainly challenged some leaders, so Timothy's correction may be partly responsible for quarrels, since name-calling and insult were common in such challenge-riposte exchanges. Further references to shame (2:15) and honor (2:20–21) add to the impression that some of the emerging leadership in Ephesus engaged in the type of honor-seeking strategies that Paul already criticized earlier in 1–2 Corinthians.

---

44. See Knight, *Pastoral Epistles*, 409–13.
45. See Malina, *The New Testament World*, 27–56.

These honor-seeking strategies most likely locate these group members at higher social levels and suggest that they were influential in Ephesus. Recent social identity research on dissent helps to clarify this situation. It was found that prototypical group members who identify strongly with a group are inclined to dissent if they believe that alternative norms, such as those from other spheres of identity, may help to improve group life.[46] Because of their social influence in the group, these high identifiers generally expect less censure from the group and evaluate their chances for successfully changing the group as relatively good. Thus, they are willing to risk deviance if they believe it will serve the group.[47] For the situation in Ephesus, this suggests that some of the emerging leaders, who were used to interacting in various social groups with alternative norms, became convinced that the honor values that determined their normal social relationships offered an alternative and better way to lead and protect the church than Paul's strategies of teaching, gentle correction and, if necessary, suffering. These emerging leaders evidently identified strongly with the group, as testified by their investment in the group through benefaction and their leadership status, and they would be motivated to do the best for the group, even at the risk of expressing dissent or deviance from the founder's teaching. Dissent, then, may well come from among those who highly identified with the community in a purposeful attempt to enhance the value and status of the group. These teachers were not marginal figures nibbling at the edges of the community to distract its weaker members, but were likely emerging leaders already well entrenched within the community with a sincere difference of opinion about the future of the church. This line of reasoning adds support to Pietersen's suggestion these teachers were among the elders.[48]

In verbal exchanges with such emerging leaders, Timothy is at a disadvantage on two counts.[49] First, Timothy does not have a local power base like other local leaders so that he was relatively powerless when local elite, through patronage and benefaction, gained influence in the church and challenged his leadership in proposing

46. Packer, "On Being Both With Us and Against Us," 53.
47. Ibid., 64.
48. Pietersen, *The Polemic of the Pastorals*, 139.
49. See also the discussion in chapter 7 about the ambiguity of Timothy's leadership status and social power in Ephesus.

alternative values and leadership styles. Second, Timothy exercised a non-competitive leadership style that was not perceived as honorable by some of the church's leaders. Timothy was to avoid shame by his handling of "the word of truth" (2:15), and to gain honor by cleansing himself from immorality (2:21–22). Although this description employs the language of honor and shame, it is quite the opposite from what local leaders might expect. In teaching and even in confrontation, Timothy is not to be quarrelsome, but "to patiently endure evil" and to correct "his opponents with gentleness" (2:24–25), behavior that would be interpreted by his opponents as an inadequate and therefore shameful response to their challenge.[50] Such a response would cause Timothy to lose honor and thus leadership influence in Ephesus, which is exactly the opposite of what the letter intends to accomplish. Paul therefore uses the language of deviance labeling to stigmatize the behavior of these deviant teachers as shameful and dishonorable, as well as to associate them with known deviants like Hymenaeus and Philetus (2:18). Timothy, on the other hand, is presented as the honorable teacher, since he is the one who reminds them of the gospel (2:14), teaches them the truth (2:15), and builds on God's firm foundation (2:19) as "the Lord's servant" (2:24). Thus, Timothy's lack of social status in Ephesus, as well as this leadership style, put him at a disadvantage in aligning the emergence of local leaders with Paul's vision of Christian social identity.

Thus, Paul attempted to prevent some teachers from emerging as fully accepted and accredited leaders, while he simultaneously sought to protect Timothy's leadership from dishonor and ineffectiveness. Some deviant leaders had already achieved a measure of social influence and social attraction, so Paul thwarted their further emergence as leader by reversing the leadership attribution process. Instead of attributing honorable leadership qualities to them, he attributed the characteristics of ingroup deviants to them and stigmatized them as comparable to known deviant leaders. Paul intended to undermine their social influence and attractiveness, and to downgrade their status as leaders.[51] At the same time, Paul reminded Timothy of his key tasks which he portrays as honorable, arguing that Timothy is the honored and duly commissioned leader for Ephesus. Furthermore,

50. Malina, *The New Testament World*, 34.
51. As argued by Pietersen, "Despicable Deviants," 349–50.

Paul's exhortations to specific leadership and teaching activities publicly constructed an alternative leadership model for Timothy to follow. This model then empowered Timothy's audience to evaluate him in the discharging of these duties, and they would undoubtedly have observed that Timothy's leadership matched the model, concluding Timothy was God's appointed leader for them. Moreover, the reference to Timothy's gift from God and the laying on of hands (1:6), as well as the solemn charge before God and Christ (2:14; 4:1) connect Timothy's routine teaching functions with a divine commission, attributing to Timothy a 'charismatic' authority much like Paul himself. In this way, Paul purposely redirects the process of leadership attribution for the benefit of Timothy and his ministry in Ephesus.

These observed social processes of leadership emergence are very similar to the leadership processes already analyzed in Corinth. Local emerging leadership seemed to derail along the cultural lines of patronage with its honor-shame values, which bred divisions and quarreling in the communities. The damage caused by these influences appears to have been far more extensive in Corinth than in Ephesus, as has been argued above, but the underlying identification processes are very similar. An important factor that may explain these different levels of damage was the availability of Paul and his team, either through brief visits or through the presence of a long-term delegate, to guide these emerging leaders into an appropriate leadership practice.

Timothy, Titus, and even Paul himself made short visits to Corinth, but no long-term delegate was left behind to implement Paul's instructions. Instead, Jewish-Christian believers arrived in Corinth from Israel and their influence became a major obstacle for the implementation of Paul's instructions, and caused serious doubt about Paul's ability as apostolic leader. Thus, Paul was forced to defend his apostolic role and authority as founder of the church in 2 Corinthians. In Ephesus, Paul was no longer personally available so Timothy had been left as long-term delegate to oversee community and leadership formation. Perhaps Paul chose to leave a delegate in Ephesus to prevent trouble similar to Corinth, because in spite of several years of independent development, the emergence of local leaders was still strongly influenced by Greco-Roman identifications and the community remained vulnerable for alternative input from elsewhere. Even so, Timothy's authority was challenged, although no outsiders appear to be involved, so that Paul was forced to defend Timothy's leadership and authority as an extension of his own apostolic commission.

Another important factor that gives the appearance of significant differences between Corinth and Ephesus are differences in the socio-rhetorical setting. In 1–2 Corinthians Paul addressed a community, which wrestled with the implications of Paul's teaching for the way they shaped their communities and their leadership, but in 2 Timothy Paul addressed a trusted close associate in Ephesus who was intimately familiar with his teaching, his vision for the Christian community and his leadership practice. When difficulties arose in Corinth, Paul needed to defend his own authority. When difficulties still arose in Ephesus, as they inevitably would for a minority community in a dominant, often oppressive environment, Paul had no need to defend his apostolic authority to Timothy, or to argue for the truth of his gospel, all of which Timothy knew well enough. Instead, Paul defended Timothy's leadership by reshaping the leadership attribution processes to Timothy's advantage and portrayed Timothy as a leader very similar to himself in order to influence the community to accept Timothy as they had accepted Paul.

These different emphases for Corinth and Ephesus do not so much reflect differences in the underlying processes of leadership emergence, but rather differences in the rhetorical setting of the letters. The differences in the availability of leadership from the apostolic team determine to whom Paul communicates, what content is needed in the communication and whose authority is in need of defense. This accounts sufficiently for the differences between 1–2 Corinthians and 1–2 Timothy and allow these letters to be situated within Paul's Aegean ministry in situations no more than 5–10 years apart.

Leadership Maintenance. The key to desirable leadership emergence in 2 Timothy is to maintain Timothy's position of leadership firmly, so that he could guide them in the right direction. This would also maintain Paul's influence as key apostolic leader and preacher. However, there is no need to revisit in detail the leadership maintenance in 2 Timothy, since this would amount to a review of Paul leadership already provided above. Suffice to say that as artist of social identity, Paul created an identity narrative which embedded Timothy in the Pauline teaching tradition, and which linked Timothy to his Jewish heritage of faith as well as to the Moses-Joshua succession narratives.

As impresario of social identity, Paul orchestrated Timothy's leadership performance before a watching a community. Paul exhorted Timothy to shape his own leadership by following himself as a model of faithful teaching, and by following Moses in resisting deviants like Jannes and Jambres. The community is implicitly enlisted to watch and affirm Timothy's appropriate leadership. As engineer of social identity, Paul initiated identity-embedding structures by affirming Timothy's status as delegate and successor, and by providing for the selection and training of faithful men as local successors.

Note that Paul appears ambivalent about Timothy's leadership. On the one hand, Paul strongly affirmed Timothy by portraying him as closely aligned to the community prototype, with himself and Moses as exemplars. On the other hand, Paul seemed seriously concerned about Timothy's faithfulness in leadership, so that he urged him to conform more to the community prototype. In other words, Paul's instructions (e.g., 2:14–26) suggest that Timothy's leadership fell short, while Paul's commendation of Timothy's imitation of himself (3:10–11) suggests the opposite. Whence then this ambivalence? Prior resolves the ambiguity by arguing that Paul was intensely concerned that Timothy might forsake him like so many others had done.[52] However, on closer inspection this ambivalence is shown to reflect the opposition's evaluation of Timothy, not Paul's. It was argued above that Paul's portrayal of Timothy intended not only to affirm Timothy in his leadership, but also to influence the community to accept Timothy. Paul's specific instructions to Timothy empowered the community to observe that Timothy's leadership matched Paul's model, as Paul already knew to be the case. Paul's ambivalence about Timothy's leadership did not rest on any personal doubts about Timothy's faithfulness, but rather showed his awareness of the critical attitude among some Ephesian leaders towards Timothy. Paul here turned these criticisms into a charge to Timothy to be faithful, but he redefined how this faithfulness is demonstrated in leadership: not in honor-seeking quarrels but in gentle teaching. Thus, he implicitly rebuked these critics who could now observe for themselves what Paul already knew: Timothy already led and taught in a way that conformed to Paul's ministry, commissioned by Christ, and parallel to Moses. Moreover, if these critics did not themselves conform their leadership to Paul's instructions, they

---

52. Prior, *Paul the Letter-Writer*, 62–64.

would thereby demonstrate to the watching community that their own leadership was problematic, not that Timothy's leadership was too timid or lacked boldness as they well might have suggested.[53]

This interpretation suggests that the sections of the letter that encourage Timothy to conform to the prototype are not to be seen as an indication that his leadership was lacking but as an indication that his critics thought so. Thus, Paul's main interest is in accentuating the prototype as already embodied by Timothy, but he casts some of his argument as a charge to conform to the prototype (knowing that Timothy already matched it) as a concession to the critics. This concession, though, is a rhetorical strategy that adeptly avoids a direct confrontation with the critics (as well as the riposte and quarrels that would be sure to follow), that rebukes them indirectly for their lack of confidence in Timothy and that exposes them to criticism from the watching congregation. Paul here played on the sensitivity of the critics to their honor and status, and anticipated that they would realize that Paul's arguments left their backs exposed to criticism from the congregation, the very ones from whom they expected honor instead. If the critics wanted to maintain their honor, they had no choice but to either increase their opposition to Paul, Timothy, and indeed the whole congregation or else to repent and acknowledge Timothy as leader—at least, these were their options in Paul's rhetorical framing of the situation. Paul gave them an honorable way out ("God may perhaps grant them repentance," 2:25), which allowed them to defer to God in accepting Timothy's leadership, instead of having to admit defeat and incur shame in public confrontation with the community. Paul thus combined his praise of Timothy's leadership as accentuating the prototype with his exhortation to Timothy as conforming to the prototype in order to maintain both Timothy's and his own leadership in Ephesus. In this way, Paul adeptly avoided a direct and humiliating confrontation with the critics, which would have estranged them from the congregation even if were made to

---

53. Note the parallels with 1–2 Corinthians where Paul had to defend himself against charges of timidity or lack of boldness against critics who were likely very similarly motivated by honor-seeking strategies and the resulting quarrels. Now, Paul defends Timothy against similar charges, but since he addresses the letter to Timothy personally, with the congregation only reading over his shoulder, the argument takes a different shape. Nevertheless, the same contours of Christian leadership with its attendant criticism from an honor-driven leadership model are evident.

accept Timothy's leadership. As a result, Timothy's leadership status is affirmed and enhanced, while the critics risk marginalizing themselves if they persist in their criticism.

Leadership Succession. In his analysis of succession in 2 Timothy, Stepp presents Paul's succession of Christ, and Timothy's succession to Paul. Unlike 1 Timothy no further succession by elders is found. Stepp confidently concludes, "the ancient audience would clearly have understood Timothy to be Paul's successor." Paul's bequest to Timothy is the "call to preserve, promote, and perpetuate the work of the gospel."[54] Stepp does not analyze Timothy's task to select and train faithful men to continue Paul's teaching tradition as a form of succession since it does not contain enough parallels with ancient succession texts. However, this additional link in the chain of succession forms a major purpose for the writing of 2 Timothy, and will thus be included in this section on leadership succession.

Paul's initiative as artist of succession is dependent on his own leadership status. Already in Ephesians and 1 Timothy, Paul had attained a high and uncontested status as apostle and teacher of the gentiles. This status was somewhat enhanced in 2 Timothy by the parallel between Paul and Moses, and by Paul's impending status as martyr for the faith. This allowed Paul to create a chain of succession, which connected Timothy to his own apostolic leadership to legitimate his function as delegate and successor. Paul extended this chain further back to their Jewish family heritage, to the Moses and Joshua narratives, and most importantly to Christ who entrusted the gospel to Paul. This chain of succession was also extended ahead with Paul's charge to entrust this gospel as a treasured deposit to faithful men who will faithfully transmit it to yet others. Note that this chain of succession seems evident from a later perspective, but that it was often challenged and criticized during Paul's and Timothy's ministry, as it would be in later generations. Thus, Paul's portrayal of this chain of succession demonstrated his artistry in identity management, since he highlighted some persons and features, and downgraded others to achieve the maximum intragroup status for Timothy in the eyes of the loyal ingroup. This empowered Timothy in his task of securing further succession, and aimed to reduce the strength of opposition.

---

54. Stepp, *Leadership Succession*, 154–78.

As impresario of succession Paul portrayed Timothy as a prototypical leader, ranking with Moses and himself, with a gift from God and a deposit from Christ to guide the community in new situations. In one sense, this may represent the routinization of charisma, as suggested by Holmberg and MacDonald,[55] since Paul's charisma is now attributed to Timothy, albeit it in a lesser quality. Yet, Timothy's portrayal as charismatic leader came at the end of a long career of cooperation with Paul. The more Timothy served faithfully in difficult situations, the more leadership abilities were attributed to him, until finally Paul was able to attribute a 'charismatic' authority to Timothy expecting that for most members and leaders in Ephesus this would prove acceptable. This may be more aptly described as a charismatization of Timothy's routine leadership functions to strengthen his leadership and authority in the perception of the community.[56] Moreover, Paul's rhetorical strategy aimed to empower the Ephesian community to evaluate and approve of Timothy's leadership, and thus also to scrutinize the leadership of the critics. Paul demonstrated his impresarioship in designing a strategy that not only raised Timothy's intragroup status to the level of charismatic leader in Ephesus, but also invited and enlisted the support of the community for both his presentation of Timothy and his censure of Timothy's critics. Even the critics are enlisted for his proposals, because only by supporting Paul's and Timothy's leadership would they be able to retain the desired position of influence and leadership, while by continued criticism they would marginalize themselves.

As engineer of succession, Paul had structured the content of his gospel, which Timothy was to teach. By thus maintaining a consistent teaching tradition as foundational beliefs of their social identity, Paul provided continuity of institutional vitality. Paul also specified the manner of Timothy's leadership (2:14–26), which provided continuity of manner in terms of leadership style. Perhaps more importantly, Paul pointed to the need of new generations of leaders that Timothy was to equip and appoint, namely the faithful men who could teach others also (2:2). Although no symbolic act of appointment men is indicated

---

55. Holmberg, *Paul and Power*, 179–92; MacDonald, *The Pauline Churches*, 203–20.

56. For a description of this phenomenon from the social sciences, see Alvesson et al., "The Charismatization of Routines," 330–51.

(cf. 1 Tim 5:22) and no explicit parallels between Timothy and these faithful men are noted, Paul's instructions assume a functioning structure of local leadership, of which Timothy became the prime example, and for which Timothy was given responsibility. In describing the content to be taught, and the manner in which it was to be taught, the new leaders were implicitly exhorted to not only faithfully handle and pass on "the word of truth" (2 Tim 2:15), just like Timothy himself, but also to conform themselves to Timothy's style of leadership as he conformed to Paul's. Thus, Paul's social engineering affirmed structures that provided continuity of institutional vitality and continuity of leadership style for the Ephesian community with the post-apostolic period already in view.

Two final observations close this overview of leadership development. First, although Paul legitimates Timothy by the closest possible connections between Timothy, himself, and Christ, he did not instruct Timothy to arrange for someone to succeed himself in his supervisory role in Ephesus. Timothy's succession of Paul mainly served to extend Paul's presence and ministry in Ephesus: retaining Timothy as his long-term delegate enabled Paul to vicariously implement stable local leadership and properly finish the community formation phase. No provisions are made for continued supra-local leadership after Timothy's commission in Ephesus is completed. Second, 2 Timothy offers little information about office. Although Timothy evidently exercised leadership and oversight, no mention is made of a particular office he fulfilled. The faithful men Timothy is to equip and appoint are likely elders who will teach and preach, but their office or status is simply assumed, not explained. Stepp concludes, "what is passed from Paul to Timothy is responsibility for and authority over the teaching and propagation of Paul's gospel." Stepp sees this as "a succession of tradition, *not* task, built on the succession between Jesus and Paul."[57] Although this is an excellent summary of 2 Timothy, its silence about other social structures does not necessarily indicate their absence. In fact, if 1 and 2 Timothy are considered authentic, the leadership structures indicated in 1 Timothy most likely continued to be operative when 2 Timothy was written so that there was no need to address these structures again.

---

57. Stepp, *Leadership Succession*, 2 and 188.

Conclusions

Patterns of Leadership and Succession in Ephesus

Leadership emergence was an important challenge in Ephesus. Timothy was to promote the emergence into leadership of those who were faithful to Paul, while obstructing the emergence into leadership of those whose leadership and teaching differed from Paul's. Timothy himself was at a disadvantage in this particular task, because he had no local power base like other householder-leaders, and because he employed a leadership style that was often perceived as timid and inefficient in comparison with cultural expectations of such leaders. Thus, Paul aimed to raise Timothy's intragroup leadership status to earn him the community's approval, and provided explicit instructions for the leadership style that Paul considered appropriate for his Christ-believing communities to allow Timothy to prove himself as a most suitable leader.

The aligning of leadership emergence depended on the community's acceptance of Timothy's leadership status and tasks. Paul therefore created a chain of succession which embedded both Timothy and himself in a common Jewish heritage, both serving the same Lord who entrusted the gospel first to Paul and then to Timothy. Thus, Paul accentuated that Timothy matched the ingroup prototype. At the same time, Paul's leadership instructions urged Timothy to conform to the prototype as it was modeled in Paul's own life and ministry. Paul may appear ambivalent in thus upholding Timothy as prototypical leader while at the same time urging him to conform to the prototype. This was shown to be a concession to the critics and for the benefit of the community, since now everyone could evaluate Timothy's leadership against Paul's standards and realize that Timothy and not the deviant leaders provided the right kind of leadership. With the church thus mobilized to align themselves with Paul and Timothy, the opportunity for deviant teachers to redefine the prototype and provide an alternative social identity was cut off—at least in Paul's rhetorical framing of the situation. Their only social option was to submit, which would ordinarily be the shameful response in an honor challenge. Thus, Paul strategically did not instruct Timothy to confront the deviant teachers about this, but empowered them instead to "repent" and claim allegiance to God in accepting Timothy's leadership. This expressed both

Paul's confidence in God's work through Timothy's leadership, as well as Paul's sensitivity to leave an honorable way back into the group for the critics.

Although leadership structures were not explicitly addressed, Timothy was to select and guide faithful men emerging into leadership. This is similar to Paul's earlier encouragement that members would do well to aspire to provide a ministry of oversight (1 Tim 3:1ff.), which suggests that in 2 Timothy as well, the emergence of new leadership is in view. Various factors contribute to this structuring of leadership. Timothy is portrayed not just as prototypical leader, but as a charismatic leader who would be able to guide the community through potential difficulties with their newly emerged leaders. This was not merely a faint reflection of Paul's original charisma; instead both Paul and Timothy appeared increasingly as charismatic leaders as their ministry continued and as they served effectively in difficult situations—which reflects the process of charismatic leadership attribution. Next, this leadership attribution process is boosted by the chain of succession from Christ to Paul to Timothy to (new) local leaders, a chain which not only legitimates Paul's and Timothy's authority, but also legitimates the faithful men whom Timothy guides into proper leadership. Their leadership status in the community is secured to the extent that they faithfully communicate Paul's vision of Christian identity to the community. Moreover, this leadership status gave them significant social power within the community, a power that was depicted as divine, exercised through the Holy Spirit in patience, suffering and gentle teaching, by contrast to the social power exercised by deviant teachers based on honor and wealth. This social power, exercised on the basis of the social identity, allowed Paul, Timothy, and faithful local leaders to cope adequately with deviant members and leaders. Finally, as key to implementing local succession, Timothy is uniquely presented as Paul's successor, which is evident both from a comparison with ancient succession texts and from a social identity analysis of his succession. No further details about leadership structures, such as office, characteristics or appointment are discussed in the letter; such structures were undoubtedly present and as such they were simply assumed rather than argued or even affirmed. The continuance of the Pauline tradition was the foremost concern, unlike in

1 Timothy where the structuring of the community was an important focus.

The present social identity and leadership analysis of 1–2 Timothy helps to resolve some old contentions about these letters that affect their social setting and authorship. The first contention is the question why Timothy needed to be instructed in these letters, if indeed the addressee is the Timothy that was one of Paul's closest coworkers. The second contention relates to the rhetorical situation of the letters, from one leader to another.

Why Did Timothy Need to Be Instructed?

The first contention asks why Timothy (and Titus) needed to be instructed in leadership. If the letters were indeed addressed to such close coworkers of Paul, why would Timothy need to be told "how one ought to behave in the household of God" (1 Tim 3:15)? Towner believes that in these instructions, Paul interacts with Timothy's Hellenistic education to provide the Christian point of view on leadership.[58] However, after fifteen years of close cooperation in leadership functions, Paul's perspective would have been abundantly clear, so this still leaves unexplained why Paul summarized his perspective in two personal letters to Timothy. Marshall believes that the problem with these instructions is greatly exaggerated, and suggests that they were provided for the benefit of the congregation.[59] This deals more directly with the question, but it tends to overlook the rhetorical setting as an internal leadership document to treat the letter as a community-wide directive without an adequate rationale.

The present analysis suggests a way forward. Essentially, 1–2 Timothy make it evident that Paul faced a double problem with the leadership in Ephesus. First, local leadership was not in all respects commendable but operated partially on the basis of patronage and honor values. In such a setting, any direct instruction or correction from Paul would be perceived as an honor challenge, which would lead to inappropriate responses, driving the parties further away from a desired resolution. This was precisely the reason why some

---

58. Towner, *Timothy and Titus*, 36.

59. He cites the third person plural verb in the ending of each of the Pastorals in support of his position. See Marshall, *Pastoral Epistles*, 75.

local leadership was not yet sufficiently qualified and deemed deviant. Second, Timothy's leadership was not well received by everyone, especially by those needing correction. Most likely his leadership was perceived as timid or cowardly, inadequate in an honor/shame culture to meet the challenges of a new social group in an oppressive social environment. In order to secure one's place in the Greco-Roman world, some may well have argued that matters of honor and challenge needed priority, even if internally these values were seen differently. In response to the double problem, Paul adopts the format of the *mandata principis* letters, where a senior official instructs a junior official in the discharge of his duties, in order to provide a recognizable instruction document for leadership in Ephesus. Although in all likelihood Paul knew that Timothy did not need these instructions and expected Timothy to fully measure up to them, this letter allowed him to make a concession to the critics. His instructions appear to instruct Timothy but he expected that they would vindicate Timothy as charismatic leader. As the Ephesian community observed Timothy's leadership, they would realize that it matched Paul's prescriptions. This turned Timothy into a practical object lesson on Christian leadership, thus indirectly modeling Paul's leadership instructions for the critics while avoiding direct confrontation and challenge. Moreover, if these critics were inclined to resist this model, they now had the majority of the community against them, since Timothy had been publicly vindicated before them all. In fact, the critics would now also be evaluated by these same criteria in their leadership. In this way, Paul mobilized the whole community in its evaluation of proper leadership and even in disciplining the critics to conform to Paul's model. Thus, Paul included specific leadership instructions, not to inform but to vindicate Timothy, as well as to motivate local leaders to conformity, both by indirect instruction and by increasing social pressure. By this mechanism, the critics would be most obliged to accept Paul's proposals for leadership.

A Leader's Perspective on Christian Social Identity in Ephesus

The second contention relates to the rhetorical setting of 1–2 Timothy. As noted in chapters 7 and 8, a discussion of social identification in Ephesus based on 1–2 Timothy is questionable because the letters present themselves as personal rather than community letters. Yet, the letters were written to an individual in his capacity of community leader, so that group concerns were never far removed from the letters' scope. Indeed, many of the instructions related to the leader's activity within the community. Thus, social identification remains an important method for assessing community and leadership formation in these letters. On the other hand, a leadership subgroup does not consist of a representative selection of group members, so that concerns expressed within a leadership subgroup are not necessarily or even likely representative for the concerns of the whole group. Thus, the leadership character of 1–2 Timothy (or at least their self-presentation as a leadership communication) suggests that these letters may express concerns that are not in every case broadly shared in the whole community. This makes it even more more challenging to reconstruct stages of community and leadership formation by a simple comparison of 1–2 Timothy with the letters 1–2 Corinthians and Ephesians.

Unfortunately, this is rarely acknowledged in historical reconstructions, which use the Pastoral Epistles to chart the development of Pauline churches.[60] For instance, Tellbe proposes to study early Christian identity formation in Ephesus, not so much by reconstructing the communities behind certain documents (1–2 Timothy, Revelation, *Ign.Eph.* and 1–3 John), but by focusing on the textual prototypes. He chooses three prototypical dimensions to analyze: leadership structures, societal relations and community metaphors. It comes as no surprise that Tellbe finds significant differences in textual prototypes for each of these (sets of) documents.[61] Next, these differences are simply juxtaposed along a tentative chronological framework of development, with each document potentially defining its textual prototype in response to the previous one. The surprising element is not his eventual reconstruction, but the complete lack of attention to the socio-rhetorical setting of each document. As is evident in the analyses completed above, the socio-rhetorical situation is crucial to explain differences from one document to another before any further social and historical reconstruction can take place, certainly with the differ-

---

60. As is evident in such studies as Verner, *The Household of God*; MacDonald, *The Pauline Churches*; Richards, *Difference and Distance*; Merz, *Selbstauslegung*; Pietersen, *Polemic of the Pastorals* and Aageson, *Pastoral Epistles*.

61. Tellbe, "The Prototypical Christ-Believer," 122–27.

ent authors, addressees, and genres in Tellbe's selection of literature. Thus, Tellbe's historical reconstruction fails to convince. Roitto uses the social identity approach to study household relationships in 1 Cor 7, Col 3:8—4:1 and Eph 5:21—6:9, and 1 Tim 3:1-13. He observes a number of differences and suggests that one's identity as a Christ-believer in 1 Cor 7 shaped the household identities in Colossians and Ephesians, but that in 1 Timothy household identity had become so dominant that it began to shape Christian identity instead of vice versa.[62] In spite of an insightful analysis, Roitto's reconstruction overlooks that household identity may be more prominent in 1 Timothy because it deals more prominently with leadership issues. Whether this reflected a church-wide household ideology that influenced constructions of Christian identity is impossible to determine without further information. Roitto supplies this information from a traditional chronological framework which assumes pseudonymous authorship—which explains why he ignores the rhetorical setting of the letter within a leadership subgroup.

Any historical reconstruction of 1–2 Timothy should take the rhetorical setting of these texts into account. A key insight for the study of 1–2 Timothy is that a leader's perspective of the church's social identity may differ from the perspective more broadly shared by group members. The leadership subgroup functions as a nested social identity within the superordinate social identity of the whole group. Such nesting implies that the leadership subgroup may have goals and functions of its own, in addition to those of the whole group. For instance, a leadership subgroup may be very concerned about a few deviant group members, while most group members are relatively unconcerned until their leaders inform them (how else could deviant members gain any influence?). Or leaders may consider themselves primarily responsible to maintain the group's belief and unity through their teaching, while most group members are more concerned to maintain unity with various levels of participation by each group member. The same applies to other subgroups within the larger community that may have additional goals or functions that are not fully shared by all members of the larger group, such as might have been the case with subgroups of Jewish believers. As long as each subgroup identifies with the foundational beliefs and values of the larger group without expecting every

---

62. Roitto, "Act as a Christ-Believer," 146–52.

member to share their subgroup's preference, this arrangement provides for a cohesive community based on the group's superordinate social identity with adequate space for subgroups and their specialized goals and functions. Thus, it is one thing to study particular documents and observe a number of differences (and similarities); it is another thing to locate these differences in an intra- or intergroup setting. Without taking the rhetorical setting into account, differences are too often simply extrapolated to reflect intergroup settings, reflecting perhaps different types of Christian communities even in one city, while alternative scenarios are rarely considered. The social identity analysis of 1–2 Timothy suggests that at least some of the differences with Paul's other letters can be located as concerns of the leadership subgroup, which complement the concerns of the group as a whole.

Two aspects of 1–2 Timothy illustrate this point: the use of stereotyping and the dominance of household language. Stereotyping takes place in referring to the Pauline teaching tradition, to Paul's opponents, and even to Paul's self-references. First, Paul's teaching in 1–2 Corinthians appears as a lively dialogue with various issues, while references to his teaching in the Pastorals appear to be static and dogmatic. Paul's gospel is now a "deposit of truth," which is the standard for "sound teaching," on the basis of which Timothy restricts the teaching of certain people.[63] Second, Paul's opponents receive personal and direct attention in Paul's early letters, while the Pastorals vilify the opponents as "puffed up with conceit," "men of depraved mind and deprived of the truth," and as "evil people and impostors."[64] Third, Paul's self-references in the early letters often provide personal details of his life, while his self-references in the Pastorals are brief and stylized. Paul was "a blasphemer, persecutor, and insolent opponent," but now he is a preacher and apostle to the gentiles. In sum, the Pastorals abound in more stereotypical references to Paul, his teaching, and his ministry.

Beker interprets this stereotypical language as a lack of concrete memory and thus as greater historical distance from Paul. The memorialized tradition spans two generations, which "brings about an increasing 'depersonalization' and 'dehistoricization' of the apostle."[65]

---

63. Beker, *Heirs of Paul*, 39–40; see also Aageson, *Pastoral Epistles*, 28–31, 50–52.
64. Beker, *Heirs of Paul*, 40–41.
65. Ibid., 39–40.

However, according to the social identity perspective, stereotyping takes place mostly in stable groups, where group characteristics are clear and acknowledged,[66] which is precisely the case in the Pauline leadership subgroup of 1–2 Timothy (even if the situation in the Ephesian church was not fully stable). Paul addressed a trusted colleague with whom he has collaborated at least 15 years.[67] Paul's call, message, and leadership, and even his opponents, are the subject of shared, uncontested memories, which can be easily evoked by brief self-references and other stereotypical language. Thus, if the rhetorical setting of a leadership subgroup is taken into account, these stereotypical references fit quite well and serve as evidence that Paul and Timothy functioned in a stable leadership subgroup at the time of composition.[68] Thus, the stereotypical language of the Pastorals provides a leadership perspective on the teaching tradition and its opponents, most likely late in Paul's ministry.[69] Whether this complements Paul's teaching as reflected in earlier letters cannot be determined by a simple comparison. The social identity analyses of this study survey more social and rhetorical variables than usual, which leads to the conclusion that the stereotypical language of the Pastorals should be read as a leadership perspective, complementing the broader congregational perspectives on Paul's gospel as reflected in Paul's community letters.

---

66. In unstable groups it is unclear what group characteristics or which group members are considered prototypical, with the result that stereotyping decreases. See Hogg, "A Social Identity Theory of Leadership," 190; Haslam, *Psychology in Organizations*, 36,

67. Timothy was associated with Paul since the beginning of Paul's second missionary journey according to Acts (ca. 48 CE, Acts 16:1–3), and appeared alongside Paul at various times until his death around 67 CE, considering Acts to be fairly historically accurate on this information.

68. One could suppose that this is still a fictional element of the pseudepigrapher, but it requires highly sophisticated social and literary skills for this author to invent such a subgroup, shape the dialogue to match these subgroups dynamics so convincingly and, finally, to blend this scenario almost perfectly into an otherwise unknown situation some 60 years prior–a feat so skillful that it took 18 centuries to discover. This is highly unlikely. The current proposal to take the leadership subgroup setting into account relieves the pressure to find a historical setting for these letters far removed from Paul's own time, since they can now be located convincingly towards the end of Paul's itinerant ministry.

69. For a more detailed analysis, see Barentsen, "Stereotyping and Leadership in 1 Timothy."

A second illustration, which indicates how the Pastorals complement earlier letters, comes from the use of household language. Household identities in 1 Corinthians and Ephesians relate primarily to individual relationships which believers have with others in the household: married or single (1 Cor 7), husband and wife, parents and children, masters and slaves (Eph 5:21—6:9). The focus of these texts is on assisting group members in negotiating their Christian social identity in the context of their day-to-day household relationships. However, in 1 Timothy household language is used to frame various relationships within the church. Gender roles in fulfilling God's mission (2:8–15) as well as the character lists for the overseer and deacons (3:1–13) are framed by the reference to the church as God's household (3:15). Timothy's relationship with older and younger men and women is framed in terms of household language (5:1–2), while the church functions as fictive household for widows whose own households can no longer support them (5:3–16). Understandably, Roitto (see above) proposed that the household became the dominant metaphor to describe Christian identity by the time of the Pastorals. Horrell speaks of a household ideology where the proper ordering of the church is modeled on the household, while Verner clarifies that the Pastorals extend household terminology beyond the actual sphere of the household.[70] These authors suppose a shift in ecclesiology because of such prominent household language in the Pastorals. Unfortunately, they do not take the rhetorical setting within a leadership subgroup into account, since they consider it fictional, and this weakens their historical reconstruction.

An alternative scenario for interpreting such dominant household terminology is provided by the rhetorical setting of the letters. Most local leaders in the early Pauline communities were relatively wealthier householders. Since the household generally and the father's role specifically were already standard metaphors in the Roman world to describe institutions and leadership outside the family,[71] this provided a readily accessible leadership model for the church—although Paul has to remind them frequently that leadership means service, not seeking honor. Moreover, since wealthier households often contained a number of subgroups (the men and women of the family, children,

---

70. Horrell, "Disciplining Performance," 133; Verner, *The Household of God*, 91–92.

71. Lassen, "The Roman Family," 110–12; Clarke, *Serve the Community*, 101.

clients and slaves), this provided a helpful organizational model for the Christ-believing community. On the other hand, most individual group members would be less concerned with leadership and organization, and more with how to integrate one's Christian identity with one's role as husband or wife, parent or child, master or slave. These day-to-day social roles were not erased, even though members could use the language of fictive kinship to address one another as brother or sister. In other words, fictive kinship was the dominant metaphor to conceptualize the group's interpersonal relationships, while fictive household was the dominant metaphor to conceptualize the group's organization and leadership.[72] These householders were also the ones most active in public settings, which is reflected in 1 Timothy's awareness of a watching world. It is thus quite likely that the household values in 1 Timothy represent a leader's perspective on the community's Christian social identity, while the household codes of Ephesians represent the perspective of individual community members in negotiating their Christian social identity in daily relationships. Although both perspectives deal with social identity, this occurs at different levels: leaders negotiate the Christian identity of the community in a larger world of institutions, while individuals negotiate Christian identity in their personal relationships. The social identity analysis in this study shows that the household language of 1 Timothy should be read as a leadership perspective, complementing the broader congregational perspectives on household relationships in a few of Paul's community letters.

The difficulty of analyzing personal letters in terms of social identity thus turns out to be an occasion for a more in-depth understanding of how rhetoric and social factors interact in the Pauline corpus. This provides additional options for including the Pastorals in a historical reconstruction of the development of Pauline churches. The pressure to interpret significant differences solely in terms of conflict and historical distance is lessened in favor of other options, which chart these differences as simultaneous and complementary perspectives.

---

72. For another perspective, see Horrell, "Social Transformation," 293–311.

9

Conclusions and Implications:
Emerging Leadership in the Pauline Mission

TO OFFER A FRESH PERSPECTIVE ON LEADERSHIP IN THE EARLY church, it was stated at the outset that this study would approach leadership as a dynamic group phenomenon, analyzing the social and psychological processes that shape and change leadership patterns. A review of the literature of church leadership studies showed the need and timeliness of such an approach in chapter 2. To accomplish this, a new methodology was required, so the social identity model of leadership was presented in chapter 3. The application of this method from social psychology is one of the key contributions of this study. Chapters 4 through 8 contain the analysis of the Pauline letters sent to Corinth and Ephesus, which required the matter of authorship to be dealt with for the Ephesian correspondence. It is time to review the results obtained and to bring them into dialogue with the debate about church office and patterns of Pauline leadership to outline the fresh perspective as promised.

The research question, guiding the current investigation, is:

> "According to the Pauline letters addressed to Corinth and Ephesus, what were the leadership patterns in these early Christ-following communities, and how did the communities as well as Paul attempt to shape these patterns?"

So far, the study has analyzed each of the Pauline letters of 1–2 Corinthians, Ephesians, and 1–2 Timothy separately to trace these leadership patterns in Paul's interaction with the community. With this analysis completed, the stage is now set to summarize the results for each community, outlining the patterns of leadership emergence, maintenance, and succession along with the forces at work to shape and change these patterns. Next, the leadership patterns in these communities will be compared with one another, investigating whether the leadership patterns in Corinth and Ephesus can be charted as segments of one relatively uniform pattern of leadership development, or whether they remain unique and distinct images of leadership formation. Paul's rising status as charismatic leader plays an important part in answering this question, from both the social and the psychological aspects. Third, this comparison will pave the way for the argument of this study that Paul advocated a relatively uniform pattern of leadership in his communities on the leadership level responsible for intragroup teaching (identity maintenance) and for intergroup communication. This section will answer the question whether Paul intended to institute a normative pattern of leadership. Finally, this chapter will close with a number of implications of the current research and suggestions for further study.

Developing Leadership Patterns in Corinth and Ephesus

Developing Leadership Patterns at Corinth

Leadership Emergence, Maintenance, Succession. The Corinthian correspondence indicates that Paul faced various challenges to his leadership and heritage in Corinth, which coincided with emerging local leadership that was not successful in stabilizing their rapidly growing communities in their Greco-Roman context. Paul faced difficulties in maintaining his leadership in Corinth, while local leaders failed to emerge to new levels of collegial leadership needed to facilitate continuing expansion. Since leadership emergence and maintenance are still in flux, the letters make no mention of leadership succession (unless Apollos, Timothy or Titus are to be considered as Paul's successors in Corinth, which is doubtful).

Paul's difficulties with leadership maintenance in 1 Corinthians are implied in the formation of subgroups around favored Jewish leaders. Paul's leadership was relegated to the level of one of the subgroups, so that he no longer had the status necessary to unify all the Corinthian house groups into one community. It appears that Paul's weak oral performance, his experiences in suffering, and his self-denial in refusing patronage support, were considered dishonorable for a leader of his ambitions by at least some in the community. Some even contradicted his teaching on such a central belief as the resurrection. This created an awkward position for Paul as leader in Corinth, since any solution he might have proposed risked being perceived as partisan, merely favoring his own party. The situation had worsened after the reception of 1 Corinthians since intruding Jewish leaders changed the community's teaching even more by focusing on Moses, and by adopting the familiar practices such as presenting letters of recommendation and accepting patronage support. It appears that Paul as apostolic leader lost his leadership influence in most of the Corinthian church. Nevertheless, Paul revisited Corinth and wrote another letter, knowing that the community had marginalized him as founder and spiritual father. Ultimately, his negotiations with Corinth were successful, in spite of the sorrow and pain along the way. At great personal cost, Paul reestablished and maintained his own leadership as divinely legitimated, directing attention to his personal self-sacrificial example and to his teaching, both his former teaching while present and his current teaching in these letters.

Paul's difficulties in maintaining his leadership reflect a breakdown in the emergence of local leadership. It appears that most of the local Corinthian leaders were caught off guard in the growing diversity of the community, with an increasing number of households and a variety of Jewish teachers. By permitting or even advocating competition over favored Jewish teachers, they resorted to community cohesion on the level of household, apparently unable to provide cohesion on the level of the whole city. Some of these leaders also faced conflicting social obligations that created tension in their relationship within the congregation. A few leaders, such as Stephanas, appeared to be aware of these difficulties, but may well have had too little influence and leadership status to handle these difficulties themselves. They turned to Paul for assistance, probably convincing the church to write Paul about some issues (although divisions were not reported in their letter), and to send a delegation. However, before Paul's answer in 1 Corinthians could establish the higher level of cohesion, itinerant Jewish-Christian teachers from Jerusalem provided this cohesion, but on a different basis. The Corinthian church was thus in danger of being lost to Paul's mission altogether, including most of its emerging leadership. Paul's confrontation and negotiations allowed him to win over the local membership and leadership once again, reestablishing his own role as apostolic founder. Presumably, Paul's restoration to apostolic leadership for Corinth allowed the earlier process of leadership emergence to be resumed, empowering the church and its leaders to establish a new cohesion for the community on a city-wide level. It is likely that stable collegial leadership was established in the aftermath of 1–2 Corinthians. This is reflected in 1 Clement some 40 years later (1 Clem. 42, 44) when difficulties of succession had arisen.

Cultural and Religious Influences. First and second Corinthians reveal a community that has grown not only numerically but has also become increasingly diverse in the 5 or 6 years since its founding. Their construction of Christian social identity had not yet broadened sufficiently to allow the local leaders to attain a new level of unity and cohesion in such a situation of dynamic growth. As a result, informal subgroups asserted their distinctiveness within the larger community, while social obligations of their Greco-Roman social identities at least sometimes took priority over the obligations of the Christian social identity. Even core identity functions, such as the Lord's Supper, manifestations of the Spirit's ministry, or belief in the resurrection were not sufficiently developed to reduce social tension within the community.

Paul evidently worked with whatever local and cultural forms of leadership were available in Corinth, but he consistently transformed these forms by orienting them towards the foundational beliefs and values of Christian social identity. Initial leadership seems to have come from the ranks of those who were able to provide benefactions for the community, Paul legitimated his own as well as local leadership in terms of self-sacrificial service for the community in the service of the gospel. He also affirmed their sensitivity to honor, but oriented it first towards God as the divine benefactor, and second to all other community members since they are sufficiently wise to judge difficult cases and sufficiently gifted to contribute to the life of the community. Some of the countercultural aspects of Paul's proposals were bound to increase social tension with the other, often cross-cutting, social identities of the group members, but Paul envisioned that his solution would bring new stability to the community after their recent expansion.

However, the reception of Paul's proposals was thwarted by the arrival of Jewish-Christian teachers from Israel, who resolved the social tension with an alternative proposal. They claimed greater allegiance from the Corinthian believers towards Moses and Jewish traditions, and adopted cultural modes of leadership based on patronage sponsorship. In essence, these teachers reduced social tension by reducing the distinctiveness of their leadership style relative to Greco-Roman identities and by reducing the distinctiveness of their teaching relative to Jewish identity. Thus, these teachers blurred the boundaries that Paul had so carefully drawn between the believing community on the one hand, and Greco-Roman and Jewish identities on the other. The Corinthian community now had a choice of two proposals for a new level of cohesion for their various house groups as one social identity: Paul's proposal for his distinct vision of Christian social identity, which heightened social tension before bringing new stability, and a Jewish-Christian proposal, which reduced social tension by slightly adapting their vision of Christian social identity. Evidently, the community and its emerging leaders chose the option of short-term reduction of social tension and simply accepted the consequence of a less distinctive form of Christian social identity.

Interestingly, Paul's negotiations with Corinth not only reestablished his role and authority as founding apostle, but also incorporated his apostolic role as a non-negotiable part of their Christian social identity. Paul's self-description as "ambassador for Christ" (2 Cor 5:20) was a formidable authority claim, which implied that the Corinthian believers could only be true adherents of the gospel if they accepted Paul's ministry; there was no gospel without Paul. The visions and revelations received and the miracles performed (12:1–12), designated Paul as an apostle on equal footing with whoever else might have claimed apostolic authority. Paul also argued that his many sufferings should have raised his status even higher in the eyes of the Corinthians (11:21–28). By contrast, his references to his apostolic authority in 1 Corinthians are more subtle. Even as a master builder, he was only a fellow worker of God alongside Apollos and others (1 Cor 3:9–10). He was entrusted with the gospel he preached in Corinth, but he made no use of the privileges of his stewardship for being financially supported (9:15–17). Though called as apostle, he presented himself as last and least of all (15:8–9). Knowing that his leadership had been relegated to the subgroup level, he downplayed his authority claims in 1 Corinthians and focused on uniting all groups in one superordinate Christian social identity. In 2 Corinthians, knowing that once again he was accepted as apostolic leader, Paul freely spoke of his authority and used it to urge the community to confirm the intended reconciliation as well as to denounce any remaining opposition.

The Corinthian troubles were finally resolved after Paul had regained his position and authority as apostle. This restored his sphere of social influence and permitted him to reconnect with their identity narrative. Through Paul's leadership, the Corinthian construction of Christian social identity was expanded to provide the needed unity and cohesion at these new levels of growth.

Developing Leadership Patterns at Ephesus

Leadership Emergence, Maintenance, Succession. The Ephesian correspondence portrays Paul as the apostle to the gentiles whose authority was well accepted in Ephesus, while local leadership appears to be functioning relatively harmoniously on a city-wide level. New leaders are discussed, either to facilitate continuing expansion or to succeed other local leaders.

Paul had less difficulty with leadership maintenance in Ephesus. The letters portray Paul as unquestioned apostle to the gentiles to reveal the mysteries of God (Eph 3:7–9), and as teacher and preacher to the gentiles (1 Tim 2:7, 2 Tim 2:11). Paul's apostolic role is explicitly connected with his divine commission and gifting for his ministry; his status as apostolic leader has now received charismatic legitimation. Both the community and the leadership subgroup surrounding Timothy appear to perceive Paul's role in this way. This increase in leadership status also increases Paul's social power, as long as he is perceived as prototypical and as serving the community's interests on Christ's behalf.

At the same time, the local leadership seems also to have stabilized in Ephesus on a collegial, city-wide level. They function in harmony with and as an extension of the foundational ministry of apostles and prophets (Eph 4:11). In 1 Timothy the increasing complexity of local leadership patterns becomes visible in the dual functions of oversight (overseer) and assistance (deacon), and with differentiated male and female participation in these functions (women allowed as deaconess). The overseers, collectively referred to as elders, also function on a city-wide level, while some of this group labored harder in leadership and teaching than others. Paul's communications to Timothy suggest that all was not quite as well as Ephesians would have it, since problems with deviance on the part of some leaders were persistent. Paul instructs Timothy to put in order the leadership subgroup for long-term maintenance as part of the overall ministry of the community and in harmony with Paul's apostolic leadership. Thus, these three letters focus largely on leadership maintenance, not in the least through the institution of various procedures for selection and appointment, remuneration, critique, and impeachment.

Leadership succession becomes an important issue. First Timothy still focused mostly on leadership maintenance, ensuring that there is sufficient leadership to facilitate the community's expansion (1 Tim 3:1), and that sufficient care is taken in examining and appointing these new leaders (5:22). Second Timothy shifts the emphasis to leadership succession. First, Timothy's succession of Paul is legitimated by their common heritage, by prophecy and ordination, by comparing Paul and Timothy with Moses and Joshua, and by Timothy's faithful following of Paul. Second, new generations of local leaders are envisioned in Paul's charge to Timothy to teach others who will be able to teach others also (2:2). Paul indicated to Timothy and other readers what these leaders should teach and how they should lead. Paul was no longer personally involved in this new generation of leaders, but his heightened status as charismatic, apostolic leader still functioned as the authority and legitimation for the succession instituted in this letter. Timothy, as Paul's delegate and successor was to oversee the appointment and training of new leaders, so that the community would be able in succeeding generations to carry out God's mission with the church in the world.

Cultural and Religious Influences. The increasing complexity of the leadership structure in Ephesus reflects the increasing social complexity of the community, which began to develop within ten years after founding the community. In Ephesians, Paul constructed a superordinate Christian social identity, rooted in Jewish identity and contextualized as an alternative to Greco-Roman identities with similar universal claims. Conflicts with nested or cross-cutting social identities are in principle resolved by making them all subordinate to the Father who named "every family on heaven and on earth" (Eph 3:15), and who gave Paul the grace to be his privileged spokesman. The integration of Christian social identity with household structures indicated not so much an accommodation to Greco-Roman social hierarchies, nor a slackening of eschatological expectation, but a realization that the vision of Christian social identity also encompassed the different household roles of group members. Christian identity needed to be clarified and further defined in its interaction with the daily life of group members in their social setting. Paul handled the increasing social complexity by expanding the Christian identity narrative, in order to ensure that Christian social identity maintained its primacy over against competing social identities and influences.

The superordinate scope of Christian social identity has implications for Paul's thinking about community leadership. Since God is the Father of the Christ-following community, and leaders are also group members, their leadership can have no other source than God himself, who through Christ gives these members as leaders to the community (Eph 4:7–11). These local leaders, labeled "shepherd and teachers" and perhaps "evangelists," function on the same level as the apostles and prophets, even though the latter have a foundational ministry (2:20). Moreover, these leaders are called to serve the united community and bring it to maturity, indicating that local leaders are to mobilize and empower group members to deepen their social identification according to the vision of Christian social identity that Paul had provided. Thus, divine institution legitimates local leadership as manner in which to maintain a clear focus on Christian social identity, thereby incorporating leadership as a structural element into Paul's conception of Christian social identity.

First and Second Timothy reflect a realistic implementation of this ideal with their instructions about deviant teachers, written within 10–14 years after the founding of the Ephesian community. Although the description of deviant teachers is colored by Paul's perspective, the letters suggest that they presented a more Jewish version of Christian identity in their emphasis on the law and on genealogies (with "myths" referring pejoratively to Jewish identity narratives). The warnings against trust in riches as well as the criticism of some that Timothy was too timid and too young suggest that these deviant teachers were closely aligned with the Greco-Roman values of honor and status. However, since the community in Ephesus was less affected by deviance than Corinth at an earlier stage, and since Timothy functioned as Paul's mouth-piece in Ephesus, 1–2 Timothy did not need to provide an extensive identity narrative, but used stereotypical language to remind Timothy of familiar expressions of Paul's teaching as well as of familiar experiences with previous deviance. This deviance, persistent though it was, had not fractured the community in Ephesus like it had in Corinth. The Ephesian leadership did not need to be rescued as in Corinth, but needed to be stabilized by a consistent orientation on God's mission with the church in the world. The increasing perception of Christian social identity in terms of household relationships seems to indicate not the growing dominance of hierarchical household structures in the community, but the perspective of the leadership subgroup as it sought to order the life of the community.

It is not surprising that Paul experienced instability and conflicts with his newly founded communities. Although they adapted some structures from their Greco-Roman environment, their leadership style and community life were so different from their environment that group members found it difficult to know how to behave or how to lead in new situations that they had not encountered before as Christ-followers. Thus, Paul's followers frequently defaulted to behavior and processes of identification that were more familiar with them. For some members, this may have involved reverting to aspects of Jewish identity, since they shared their Scriptures and many of their stories. Moreover, Jewish identity was a known and usually accepted identity in the Greco-Roman world, offering social and political stability in a way that Paul was not yet able to do. For almost all members, with or without prior experience with Jewish identity, Greco-Roman values of honor, status, and competition presented a constant pull away from such important distinctives as self-sacrifice and mutual service in Christian social identity. Paul's communities evidently did not have a natural 'home' in the Greco-Roman world. "Paul's new communities of varying social levels of gentiles did not quite fit in or easily relate to the known patterns of the ancient world. Sometimes it seemed as if this Diaspora-born Jew [Paul] understood neither his own people's not the gentiles' traditions."[1]

---

1. Campbell, *Paul and the Creation of Christian Identity*, 55.

Comparison of Leadership Patterns in Corinth and Ephesus

After summarizing the leadership patterns in Corinth and Ephesus separately, this section will compare them with one another to investigate whether these different patterns are in some way related to one another as stages of community and leadership formation.

Differences. Leadership patterns in Corinth and Ephesus differed significantly. In Corinth, the community struggled with proper leadership emergence, symptomatic of the broader struggles in defining Christian social identity, while in Ephesus local leadership had already successfully emerged, functioning on a city-wide level of coordination. The available evidence shows explicit provisions for succession along with several indicators of established leadership offices only for Ephesus. Put differently, the Corinthian community struggled to move the coordination of local leadership from the level of households to the level of the city, while the Ephesian community needed structures for their city-wide level of leadership to be transferrable to the next generation of leaders.

This basic difference provides the background to most other differences observed. First, the Corinthian troubles fragmented the community and even threatened its total loss for the Pauline mission, while the deviance in Ephesus was troublesome—since it probably originated from a few of its committed leaders—but the level of threat was significantly lower. Second, the Corinthian correspondence is mostly reactive, resolving problems that had already occurred, while the Ephesian correspondence is more proactive, providing the communities with an ideological framework for principled solutions in order to safeguard future leadership maintenance and succession. Third, as a result, the Corinthian letters are full of concrete indications of social tension and conflict, while the Ephesian correspondence situates current or potential issues, including opposition, within this ideological framework; even 1–2 Timothy present opposition in stereotyped fashion more than in detailed concrete narrative. This more prominent ideological framework thus does not seek to institute new levels of organizational hierarchy in parallel with their Greco-Roman neighbors, but seeks ways in which the connections between various groups in the city can be conceptualized and managed.

Fourth, these reactive and proactive stances are visible in Paul's leadership practice. In Corinth, Paul directly disciplined the participation of various group members and subgroups in the larger community. In Ephesus he does this indirectly by presenting an ideology of divinely legitimated leadership (Ephesians) and by instructing Timothy and other local leaders in how to discipline the various subgroups in the congregation (1–2 Timothy). As a consequence, fifth, leadership is discussed mostly implicitly in 1–2 Corinthians, often by way of Paul's example in suffering and self-denial, while in Ephesians leadership seems to have attained higher status within the community, with especially their teaching function theologically legitimated. In 1–2 Timothy these strands converge with suffering and teaching as leadership characteristics, along with provisions for long-term maintenance of the teaching tradition through office-like structures.

Finally, Paul's leadership in Corinth faced continual challenges, while in Ephesus it generally appeared to be well accepted since the Ephesian correspondence puts forward strong authority claims on Paul's behalf, which remain essentially uncontested. It is possible, though, that this last difference is more rhetorical than social, since Ephesians is written from greater social distance than 1–2 Corinthians, and from a more ideological perspective, possibly glossing over real Ephesian tensions over Paul's status. However, authority claims of this nature are only effective in a group climate where such claims are perceived as beneficial, serving the group's interests, which suggests that Paul estimated that his leadership was perceived as prototypical, not just by Timothy but also by the Ephesian community. This warrants the conclusion that the acceptance of Paul's apostolic leadership in Ephesus was not only a rhetorical device but also for the most part a social reality.

Similarities. In spite of the significant differences pointed out, a number of basic similarities are also evident. Leadership patterns in both communities were mostly based on household leadership, while gradually a new level of coordination developed as the house groups in each city perceived themselves as belonging to a broader community of households. Although the timing and progress of this development may have differed, the basic pattern is similar.

Moreover, both communities wrestled with similar social tensions over Greco-Roman and Jewish values and identities. Greco-Roman values of patronage, honor, and status caused considerable tension in Corinth, but also caused significant distress in the Ephesian community and its leadership. Both communities experienced additional stress over their relationship to Jewish identity, with its greater emphasis on Moses and the law. In Corinth, this tension arose most likely through the intrusion of Jewish Christ-followers from Israel, while in Ephesus the source appears to be local elders and teachers, but the basic patterns of social tension are similar. It may easily be granted that these struggles appear in more concrete fashion in the reactive Corinthian letters than in the proactive Ephesian letters, and that they appear to have been more disruptive in Corinth than in Ephesus. However, these reflect merely different perspectives on and different degrees of a similar pattern of social tension.

Two additional points of social tension are similar in both cities. One point relates to the role of women in the community, which in both locations led to instructions about the public speech of female members, allowing some forms of speech (praying, prophesying) but not all (evaluative leadership, teaching). Since both communities are to maintain this balance of permission and restriction, it is hard to see how Capper's proposal that the church moved increasingly into public space where women did not have voice, accounts for the similarity.[2] A second point of social tension relates to the participation in the life of the community by the community's leaders, while ordinarily patrons and other benefactors did not do so.[3] This countercultural pattern is similar in both communities.

Evaluation. The key question is how to evaluate these differences and similarities. The differences outlined are generally due to different stages of community and leadership formation, to differences in Paul's personal accessibility for the community in Corinth or Ephesus (implying less or more social distance), and thus to differences in available strategies for intervention on the local level. An additional factor is the personal development of Paul and his missionary team, who undoubtedly would have applied lessons learned in the Corinthian situation to their early and later ministries in Ephesus, which would also be reflected in the available correspondence. The similarities outlined are

---

2. See Capper, "The Transition from Gathering in Private," Part 1, 117–27, and Part 2, 311–14.

3. Schmeller, *Hierarchie und Egalität*, 61–62.

mostly due to social and cultural similarities in Corinth and Ephesus. Leadership by householders as patrons or benefactors is a basic feature of antiquity in the Roman world, and so is patronage and honor competition to enhance one's social status. The influence of Jewish identity in both locations had similar impact on the communities. Thus, the similarities are attributable to basic similarity in social and cultural patterns of both locations, while the differences are mainly attributable to differences in timing, availability, style of intervention, and personal growth. This suggests the possibility that Corinthian and Ephesian communities operate on similar patterns of social identification and leadership formation, while their different stages of development account for the differences.

Thus, this study proposes that the later developments in Corinth probably paralleled what is known from Ephesus, but they remain beyond the horizon of our current sources. First Clement 42–44 provide a little window on this situation, confirming the idea that later developments in Corinth paralleled those in Ephesus. Furthermore, our evidence for Ephesus starts with a functioning leadership subgroup, and any earlier development in Ephesus also remains beyond the horizon. Even if the emerging Ephesian leadership had faced conflict similar to Corinth, the Corinthian correspondence—either in manuscript form or by way of oral instruction—would have been called upon to help settle the matter, thus hiding these developments from the scrutiny of historians. Thus, it is warranted to suppose that Ephesians and 1–2 Timothy purposely build on the information available in the Corinthian correspondence, and that the patterns of social identification and leadership formation in these communities can be connected as different stages of a similar development.

This is also affirmed by the process of leadership legitimation. In Corinth, Paul had to reestablish the legitimacy of his own leadership, which he accomplished with reference to his sacrificial behavior, his own teaching authority, and his divine commission. In Ephesus, his divine commission and teaching authority were less contested so that Paul no longer needed to legitimate his own leadership. Instead, he legitimated the local leaders, first in terms of their role in teaching and maintaining the unity of the community (Ephesians), but also in terms of self-sacrifice and suffering (1–2 Timothy). This also included legitimation for Timothy's task as delegate and successor. The process of legitimation is thus similar in both communities, but applied to different leaders as relevant to their particular stage of development.

Paul's Rising Charismatic Status in Historical Context

It was noted above that Paul's authority claims seem much bolder and less contested in Ephesus than in Corinth. The portrayal of Paul in Ephesians as well as in 1–2 Timothy position him in a nearly unassailable authority as revealer of God's mysteries and teacher of the gentiles; his authority claims in 2 Corinthians are perhaps just as strong, but had been strongly contested just prior to the writing of the letter. It seems that Paul's success in his negotiation of the Corinthian conflict not only allowed him to regain his leadership position in Corinth, but also occasioned a significant rise in Paul's status as leader. This should not be surprising, for Paul had persuaded the community and its leadership to accept once again his own proposal for Christian social identity, which had caused them such serious social tension before, while a socially more attractive option was available from the itinerant Jewish-Christian teachers (a more Jewish-Christian identity with more lenience towards Greco-Roman values). In other words, Paul succeeded in winning over the Corinthians and defeating the opponents, not because his option for Christian social identity offered a better social and cultural fit, but because his ideology of Christian identity was so compelling that the social tension it caused was reinterpreted as suffering for the sake of Christ and the gospel. The social tension was valorized as an important although not always necessary component of Christian social identity. Since Paul was able to mobilize the Corinthian believers to identify with his vision of Christian social identity, against the grain of deep-seated Greco-Roman values of honor and status, even in competition with Jewish-Christian identity narratives, which represented another powerful social force, he became the champion of Christian identity. The process of leadership attribution led to Paul being perceived as close to God, commissioned by Christ, empowered by the Spirit, just as Paul himself claimed. Thus, Paul rose to the status of a charismatic leader as modern social theory would predict in such a situation.

Paul's triumph in Corinth did not go without notice in Ephesus. Paul's authority claims in Ephesians, even if they contained new information for the addressees, would have been readily accepted by anyone familiar with Paul's history in Corinth. Similarly, Paul's unassailable authority in 1–2 Timothy seems to rest on this process of charismatic leadership attribution, even if Paul was writing directly to one of his most loyal associates, since the community read along over Timothy's shoulders. Paul's portrayals of Timothy as very similar to himself, as his delegate and eventually as his successor, can be read as Paul's efforts to stimulate a similar process of leadership attribution on Timothy's behalf, obtaining for Timothy a similar level of social power to carry out Paul's own agenda.

This process of charismatic leadership attribution is a key feature to explain some of the differences in the portrayal of Paul's authority in earlier and later letters. The lofty portrayal of Paul the Apostle in Ephesians and especially in 1–2 Timothy need not be attributed to the hindsight of later generations who made Paul their hero to advance their own particular interpretation of Paul's teaching. Following the Holtzmann-Sohm hypothesis, scholars have often portrayed Paul as charismatic leader in Corinth, while the later lofty picture was considered the result of two generations of institutionalization. However, the social development as proposed in this study is quite different. In Corinth, in spite of his own claims, Paul was not considered a suitable or charismatic leader when new challenges of expansion presented themselves; rather, he was marginalized and then even hotly contested and rejected. It was not until Paul emerged successfully from a few difficult years of conflict that his leadership status rose to what leadership research today would call a charismatic status. Ironically, this occurred precisely after resolving one of the Corinthian problems relating to charismatic excesses, and after leadership emergence had been restored to its proper place with Paul as the most significant exemplar. That is, when a new level of leadership stabilization and thus a new stage of institutionalization had been successfully implemented, Paul emerged with the status of a charismatic leader. In turn, Paul's increased status enabled him to institute the community structures for leadership maintenance and succession in 1–2 Timothy. Thus, the differences in Paul's leadership status across the Corinthian and Ephesian correspondence do not necessarily reflect generations of development, but easily fit a scenario where Paul's status rises simultaneously in Corinth and Ephesus because of Paul's successful conflict resolution in Corinth. In 2 Corinthians this is a brand new development from the conflictual setting, while a few years later in Ephesians and 1–2 Timothy the conflictual setting has faded into the background, heightening even further Paul's status as apostolic authority.

Corinth and Ephesus as Stages of Similar Developing Leadership Patterns

The above evaluation of the differences and similarities in leadership patterns as well as Paul's increasing status as charismatic leader during his career suggest that Ephesus followed Corinth after an interval of only a few years in a similar scenario of community and leadership formation. These observations harmonize well with several other aspects of the Pauline mission in the Aegean region. First, both churches were founded during Paul's Aegean mission in 'virgin' territory, so that Paul and his missionary team developed these communities and their leadership from the start, most likely using relatively similar missionary strategies. Second, the constraints of local culture and of Jewish-Christian competition were relatively similar in both locations, so that these factors would have shaped the developments in similar ways. Third, both churches were part of Paul's network of churches and coworkers, maintaining contact through visits of missionary coworkers and local leadership as well as through correspondence. In such a setting, the development or practice in one community could easily become model for another, as Paul explicitly writes on several occasions. Fourth, it is likely that Paul's letters were available across this entire region soon after their publication and delivery to a particular community (assuming the authenticity of Ephesians and 1–2 Timothy, as argued above). This would have had a standardizing influence on the Pauline churches in the whole region, with churches that were started later, such as in Ephesus, benefiting from the lessons learned in churches started earlier, such as in Corinth and elsewhere in Macedonia. These observations support the earlier conclusion that the patterns of leadership development in Corinth and Ephesus can be read as segments or stages of community and leadership formation that are likely to indicate a similar progression in each location.

It has often been noted that the variation in local culture, social structures, and titles is too great and the available evidence too sparse to bear the weight of such a reconstruction.[4] However, in spite of various idiosyncratic features in each location, cognitive processes relating to group dynamics and leadership can be assumed to be fairly constant as part of the human condition. It is therefore not surprising that the above analysis of the letters through the lens of social identity theory suggests similar lines of social development across the region that allow sufficient room for a variety of local expressions while pointing to underlying similarities in process. This opens up a credible way for the reconstruction of both Christian social identity and leadership formation, balancing between the two extremes of seeing an identical pattern in every situation, and seeing each situation as unique and incomparable.

This study, then, proposes similar patterns of leadership in Paul's Aegean churches that developed within a span of about 16 years (from the founding of the Corinthian community to the writing of 2 Timothy). Definitive proof for such a short period of social development cannot be attained with a social identity or any other type of analysis. At best, various scenarios can be compared for their likelihood and explanatory potential of the observed social phenomena. This study, assisted by social identity theory, suggests that the observed social phenomena can be explained reasonably and credibly within the time frame indicated. One could, of course, propose a greater lapse of time between the writing of 1–2 Corinthians on the one hand, and Ephesians and 1–2 Timothy on the other, but this only makes it more difficult to explain the social and rhetorical similarities observed and to reconstruct a credible and coherent social setting for the later letters. This in turn makes it virtually impossible to suggest lines of social as well as ideological development that can be expected to garner broad scholarly support. Additional hypotheses are needed to explain similarities and divergences, creating a more complex theory. Generally, the simpler theory with fewer hypotheses is to be preferred over more complex theories if their explanatory potential is the same. The present social identity analysis has sufficient explanatory power to postulate the shorter time frame with fewer supporting hypotheses, so that the resulting social reconstruction of developing leadership

---

4. E.g., Streeter, *The Primitive Church*, 75–76, Clarke, *Serve the Community*, 207 and most recently in a personal conversation with John Kloppenborg, at the International Conference on Matthew, James, and Didache at the University of Tilburg, Netherlands, April 13, 2007.

patterns, including its time frame, deserves to be considered as a serious candidate to model the development of the Pauline mission and indeed of the first century church.

Paul's Advocacy of Uniform Patterns of Leadership

Up to this point, this chapter summarized historical findings. Differences and similarities were listed and compared, with an attempt to generate a social scenario that could account for them within the context of Paul's Aegean mission, in spite of our limited knowledge of this mission. This attempt was undergirded by the social identity model of leadership. This answers the first part of the research question, which is mainly historical in nature: *"according to the Pauline letters addressed to Corinth and Ephesus, what were the leadership patterns in these early Christ-following communities?"* The second part of this question is mainly ideological, *"how did the communities as well as Paul attempt to shape these patterns?"* which will be addressed next.

An interesting question, that has been dropped from recent research into church leadership patterns, but featured dominantly in older studies, is whether Paul (or other NT writers) advocated any patterns of leadership as normative for his and all other Christ-following communities. It appears that purely historical research cannot answer this question, since that would imply that a particular leadership pattern at a particular time and place is to be identified as normative. It would amount to raising a particular slice of history to the status of universal norm. However, the developing leadership patterns in Paul's Aegean mission did not simply stop when they arrived at a particular point, but continued to develop towards monepiscopacy and beyond as is evident from the Apostolic Fathers and later Christian literature. What stops is our evidence from Paul's hand. It is impossible methodologically to 'freeze history' at a particular time and place, and uphold that situation as a universal pattern. This would, in effect, bring an end to history, since any further development is denied legitimacy.[5] Such use of historical research to legitimate a particular historical pattern as universal standard was found guilty of denominational ideology, against which such a strong suspicion developed in recent decades,

---

5. See a similar argument on some social science practices by Reicher and Hopkins, "Psychology and the End of History," 391–92.

explaining the fact that questions about normative patterns were simply dropped from the research agenda.

However, it is increasingly recognized today that ideological motives, usually based on one's group membership, continue to play a role and that a better method is to consciously account for ideology and group membership, ancient as well as modern. It has been argued that social identity theory provides the tools to give such an account, since it studies not only social fact (e.g., history), but also the psychological processes that underpin of these social facts (e.g., group ideology). Seen from this perspective, group ideology is an integral part of historical research, which investigates Paul's letters to uncover the ideology with which he aimed to shape the communities of which he considered himself a member, often in competition with deviant members or opponents and their differing ideologies. The question "how the communities as well as Paul attempted to shape these patterns" thus asks if Paul and his communities were motivated by their group ideology to advocate a particular leadership pattern as normative, and if so, what that pattern was. This, too, is a matter of historical research, and thus a legitimate part of this study.

One way to proceed to answer this question is to ask whether the similar developmental patterns that emerged from the present study were, at least to some extent, intentional, or whether the similarity is mostly contextually determined. In other words, did Paul and his communities intentionally direct the development of patterns of leadership in a particular direction, or did they simply seek to adapt leadership function to what was required in a particular social context? The answer will not be an either/or choice, as if intention and social context are mutually exclusive but an assessment of the relative weight of intention versus social context in these developing patterns.

An answer to the ideological question can be formulated as follows, taking as basis the historical conclusion that the variety of leadership patterns visible in the Pauline communities at Corinth and Ephesus can be credibly charted as segments of similar patterns of leadership development. First, then, Paul's correspondence to Corinth and Ephesus testifies to a convergence towards a fairly standardized pattern of householder-overseers, united for the city as a college of elders, assisted by deacons as the needs and size of the community require. This fits well with evidence that in Philippi the leadership group could be identified with "overseers and deacons" (Phil 1:1, written at about the same time as Ephesians), and that in Crete, no provisions were (yet) made for deacons since most likely the communities were too young and small to need this (cf. Tit 1:5–9). At the same time, Paul's letters indicate a variety of other gifts or functions at either Corinth or Ephesus, and while these are presented as important elements of Christian social identity, no standardized pattern seems to be advocated. Thus, convergence towards a standardized pattern seems to be indicated only for some of the leadership functions. Even at that level, some variety is visible, since 1–2 Corinthians speak of apostles, prophets, and teachers, Ephesians adds evangelists and pastors, while 1–2 Timothy speak in addition of elders and deacons. The main point is not convergence towards identical leadership structures, but towards a standardized leadership pattern as historical fact.

Second, this convergence seems to be intentional, since Paul is clearly concerned to institute specific patterns of leadership in these communities. He identifies leadership character, function, appointment, and accountability as defining elements of these Christian patterns of leadership. Moreover, his concern for standardized leadership patterns is connected to his concern for future generations of believers, since he charges Timothy and the local leaders he appoints to maintain these patterns. In other words, Paul advocates this relative uniformity of leadership patterns not merely for a sense of order in the present but for stability and cohesion in the future. Paul's advocated uniformity is admittedly ideal, presenting a point of convergence towards which communities may strive; the historical convergence already noted reflects this ideological point of convergence. This does not describe the full breadth of patterns of function and leadership in the entire community or network, but only the most important leadership patterns.

Third, these standardized patterns apply to leaders who maintain the vision of Christian social identity as proclaimed by Paul and his coworkers, and who also maintain the relationship of their own community with other communities in Paul's network. Paul's strongest advocacy relates to the consistent and full communication of his group ideology in each community, a task on which he focused in his own ministry in Corinth and Ephesus, and which he later committed to Timothy and other local leaders. Ephesians legitimates local leadership as Christ's gift for the community's continuing growth and cohesion, implying that these leaders continue to communicate the mystery of the gospel, which Paul received from God. In 1–2 Timothy, the faithful proclamation of Paul's gospel and its protection from deviant influences are presented as key leadership responsibilities, which are to be transferred to faithful men, trained to be knowledgeable about the gospel and to teach it consistently whatever the cost. The connections within Paul's network of communities serve to stabilize and standardize the communication of group ideology, initially by virtue of their connection with the apostle Paul as recipient of divine revelation and founder of the communities, and later as his delegates and their trainees continue to encourage one another and keep each other accountable.

Fourth, Paul's advocacy of these relatively uniform patterns of leadership is driven by his awareness that leadership must be embedded in his vision of Christian social identity if it is to provide long-term continuity for his communities. Communities and their sense of social identity remain stable if they have strong identity-embedding structures. Thus, leaders interested in maintaining their leadership often provide such identity-embedding structures, which not only bring continuity for their vision of social identity but also protect their own role as leader. Thus, Paul was not content to leave patterns of leadership up to the social and cultural context, but integrated leadership patterns in his vision of Christian social identity. Leaders were to become the champions of the foundational beliefs and values of his communities, implying that their function centered on the communication of these beliefs and the modeling of these values, which makes them key proponents of the group's ideology. Therefore, Paul advocates standardized leadership patterns because they represent identity-embedding structures for his vision of Christian social identity, needed for long-term continuity and stability. Paul uses his rising status as charismatic leader to make his advocacy of these leadership patterns as persuasive as possible, thus intending to secure the succession needed to maintain and protect his vision of Christian social identity.

Fifth, Paul advocated the norm of uniform leadership patterns to facilitate communication within and networking between different Christian communities, but it is unlikely that Paul intended for these uniform patterns to become normative in their specific structures. It is doubtful that a specific two or threefold structure of leadership ([bishop]-elder-deacon), or their specific titles, can be considered normative in themselves, except in so far as they contribute towards the long-term maintenance of Christian social identity. Instead, Paul's focus on intra- and intergroup communication suggests uniformly recognizable leadership structures for key leadership levels as the normative pattern, with latitude for local adaptation and expansion. In advocating such uniform patterns, Paul looked towards future stability and cohesion within Greco-Roman culture with its leadership patterns as he knew them. The specific structures he advocates are not necessarily intended to transcend Paul's culture; instead, Paul's concern to ensure that leadership structure is embedded in Christian social identity as the guarantor of its future stability and cohesion is the cross-cultural principle.

In conclusion, Paul transformed leadership patterns in both Corinth and Ephesus to converge on a standardized pattern in order to facilitate the intra- and intergroup communication of the gospel as the defining message that shaped their Christian social identity over against Jewish and Greco-Roman influences. These similar patterns of leadership are presented as universal and normative, not in their specific structures and titles but as a condition for this intra- and intergroup communication to provide long-term stability and cohesion for Christ-following communities in their understanding of Christian social identity.

A caveat remains. Speaking of "Paul's gospel," of his "vision of Christian social identity" and of "group ideology" assumes that these refer to an identifiable set of beliefs, values, and identity narratives that function as the standard against which long-term stability and cohesion can be measured. Paul himself already spoke of "the deposit" entrusted to him (1 Tim 6:20; 2 Tim 1:12, 14), so this assumption seems warranted. Yet, it has not been easy to delineate precisely what this message contains, as centuries of lively theological debate show.[6] This is partly due to the nature of Paul's letters as responses to particular situations—with the possible exception of Romans and Ephesians. This happens piecemeal, with most of the message remaining implicit, simply assumed to be known, as in Paul's reference to "the deposit." It is also due to the nature of the concept of social identity, which represents a continuing adaptation of beliefs, identity narratives, and

---

6. For a recent contribution, see Campbell, *The Quest for Paul's Gospel*.

ideology to shape the group's identity in each new social context. For the present purpose, therefore, it is sufficient to demonstrate that Paul's advocacy of uniform leadership patterns is founded upon his understanding of Christian social identity, even if a full description of these concepts remain beyond the limits of this study.

Implications for Further Research

With these conclusions, the research question has been answered and study completed. In closing, some of the more important implications of this project for further research should be noted. The study answers some long-standing questions about the historical development of church office and contributes to a further understanding of the later rise of the monepiscopacy. Next, this project points to new ways of charting the Pauline mission and studying Paul's opponents. Finally, the methodology used in this study suggests a reading strategy for the Pauline letters, has broader hermeneutical implications for NT studies and offers an integrative method for current Christian leadership studies.

Aspects of the Historical Development of Church Office

This study answers two long-standing questions about the historical development of offices. First, it remains difficult to discern whether the bishop rose to higher status from among the elders through specialization of function, or whether he attained such status by apostolic appointment. Both lines are visible in the evidence, which is what SIMOL would lead one to expect: leadership appointment is effective only when supported by the group. This is illustrated by Timothy's unsuccessful mission in Corinth after the delivery of 1 Corinthians, where Paul's appointment of Timothy failed because of lack of congregational support. It is illustrated positively by Paul's affirmation of the already functioning body of elders in Ephesus (Eph 4:11ff.), and by his legitimation of the rise of specialized functions within that body by acknowledging them and providing financial compensation (1 Tim 5:17ff). Thus, differentiation in leadership function as an internal group dynamic and legitimation by apostolic or other leadership are necessary complements in the rise of new levels of leadership. Thus, the question whether the monarchical bishop arose by specialization from among the elders or by apostolic appointment, is a false dilemma since these are complementary processes.

Second, the question whether the origin of church offices—in either its two- or threefold structure—is to be traced to the synagogue, to the Hellenistic association or to some other first century form of leadership, remains unresolved. In light of the social identity analysis, this seems a moot point. Paul willingly works with local leadership structures, but consistently reinterprets cultural standards of patronage and honor in ways that accord with his vision of Christian social identity. Since the Christ-following communities are threatened by both Jewish and Greco-Roman institutions, Paul does his utmost to maintain the distinctiveness of Christian social identity over against these competing identities. Competition from Jewish identity seems most damaging, precisely because Christian social identity is relatively close to it. Thus, even if the threefold office structure derives early on from the synagogue, as Burtchaell maintains,[7] Paul would have emphasized the distinctions in nomenclature, function, and orientation to maintain the distinctiveness of Christ-following leadership structures. Social continuities with Jewish communities would be suppressed in order to avoid or reduce the social tension caused by contact with the synagogue. Thus, since our sources for early Christian community formation are all documents emphasizing the distinctiveness of the Christ-movement, it will probably be impossible to gain more certainty about the historical origin of church office than can be suggested simply by comparing community and leadership structures of different ancient organizations with those of the Christ-movement.

Paul and Monepiscopacy: A Social Psychological Framework

This study has several implications for investigating the later rise of a single bishop among a group of local elders (monepiscopacy), a familiar and frequently contested topic in the history of research on church leadership. Since in the Pauline letters, the term 'bishop' or 'overseer' (ἐπίσκοπος) occurs only in the singular (1 Tim 3:2; Titus 1:7),[8] the suggestion has often made that these letters offer the first

---

7. See Burtchaell, *Synagogue*.
8. The only plural reference is in Phil 1:1.

available evidence of leadership structures that move towards monepiscopacy.[9] This development in the Pastorals is then compared with the letters of Ignatius of Antioch, dated around 110–117 CE,[10] which are the first post-apostolic documents to clearly position the bishop above the local elders. Paul is not held directly responsible for the rise of the monepiscopacy, but it is attributed to the Pauline tradition several generations after Paul as the institutionalization of Christian communities proceeded.

The present study proposes that Paul is not directly but indirectly responsible for the development of the monepiscopacy. It has been argued above that 1 Timothy, considered to be Pauline, did not in 3:1 institute a new office of bishop as a single leader above the elders, but that instead it encouraged new householders to host a church in their house. These overseer-householders formed a college of elders to oversee the house churches in their city (cf. πρεσβυτέριον, 4:14), in which context some overseer-elders devoted themselves more than some others to ruling and teaching. No development towards a single city-church leader is evident in 1 Timothy. Paul is not directly responsible for the rise of the monepiscopacy.

Yet, 1 Timothy prepared for this later development in important ways. Note first that specialization of function within the college of elders is acknowledged and further development is not in principle ruled out. Second, although Paul's charge to Timothy is not presented as a pattern for institutional imitation, it presented a practical model for how apostolic authority is delegated to a non-apostolic leader who, moreover, received an apostolic mandate to oversee the church in a city. Third, Paul acknowledged his high status as apostolic leader and portrayed Timothy as similar, stimulating the community to view and accept Timothy as they had accepted him. In the collectivist, hierarchical culture of the Mediterranean world, such a high status for Timothy would have suggested a developing hierarchy as the natural mechanism to maintain the unity and cohesion of the city-church. Thus, further specialization and an apostolic succession model in a hierarchical society provided the seeds that would later develop into

---

9. See for instance, Campbell, *The Elders*. The plural ἐπίσκοποι in Phil 1:1 refers to a several overseers in the church in Philippi, thus preventing the conclusion that this church moved towards monepiscopacy. For a detailed discussion, see Chapple, "Local Leadership," 544–90.

10. Holmes et al., *The Apostolic Fathers*, 131.

monepiscopacy. Paul, therefore, is indirectly responsible for the development of monepiscopacy.

Would Paul have welcomed or even encouraged such a development? Although Paul did not address this directly (the issue had simply not come up), several key elements in Paul's ideology of leadership suggest that he would have resisted this. First, Paul portrayed leaders always as members of the community, who participated in the community even if their particular contribution is distinct. Although leaders formed a subgroup within the community, they were not portrayed as a distinct group over against the larger believing community, a trend observable in Ignatius (e.g., *Ign. Eph.* 2–4). When a leadership subgroup begins to form a leadership clique over against the majority of group members, the basis for influence and leadership shifts from social identification to intergroup competition and the use of power changes.[11] Second, Paul, Timothy, and other leaders are portrayed as workers in God's field, servants of Christ, or even stewards of God's grace and power, which implies that they participate in the status, honor, and authority of Christ.[12] Yet, the emphasis is on their service of and sacrifice for the community. Leaders serve God by serving and sacrificing for the community. To the extent that in later centuries the church is at times portrayed as serving its leaders or as consisting in its leaders, a different leadership model has replaced Paul's model of identity-based leadership. Third, Paul's continual anti-patronage and anti-honor rhetoric is at tension with the tendency towards increased leadership status and power in Corinth and Ephesus, as well as in later forms of leadership. To the extent that the monarchical bishop developed a high social status and powers of reward and coercion over the communities, Paul's ideology of leadership suggests that he would resist this development. This is not to say that Paul in principle resisted the convergence of city-wide leadership in the single person of the bishop, but that he would object to the increase in status and honor at the expense of empowerment of the community that later became features of the office of monarchical bishop.[13]

11. Hogg and Reid, "Social Identity, Leadership, and Power," 172ff.

12. Williams, *Stewards, Prophets*, 82–83.

13. Ehrensperger concludes much more boldly that the development of hierarchy and the exercise of power-over goes beyond the limitations imposed by the message of the gospel. "Although asymmetrical relationships are not ruled . . . hierarchies cannot be established on a permanent basis, they can only be functional in nature,

These observations derive from a view of leadership based on prototypicality and self-sacrifice on behalf of the group. Leading group members gain status within the group, but if their status becomes too much distinct from that of other group members, leaders are no longer prototypical and loose the social influence and attraction that empowered them as leaders initially. Instead, they begin to lead by virtue of their office and ascribed authority. Such leaders tend to categorize themselves (and be categorized by other group members) as a subgroup with a social identity distinct from the main body of the group. This would create an us-versus-them mentality within the Christian community, activating the comparative and competitive dynamics of an *inter*group relationship rather than the cooperative and supportive dynamics of an *intra*group relationship. Such leadership, it is argued here, no longer corresponds to Paul's vision of Christian identity and has moved into the area of illegitimacy. Instead, Paul's vision of Christian social identity and of leadership as an identity-embedding structure within that social identity remain the most important factors in how Paul developed leadership patterns in his churches.[14]

Charting the Pauline Mission

This study has frequently referred to the Pauline network of churches as representing not merely the historical accident that Paul happened to work with missionary teams who traveled from place to place, but as an important social instrument for aligning his communities with one another in their common vision of Christian social identity. The network provided opportunities for quick exchange of information, so that lessons learned in one place could be taught and implemented in another. The various communities that were established were not independent movements with their own independent trajectory—although each had its own social and cultural background—but from their earliest stages, they appear to function in connection with other groups of believers in nearby cities and across the Aegean region.

---

serving limited purposes for a limited time. Moreover, any position of superiority is granted only as a means to serve the gospel, that is, to serve people" (*Paul and the Dynamics of Power*, 186).

14. For further study of Ignatius and his impact of the development of the monepiscopacy, a few studies are noteworthy: Brent, *Ignatius of Antioch*; Trevett, *Ignatius of Antioch in Syria and Asia*; and Williams, "Charismatic Patronage and Brokerage."

Conclusions and Implications: Emerging Leadership in the Pauline Mission   317

These groups build a common social memory and share an identity narrative, which accounts for the continuity and social development in Paul's Aegean mission. In this way, Paul's network became an identity-embedding structure, which provided a stabilizing factor for all the linked communities, whatever their stage of community formation and leadership development. It may well be that Corinth and Ephesus, on which this study focused, functioned as hubs or missionary centers within this network, which deserves further investigation.[15] Perhaps this reflects earlier missionary patterns that were already in use in Antioch and Jerusalem; these also seem to have functioned as hubs in a growing network of communities. In such a case, Paul's missionary patterns may well be adapted from similar patterns used by the other apostles already in Jerusalem.[16] Paul's interest in the church in Rome and his intentions for ministry there and beyond may suggest a similar missionary strategy for that city.[17]

A major challenge will be to broaden the current study to an investigation of other literature related to the Aegean region: the Johannine and Petrine literature, the letters of Ignatius, and 1 Clement. In this way, studies on church leadership in post-apostolic literature can also benefit from a social identity approach.

Implications for the Study of Paul's Opponents

An important aspect of the Pauline mission is his interaction with opponents. If it should be granted that leadership should not be studied apart from group dynamics, then this applies even more to the study of opposition and deviance. Research on deviance in groups demonstrates that deviants usually attract the greater share of communication from the majority in order to persuade them to change their mind. Given the potential influence of deviant minorities in influencing the majority, the amount of rhetoric is justified not so much by the relative numbers, but by the potential danger.[18] This suggests that the relative length of Paul's communication about his critics as well as

15. See Donfried, "Rethinking Scholarly Approaches to 1 Timothy," 158–59.

16. See, e.g., Campbell, *Paul and the Creation of Christian Identity*, 38–42 on Paul's relationship with other leaders and their missions.

17. Barentsen, "Pre-Pauline Leadership in the Roman Church," 589–610.

18. Brown, *Group Processes*, 141–42.

the intensity of his polemic cannot simply be interpreted as evidence for a sizeable proportion of Corinthians who opposed Paul, nor for the supposed lack of conviction or action on the part of the majority. Rather, it is evidence for Paul's estimate of the danger these few critics still pose, and—in the case of 2 Cor 10–13—of the renewed trust in Paul as apostolic leader. Therefore, Paul's warnings do not necessarily imply that the false teachers had great influence, or that the majority of Christians were wavering in their beliefs and commitments. Rather, Paul follows up Titus' report of the reconciliation by encouraging the majority, convinced as they are that Paul deserves recognition as apostolic founder, to demonstrate their loyalty to Paul, and to either dissociate from the critics or to convince them of their errors with the arguments that he supplies in the letter.

Methodologically, the chosen approach offers a different and socially better-anchored way to interpret Paul's stereotypical language about his opponents. The forcefulness of the rhetoric and the amount of space dedicated to communication about an opponent primarily indicate the danger this person or teaching poses for Christian social identity. Generally, the more closely a deviant person or teaching is connected to Christian social identity, the more dangerous his or its potential influence, and the stronger the rhetoric. Thus, deviance from Jewish sources is likely to receive more intense and derogatory attention than from Greek or Roman sources. However, the intensity of derogation has often been interpreted as an indication of large numbers of deviants, which in turn was considered as the most likely explanation for the dangers. The latter interpretation results in the impression that Paul was surrounded by influential and sizeable deviant segments of Christianity, the former interpretation results in a scenario of a network of churches essentially in harmony with Paul's gospel and leadership style, but with dangers of deviance from Jewish and other sources infiltrating mostly at the edges.

Moreover, Paul's strong polemical rhetoric has often been interpreted as an indication that Paul resorted to vilification or other denunciatory strategies because he was losing influence and in danger of being marginalized—as if Paul merely shouted louder the more he was marginalized. This is admittedly the strategy of some, but people who make thunderous denunciations of their opponents are either applauded as strong leaders, or else considered deranged for lack of touch with reality. In more sober wording, the acceptance of Paul as community leader determines whether his forceful stereotypes are perceived as beneficial. Without significant leadership attribution by the community, Paul's stereotypes would be considered as an instance of the very slander that he warned against. This again results in significantly different scenarios of early Christian community formation. One scenario conceived of Paul as a marginalized leader unable to direct the identification processes for several of the communities he himself had founded, with control wrested away from him at various occasions. The other scenario pictures Paul as entrenched and esteemed leader of the communities he founded, with serious but resolved challenges in the Corinthian and Galatian communities that had threatened to remove him from his place of apostolic leadership.[19]

A Reading Strategy for the Corpus Paulinum

This study used social identity theory to locate Paul's rhetoric in its social setting. Rhetorical criticism is well established in the study of the Pauline letters.[20] However, it is not enough to trace the intricacies of Paul's argumentation solely within the text itself. The social setting of the text needs to be investigated to enlighten why Paul argued in a particular way and what he intended to accomplish with it. This hermeneutical maneuver is not everywhere accepted in NT studies,[21] but this study's use of the social identity model of leadership has demonstrated the use of one particular scientific model to make this connection. As a result Paul's letters were read as instruments of leadership, as ways in which he exercised his leadership in absentia in his churches[22]; his letters are not merely documents that might contain a few nuggets of information about leadership.

---

19. These concerns also apply to the investigation of the relationship between Paul and the other apostles, possible varieties in the early Christ-movement, and the scholarly discussion of the "parting of the ways" of Christianity and Judaism.

20. See for instance Witherington, *New Testament Rhetoric*, Robbins, *The Invention of Christian Discourse*, and Vos, *Die Kunst der Argumentation bei Paulus*.

21. E.g., in Lieu's skepticism in making any connections to the historical reality 'beyond' the text. See Lieu, *Christian Identity*, 9, 28ff.; and Holmberg's comments thereon in "Understanding the First Hundred Years," 6–9.

22. For this way of phrasing it, I am indebted to Agosto, *Servant Leadership*, 11, 119.

The concept that Paul's letters are instruments to influence and shape the socio-historical situations they address deserves further exploration. Paul's earliest letters can for the most part be characterized as reactive problem solving letters: 1–2 Thessalonians, 1–2 Corinthians, and Galatians. Similarly, Philippians, Philemon, and Colossians appear to respond to particular situations or problems and are mostly reactive. A next set of letters is more reflective: Romans and Ephesians, both of which have been proposed as Paul's theological resume or testament; whether or not this is the correct perspective, such proposals arise from their different character as compared with the reactive letters. Then follow 1 Timothy and Titus, the more official letters of instruction to a junior official, and 2 Timothy as Paul's testament. There appears to be a shift during the course of Paul's letter writing career from a situational, reactive perspective to a more proactive perspective, inspired by the expanding network of churches and the need to provide for his own increasing absence and inaccessibility. While Paul's early letters were perhaps not written with succeeding generations in view (although they do appear to have a larger contemporary audience in mind than only the immediate addressees), the more proactive letters move in that direction, while the Pastorals demonstrate a beginning awareness that they would soon become important elements of Paul's heritage. Paul seems increasingly aware of a readership beyond the immediate addressees and aims to provide continuity for his communities for the time after his own death. Thus, his later letters are purposely written to be disseminated to extend their social influence, while earlier dissemination was more a local solution to particular communication problems, explaining perhaps the loss of two out of four of Paul's letters to Corinth. Although such a reading strategy needs further investigation than these few comments permit, this may have important implications both for the exegesis of the letters (as is already evident in this study), as well as for theories about the collection of the letters and their eventual canonization.

Social Identity Theory as Hermeneutical Tool

Social identity theory, then, functions as a hermeneutical tool for analyzing texts in their context. This theory from social psychology works well with the rich contextual data of the Pauline letters because it is primarily concerned with how individual psychological processes and social group phenomena interact with one another, which is precisely the kind of concerns evident in Paul's letters (as well as in other parts of the NT). These psychological processes find expression in letters and gospels, which represent the movement's rhetoric about their foundational identity narratives, beliefs, and behaviors. They are intended to define Christian social identity, and to shape and transform the thinking of group members to deepen their social identification with the movement, and to mobilize them to behave in accordance with it. In the process, these texts provide some information about the social development of these communities, although this needs to be discerned with great methodological care.[23] Without wishing to reduce the NT to a compendium of rhetorical instruments for (Christian) social identity formation, it is clear that this is at least one major purpose of these documents. Thus, the nature of the NT documents and their social and psychological evidence provides the kinds of data that the social identity theory is designed to analyze.

If correct, this estimate of the role of social identity theory has some important ramifications. First, the continuities and discontinuities across Paul's letters should most likely be interpreted as a reflection of the continuities and discontinuities of the formation of Christian (Pauline) social identity. Studies on literary relationships, intertextuality, and theological development in the Pauline corpus all have their place, but unless they are connected with their social setting, they are disembodied abstractions of some phenomena in Paul's mission and communities that will only be explained sufficiently when the social context is also taken into account.

Second, the concept of identity revolves around sameness and difference, presenting another way to approach the discussion of unity and diversity in the NT. For instance, Paul's extended argument in 1 Corinthians and Ephesians for the superordinate position of Christian social identity is not so much a plea for a universal theology that erases all local distinctions, but is rather a way to bind existing social and ethnic differences together in a higher level of unity without denying or erasing these differences. Thus, Jewish Christ-followers were not necessarily required to abandon their ethnic Jewish identity, but to value it differently in light of their new Christian social identity.

23. See Barentsen, "Early Christian Identity Formation," 245–52.

Similarly, gentile Christ-followers did not need to adopt a Jewish identity, while they also learned to value their Greco-Roman identity in light of their Christian social identity. This provides a more sophisticated model for accommodating difference and sameness within the Christ-movement, allowing different subgroups to function unitedly by maintaining the superordinate nature of Christian social identity for all subgroups, whoever of the apostles might have been instrumental in their founding.

Third, the ability of social identity theory to link socio-historical data with cognitive processes presents a different way of thinking about the connection between history and theology, often considered problematic in NT studies for fear of how theology may distort accurate historical perception.[24] To be sure, there is good reason to be alert to this danger, but over the last decades the realization has grown that a neutral, non-ideological stance is principally impossible. This favors a method like the social identity theory that enables the scholar to make both history and ideology explicit topics of research. This includes both ancient ideology (such as, for instance, Paul's ideology of leadership and community identity) and modern ideology (such as, for instance, the denominational bias in earlier church leadership studies). Could it be, for instance, that the Holtzmann-Sohm hypothesis, that the church developed from pristine innocence to thoroughgoing institutionalization, is an expression or even critique of western, colonial ideology where "civilized" institutions override the "spiritual" freedom of the natives, reflecting the exegete's experience in theological debate and denominational life in the 19th century? And how does the postmodern ideology of authentic cultural and local truths without an overarching meta-narrative affect the current scholarly perception of the variety of Christian communities in the ancient sources, even in this current study? Of course, things are never quite that simple, but it serves to highlight that ideology—ancient as well as modern—plays an important role in research, and that adequate tools are needed to handle this explicitly. Even if the current application of one such tool, the social identity theory, were to be evaluated as less than felicitous, at least an attempt has been made to take account of this aspect in a responsible manner, which is in itself already a step forwards in the research.

24. See for instance Räisänen, *Beyond New Testament Theology*.

Implications for Modern Christian Leadership Studies

The opening lines of chapter 1 situated this study in a context of major social change at the beginning of the 21st century, where social identity and leadership have become key issues. Renewal movements within the church look for fresh input into these matters to help them contextualize the gospel and its community structures for yet uncharted territories. In closing, it is fruitful to connect with this search for renewal.

A recent overview of some current Christian leadership studies observed that the approaches used are very diverse, but that four areas of convergence are discernible in the surveyed methods.[25] Christian leadership is

a. mimetic with its focus on serving, humility and obedience,

b. concerned with a correct understanding of power, focusing on influence and authenticity rather than asserting authority or even coercion,

c. follower-centered, focusing on inspiring and transforming followers, and

d. christological, since Christ serves as ultimate model and authority.

Overall, however, the author believes that "little work has been done to synthesize all these approaches and to provide a 'mega-theory' of the concept [of Christian leadership]."[26]

At the conclusion of the present study, it should be evident that the social identity model of leadership addresses these areas and more besides. The mimetic dimension of Paul's (and even Timothy's) leadership was analyzed in 1–2 Corinthians and 1–2 Timothy. Paul's sensitivity to the use of power was noted in how he addressed division and his own marginalized leadership in Corinth, and how he instituted leadership maintenance and succession in Ephesus. Throughout, this study observed Paul's focus on empowering and mobilizing his followers through strategies of identity management and social creativity. Christ was the key reference point as model of suffering, as legitimation for Paul's leadership, as the one who instituted local leadership,

---

25. Bekker, "Towards a Theoretical Model of Christian Leadership," 148–49. The research by Andrew Clarke, used in this study, is among the seven authors reviewed.

26. Ibid.

and as the object and source of Paul's gospel which defined Christian social identity.

Moreover, SIMOL was instrumental in situating leadership in the context of intra- and intergroup dynamics, and in explaining the rise of some group members into leadership through the processes of leadership emergence and maintenance. Aspects of leadership formation received attention, while specifications for leadership character and leadership function were seen to be connected contextually to the identity of the group in which the leaders functioned. In this way, the interaction between Christian leadership, group dynamics, and Christian social identity is brought into focus, which should also be part of the 'mega-theory' of Christian leadership. For these reasons, it is proposed that the social identity model of leadership has much to offer current research on Christian leadership and may well provide some tools to recontextualize the gospel in community and leadership structures that fit today's culture and challenges. With the study now completed, this proposal is offered in the hope that it says as much about the model as it does about the enthusiasm of the current author.

Paul: Social Strategist, Situational Theologian

The application of SIMOL opened up new avenues for historical reconstruction, and promises advances for research into Christian leadership, both ancient and modern. Paul's Aegean mission is one unified missionary effort with similar patterns of community and leadership formation, patterns that may be replicated in other areas of the Pauline and the larger Christian mission. Paul himself emerges from this study as an entrepreneur of social identity, not only by virtue of the theological and ideological sources he employed, amongst which the revelation he received played a key role, but also by virtue of the social strategies with which he sought to contextualize his theology. Whether and to what extent he was outwitted as entrepreneur in his own time remains a subject of debate. We may not be confident that Paul's attitudes towards female leadership and slavery are model for today, but later generations have often turned to Paul as their key authority, accepting his vision of Christian social identity as normative. Subsequently, churchmen adopted patterns of leadership that they considered most suitable for their time and culture to faithfully implement and embed this vision of Christian identity in the church. It remains a challenge today to adapt Paul's vision of Christian identity and his patterns of leadership to the demands of our own time and culture in order to provide the vitality, continuity and cohesion for today's churches that Paul envisioned for the churches of his own time.

Bibliography

Aageson, James W. *Paul, the Pastoral Epistles, and the Early Church*. Library of Pauline Studies. Peabody, MA: Hendrickson, 2008.
Abrams, Dominic, and Michael A. Hogg. "Metatheory: Lessons from Social Identity Research." *PSPR* 8:2 (2004) 98–106.
———. "Social Identity and Social Cognition: Historical Background and Current Trends." In *Social Identity and Social Cognition*, edited by D. Abrams, and M. A. Hogg, 1–25. Malden, MA: Blackwell, 1999.
Adams, Edward, and David G. Horrell. *Christianity at Corinth: The Quest for the Pauline Church*. Louisville: Westminster John Knox, 2004.
Agosto, Efrain. *Servant Leadership: Jesus and Paul*. St. Louis: Chalice, 2005.
Alvesson, Mats, et al. "The Charismatization of Routines: Management of Meaning and Standardization in an Educational Organization." *Scandinavian Journal of Management* 22:4 (2006) 330–51.
———. "Identity Matters: Reflections on the Construction of Identity Scholarship in Organization Studies." *Organization* 15:1 (2008) 5–28.
Alvesson, Mats, and Kaj Sköldberg. *Reflexive Methodology: New Vistas for Qualitative Research*. 2nd ed. London: Sage, 2009.
Alvesson, Mats, and Hugh Willmott. "Identity Regulation as Organizational Control: Producing the Appropriate Individual." *JMS* 39:5 (2002) 619–44.
Anderson, R. Dean. *1 Korintiërs: Orde op zaken in een jonge stadskerk*. Commentaar op het Nieuwe Testament. Kampen: Kok, 2008.
D'Angelo, Mary R. "Εὐσέβεια: Sexual Politics and True Piety in 4 Maccabees and the Pastorals." *Biblical Interpretation* 11:2 (2003) 139–65.
Arnold, Clinton E. "Ephesus." In *DPL*, 249–52.
———. *Power and Magic: The Concept of Power in Ephesians*. 2nd ed. Grand Rapids, MI: Baker Book House, 1997.
Ashforth, Blake E., et al. "Identification in Organizations: An Examination of Four Fundamental Questions." *Journal of Management* 34:3 (2008) 325–74.
Ashforth, Blake E., and Fred Mael. "Social Identity Theory and the Organization." *AMR* 14 (1989) 20–39.
Aune, David E. "Distinct Lexical Meanings of ἀπαρχή in Hellenism, Judaism, and Early Christianity." In *Early Christianity and Classical Culture: Comparative Studies in Honor of Abraham J. Malherbe*, edited by J. T. Fitzgerald, et al. Supplements to NT 110, 103–29. Leiden: Brill, 2003.
Avemarie, Friedrich. "The Notion of a 'New Covenant' in 2 Corinthians 3: Its Function in Paul's Argument and Its Jewish Background." Paper presented at the Conference on Jewish Perspectives on Paul: 2 Corinthians and Late Second Temple Judaism. Leuven: Katholieke Universiteit Leuven, March 30, 2009.
Balch, David L. *Let Wives Be Submissive: The Domestic Code in 1 Peter*. Society of Biblical Literature Monograph Series 26. Chico, CA: Scholars, 1981.

Bar-Tal, Daniel. "Group Beliefs as an Expression of Group Identity." In *Social Identity: International Perspectives*, edited by S. Worchel, et al, 93–113. London: Sage, 1999.

Barentsen, Jack. "Destabilisatie van opkomend leiderschap. Wisselwerking tussen cultuur en apostolisch gezag bij leiderschapspatronen te Korinte." In *Gezag in beweging: Kerkelijk leiderschap tussen tekst en context*, edited by P. Boersema, et al., 193–210. Heerenveen: Protestantse Pers, 2008.

———. "Early Christian Identity Formation, A Review Article (Holmberg, *Exploring Early Christian Identity* and Holmberg & Winnenge, *Identity Formation in the New Testament*)." *Biblische Zeitschrift* 54:2 (2010) 245–52.

———. "Pre-Pauline Leadership and Pauline Constitution in the Roman Church: An Alternative Interpretation of Romans 12 and 16." In *The Letter to the Romans*, edited by U. Schnelle. BETL 226, 589–610. Leuven: Peeters, 2009.

———. "Stereotyping and Leadership in 1 Timothy: A Social Identity Perspective." In Annual Meeting of the NOSTER Conference, 10. Leuven: ETF, 2009.

Barnett, Paul. *The Second Epistle to the Corinthians*. NICNT. Grand Rapids, MI: Eerdmans, 1997.

Barrett, C. K. *The First Epistle to the Corinthians*. BNTC. Peabody, MA: Hendrikson, 1968.

———. *The Second Epistle to the Corinthians*. BNTC. Peabody, MA: Hendrikson, 1973.

Bartchy, S. Scott. "Who Should Be Called Father? Paul of Tarsus between the Jesus Tradition and Patria Potestas." *BTB* 33:4 (2003) 135–47.

Barth, Markus. *Ephesians 1–3: Introduction, Translation, and Commentary*. AB 34A. Garden City, NY: Doubleday, 1973.

Barton, Stephen C. "Memory and Remembrance in Paul." In *Memory in the Bible and Antiquity: The Fifth Durham-Tübingen Research Symposium (Durham, September 2004)*, edited by S. C. Barton, et al. WUNT 212, 321–40. Tübingen: Mohr/Siebeck, 2006.

Bass, Bernard M., et al. *Handbook of Leadership: Theory, Research, and Application*. 4th ed. New York: Free Press, 2008.

Batten, Alicia. "The Patron-Client Institution: God in the Letter of James: Patron or Benefactor?" In *The Social World of the New Testament: Insights and Models*, edited by J. H. Neyrey, and E. C. Stewart, 47–61. Peabody, MA: Hendrickson, 2008.

Bauer, Walter. *Orthodoxy and Heresy in Earliest Christianity*. Translated by R. A. Kraft, and G. Krodel. Philadelphia: Fortress, 1971.

Baugh, S.M. "A Foreign World: Ephesus in the First Century." In *Women in the Church: An Analysis and Application of 1 Timothy 2:9–15*, edited by A. J. Köstenberger, and T. R. Schreiner, 13–38. Grand Rapids, MI: Baker Academic, 2005.

Baum, Armin D. *Pseudepigraphie und literarische Fälschung im frühen Christentum: Mit ausgewählten Quellentexten samt deutscher Übersetzung*. WUNT 2nd ser., 138. Tübingen: Mohr/Siebeck, 2001.

———. "Semantic Variation within the Corpus Paulinum: Linguistic Considerations Concerning the Richer Vocabulary of the Pastoral Epistles." *TB* 59:2 (2008) 271–92.

Beech, Nic. "On the Nature of Dialogic Identity Work." *Organization* 15:1 (2008) 51–74.
Beker, Johan C.. *Heirs of Paul: Paul's Legacy in the New Testament and in the Church Today*. Minneapolis: Fortress, 1991.
Bekker, Corné J. "Towards a Theoretical Model of Christian Leadership." *Journal of Biblical Perspectives in Leadership* 2:2 (2009) 142–52.
Berding, Kenneth. "The Hermeneutical Framework of Social-Scientific Criticism: How Much Can Evangelicals Get Involved?" *EQ* 75:1 (2003) 3–22.
———. *Polycarp and Paul: An Analysis of Their Literary and Theological Relationship in Light of Polycarp's Use of Biblical and Extra-Biblical Literature*. Supplements to Vigiliae Christianae 62. Leiden: Brill, 2002.
Best, Ernest. *A Critical and Exegetical Commentary on Ephesians*. ICC. Edinburgh: T. & T. Clark, 1998.
Best, Thomas F. "The Sociological Study of the New Testament: Promise and Peril of a New Discipline." *Scottish Journal of Theology* 36 (1983) 181–94.
Betz, Hans D. "2 Cor 6:14—7:1: An Anti-Pauline Fragment?" *Journal of Biblical Literature* 92:1 (1973) 88–108.
Bieringer, Reimund. "2 Korinther 6,14–7,1 im Kontext des 2. Korintherbriefes. Forschungsüberblick und Versuch eines eigenen Zugangs." In *Studies on 2 Corinthians*, edited by R. Bieringer, and J. Lambrecht, BETL 112, 551–70. Leuven: Peeters, 1994.
———. "Plädoyer für die Einheitlichkeit des 2. Korintherbriefes. Literarkritische und inhaltliche Argumente." In *Studies on 2 Corinthians*, edited by R. Bieringer, and J. Lambrecht, BETL 112, 131–79. Leuven: Peeters, 1994.
Blanz, Mathias, et al. "Responding to Negative Social Identity: A Taxonomy of Identity Management Strategies." *European Journal of Social Psychology* 28:5 (1998) 697–729.
Blomberg, Craig L. "The Structure of 2 Corinthians 1–7." *Criswell Theological Review* 4:1 (1989) 3–20.
Brent, Allen. *Ignatius of Antioch: A Martyr Bishop and the Origin of Monarchial Episcopacy*. T. & T. Clark Theology. London: Continuum, 2007.
Brockhaus, Ulrich. *Charisma und Amt: Die paulinische Charismenlehre auf dem Hintergrund der frühchristlichen Gemeindefunktionen*. Wuppertal: Theologischer Verlag Brockhaus, 1972.
Brown, Andrew D. "A Narrative Approach to Collective Identities." *JMS* 43:4 (2006) 731–53.
Brown, Raymond E. *An Introduction to the New Testament*. The Anchor Yale Bible Reference Library. New York: Doubleday, 1997.
Brown, Rupert. *Group Processes: Dynamics Within and Between Groups*. 2nd ed. Oxford: Blackwell, 2001.
———. "Social Identity Theory: Past Achievements, Current Problems and Future Challenges." *European Journal of Social Psychology* 30:6 (2000) 745–78.
Bruggen, Jakob van. *Ambten in de apostolische kerk: Een exegetisch mozaïek*. Kampen: Kok, 1984.
———. *Paulus: Pionier voor de Messias van Israël*. Commentaar op het Nieuwe Testament 3rd ser. Kampen: Kok, 2001.
Burke, Peter J., and Jan E. Stets. *Identity Theory*. New York: Oxford University Press, 2009.

Burkett, Delbert R. *An Introduction to the New Testament and the Origins of Christianity*. Cambridge: Cambridge University Press, 2002.
Burtchaell, James T. *From Synagogue to Church: Public Services and Offices in the Earliest Christian Communities*. Cambridge: Cambridge University Press, 1992.
Campbell, Douglas A. *The Quest for Paul's Gospel: A Suggested Strategy*. JSNTSS 274. Edinburgh: T. & T. Clark, 2005.
Campbell, R. Alastair. *The Elders: Seniority Within Earliest Christianity*. Studies in the New Testament and Its World. London: T. & T. Clark, 1994.
Campbell, William S. *Paul and the Creation of Christian Identity*. LNTS 322. London: T. & T. Clark, 2008.
Campenhausen, Hans F. von. *Ecclesiastical Authority and Spiritual Power in the Church of the First Three Centuries*. Translated by J. A. Baker. Reprint of 1969 ed. Peabody, MA: Hendrickson, 1997.
Capes, David B., et al. *Rediscovering Paul: An Introduction to His World, Letters, and Theology*. Downers Grove, IL: IVP Academic, 2007.
Capozza, Dora, and Rupert Brown. "Conclusion: New Trends in Theory and Research." In *Social Identity Processes: Trends in Theory and Research*, edited by D. Capozza and R. Brown, 184–9. London: Sage, 2000.
Capper, Brian J. "The Transition from Gathering in Private to Meeting in Public Space in Second Generation Christianity and the Exclusion of Women from Leadership of the Public Assembly, Part 1." *Theologische Zeitschrift* 61:2 (2005) 113–31.
———. "The Transition from Gathering in Private to Meeting in Public Space in Second Generation Christianity and the Exclusion of Women from Leadership of the Public Assembly, Part 2." *Theologische Zeitschrift* 61:6 (2005) 301–19.
Carter, Warren. *The Roman Empire and the New Testament: An Essential Guide*. Abingdon Essential Guides. Nashville: Abingdon, 2006.
Castelli, Elizabeth A. *Imitating Paul: A Discourse of Power*. Literary Currents in Biblical Interpretation. Louisville: Westminster John Knox, 1991.
Chapple, Allen L. "Local Leadership in the Pauline Churches: Theological and Social Factors in Its Development. A study based on 1 Thessalonians, 1 Corinthians and Philippians." PhD diss., University of Durham, 1984.
Chemers, Martin M. *An Integrative Theory of Leadership*. Mahwah: Erlbaum, 1997.
Chow, John K. *Patronage and Power: A Study of Social Networks in Corinth*. JSNTSS 75: Sheffield Academic, 1992.
Chryssochoou, Xenia. *Cultural Diversity: Its Social Psychology*. Oxford: Blackwell, 2004.
Clarke, Andrew D. *A Pauline Theology of Church Leadership*. LNTS 362. London: T. & T. Clark, 2008.
———. *Secular and Christian Leadership in Corinth: A Socio-Historical and Exegetical Study of 1 Corinthians 1–6*. 2nd ed. PBM. Milton Keynes, UK: Paternoster, 2006.
———. *Serve the Community of the Church: Christians As Leaders and Ministers*. First-Century Christians in the Graeco-Roman World. Grand Rapids, MI: Eerdmans, 2000.
Collins, John N. *Deacons and the Church: Making Connections between Old and New*. Harrisbur, PA: Morehouse, 2002.

———. *Diakonia: Re-Interpreting the Ancient Sources*. New York: Oxford University Press, 1990.
Conger, Jay A., and Rabindra N. Kanungo. "Toward a Behavioral Theory of Charismatic Leadership in Organizational Settings." *AMR* 12:4 (1987) 637–47.
Conger, Jay A., et al. "Charismatic Leadership and Follower Effects." *Journal of Organizational Behavior* 21:7 (2000) 747–67.
Copan, Victor. *Saint Paul as Spiritual Director: An Analysis of the Concept of the Imitation of Paul with Implications and Applications to the Practice of Spiritual Direction*. PBM. Milton Keynes, UK: Paternoster, 2007.
Cornelissen, Joep P., et al. "Social Identity, Organizational Identity and Corporate Identity: Towards an Integrated Understanding of Processes, Patternings and Products." *BJM* 18:S1 (2007) S1–S16.
Couser, Greg A. "The Mystery of Godliness is Great: Christology in the Pastoral Epistles." In *Entrusted with the Gospel: Paul's Theology in the Pastoral Epistles*, edited by A. J. Köstenberger, and T. L. Wilder, 137–52. Nashville: B & H Academic, 2010.
Crook, Zeba A. "Reflections on Culture and Social-Scientific Models." *Journal of Biblical Literature* 124:3 (2005) 515–20.
Crossan, John D., and Jonathan L. Reed. *In Search of Paul: How Jesus's Apostle Opposed Rome's Empire with God's Kingdom: A New Vision of Paul's Words and World*. San Francisco: HarperSanFrancisco, 2005.
Dahl, Nils A., et al. *Studies in Ephesians: Introductory Questions, Text- and Edition-Critical Issues, Interpretation of Texts and Themes*. WUNT 131. Tübingen: Mohr/Siebeck, 2000.
Danker, Frederick W., et al. *A Greek-English Lexicon of the New Testament and Other Early Christian Literature*. 3rd ed. Chicago: University of Chicago Press, 2000.
Darko, Daniel K. *No Longer Living as the Gentiles: Differentiation and Shared Ethical Values in Ephesians 4.17–6.9*. LNTS 375. London: T. & T. Clark, 2008.
Deaux, Kay. "Models, Meanings and Motivations." In *Social Identity Processes: Trends in Theory and Research*, edited by D. Capozza, and R. Brown, 1–14. London: Sage, 2000.
Delling, G. "ἄρχω, ἀρχή, ἀπαρχή, ἀρχαῖος, ἀρχηγός, ἄρχων." In *TDNT* 1, 478–90.
DeSilva, David A. *An Introduction to the New Testament: Contexts, Methods and Ministry Formation*. Downers Grove, IL: InterVarsity, 2004.
———. "Measuring Penultimate against Ultimate Reality: An Investigation of the Integrity and Argumentation of 2 Corinthians." *JSNT* 52 (1993) 41–70.
———. "Recasting the Moment of Decision: 2 Corinthians 6:14—7:1 in Its Literary Context." *Andrews University Seminary Studies* 31:1 (1993) 3–16.
Dibelius, Martin, and Hans Conzelmann. *The Pastoral Epistles*. Translated by P. Buttolph, and A. Yarbro. Hermeneia: A Critical and Historical Commentary on the Bible. Philadelphia: Fortress, 1972.
Dix, Gregory. "The Ministry in the Early Church, c. AD 90–410." In *The Apostolic Ministry: Essays on the History and Doctrine of Episcopacy*, edited by K. E. Kirk, 183–303. London: Hodder & Stoughton, 1946.
Dodd, Brian J. *Paul's Paradigmatic "I": Personal Example as Literary Strategy*. JSNTSS 177. Sheffield: Sheffield Academic, 1999.

Donelson, Lewis R. *Pseudepigraphy and Ethical Argument in the Pastoral Epistles*. Hermeneutische Untersuchungen zur Theologie 22. Tübingen: Mohr/Siebeck, 1986.

Donfried, Karl P. "Rethinking Scholarly Approaches to 1 Timothy." In *1 Timothy Reconsidered*, edited by K. P. Donfried. COP 18, 153–82. Leuven: Peeters, 2008.

Dudrey, Russ. "'Submit Yourselves to One Another': A Socio-historical Look at the Household Code of Ephesians 5:15—6:9." *RQ* 41:1 (1999) 27–44.

Dunn, James D. G. "Pseudepigraphy." In *Dictionary of the Later New Testament and Its Developments*, edited by R. P. Martin, and P. H. Davids, 977–84. Downers Grove, IL: InterVarsity Press, 1997.

Dunning, Benjamin H. "Strangers and Aliens No Longer: Negotiating Identity and Difference in Ephesians 2." *Harvard Theological Review* 99:1 (2006) 1–16.

Ehrensperger, Kathy. *Paul and the Dynamics of Power: Communication and Interaction in the Early Christ-Movement*. LNTS 325. London: T. & T. Clark, 2007.

Ehrman, Bart D. *The New Testament: A Historical Introduction to the Early Christian Writings*. 3rd ed. Oxford: Oxford University Press, 2004.

Elliott, John H. "Elders as Honored Household Heads and Not Holders of 'Office' in Earliest Christianity. Review of *The Elders: Seniority within Earliest Christianity* by R. Alastair Campbell." *BTB* 33:2 (2003) 77–82.

———. "From Social Description to Social-Scientific Criticism: The History of a Society of Biblical Literature Section 1975–2005." *BTB* 38:1 (2008) 26–36.

Ellis, E. Earle. "Pastoral Letters." In DPL, 658–66.

———. "Paul and His Coworkers." In DPL, 183–88.

Esler, Philip F. *Conflict and Identity in Romans: The Social Setting of Paul's Letter*. Minneapolis: Fortress, 2003.

———. *Galatians*. New Testament Readings. London: Routledge, 1998.

———. "Glossolalia and the Admission of Gentiles into the Early Christian Community." In *The First Christians in Their Social Worlds: Social-Scientific Approaches to New Testament Interpretation*, 37–51. London: Routledge, 1994.

———. "Group Boundaries and Intergroup Conflict in Galatians: A New Reading of Gal. 5:13—6:10." In *Ethnicity and the Bible*, edited by M. G. Brett, 215–40. Leiden: Brill, 1996.

———. "'Remember My Fetters': Memorialisation of Paul's Imprisonment." In *Explaining Christian Origins and Early Judaism: Contributions from Cognitive and Social Science*, edited by P. Luomanen et al. BIS 89, 231–58. Leiden: Brill, 2007.

———. "Social Identity, the Virtues, and the Good Life: A New Approach to Romans 12:1–15:13." *BTB* 33:2 (2003) 51–63.

Fee, Gordon D. *The First Epistle to the Corinthians*. NICNT. Grand Rapids, MI: Eerdmans, 1987.

Fiore, Benjamin. *The Function of Personal Example in the Socratic and Pastoral Epistles*. Analecta Biblica 105. Rome: Biblical Institute Press, 1986.

———. *The Pastoral Epistles: First Timothy, Second Timothy, Titus*. SP 12. Collegeville, MD: Liturgical, 2007.

Fitzmyer, Joseph A. *The Acts of the Apostles: A New Translation with Introduction and Commentary*. AB 31. New York: Doubleday, 1998.

Forbes, Christopher. "Early Christian Inspired Speech and Hellenistic Popular Religion." *NT* 28:3 (1986) 257–70.
French, John R.P., and Bertram H. Raven. "The Bases of Social Power." In *Studies in Social Power*, edited by D. Cartwright, 150–67. Ann Arbor, MI: Institute of Social Research, 1959.
Fuchs, Rüdiger. *Unerwartete Unterschiede: Müssen wir unsere Ansichten über die Pastoralbriefe revidieren?* Bibelwissenschaftliche Monographien 12. Wuppertal: Brockhaus, 2003.
Furnish, Victor P. *II Corinthians*. AB 32A. Garden City, NY: Doubleday, 1984.
Gamble, Harry Y. *The New Testament Canon: Its Making and Meaning*. Guides to Biblical Scholarship, New Testament Series. Philadelphia: Fortress, 1985.
Garland, David E. *1 Corinthians*. Baker Exegetical Commentary on the New Testament 7. Grand Rapids, MI: Baker Academic, 2003.
———. *2 Corinthians*. NAC 29. Nashville: Broadman & Holman, 1999.
Gehring, Roger W. *House Church and Mission: The Importance of Household Structures in Early Christianity*. Peabody, MA: Hendrickson, 2004.
Gill, David W. J. "The Importance of Roman Portraiture for Head Coverings in 1 Corinthians 11:2–16." *TB* 41 (1990) 245–60.
Gombis, Timothy G. "A Radically New Humanity: The Function of the Haustafel in Ephesians." *JETS* 48:2 (2005) 317–30.
Gore, Charles. *The Church and the Ministry*. 4th rev. ed. London: Longmans, Green, 1900.
Gorman, Michael J. *Apostle of the Crucified Lord: A Theological Introduction to Paul and His Letters*. Grand Rapids, MI: Eerdmans, 2004.
Gosnell, Peter W. "Honor and Shame Rhetoric as a Unifying Motif in Ephesians." *Bulletin for Biblical Research* 16:1 (2006) 105–28.
Grieve, Paul G., and Michael A. Hogg. "Subjective Uncertainty and Intergroup Discrimination in the Minimal Group Situation." *PSPB* 25:8 (1999) 926–40.
Grindheim, Sigurd. "The Law Kills but the Gospel Gives Life: The Letter-Spirit Dualism in 2 Corinthians 3:5–18." *JSNT* 84 (2001) 97–115.
Grudem, Wayne A. *The Gift of Prophecy in 1 Corinthians*. Washington, DC: University Press of America, 1982.
Hafemann, Scott J. *Suffering and Ministry in the Spirit: Paul's Defense of his Ministry in II Corinthians 2:14—3:3*. Grand Rapids, MI: Eerdmans, 1990.
Hainz, Josef. *Ekklesia: Strukturen paulinischer Gemeinde-Theologie und Gemeinde-Ordnung*. Regensburg: F. Pustet, 1972.
Haley, Peter. "Rudolph Sohm on Charisma." *The Journal of Religion* 60:2 (1980) 185–97.
Hall, David R. *The Unity of the Corinthian Correspondence*. JSNTSS 251. London: T. & T. Clark, 2003.
Hansen, Bruce. *'All of You Are One': The Social Vision of Galatians 3.28, 1 Corinthians 12.13 and Colossians 3.11*. LNTS 409. London: T. & T. Clark, 2010.
Harland, Philip A. *Associations, Synagogues, and Congregations. Claiming a Place in Ancient Mediterranean Society*. Minneapolis: Fortress, 2003.
———. *Dynamics of Identity in the World of the Early Christians: Associations, Judeans, and Cultural Minorities*. New York: T. & T. Clark, 2009.

———. "Honours and Worship: Emperors, Imperial Cults, and Associations at Ephesus (First to Third Centuries C.E.)." *Studies in Religion/Sciences Religieuses* 25 (1996) 319–34.

Harnack, Adolf von. *The Constitution and Law of the Church in the First Two Centuries*. Translated by F. L. Pogson. London: Williams & Norgate, 1910.

Harris, Murray J. *The Second Epistle to the Corinthians: A Commentary on the Greek Text*. The New International Greek Testament Commentary. Grand Rapids, MI: Eerdmans, 2005.

Harrison, James R. "Paul and the Gymnasiarchs: Two Approaches to Pastoral Formation in Antiquity." In *Paul as Jew, Greek and Roman*, edited by S. E. Porter. Pauline Studies 5, 141–78. Leiden: Brill, 2008.

Harrison, Percy N. *The Problem of the Pastoral Epistles*. Oxford: Oxford University Press, 1921.

Hart, Ann W. "Leader Succession and Socialization: A Synthesis." *Review of Educational Research* 61:4 (1991) 451–74.

Hartog, Paul. *Polycarp and the New Testament: The Occasion, Rhetoric, Theme, and Unity of the Epistle to the Philippians and Its Allusions to New Testament Literature*. WUNT 2nd ser., 134. Tübingen: Mohr/Siebeck, 2002.

Haslam, S. Alexander. *Psychology in Organizations: The Social Identity Approach*. 2nd ed. London: Sage, 2004.

Haslam, S. Alexander, and Naomi Ellemers. "Social Identity in Industrial and Organizational Psychology: Concepts, Controversies and Contributions." In *International Review of Industrial and Organizational Psychology*, edited by G. P. Hodgkinson, and J. K. Ford 20, 39–118. Hoboken: Wiley, 2005.

Haslam, S. Alexander, and Michael J. Platow. "The Link between Leadership and Followership: How Affirming Social Identity Translates Vision into Action." *PSPB* 27:11 (2001) 1469–79.

———. "Social Identity and the Romance of Leadership: The Importance of Being Seen to Be 'Doing It for Us.'" *Group Processes and Group Interrelations* 4:3 (2001) 191–205.

———. "Your Wish Is Our Command: The Role of Shared Social Identity in Translating a Leader's Vision into Followers' Action." In *Social Identity Processes in Organizations*, edited by M. A. Hogg, and D. J. Terry, 213–28. New York: Psychology Press, 2001.

Haslam, S. Alexander, and Stephen Reicher. "Social Identity and the Dynamics of Organizational Life: Insights from the BBC Prison Study." In *Identity and the Modern Organization*, edited by C. Bartel et al. Lea's Organization and Management Series, 135–66. Mahwah: Erlbaum, 2007.

Haslam, S. Alexander, Stephen Reicher, and Michael J. Platow. *The New Psychology of Leadership: Identity, Influence and Power*. New York: Psychology Press, 2011.

Haslam, S. Alexander, et al. "More Than a Metaphor: Organizational Identity Makes Organizational Life Possible." *BJM* 14:4 (2003) 357–69.

Hatch, Edwin. *The Organization of the Early Christian Churches*. 2nd ed. London: Rivingtons, 1882.

Heiligenthal, R. "Τό Ἔργον, Ergon, Work, Task." In *EDNT* 2, 49–51.

Heitink, Gerben. *Praktische theologie: Geschiedenis, theorie, handelingsvelden*. Handboek praktische theologie. Kampen: Kok, 1993.

Hendrix, Holland. "On the Form and Ethos of Ephesians." *Union Seminary Quarterly Review* 42:4 (1988) 3–15.

Hering, James P. *The Colossian and Ephesian Haustafeln in Theological Context: An Analysis of Their Origins, Relationship, and Message*. Theology and Religion 260. New York: Peter Lang, 2007.

Herzer, Jens. "Abschied vom Konsens? Die Pseudepigraphie der Pastoralbriefe als Herausforderung an die neutestamentliche Wissenschaft." *Theologische Literaturzeitung* 129:12 (2004) 1267–82.

———. "Rearranging the 'House of God': A New Perspective on the Pastoral Epistles." In *Empsychoi Logoi, Religious Innovations in Antiquity: Studies in Honour of Pieter Willem Van Der Horst*, edited by A. Houtman et al. Ancient Judaism and Early Christianity 73, 547–66. Leiden: Brill, 2008.

Hiigel, John L. *Leadership in 1 Corinthians: A Case Study in Paul's Ecclesiology*. Studies in the Bible and Early Christianity 57. Lewiston: Mellen Press, 2003.

Hoehner, Harold W. *Ephesians: An Exegetical Commentary*. Grand Rapids, MI: Baker Academic, 2002.

Hogg, Michael A. "From Prototypicality to Power: A Social Identity Analysis of Leadership." In *Advances in Group Processes* 18, edited by S. R. Thye, et al, 1–30. Oxford: Elsevier, 2001.

———. "Social Identification, Group Prototypicality, and Emergent Leadership." In *Social Identity Processes in Organizational Contexts*, edited by M. A. Hogg, chapter 13, 197–213. Philadelphia: Psychology Press, 2001.

———. "A Social Identity Theory of Leadership." *PSPR* 5:3 (2001) 184–200.

Hogg, Michael A., and Dominic Abrams. *Social Identifications: A Social Psychology of Intergroup Relations and Group Processes*. London: Routledge, 1988.

Hogg, Michael A., and Paul Grieve. "Social Identity Theory and the Crisis of Confidence in Social Psychology: A Commentary, and Some Research on Uncertainty Reduction." *Asian Journal of Social Psychology* 2 (1999) 79–93.

Hogg, Michael A., and Scott A. Reid. "Social Identity, Leadership, and Power." In *The Use and Abuse of Power: Multiple Perspectives on the Causes of Corruption*, edited by A. Y. Lee-Chai, and J. A. Bargh, 159–80. Philadelphia: Psychology Press, 2001.

Hogg, Michael A., et al. "The Social Identity Perspective: Intergroup Relations, Self-Conception, and Small Groups." *Small Group Research* 35:3 (2004) 246–76.

———. "Identification and Leadership in Small Groups: Salience, Frame of Reference, and Leader Stereotypicality Effects on Leader Evaluations." *JPSP* 75 (1998) 1248–63.

Holmberg, Bengt. *Paul and Power: The Structure of Authority in the Primitive Church as Reflected in the Pauline Epistles*. Lund: CWK Gleerup, 1978.

———. *Sociology and the New Testament: An Appraisal*. Minneapolis: Fortress, 1990.

———. "Understanding the First Hundred Years of Christian Identity." In *Exploring Early Christian Identity*, edited by B. Holmberg. WUNT 226, 1–32. Tübingen: Mohr/Siebeck, 2008.

Holmberg, Bengt, and Mikael Winninge. *Identity Formation in the New Testament*. WUNT 227. Tübingen: Mohr/Siebeck, 2008.

Holmes, Michael W., et al. *The Apostolic Fathers: Greek Texts and English Translations*. 2nd ed. Grand Rapids, MI: Baker, 1999.

Holtzmann, Heinrich J. *Die Pastoralbriefe kritisch und exegetisch behandelt.* Leipzig: Wilhelm Engelmann, 1880.

Hornsey, Matthew J. "Social Identity Theory and Self-Categorization Theory: A Historical Review." *Social and Personality Psychology Compass* 2:1 (2008) 204–22.

Hornsey, Matthew J., and Michael A. Hogg. "Assimilation and Diversity: An Integrative Model of Subgroup Relations." *PSPR* 4:2 (2000) 143–56.

Horrell, David G. "Disciplining Performance and 'Placing' the Church: Widows, Elders and Slaves in the Household of God (1 Tim 5,1–6,2)." In *1 Timothy Reconsidered*, edited by K. P. Donfried. COP 18, 109–34. Leuven: Peeters, 2008.

———. "Leadership Patterns and the Development of Ideology in Early Christianity." *Sociology of Religion* 58 (1997) 323–41.

———. "From ἀδελφοί to οἶκος θεοῦ: Social Transformation in Pauline Christianity." *Journal of Biblical Literature* 120:2 (2001) 293–311.

Horsley, Richard A. *Paul and Empire: Religion and Power in Roman Imperial Society.* Harrisburg, PA: Trinity, 1997.

Houwelingen, P. H. R. van. *Timoteüs en Titus: Pastorale instructiebrieven.* Commentaar op het Nieuwe Testament. Kampen: Kok, 2009.

Jennings, Mark A. "Patronage and Rebuke in Paul's Persuasion in 2 Corinthians 8–9." *Journal of Greco-Roman Christianity and Judaism* 6 (2009) 107–27.

Johnson, Luke T. *The First and Second Letters to Timothy: A New Translation with Introduction and Commentary.* AB 35A. New York: Doubleday, 2001.

———. "First Timothy 1,1–20: The Shape of the Struggle." In *1 Timothy Reconsidered*, edited by K. P. Donfried, 19–39. Leuven: Peeters, 2008.

Joubert, Stephan J. *Paul as Benefactor: Reciprocity, Strategy and Theological Reflection in Paul's Collection.* WUNT 2nd ser., 4. Tübingen: Mohr/Siebeck, 2000.

Judge, Edwin A. "The Social Identity of the First Christians: A Question of Method in Religious History." *Journal of Religious History* 11 (1980) 201–17.

———. "The Teacher as Moral Exemplar in Paul and in the Inscriptions of Ephesus." In Edwin A. Judge, and David M. Scholer, *Social Distinctives of the Christians in the First century: Pivotal Essays by E. A. Judge*, 175–88. Peabody, MA: Hendrickson, 2008.

Kanungo, Rabindra N., and Jay A. Conger. "Charisma: Exploring New Dimensions of Leadership Behaviour." *Psychology of Developing Societies* 4:1 (1992) 21–37.

Karris, Robert J. "Background and Significance of the Polemic of the Pastoral Epistles." *Journal of Biblical Literature* 92:4 (1973) 549–64.

Keay, Robert. "Paul the Spiritual Guide: A Social Identity Perspective on Paul's Apostolic Self-Identity." PhD diss., St. Andrews University, 2004.

Kelly, John N. D. *A Commentary on the Pastoral Epistles.* BNTC 14. Peabody, MA: Hendrickson, 1963.

Kidd, Reggie M. *Wealth and Beneficence in the Pastoral Epistles: A "Bourgeois" Form of Early Christianity?* Society of Biblical Literature Dissertation Series 122. Atlanta: Scholars, 1990.

Kim, Seyoon. *Christ and Caesar: The Gospel and the Roman Empire in the Writings of Paul and Luke.* Grand Rapids, MI: Eerdmans, 2008.

Klauck, Hans-Josef. *Die antike Briefliteratur und das Neue Testament: Ein Lehr- und Arbeitsbuch.* Paderborn: UTB für Wissenschaft, 1998.

Klein, Olivier, et al. "Social Identity Performance: Extending the Strategic Side of SIDE." *PSPR* 11:1 (2007) 28–45.

Knight, George W. *The Faithful Sayings in the Pastoral Letters*. Kampen: Kok, 1968.
———. *The Pastoral Epistles: A Commentary on the Greek Text*. NIGTC. Carlisle: Paternoster, 1992.
Knippenberg, Barbara van, and Daan van Knippenberg. "Leader Self-Sacrifice and Leadership Effectiveness: The Moderating Role of Leader Prototypicality." *Journal of Applied Psychology* 90:1 (2005) 25–37.
Knippenberg, Daan van, and Michael A. Hogg. "A Social Identity Model of Leadership Effectiveness in Organizations." In *Research in Organizational Behavior* 25, edited by B. E. Staw, and R. M. Kramer, 243–95. Greenwich, CT: JAI Press, 2003.
Knippenberg, Daan van, et al. "Leadership, Self, and Identity: A Review and Research Agenda." *LQ* 15 (2004) 825–56.
———. "Who Takes the Lead in Risky Decision Making? Effects of Group Members' Individual Riskiness and Prototypicality." *Organizational Behavior and Human Decision Processes* 83:2 (2000) 213–34.
Koester, Helmut. *Ephesos, Metropolis of Asia: An Interdisciplinary Approach to Its Archaeology, Religion, and Culture*. HThS 41. Valley Forge, PA: Trinity, 1995.
Küng, Hans. *Strukturen der Kirche*. Quaestiones Disputatae 17. Freiburg: Herder, 1962.
Lambrecht, Jan. *Second Corinthians*. SP 8. Collegeville, MN: Liturgical, 2006.
Lampe, Peter. *From Paul to Valentinus: Christians at Rome in the First Two Centuries*. Translated by M. Steinhauser. Minneapolis: Fortress, 2003.
Lassen, Eva M. "The Roman Family: Ideal and Metaphor." In *Constructing Early Christian Families: Family as Social Reality and Metaphor*, edited by H. Moxnes, 103–20. London: Routledge, 1997.
Lawler, Steph. *Identity: Sociological Perspectives*. Cambridge: Polity Press, 2008.
Lea, Thomas D., and Hayne P. Griffin. *1, 2 Timothy, Titus*. NAC 34. Nashville: Broadman, 1992.
Liddell, Henry G., et al. *A Greek-English Lexicon*. 9th ed. Oxford: Clarendon, 1996.
Lieu, Judith M. *Christian Identity in the Jewish and Graeco-Roman World*. Oxford: Oxford University Press, 2004.
Lightfoot, Joseph B. *Saint Paul's Epistle to the Philippians*. London: Macmillan, 1868.
Lincoln, Andrew T. *Ephesians*. Word Biblical Commentary 42. Dallas: Word, 2002.
Lindemann, Andreas. *Die Aufhebung der Zeit: Geschichtsverständnis und Eschatologie im Epheserbrief*. Studien zum Neuen Testament 12. Gütersloh: Mohn, 1975.
Long, Fredrick J. *Ancient Rhetoric and Paul's Apology: The Compositional Unity of 2 Corinthians*. SNTSMS 131. Cambridge: Cambridge University Press, 2004.
Lord, Robert G., and Cynthia G. Emrich. "Thinking Outside the Box by Looking Inside the Box: Extending the Cognitive Revolution in Leadership Research." *LQ* 11:4 (2000) 551–79.
Lord, Robert G., et al. "System Constraints on Leadership Perceptions, Behavior, and Influence: An Example of Connectionist Level Processes." In *Blackwell Handbook of Social Psychology: Group Processes*, edited by M. A. Hogg, and R. S. Tindale, 283–310. Malden: Blackwell, 2002.
———. "Understanding the Dynamics of Leadership: The Role of Follower Self-Concepts in the Leader/Follower Relationship." *Organizational Behavior and Human Decision Processes* 78:3 (1999) 167–203.

Louw, Johannes P., and Eugene A. Nida. *Greek-English Lexicon of the New Testament Based on Semantic Domains.* 2nd ed. New York: United Bible Societies, 1989.

Luomanen, Petri. "The Sociology of Knowledge, the Social Identity Approach and the Cognitive Science of Religion." In *Explaining Christian Origins and Early Judaism: Contributions from Cognitive and Social Science,* edited by P. Luomanen et al., BIS 89, 199–230. Leiden: Brill, 2007.

Luomanen, Petri, et al. *Explaining Christian Origins and Early Judaism: Contributions from Cognitive and Social Science.* BIS 89. Leiden: Brill, 2007.

MacDonald, Margaret Y. *Colossians and Ephesians.* SP 17. Collegeville, MN: Liturgical, 2000.

———. *The Pauline Churches: A Socio-Historical Study of Institutionalization in the Pauline and Deutero-Pauline Writings.* Cambridge: Cambridge University Press, 1988.

———. "The Politics of Identity in Ephesians." *JSNT* 26:4 (2004) 419–44.

Maier, Harry O. *The Social Setting of the Ministry as Reflected in the Writings of Hermas, Clement and Ignatius.* Studies in Christianity and Judaism 12. Waterloo, ON: Wilfrid Laurier University Press, 2002.

Malina, Bruce J. "Early Christian Groups: Using Small Group Formation Theory to Explain Christian Organizations." In *Modelling Early Christianity: Social-Scientific Studies of the New Testament in Its Context,* edited by P. F. Esler, 96–113. London: Routledge, 1995.

———. *The New Testament World: Insights from Cultural Anthropology.* Third revised and expanded ed. Louisville: Westminster John Knox, 2001.

———. *Timothy: Paul's Closest Associate.* Paul's Social Network, Brothers and Sisters in Faith Series. Collegeville, MN: Liturgical, 2008.

Malina, Bruce J., and Jerome H. Neyrey. "Conflict in Luke-Acts: Labelling and Deviance Theory." In *The Social World of Luke-Acts: Models for Interpretation,* edited by J. H. Neyrey, 97–124. Peabody, MA: Hendrickson, 1991.

Marshall, I. Howard. "Congregation and Ministry in the Pastoral Epistles." In *Community Formation in the Early Church and the Church Today,* edited by R. N. Longenecker, 105–25. Peabody, MA: Hendrickson, 2002.

———. *The Pastoral Epistles.* ICC. Edinburgh: T. & T. Clark, 2004.

Martin, Dale B. "Tongues of Angels and Other Status Indicators." *Journal of the American Academy of Religion* 59 (1991) 563–9.

Martin, Jochen. *Der priesterliche Dienst. Die Genese des Amtspriestertums in der frühen Kirche.* Freiburg: Herder, 1972.

Martin, Ralph P. *2 Corinthians.* Word Biblical Commentary 40. Waco, TX: Word, 1986.

Martin, Seán C. *Pauli Testamentum: 2 Timothy and the Last Words of Moses.* Tesi Gregoriana Serie Teologia 18. Rome: Pontificia Università Gregoriana, 1997.

McDonald, Lee M., and Stanley E. Porter. *Early Christianity and Its Sacred Literature.* Peabody, MA: Hendrickson, 2000.

Meeks, Wayne A. *The First Urban Christians: The Social World of the Apostle Paul.* New Haven, CT: Yale University Press, 1983.

Merklein, Helmut. *Das kirchliche Amt nach dem Epheserbrief.* Studien zum Alten und Neuen Testament 33. München: Kösel, 1973.

Merz, Annette. "Amore Pauli: Das Corpus Pastorale und das Ringen um die Interpretationshoheit bezüglich des paulinischen Erbes." *Theologische Quartalschrift* 187:4 (2007) 274–94.

———. "The Fictitious Self-Exposition of Paul: How Might Intertextual Theory Suggest a Reformulation of the Hermeneutics of Pseudepigraphy?" In *The Intertextuality of the Epistles: Explorations of Theory and Practice*, edited by T. L. Brodie et al. New Testament Monographs 16, 113–32. Sheffield: Sheffield Phoenix, 2006.

———. *Die fiktive Selbstauslegung des Paulus: Intertextuelle Studien zur Intention und Rezeption der Pastoralbriefe*. Novum Testamentum et Orbis Antiquus 52. Göttingen: Vandenhoeck & Ruprecht, 2004.

Metzger, Bruce M. *The Text of the New Testament: Its Transmission, Corruption, and Restoration*. 4th rev. ed. Oxford: Oxford University Press, 1994.

Mitchell, Margaret M. "Corrective Composition, Corrective Exegesis: Teaching on Prayer in 1T2,1–15." In *1 Timothy Reconsidered*, edited by K. P. Donfried, 41–62. Leuven: Peeters, 2008.

Morgenthaler, Robert. *Statistik des neutestamentlichen Wortschatzes*. 4th ed. Zürich: Gotthelf, 1992.

Mounce, William D. *Pastoral Epistles*. Word Biblical Commentary 46. Nashville: Nelson, 2000.

Mouton, A. Elna J. "The Communicative Power of the Epistle to the Ephesians." In *Rhetoric, Scripture, and Theology: Essays from the 1994 Pretoria Conference*, edited by S. E. Porter, and T. H. Olbricht. JSNTSS 131, 280–307. Sheffield: Sheffield Academic, 1996.

———. *Reading a New Testament Document Ethically*. Academia Biblica 1. Atlanta: Society of Biblical Literature, 2002.

Murphy-O'Connor, Jerome. *St. Paul's Corinth: Text and Archaeology*. 3rd rev. and expanded ed. Collegeville, MN: Liturgical, 2002.

———. *St. Paul's Ephesus: Texts and Archaeology*. Collegeville, MN: Liturgical, 2008.

Neumann, Kenneth J. *The Authenticity of the Pauline Epistles in the Light of Stylostatistical Analysis*. Society of Biblical Literature Dissertation Series 120. Atlanta: Scholars, 1990.

Neyrey, Jerome H. "God, Benefactor and Patron: The Major Cultural Model for Interpreting the Deity in Greco-Roman Antiquity." *JSNT* 27:4 (2005) 465–92.

———. "'Teaching You in Public and from House to House' (Acts 20.20): Unpacking a Cultural Stereotype." *JSNT* 26:1 (2003) 69–102.

Nguyen, V. Henry T. *Christian Identity in Corinth: A Comparative Study of 2 Corinthians, Epictetus and Valerius Maximus*. WUNT/2, 243. Tübingen: Mohr/Siebeck, 2008.

Niens, Ulrike, and Ed Cairns. "Explaining Social Change and Identity Management Strategies: New Directions for Future Research." *Theory and Psychology* 13:4 (2003) 489–509.

Northouse, Peter G. *Leadership: Theory and Practice*. 4th ed. Thousand Oaks, CA: Sage, 2007.

O'Brien, Peter T. *The Letter to the Ephesians*. Pillar New Testament Commentary. Grand Rapids, MI: Eerdmans, 1999.

Oakes, Penelope J., et al. "The Role of Prototypicality in Group Influence and Cohesion: Contextual Variation in the Graded Structure of Social Categories." In *Social Identity: International Perspectives*, edited by S. Worchel, 75–92. London: Sage, 1998.

Oberlinner, Lorenz. *Der erste Timotheusbrief, der zweite Timotheusbrief.* Ungekürzte Sonderausgabe. Herders theologischer Kommentar zum Neuen Testament. Freiburg: Herder, 2002.

Operario, Don, and Susan T. Fiske. "Integrating Social Identity and Social Cognition: A Framework for Bridging Diverse Perspectives." In *Social identity and Social Cognition*, edited by D. Abrams, and M. A. Hogg, 26–54. Malden, MA: Blackwell, 1999.

Osiek, Carolyn, et al. *A Woman's Place: House Churches in Earliest Christianity*. Minneapolis: Fortress, 2006.

Packer, Dominic J. "On Being Both With Us and Against Us: A Normative Conflict Model of Dissent in Social Groups." *PSPR* 12:1 (2008) 50–72.

Page, Sydney H. T. "Whose Ministry? A Re-appraisal of Ephesians 4:12." *NT* 47:1 (2005) 26–46.

Paschke, Boris A. "The *cura morum* of the Roman Censors as Historical Background for the Bishop and Deacon Lists of the Pastoral Epistles." *Zeitschrift für die neutestamentliche Wissenschaft und Kunde der älteren Kirche* 98:1 (2007) 105–19.

Paul, Jim, et al. "The Mutability of Charisma in Leadership Research." *Management Decision* 40:2 (2002) 192–200.

Perkins, Pheme. *Ephesians*. Abingdon New Testament Commentary. Nashville: Abingdon, 1997.

Perrin, Nicholas. *Thomas and Tatian: The Relationship between the Gospel of Thomas and the Diatessaron*. Academia Biblica 5. Leiden: Brill, 2002.

Pietersen, Lloyd. "Despicable Deviants: Labelling Theory and the Polemic of the Pastorals." *Sociology of Religion* 58:4 (1997) 343–52.

———. *The Polemic of the Pastorals: A Sociological Examination of the Development of Pauline Christianity*. JSNTSS 264. London: T. & T. Clark, 2004.

Platow, Michael J., and Daan van Knippenberg. "A Social Identity Analysis of Leadership Endorsement: The Effects of Leader Ingroup Prototypicality and Distributive Intergroup Fairness." *PSPB* 27:11 (2001) 1508–19.

Platow, Michael J., et al. "A Special Gift We Bestow on You for Being Representative of Us: Considering Leader Charisma from a Self-Categorization Perspective." *British Journal of Social Psychology* 45 (2006) 303–20.

Polaski, Sandra Hack. "'Let No One Despise Your Youth': The Deconstruction of Traditional Authority in the Pastoral Epistles." *Lexington Theological Quarterly* 40:4 (2005) 249–63.

———. *Paul and the Discourse of Power*. The Biblical Seminar 62. Sheffield: Sheffield Academic, 1999.

Prior, Michael. *Paul the Letter-Writer and the Second Letter to Timothy*. JSNTSS 23. Sheffield: JSOT Press, 1989.

Quinn, Jerome D., and William C. Wacker. *The First and Second Letters to Timothy: A New Translation with Notes and Commentary*. The Eerdmans Critical Commentary. Grand Rapids, MI: Eerdmans, 2000.

Räisänen, Heikki. *Beyond New Testament Theology: A Story and a Programme*. London: SCM, 1990.

Raven, Bertram H. "The Bases of Power and the Power/Interaction Model of Interpersonal Influence." *Analyses of Social Issues and Public Policy* 8:1 (2008) 1–22.
Reasoner, Mark. "Rome and Roman Christianity." In DPL, 850–54.
Redalié, Yann. *Paul après Paul:Lle temps, le salut, la morale selon les épîtres à Timothé et à Tite.* Le monde de la Bible 31. Geneva: Labor et Fides, 1994.
———. "'Sois un modèle pour les croyants.' Timothée, un portrait exhortatif, 1 Tm 4." In *1 Timothy Reconsidered*, edited by K. P. Donfried, 87–108. Leuven: Peeters, 2008.
Reicher, Stephen. "Biography of Henri Tajfel (1919–1982)." European Association of Experimental Social Psychology. Online: http://www.eaesp.org/activities/own/ awards/tajfel.htm.
———. "The Context of Social Identity: Domination, Resistance, and Change." *Political Psychology* 25:6 (2004) 921–45.
Reicher, Stephen, and Nick Hopkins. "Psychology and the End of History: A Critique and a Proposal for the Psychology of Social Categorization." *Political Psychology* 22:2 (2001) 383–407.
Reicher, Stephen, et al. "Social Identity and the Dynamics of Leadership: Leaders and Followers as Collaborative Agents in the Transformation of Social Reality." *LQ* 16:4 (2005) 547–68.
Reicke, Bo I. *Re-Examining Paul's Letters: The History of the Pauline Correspondence.* Edited by D. P. Moessner. Harrisburg, PA: Trinity, 2001.
Reiser, Marius. "Paulus als Stilist." *Svensk Exegetisk Årsbok* 66 (2001) 151–65.
Richards, E. Randolph. *Paul and First-Century Letter Writing: Secretaries, Composition and Collection.* Downers Grove, IL: Apollos, 2005.
———. *The Secretary in the Letters of Paul.* WUNT/2, 42. Tübingen: Mohr/Siebeck, 1991.
Richards, William A. *Difference and Distance in Post-Pauline Christianity: An Epistolary Analysis of the Pastorals.* Studies in Biblical Literature 44. New York: Lang, 2002.
Ritter, Barbara A., and Robert G. Lord. "The Impact of Previous Leaders on the Evaluation of New Leaders: An Alternative to Prototype Matching." *Journal of Applied Psychology* 92:6 (2007) 1683–95.
Robbins, Vernon K. *The Invention of Christian Discourse.* Rhetoric of Religious Antiquity. Leiden: Deo, 2008.
Robertson, Joseph M. "The Basis for Paul's Claim to Authority in 1 and 2 Corinthians: A Reappraisal." PhD diss., Golden Gate Baptist Theological Seminary, 1994.
Robinson, W. Peter. *Social Groups and Identities: Developing the Legacy of Henri Tajfel.* International Series in Social Psychology. Oxford: Butterworth-Heinemann, 1996.
Rohde, Joachim. "Ἐπίσκοπος, *Episkopos*, Bishop (Overseer)." In *EDNT* 2, 35–36.
Rohrbaugh, Richard L. "Hermeneutics as Cross-Cultural Encounter: Obstacles to Understanding." *HTS* 62:2 (2006) 559–76.
Roitto, Rikard. "Act as a Christ-Believer, as a Household Member or Both? A Cognitive Perspective on the Relation between the Social Identity in Christ and Household Identities in Pauline and Deutero-Pauline Texts." In *Identity Formation in the New Testament*, edited by B. Holmberg and M. Winninge. WUNT 227, 141–61. Tübingen: Mohr/Siebeck, 2008.

———. *Behaving as a Christ-Believer: A Cognitive Perspective on Identity and Behavior Norms in Ephesians*. Linköping Studies in Arts and Science 493. Linköping: Linköping University, Department of Culture and Communication, 2009.

Runesson, Anders. "Inventing Christian identity: Paul, Ignatius, and Theodosius I." In *Exploring Early Christian Identity*, edited by B. Holmberg. WUNT 226, 59–92. Tübingen: Mohr/Siebeck, 2008.

Sani, Fabio. "When Subgroups Secede: Extending and Refining the Social Psychological Model of Schism in Groups." *PSPB* 31:8 (2005) 1074–86.

Sashkin, Marshall. "Transformational Leadership Approaches: A Review and Synthesis." In *The Nature of Leadership*, edited by J. Antonakis, et al, 171–96. Thousand Oaks, CA: Sage, 2004.

Scherrer, Peter. *Ephesus: The New Guide*. Translated by L. Bier, and G. M. Luxon. Rev. ed. Istanbul: Österreichisches Archäologisches Institut, 2000.

Schlier, Heinrich. *Der Brief an die Epheser: Ein Kommentar*. 2nd ed. Düsseldorf: Patmos, 1958.

Schmeller, Thomas. *Hierarchie und Egalität: Eine sozialgeschichtliche Untersuchung paulinischer Gemeinden und griechisch-römischer Vereine*. Stuttgarter Bibelstudien 162. Stuttgart: Verlag Katholisches Bibelwerk, 1995.

Schnackenburg, Rudolf. *Die Kirche im Neuen Testament: Ihre Wirklichkeit und theologische Deutung, ihr Wesen und Geheimnis*. Quaestiones Disputatae 14. Freiburg: Herder, 1961.

Schowalter, Daniel N., and Steven J. Friesen. *Urban Religion in Roman Corinth: Interdisciplinary Approaches*. HThS 42. Cambridge: Harvard Divinity School, 2005.

Schreiber, Alfred. *Die Gemeinde in Korinth: Versuch einer gruppendynamischen Betrachtung der Entwicklung der Gemeinde von Korinth auf der Basis des ersten Korintherbriefes*. Neutestamentliche Abhandlungen, Neue Folge 12. Münster: Aschendorff, 1977.

Schüssler Fiorenza, Elisabeth. *In Memory of Her: A Feminist Theological Reconstruction of Christian Origins*. New York: Crossroad, 1983.

Schütz, John H. *Paul and the Anatomy of Apostolic Authority*. Society of New Testament Studies Monograph Series 26. London: Cambridge University Press, 1975.

Schweizer, Eduard. *Church Order in the New Testament*. Translated by F. Clarke. Studies in Biblical Theology 32. London: SCM, 1961.

Shkul, Minna. *Reading Ephesians: Exploring Social Entrepreneurship in the Text*. LNTS 408. London: T. & T. Clark, 2009.

Simon, Bernd, and Penelope J. Oakes. "Beyond Dependence: An Identity Approach to Social Power and Domination." *Human Relations* 59:1 (2006) 105–39.

Sluss, David M., and Blake E. Ashforth. "Relational Identity and Identification: Defining Ourselves through Work Relationships." *AMR* 32:1 (2007) 9–32.

Smink, Geurt J. *Het kerkelijk ambt naar een nieuw paradigma: De ambtstheologie van Hans Küng*. Zoetermeer: Meinema, 2006.

Söding, Thomas. "1 Timotheus 3: Der Episkopos und die Diakone in der Kirche." In *1 Timothy Reconsidered*, edited by K. P. Donfried. COP 18, 63–86. Leuven: Peeters, 2008.

Sohm, Rudolf. *Kirchenrecht I: Die geschichtlichen Grundlagen.* Leipzig: J. C. Henrich, 1892.
Stagaman, David J. *Authority in the Church.* Collegeville, MN: Liturgical, 1999.
Standhartinger, Angela. "*Eusebeia* in den Pastoralbriefen. Ein Beitrag zum Einfluss römischen Denkens auf das entstehende Christentum." *NT* 48:1 (2006) 51–82.
Stegman, Thomas. *The Character of Jesus: The Linchpin to Paul's Argument in 2 Corinthians.* Analecta Biblica 158. Rome: Editrice Pontificio Istituto Biblico, 2005.
Stepp, Perry L. *Leadership Succession in the World of the Pauline Circle.* New Testament Monographs 5. Sheffield: Sheffield Phoenix, 2005.
Streeter, Burnett H. *The Primitive Church, Studied with Special Reference to the Origins of the Christian Ministry; Lectures Delivered on the Hewett Foundation.* New York: Macmillan, 1929. Reprint, Kessinger, 2003.
Strelan, Rick. *Paul, Artemis, and the Jews in Ephesus.* Beihefte zur Zeitschrift für die neutestamentliche Wissenschaft und die Kunde der älteren Kirche 80. Berlin: De Gruyter, 1996.
Suh, Robert H. "The Use of Ezekiel 37 in Ephesians 2." *JETS* 50:4 (2007) 715–34.
Sullivan, Francis A. *From Apostles to Bishops: The Development of the Episcopacy in the Early Church.* New York: Newman, 2001.
Sumney, Jerry L. *Identifying Paul's Opponents: The Question of Method in 2 Corinthians.* JSNTSS. Sheffield: JSOT Press, 1990.
———. *'Servants of Satan', 'False Brothers' and Other Opponents of Paul.* JSNTSS 188. Sheffield: Sheffield Academic, 1999.
Tajfel, Henri. *Differentiation between Social Groups: Studies in the Social Psychology of Intergroup Relations.* European Monographs in Social Psychology 14. London: Academic, 1978.
———. *Human Groups and Social Categories: Studies in Social Psychology.* Cambridge: Cambridge University Press, 1981.
Talbert, Charles H. *Ephesians and Colossians.* Paideia Commentary on the New Testament. Grand Rapids, MI: Baker Academic, 2007.
Tamez, Elsa. *Struggles for Power in Early Christianity: A Study of the First Letter to Timothy.* Translated by G. Kinsler. Maryknoll: Orbis, 2007.
Taylor, Nicholas H. "Conflict as Context for Defining Identity: A Study of Apostleship in the Galatian and Corinthian Letters." *HTS* 59:3 (2003) 915–45.
Tellbe, Mikael. *Christ-Believers in Ephesus: A Textual Analysis of Early Christian Identity Formation in a Local Perspective.* WUNT 242. Tübingen: Mohr/Siebeck, 2009.
———. "The Prototypical Christ-Believer: Early Christian Identity Formation in Ephesus." In *Exploring Early Christian Identity*, edited by B. Holmberg, 115–38. Tübingen: Mohr/Siebeck, 2008.
Theissen, Gerd. *The Social Setting of Pauline Christianity: Essays on Corinth.* Translated by J. H. Schütz. Philadelphia: Fortress, 1982.
Thiselton, Anthony C. *The First Epistle to the Corinthians: A Commentary on the Greek Text.* NIGTC. Carlisle, UK: Paternoster, 2000.
———. "Realized Eschatology at Corinth." In *Christianity at Corinth: The Quest for the Pauline Church*, edited by E. Adams, and D. G. Horrell, 107–18. Louisville: Westminster John Knox, 2004.

Thrall, Margaret E. *A Critical and Exegetical Commentary on the Second Epistle to the Corinthians 1–7*. ICC 47A. Edinburgh: T. & T. Clark, 1994.

———. *A Critical and Exegetical Commentary on the Second Epistle to the Corinthians 8–13*. ICC 47B. Edinburgh: T. & T. Clark, 2000.

Thurén, Lauri. "The Antagonists: Rhetorically Marginalized Identities in the New Testament." In *Identity Formation in the New Testament*, edited by B. Holmberg, and M. Winninge. WUNT 227, 79–95. Tübingen: Mohr/Siebeck, 2008.

Towner, Philip H. *The Goal of Our Instruction: The Structure of Theology and Ethics in the Pastoral Epistles*. JSNTSS 34. Sheffield: Sheffield Academic, 1989.

———. *The Letters to Timothy and Titus*. NICNT. Grand Rapids, MI: Eerdmans, 2006.

Trebilco, Paul R. *The Early Christians in Ephesus from Paul to Ignatius*. Grand Rapids, MI: Eerdmans, 2007.

———. *Jewish Communities in Asia Minor*. Cambridge: Cambridge University Press, 1991.

Trevett, Christine. *A Study of Ignatius of Antioch in Syria and Asia*. Lewiston, NY: Mellen, 1992.

Triandis, Harry C., and Michele J. Gelfand. "Converging Measurement of Horizontal and Vertical Individualism and Collectivism." *JPSP* 74:1 (1998) 118–28.

Triandis, Harry C., et al. "Individualism and Collectivism: Cross-Cultural Perspectives on Self-Ingroup Relationships." *JPSP* 54:2 (1988) 323–38.

Tucker, Brian J. "'You Belong to Christ': Paul and the Formation of Social Identity in 1 Cor 1–4." PhD diss., Lampeter, University of Wales, 2009. Published by the same title at Eugene, OR: Pickwick, 2011.

Turner, John C. "Explaining the Nature of Power: A Three-Process Theory." *European Journal of Social Psychology* 35:1 (2005) 1–22.

———. "Towards a Cognitive Redefinition of the Social Group." In *Social Identity and Intergroup Relations*, edited by H. Tajfel, 15–40. Cambridge: Cambridge University Press, 1982.

Turner, John C., et al. *Rediscovering the Social Group: A Self-categorization Theory*. Oxford: Basil Blackwell, 1987.

Tyler, Tom R. "The Psychology of Legitimacy: A Relational Perspective on Voluntary Deference to Authorities." *PSPR* 1:4 (1997) 323–45.

Ubieta, Carmen B. "'Neither *Xenoi* nor *paroikoi*, *sympolitai* and *oikeioi tou theou*' (Eph. 2:19). Pauline Christian Communities: Defining a New Territoriality." In *Social Scientific Models for Interpreting the Bible: Essays by the Context Group in Honor of Bruce J. Malina*, edited by J. J. Pilch, 260–80. Leiden: Brill, 2001.

Van Neste, Ray. *Cohesion and Structure in the Pastoral Epistles*. JSNTSS 280. London: T. & T. Clark, 2004.

Vegge, Ivar. *2 Corinthians, A Letter about Reconciliation: A Psychagogical, Epistolographical, and Rhetorical Analysis*. WUNT 2nd ser., 239. Tübingen: Mohr/Siebeck, 2008.

Verner, David C. *The Household of God: The Social World of the Pastoral Epistles*. Chico, CA: Scholars, 1983.

Vignoles, Vivian L. "The Motive for Distinctiveness: A Universal, but Flexible Human Need." In *Oxford Handbook of Positive Psychology*, edited by C. R. Snyder, and S. Lopez. Oxford Library of Psychology, 491–500. Oxford: Oxford University Press, 2009.

Vignoles, Vivian L., et al, "Beyond Self-Esteem: Influence of Multiple Motives on Identity Construction." *Journal of Personality and Social Psychology* 90:2 (2006) 308–33.

Vitringa, Campegius. *De synagoga vetere libri tres: Quibus tum de nominibus, structura, origine, præfectis, ministris, and sacris synagogarum, agitur; tum præcipue, formam regiminis and ministerii earum in ecclesiam christianam translatam esse, demonstratur; cum prolegomenis.* Franequeræ: Typis & impensis J. Gyzelaar, 1696.

Vleugels, Gie A. M., and Maria Verhoeff. *De leer van de twaalf.* Heerenveen: Uitgeverij Protestantse Pers, 2006.

Vos, Johan S. *Die Kunst der Argumentation bei Paulus: Studien zur antiken Rhetorik.* WUNT 149. Tübingen: Mohr/Siebeck, 2002.

Wainwright, John J. "*Eusebeia*: Syncretism or Conservative Contextualization?" *EQ* 65 (1993) 211–24.

Wallace, Daniel B. *Greek Grammar beyond the Basics: An Exegetical Syntax of the New Testament.* Grand Rapids, MI: Zondervan, 1996.

Weber, Max. *Wirtschaft und Gesellschaft.* Grundriss der Sozialökonomik 3. Tübingen: Mohr/Siebeck, 1922.

Weber, Max, and S. N. Eisenstadt. *Max Weber on Charisma and Institution Building, Selected Papers.* The Heritage of Sociology 322. Chicago: University of Chicago Press, 1968.

Weiser, Alfons. "Διακονέω, *Diakoneo*, Serve; Διακονία, *Diakonia*, Service, Ministry; Office; Διάκονος, *Diakonos*, Servant." In *EDNT* 1, 302–4.

Weiss, Hans-F. "Διδασκαλία, *didaskalia*, teaching." In *EDNT* 1, 317.

Westcott, Brooke F. *Saint Paul's Epistle to the Ephesians: The Greek Text.* ed. J. M. Schulhof. Logos electronic ed. London: Macmillan, 1909.

White, Joel. *Die Erstlingsgabe im Neuen Testament.* Texte und Arbeite zum neutestamentlichen Zeitalter 45. Tübingen: Francke, 2007.

White, L. Michael. "Social Authority in the House Church Setting and Ephesians 4:1–16." *RQ* 29:4 (1987) 209–28.

Wilder, Terry L. *Pseudonymity, the New Testament, and Deception: An Inquiry into Intention and Reception.* Lanham: University Press of America, 2004.

Williams, Ritva H. "Charismatic Patronage and Brokerage: Episcopal Leadership in the Letters of Ignatius of Antioch." Doctoral Dissertation, University of Ottawa, 1997.

———. *Stewards, Prophets, Keepers of the Word: Leadership in the Early Church.* Peabody, MA: Hendrickson, 2006.

Winter, Bruce W. *After Paul Left Corinth: The Influence of Secular Ethics and Social Change.* Grand Rapids, MI: Eerdmans, 2001.

———. *Philo and Paul among the Sophists: Alexandrian and Corinthian Responses to a Julio-Claudian Movement.* 2nd ed. Grand Rapids, MI: Eerdmans, 2002.

———. *Roman Wives, Roman Widows: The Appearance of New Women and the Pauline Communities.* Grand Rapids, MI: Eerdmans, 2003.

Witherington, Ben. *The Acts of the Apostles: A Socio-Rhetorical Commentary.* Grand Rapids, MI: Eerdmans, 1998.

———. *Conflict and Community in Corinth: A Socio-Rhetorical Commentary on 1 and 2 Corinthians.* Grand Rapids, MI: Eerdmans, 1995.

———. *Letters and Homilies for Hellenized Christians: A Socio-Rhetorical Commentary of Titus, 1-2 Timothy and 1-3 John*. Downers Grove, IL: IVP Academic, 2006.

———. *Letters to Philemon, Colossians and Ephesians: A Social-Rhetorical Commentary on the Captivity Epistles*. Grand Rapids, MI: Eerdmans, 2007.

———. *New Testament Rhetoric*. Eugene, OR: Cascade, 2009.

———. *Women in the Earliest Churches*. SNTSMS 58. Cambridge: Cambridge University Press, 1988.

Wolter, Michael. *Die Pastoralbriefe als Paulustradition*. Forschungen zur Religion und Literatur des Alten und Neuen Testaments 146. Göttingen: Vandenhoeck & Ruprecht, 1988.

Worchel, Stephen, et al. "A Multidimensional Model of Identity: Relating Individual and Group Identities to Intergroup Behaviour." In *Social Identity Processes: Trends in Theory and Research*, edited by D. Capozza, and R. Brown, 15-32. London: Sage, 2000.

Wright, N. T. *The Resurrection of the Son of God*. Christian Origins and the Question of God 3. Minneapolis: Augsburg Fortress, 2003.

Wright, N. T., and John D. Crossan. "The Resurrection: Historical Event or Theological Explanation? A Dialogue." In *The Resurrection of Jesus: John Dominic Crossan and N. T. Wright in Dialogue*, edited by R. B. Stewart, 16-47. Minneapolis: Fortress, 2006.

Wyrick, Jed. *The Ascension of Authorship: Attribution and Canon Formation in Jewish, Hellenistic, and Christian Traditions*. Harvard Studies in Comparative Literature. Cambridge: Harvard University, 2004.

Yee, Tet-Lim N. *Jews, Gentiles, and Ethnic Reconciliation: Paul's Jewish Identity and Ephesians*. SNTSMS 130. Cambridge: Cambridge University Press, 2005.

Author Index

Aageson, James W., 21, 186, 284, 286, 327
Abrams, Dominic, 36–38, 327, 335, 340
Adams, Edward, 76, 327, 343
Agosto, Efrain, 29, 319, 327
Alvesson, Mats, 7–8, 37, 51, 68, 70, 278, 327
Anderson, R. Dean, 82, 107, 327
Arnold, Clinton E., 163–64, 181, 182, 327
Ashforth, Blake E., 34, 51–52, 55, 62, 327, 342
Aune, David E., 88, 327
Avemarie, Friedrich, 116, 327

Balch, David L., 159, 327
Barentsen, Jack, 29, 79, 81, 87, 182, 287, 317, 321, 328
Barnett, Paul, 117, 328
Barrett, C. K., 76, 84, 114, 130, 328
Bar-Tal, Daniel, 2, 45, 85, 328
Bartchy, S. Scott, 160, 328
Barth, Markus, 144, 151, 156, 167, 168, 180, 328
Barton, Stephen C., 173, 328
Bass, Bernard M., 52, 328
Batten, Alicia, 80, 328
Bauer, Walter, 21, 328

Baugh, S. M., 217, 328
Baum, Armin D., 192, 193, 195, 196, 328
Beech, Nic, 329
Beker, Johan C., 213, 216, 228, 286, 329
Bekker, Corné J., 323, 329
Berding, Kenneth, 42, 190, 329
Best, Ernest, 153, 329
Best, Thomas F., 32, 42, 329
Betz, Hans D., 117, 329
Bieringer, Reimund, 113, 117, 129, 329
Blanz, Mathias, 50, 329
Blomberg, Craig L., 113, 329
Brent, Allen, 173, 316, 329
Brockhaus, Ulrich, 9, 20, 23, 88, 175, 239, 242, 329, 333
Brown, Andrew D., 51, 329
Brown, Raymond E., 141, 198, 329
Brown, Rupert, 34, 36–39, 135, 227, 317, 329, 330
Burke, Peter J., 36, 329
Burkett, Delbert R., 193, 197, 330
Burtchaell, James T., 24, 141, 313, 330

Cairns, Ed, 50, 339
Campbell, Douglas A., 311, 330

Campbell, R. Alastair, 24, 141, 184, 229–30, 233–34, 240–41, 314, 330, 332
Campbell, William S., 9, 21, 298, 317, 330
Capes, David B., 192, 214, 330
Capozza, Dora, 34, 330,
Capper, Brian J., 217, 301, 330
Carter, Warren, 159, 165, 330
Castelli, Elizabeth A., 26, 76, 99, 108, 330
Chapple, Allen L., 28, 75–76, 86, 88–89, 91, 141, 314, 330
Chemers, Martin M., 52, 330
Chow, John K., 24, 79, 81, 330
Chryssochoou, Xenia, 42, 330
Clarke, Andrew D., 6, 24, 26, 30–31, 76, 79, 81, 87, 112, 114, 119, 141, 242, 288, 306, 323, 330
Collins, John N., 87, 107, 243–45, 330
Conger, Jay A., 65, 331, 336
Conzelmann, Hans, 184, 188, 190, 197, 232, 331
Copan, Victor, 26, 331
Cornelissen, Joep P., 35–37, 139, 331
Couser, Greg A., 207, 331
Crook, Zeba A., 42, 331
Crossan, John D., 85, 165, 331, 346
Dahl, Nils A., 151, 331
Danker, Frederick W., xv, 331
Darko, Daniel K., 147, 157, 158–60, 331
Deaux, Kay, 45, 331
Delling, G., 88, 331

deSilva, David A., 77, 113, 115, 117, 129, 144–45, 201, 253–54, 331
Dibelius, Martin, 184, 188, 190, 197, 232, 331
Dix, Gregory, 19, 331
Dodd, Brian J., 28, 331
Donelson, Lewis R., 193, 332
Donfried, Karl P., 77, 188, 317, 332
Dudrey, Russ, 160, 332
Dunn, James D. G., 175, 193, 332
Dunning, Benjamin H., 154, 155, 156, 332

Ehrensperger, Kathy, 27, 94, 108, 112, 130, 315, 332
Ehrman, Bart D., 193, 332
Eisenstadt, S.N., 66, 67, 345
Ellemers, Naomi, 34, 37, 139, 334
Elliott, John H., 3, 41, 332
Ellis, E. Earle, 87, 190, 191, 332
Emrich, Cynthia G., 61, 337
Esler, Philip F., 7–9, 29, 41, 49, 57, 85, 172–73, 260, 332

Fee, Gordon D., 107, 332
Fiore, Benjamin, 21, 25, 106, 184, 186, 188, 199, 207, 209, 218, 221–22, 227, 249, 252, 267, 332
Fiske, Susan T., 36–37, 340
Fitzmyer, Joseph A., 76, 233, 332
Forbes, Christopher, 85, 333
French, John R. P., 54–55, 333
Friesen, Steven J., 4, 342
Fuchs, Rüdiger, 186, 333
Furnish, Victor P., 113, 117, 127, 130, 333

Gamble, Harry Y., 191, 333
Garland, David E., 76, 83, 85, 104–5, 114, 118, 123, 133, 333
Gehring, Roger W., 23–24, 90, 333
Gelfand, Michele J., 43, 344
Gill, David W. J., 84, 333
Gombis, Timothy G., 159, 160, 333
Gore, Charles, 19, 333
Gorman, Michael J., 160, 333
Gosnell, Peter W., 153, 333
Grieve, Paul G., 33, 45, 333, 335
Griffin, Hayne P., 201, 260–61, 269, 337
Grindheim, Sigurd, 116, 333
Grudem, Wayne A., 167, 333

Hafemann, Scott J., 122, 333
Hainz, Josef, 19, 333
Haley, Peter, 21, 333
Hall, David R., 113, 333
Hansen, Bruce, 78, 333
Harland, Philip A., 91, 173, 236, 333
Harnack, Adolf von, 18–19, 22, 334
Harris, Murray J., 113–14, 118, 123, 129, 133, 334
Harrison, James R., 25, 184, 218, 221, 334
Harrison, Percy Neale, 195–96, 334
Hart, Ann W., 69, 334
Hartog, Paul, 190, 334
Haslam, S. Alexander, 11, 34–38, 40, 42, 44, 46, 49, 52–61, 66, 139, 287, 334
Hatch, Edwin, 18, 334
Heiligenthal, R., 218, 334
Heitink, Gerben, 26, 334
Hendrix, Holland, 153, 335

Hering, James P., 160, 335
Herzer, Jens, 5, 186, 195, 208, 228, 335
Hiigel, John L., 28–29, 86, 97, 99, 335
Hoehner, Harold W., 5, 141, 143–45, 156, 158, 162, 167, 170, 335
Hogg, Michael A., 33, 35–38, 40, 45, 52, 58–60, 64, 95, 214, 287, 315, 327, 333, 335–37
Holmberg, Bengt, 7, 22–23, 31, 141, 143, 278, 319, 328, 335
Holmes, Michael W., 314, 335
Holtzmann, Heinrich J., 18–23, 29–30, 101, 185, 195–96, 304, 322, 336
Hopkins, Nick, 37, 139, 307, 341
Hornsey, Matthew J., 37, 40, 95, 336
Horrell, David G., 76, 161, 184, 188, 208, 224, 236–37, 246, 288–89, 327, 336
Horsley, Richard A., 165, 336

Jennings, Mark A., 129, 336
Johnson, Luke T., 186–88, 210, 212, 216, 222, 244, 246, 249, 253–54, 261, 265, 269, 336
Joubert, Stephan J., 129–30, 336
Judge, Edwin A., 7, 102, 174, 336

Kanungo, Rabindra N., 65, 331, 336
Karris, Robert J., 222, 225, 336
Keay, Robert, 41, 78, 336
Kelly, John N. D., 201, 204, 225, 231, 234, 263–64, 336

Kidd, Reggie M., 186, 205, 225, 336
Kim, Seyon, 165, 336
Klauck, Hans-Josef, 144, 336
Klein, Olivier, iv, 47–48, 336
Knight, George W., 189, 201, 229, 232, 247, 253, 265, 267, 270, 337
Koester, Helmut, 4, 337
Küng, Hans, 20, 337, 342

Lambrecht, Jan, 113, 329, 337
Lampe, Peter, 182, 337
Lassen, Eva M., 154, 288, 337
Lawler, Steph, 36, 50, 337
Lea, Thomas D., 201, 260–61, 269, 334, 337
Liddell, Henry G., 337
Lieu, Judith M., 146, 319, 337
Lightfoot, Joseph B., 17–18, 337
Lincoln, Andrew T., 142–44, 149, 152, 155, 161, 168–69, 172, 174, 337
Lindemann, Andreas, 142, 337
Long, Frederick J., 113, 136, 337
Lord, Robert G., 12, 53, 61–62, 64, 84, 90, 92, 97–98, 102–3, 110, 148–49, 159–60, 162, 165, 230, 265–66, 272, 280, 293, 333, 337, 341
Louw, Johannes P., 338
Luomanen, Petri, 7, 41, 50, 332, 338

MacDonald, Margaret Y., 22, 141–42, 146, 148–49, 155–59, 162–63, 169–70, 216, 225, 278, 284, 338
Mael, Fred, 34, 327

Maier, Harry O., 17, 18, 338
Malina, Bruce J., 23, 43, 78, 88, 126, 128, 166, 178, 215, 222, 236, 259, 270, 272, 338, 344
Marshall, I. Howard, 186, 190–91, 197–99, 203–4, 206, 211, 218, 224, 232–33, 241–44, 248, 253, 263, 282, 338
Martin, Dale B., 85, 338
Martin, Jochen, 174, 338
Martin, Ralph P., 113, 118–19, 126, 131, 338
Martin, Seán C., 188, 199, 252, 258, 260, 263, 266, 268, 338
McDonald, Lee M., 77, 115, 192, 338
Meeks, Wayne A., 83, 338
Merklein, Helmut, 9, 141, 156, 162, 168–69, 174–76, 178, 338
Merz, Annette, 21, 186, 187, 190, 193–94, 284, 339
Metzger, Bruce M., 144, 339
Mitchell, Margaret M., 188, 216, 339
Morgenthaler, Robert, 143, 195, 339
Mounce, William D., 186, 189, 197, 199, 243–44, 253, 264, 339
Mouton, A. Elna J., 153, 154, 339
Murphy-O'Connor, Jerome, 4, 149, 164, 181, 339

Neumann, Kenneth J., 195, 339
Neyrey, Jerome H., 80, 128, 162, 222, 233, 338, 339
Nguyen, V. Henry T., 126–27, 339
Nida, Eugene A., xvi, 338
Niens, Ulrike, 50, 339

Northouse, Peter G., 52–53, 57, 65, 339
Oakes, Penelope J., 41, 54, 132, 340, 342
Oberlinner, Lorenz, 188, 208–9, 253, 340
Operario, Don, 36–37, 340
Osiek, Carolyn, 246–48, 340

Packer, Dominic J., 271, 340
Page, Sydney H. T., 170, 340
Paschke, Boris A., 25, 184, 218, 221, 340
Paul, Jim, 65, 340
Perkins, Pheme, 144, 158, 340
Perrin, Nicholas, 193, 340
Pietersen, Lloyd, 128, 204, 265, 268, 271–72, 284, 340
Platow, Michael J., 11, 36, 55, 58–59, 66, 334, 340
Polaski, Sandra Hack, 26, 27, 99, 184, 236–37, 340
Porter, Stanley E., 77, 115, 192, 334, 338, 339
Prior, Michael, 252–53, 275, 340

Quinn, Jerome D., 186, 223, 254, 259, 340

Räisänen, Heikki, 322, 340
Raven, Bertram H., 54–55, 333, 341
Reasoner, Mark, 182, 341
Redalié, Yann, 211, 261, 341
Reed, Jonathan L., 165, 331
Reicher, Stephen, 11, 33, 37, 42, 49, 55, 58, 61, 139, 307, 334, 341
Reicke, Bo I., 199, 201–2, 341

Reid, Scott A., 36, 315, 335
Reiser, Marius, 196, 341
Richards, E. Randolph, 144, 191, 196, 341
Richards, William A., 21, 186, 249, 255, 284, 341
Ritter, Barbara A., 61–62, 64, 341
Robbins, Vernon K., 319, 341
Robertson, Joseph M., 109, 341
Robinson, W. Peter, 34, 341
Rohde, Joachim, 242, 341
Rohrbaugh, Richard L., 213, 341
Roitto, Rikard, 147–48, 150, 156, 161, 285, 288, 341
Runesson, Anders, 9, 342

Sani, Fabio, 90, 342
Sashkin, Marshall, 65, 342
Scherrer, Peter, 4, 342
Schlier, Heinrich, 151, 342
Schmeller, Thomas, 24, 301, 342
Schnackenburg, Rudolf, 19, 342
Schowalter, Daniel N., 4, 342
Schreiber, Alfred, 28, 342
Schüssler Fiorenza, Elisabeth, 224, 246, 342
Schütz, John H., 21–23, 342, 343
Schweizer, Eduard, 19, 342
Shkul, Minna, 8, 142, 146–48, 159, 342
Simon, Bernd, 54, 132, 342
Sköldberg, Kaj, 7–8, 327
Sluss, David M., 62, 342
Smink, Geurt J., 20, 342
Söding, Thomas, 184, 188, 220, 230, 240–41, 342

Sohm, Rudolf, 18–23, 29–30, 65, 67, 101, 185, 304, 322, 333, 343
Stagaman, David J., 27, 214, 343
Standhartinger, Angela, 219–20, 343
Stegman, Thomas, 113, 121–22, 126, 343
Stepp, Perry L., 25, 62, 71, 184, 186, 235, 249, 252, 258, 277, 279, 343
Stets, Jan E., 36, 329
Streeter, Burnett H., 20, 30, 306, 343
Strelan, Rich, 149, 164, 343
Suh, Robert H., 155, 343
Sullivan, Francis A., 20, 184, 343
Sumney, Jerry L., 112, 116, 343

Tajfel, Henri, 33–35, 38, 57, 341, 343
Talbert, Charles H., 142, 343
Tamez, Else, 99, 209, 215–16, 225, 237, 343
Taylor, Nicholas H., 98, 120, 128, 343
Tellbe, Mikael, 146, 284–85, 343
Theissen, Gerd, 75–76, 82, 87, 343
Thiselton, Anthony C., 76–77, 79, 82–84, 88, 95, 104, 122, 343
Thrall, Margaret E., 114, 121–22, 344
Thurén, Lauri, 344
Towner, Philip H., 186, 188–89, 197, 199, 204, 207, 218–19, 223, 282, 344
Trebilco, Paul R., 145–46, 149, 344
Trevett, Christine, 316, 344

Triandis, Harry C., 42–43, 344
Tucker, Brian J., 78, 80, 94, 344
Turner, John C., 27, 34, 54, 132, 264, 344
Tyler, Tom R., 55, 344

Ubieta, Carmen B., 156, 166, 344

van Bruggen, Jakob, 88, 201, 329
van Houwelingen, P. H. R., 199, 201, 233–34, 264, 336
van Knippenberg, Barbara, 59, 337
van Knippenberg, Daan, 35, 58–59, 64, 67, 337, 340
Vegge, Ivar, 113, 344
Verhoeff, Maria, 264, 345
Verner, David C., 21, 24, 203, 205, 208, 218–19, 284, 288, 344
Vignoles, Vivian L., 38, 45, 47, 344–45
Vitringa, Campegius, 17–18, 345
Vleugels, Gie A. M., 264, 345
von Campenhausen, Hans F., 19, 173, 330
Vos, Johan S., 319, 345

Wacker, William C., 186, 223, 254, 259, 340
Wainwright, John J., 220, 345
Wallace, Daniel B., 167, 345
Weber, Max, 21–23, 29, 65–68, 345
Weiser, Alfons, 243, 345
Weiss, Hans-F., 204, 345
Westcott, Brooke F., 169, 176, 345
White, Joel, 88, 345
White, L. Michael, 134–35, 176. 345
Wilder, Terry L., 193–94, 331, 345

Williams, Ritva H., 79, 95, 102, 107, 159, 315–16, 345
Willmott, Hugh, 51, 327
Winninge, Mikael, 7, 335
Winter, Bruce W., 79–80, 83, 85, 105, 217, 345
Witherington, Ben, 76, 82, 84–85, 97, 107, 132, 158, 189, 201, 204–5, 215, 217, 233, 247, 250, 254, 259, 261, 269, 319, 345

Wolter, Michael, 199, 232, 252, 346
Worchel, Stephen, 34, 328, 340, 346
Wright, N. T., 85, 346
Wyrick, Jed, 192, 346

Yee, Tit-Lim N., 142, 149, 155, 346

Subject Index

agency, 15, 54, 98, 100, 108, 124, 162–63, 168, 235
ambassador, 107, 127, 133, 138, 142, 294
ambiguity, 67, 156–57, 199, 206, 236, 237, 271, 275
anthropology, 10, 22, 23, 31, 215, 232
appoint, ordain, 9, 13, 17, 66, 88, 96, 104–5, 107, 139, 140, 173, 175, 210, 229, 237, 240, 244, 260–61, 273, 278–79, 281, 312–13
apprenticeship, 244
Architecture, 119, 156, 164
  building, 10, 94, 119, 156, 170, 233
  buttress, 28, 194, 208, 219
  pillar, 208, 219
  temple, 82, 94, 96, 156, 164, 208, 220–21, 243, 259
Artemis, 148–49, 164–65, 181, 197, 343
associations, see collegia
authoritarian, 99, 213–14
Authorship, 1, 5, 12, 13, 21–22, 89, 110, 141–52, 155–57, 161–62, 166, 168–69, 172, 185–201, 216, 218–20, 228, 232, 237, 252, 282, 285, 287, 290, 323–24

deutero-Pauline, 141, 185
pseudepigraphy, 5, 13, 21, 144, 148, 185–95, 198–200, 222, 267, 285
scribes, 13, 77, 146, 189, 191–92, 200
secretaries, 191, 196
trito-Pauline, 185

benefaction, 79, 80, 130, 153–57, 159, 162, 173–74, 209, 216–17, 225, 234, 237, 250, 270–71, 293
boast, 81, 90, 92, 99, 102, 118–19, 126
boundary, 50, 94, 150, 155–60, 204, 213, 294
broker, 26, 107, 153, 162
building, see Architecture
buttress, see Architecture

categorization, see self-categorization
category accessibility, see Social Comparison
censure, 25, 43, 92, 209, 271, 278
character list, 25, 184, 205, 217–18, 228–30, 239, 246–47, 288
charismatic leadership, see Leadership Theory

Subject Index

christology, 121–22, 160, 207, 220–21, 323
church-sect, 23
circumcision, 82, 155–56, 256, 259, 267–68
citizenship, 156
civic identy, see Social Identities
cognitive psychology, see Psychology
cohesion, see Social Identification
collection, see Finances
collectivism, 42–43, 213, 238, 314
collegia, associations, 14, 18, 23–24, 39, 80, 91, 135, 213, 313
collegial, 12–13, 15, 104, 106, 111, 115, 120, 125, 135–39, 152, 170–71, 210, 233, 249, 291, 293, 295
commission, 127, 138, 162, 175, 211–12, 240, 261–62, 264, 273–74, 279, 295, 302
comparative fit, see Social Comparison
conflict, 19, 21, 35, 39, 78, 81–83, 95, 97, 99–100, 107, 113, 116–17, 150, 163, 180–81, 187, 194, 198, 205, 209, 215, 235–36, 238, 289, 299, 302–4
consensus, 1, 3, 5, 20–21, 23, 34, 68, 187, 199
contextualization, 13, 118, 157, 164–65, 182–83, 197, 200, 230, 247, 257, 296, 323–324
continuity, 13, 25, 51–52, 60, 63, 71–72, 176, 229, 235, 238, 255, 269, 278–79, 310, 317, 320, 325
contrast, 18, 40, 79, 122, 124, 149, 155, 170, 195, 212–13, 222–23, 227, 246, 258, 267–68, 281, 294

conversion, 4, 82, 84, 95, 170, 212–13, 231
Corinth, see Locations
cosmic, 142–43, 149–50, 153–54, 157, 164, 182–83
countercultural, 102, 117, 209, 293, 301
courts, 19, 81–82, 90–91, 96, 103, 175, 182, 239, 240, 244–45, 261–62, 268–69
covenant, 116–17, 127, 156
coworker, 105, 110, 213, 232, 236
creation, 84, 97–98, 208, 217
crisis, 26, 33, 35, 136, 142, 172, 177, 210
cross-cultural, 4, 15, 42, 311
cross-cutting identy, see Social Identities
cura morum, 25, 184, 218, 221, 340

deception, 13, 128, 225
deconstruction, 26
degradation, 128, 131, 265
Delphic Canon, 25
demonization, see Deviance
denomination, 1, 10, 16, 19–21, 23, 39, 307, 322
deutero-Pauline, see Authorship
Deviance, 13, 14, 26–27, 43, 55, 60, 85, 96, 113, 128, 133, 135–39, 170, 190, 203–17, 222, 225, 227–28, 231–32, 241–42, 249–51, 254–58, 262, 265–72, 280–81, 283, 285, 296–99, 308, 310, 317–18
  demonization, 60, 221, 265, 267
  labeling, 120, 128, 204, 212, 227, 265, 272
  stigmatization, 96, 123, 231, 266–67, 272

Subject Index 357

vilification, 120, 128–29, 133, 318
discourse, 108, 116–17, 126, 159–60, 219, 221–22
discrimination, 33, 92
disobedience, 155
dissociation, 128, 135, 155, 204–5, 266–67, 318
distinctiveness, 45, 64, 85, 94, 149, 151, 154–57, 160, 172, 221, 257–58, 293–94, 313
duty, 25, 104, 161

early Christian identity, 7, 31, 284
embedding, see Social Identification
enthronement, 155
Ephesus, see Locations
equality, 101, 107–8, 159
eschatology, 83–84, 95, 122, 131, 143, 197, 297
ethics, 25, 158–59, 160, 161
ethnic identity, see Social Identities
eucharist, 18, 151
exhortation, see paraenesis
expansion, 13, 18, 62, 78, 93, 109, 112, 120, 143, 145, 148, 162, 164, 168, 180–81, 232, 255, 263, 267, 295, 338–39
external attestation, 13, 188–91, 195
eyewitness, 190, 192, 198

faithfulness, 13, 69, 110, 126, 137, 163–64, 173, 178, 199, 207, 219, 222, 226, 230–35, 253–54, 260, 263–70, 275, 277–81, 296, 310, 324
father, 25, 107, 131, 154, 259, 267, 288, 292

Father, 18, 150, 153–54, 160, 163, 190, 194, 264, 297, 307, 314, 328, 335
Finances, 123, 134, 136, 175–76, 203, 205–6, 224–25, 234, 240–41, 244–46, 250, 264, 312
  abuse, 128, 207, 225
  collection, 12, 33–34, 42, 50, 76, 78, 98, 114, 129, 130, 136, 191–92, 196, 201, 246, 253, 298, 320
  wealth, riches, 1, 5, 7, 22–23, 25, 81–82, 84, 87, 96, 99, 101, 111, 124–25, 132, 151, 153, 155, 161–62, 166, 201, 203, 205, 208, 215–16, 225, 237, 281, 288, 297, 320
first century, 7, 8, 10, 17, 23, 25–26, 29, 42, 44, 122, 139, 182, 187, 192, 199, 213, 230, 237, 307, 313
followers, 3, 8–9, 25, 27, 44, 53–57, 60–61, 65–66, 69, 81, 109, 148, 177, 216, 227–28, 231, 238, 267, 298, 301, 321–23
food, 84, 97, 221–22, 225
Foucault, 26
foundational beliefs, 45, 94, 97, 100, 106, 153, 205, 210, 212, 214, 224, 226, 258, 260, 278, 285, 293, 310
freedom, 18–19, 67, 83, 197, 246, 322

gender roles, 5, 10, 14, 39, 42, 45, 83, 84, 87, 97, 150, 203, 205, 208, 211–12, 215, 217, 224–26, 236, 245–50, 257, 288, 295–96, 301, 324
genealogy, 203–4, 297
genre, 75, 153, 184, 199

Subject Index

gift, 65–66, 88–89, 92, 106–7, 109, 129–30, 150, 169, 174, 177, 232, 260, 273, 278, 309
glory, 153–54, 162, 207, 212, 220, 231, 265
glossolalia, 85, 106–7
gnosticism, 121, 197
godliness (*eusebeia*), 197, 219, 221–23, 245, 247
grace, 26, 27, 212, 231, 297, 315
Greco-Roman identity, see Social Identities
Group Dynamics, 1, 33, 35, 188, 203, 306, 317, 324
  group formation, 78, 166
  intergroup relationships, 34, 43, 51, 80, 81, 90, 154–55, 158, 202–3, 227, 286, 291, 311, 315–16, 324
  intragroup relationships, 40, 43, 51, 64, 67, 94, 96, 102–3, 105, 107, 111, 113, 155, 174, 176–77, 202–3, 206–7, 229, 235, 237, 245, 257, 265–66, 277–78, 280, 291, 316

heresy, 190, 197, 204, 219, 229, 231
heritage, 28, 33, 63, 187, 193–94, 238, 255, 258–62, 267–68, 274, 277, 280, 291, 296, 320
hermeneutics, 26, 28, 41, 43–44, 51, 68, 74, 105, 130, 162, 164, 180, 187, 194, 227, 229, 233, 247, 276, 304, 312, 318–20
hierarchy, 15, 17, 39, 88, 99, 101, 111, 130, 132, 159, 176, 228, 238, 243, 298–99, 314–15
historical, 2–4, 6–8, 10, 13, 15–17, 19–23, 25, 28–32, 35, 41–42, 52, 76, 95, 113, 122, 141–42, 146–48, 160, 162, 166, 168, 172, 185–90, 192, 195–202, 220, 222, 228, 252, 255, 284–89, 319–24, 332
history, 5, 10, 19, 21, 32, 35, 45–47, 50–52, 56, 65, 69, 75, 113, 140, 198, 304, 307–8, 313, 322
Holtzmann-Sohm hypothesis, 19–23, 29, 30, 101, 185, 304, 322
honor, shame, 24, 58, 79, 80–82, 84–86, 90–92, 97, 99, 101–2, 105, 107, 111, 114, 122, 124, 127, 129, 140, 148, 153–57, 162, 173–74, 193, 205–10, 215–17, 221, 224–25, 234, 249, 254, 256–57, 260–63, 268, 270–76, 280–83, 288, 293, 298, 301–3, 313, 315
hortatory letters, 25, 106, 186, 252
Household, 14, 22–23, 79, 87–88, 90, 103–4, 106–7, 115, 150, 156, 159–61, 164, 170–71, 203, 205, 208, 210, 215, 218, 220–24, 228–30, 233–41, 244–50, 253, 268, 282, 285, 286, 288–89, 292, 297–300
  household code, 22, 150, 156, 159–60, 164, 170, 223–24, 289
  householders, 23, 87, 91, 205, 210, 215, 229, 230–31, 233–34, 236, 241, 249, 262, 280, 308

idealism, 22, 143
identity narrative / construction / performance, see Social Identification
ideology, 2, 6–7, 10, 13, 16–23, 26–31, 75, 95, 139, 142, 159–60, 165, 169, 172, 174, 176, 180–81, 194, 208, 215, 226,

258, 285, 288, 299–300, 303, 307–12, 315, 322, 324
imprisonment, 12–14, 143, 145, 164, 166, 171–72, 181–83, 196, 198, 201–2, 253–54, 260–62
incest, 81, 90–91, 96, 99, 103, 114
individualism, 42
inequality, 84
inscriptions, 4, 173–74, 250
institutional vitality, 25, 71–72, 238, 278–79
institutionalization, 1, 13, 21–22, 63, 68, 70–71, 98, 149, 153–54, 169, 173–75, 242, 288–89, 296–97, 304, 313–14, 322
integration, 7, 16, 26, 29–31, 51, 62, 159–60, 180, 188, 198, 211, 289, 297, 310
inter- and intragroup relationships, see Group Dynamics
itinerant, 12, 113–14, 123, 134, 136–38, 230, 236, 287, 292, 303

Jesus, 29, 85, 94, 113, 119, 121–23, 125–28, 131, 138, 164–65, 172, 207, 222, 230–31, 244, 259–61, 264–65, 279, 327–28, 331, 343, 346
Jewish identity, see Social Identities

kerygma, 261
kingdom, 156, 182, 268
kingship literature, 25

labeling, see Deviance
labor, 87, 102, 224, 233–34
law, 9, 18–19, 67, 115–17, 156, 203–4, 206, 211–12, 235, 263, 297, 301

Leader as
  artist, 56–57, 60, 63–64, 68, 73, 91, 93, 109, 121–22, 126, 154, 157, 177, 208, 211, 214, 231, 235, 262, 274, 277
  engineer, 56–57, 58, 60–61, 72–73, 97, 110, 120, 123, 129, 161, 165, 178, 210–11, 224, 226, 235, 238, 275, 278, 279
  entrepreneur, 146–48, 166, 324
  impresario, 56–57, 60, 63, 69, 71, 73, 92, 123, 127, 137, 163, 177, 208, 211, 217, 221, 223, 232, 237, 266, 268, 275, 278
  manager of identity, 15, 28, 32, 34–35, 44, 55, 58, 61, 72, 74, 91–92, 95, 98, 100, 120, 124, 142, 147, 150, 152, 164, 179, 180–181, 226, 248, 250, 258, 277, 323
Leadership
  attribution, 13, 15, 58, 64–68, 70, 80, 94, 105, 110, 139, 154, 156, 172, 177, 179–80, 188, 192–94, 237, 241, 245, 272–74, 278, 281, 303–4, 314, 319
  authority, 3, 9, 16–23, 26–31, 43, 65–68, 76, 84, 88, 98–100, 104, 108–11, 132, 153, 155, 162, 165, 168–69, 175–76, 179–82, 187, 193–94, 198, 213–17, 228, 232–35, 238–40, 244, 248–49, 260, 264–66, 273–74, 278–81, 294–96, 300–5, 314–16, 323–24
  development, 1–6, 9–23, 26–34, 37, 41–45, 52, 58, 61, 67–68, 73–74, 77–78, 83, 91–94, 101–4, 117–18, 123–24, 132, 135–39, 145, 151, 153, 165–66, 171–79, 182–83, 193,

199, 202–3, 210, 223, 227–28, 232, 236–43, 261, 273, 279, 284, 289, 291, 293, 296, 300–8, 312–17, 321–22

effectiveness, 12, 57, 60–65, 69–71, 93, 102, 104, 106, 109–10, 114, 121, 124, 128, 172, 177–78, 229, 231, 238, 245, 300, 312

emergence, 2, 11–12, 15, 17, 21, 44, 58, 61, 68, 74, 104–10, 116, 132–35, 138–39, 167–72, 178–79, 228–30, 244, 270–74, 280–81, 290–93, 299, 304, 308, 324

empowerment, 2, 11–13, 27, 99–100, 108, 110, 127, 133, 160–161, 179–81, 185, 210, 215, 223, 226, 238, 247–51, 268, 273, 275–78, 280, 293, 297, 303, 315–16, 323

formation, 9, 12, 15, 28, 43–44, 52, 67, 77–78, 86, 91, 102, 150, 166, 176, 184–85, 206, 227, 236, 273, 279, 284, 291, 299–302, 305–6, 313, 317, 319, 321, 324

intragroup status, 14, 20, 22, 24, 31, 33, 44–45, 49–50, 55–56, 61–64, 67–71, 79–97, 100–6, 109–11, 124–28, 131–32, 136–39, 147–48, 153–56, 162–65, 170–79, 182–83, 203–8, 212, 215–18, 221, 225, 229, 235–41, 244–45, 249, 254–59, 262, 265–68, 271–72, 275–81, 291–7, 310–16

legitimacy, 3, 9, 12–13, 22, 26, 55, 61, 71–72, 85, 88, 95, 107, 111, 116, 122–23, 126–28, 131–33, 146, 148, 152, 156, 162–63, 167, 169, 171–80, 183, 187, 201–2, 212, 223, 231–32, 235–40, 244–46, 260, 264, 266, 277, 292–96, 300–3, 307–8, 312, 323

maintenance, 2, 11, 13–15, 25, 27, 43–44, 50–51, 56–61, 68, 71–74, 81–82, 84, 90–91, 102–6, 111, 130, 132, 135, 146–47, 150, 159, 164, 172–83, 204, 210, 214, 217, 219, 226–35, 239–41, 249, 257–58, 263–64, 270, 274, 276, 285, 290–92, 295–301, 304, 309–14, 323–24

manner, 71, 72, 97, 165, 169, 187, 197, 215, 232, 238, 239, 265, 266, 278, 279, 279, 322

patterns, 1–3, 5–6, 9–17, 23, 26, 29–32, 37, 43–44, 52, 58, 61, 67, 74, 78, 80, 86, 89–91, 101–4, 111–12, 134–37, 142, 144, 161, 171–74, 183–85, 188, 199, 217, 226, 235, 239, 262–63, 290–91, 295, 298–2, 305–17, 324–25

perception, 9, 38–41, 45, 47, 50, 53–55, 59–62, 64, 67–69, 80, 90, 100, 102, 105–6, 109–12, 124, 126, 128, 132–35, 139, 142, 144, 148, 152, 157, 165, 178, 180, 182, 187, 194, 229, 232, 235–38, 244–45, 259, 261, 267, 272, 278–83, 292, 295, 298, 300, 303, 319, 322

position, 3–10, 13, 18, 20, 26–29, 32, 37, 40–41, 49, 59, 60–61, 64, 69, 79, 94, 100, 102, 105, 108, 116, 121–22, 126, 139, 141, 145, 149–50, 153, 167, 174–75, 185–88, 198–99, 209, 226, 229, 233–44, 247–50,

Subject Index   361

253, 266, 274, 278, 282, 292, 295, 303, 316, 321
power, 3, 9, 11, 15, 22, 26–28, 31, 35, 42, 54–55, 64, 70, 83, 90, 93, 98, 107, 108–9, 124, 131–36, 153–55, 172, 177, 182, 214–15, 235–38, 264, 267, 271, 280–81, 295, 304, 306, 315, 323
sacrificial, 14, 43, 60, 65, 82, 90, 92, 96–97, 102, 105–11, 125, 138, 148, 150, 159, 167, 169, 172, 177, 224, 237, 242, 269, 292–93, 298, 302, 315–16
style, 13, 30–31, 35, 39, 72, 89–90, 99, 103, 112–17, 133–38, 141–45, 188–91, 195, 199, 206, 208, 223, 226, 238, 257–58, 266, 272, 278–80, 294, 298, 302, 318
succession, 2, 11, 14–15, 18, 21, 25, 28, 44, 58, 61–64, 68–74, 104, 108–10, 121, 132, 136–40, 174, 175–79, 183–84, 202, 207, 213–14, 226, 228, 235–40, 244, 252, 257–68, 274–81, 290–96, 299, 302, 304, 310, 314, 323
tasks, 31, 43, 52, 71–72, 87, 104, 115, 137, 170, 185, 205, 209–12, 215, 218–19, 231–32, 236, 245, 263, 269, 272, 277–80, 302, 309
titles, 13, 15, 31, 36, 88, 241, 252, 266, 305, 311, 344
tools, 30–31, 41, 43, 52, 74, 180, 228, 308, 320, 322, 324
Leadership Structure
apostle, 12, 100, 105–9, 126–28, 131, 134–35, 139, 169–70, 173–74, 177, 180, 194, 209,
216, 231–32, 236, 249, 260–61, 263, 277, 286, 294–95, 310
bishop, episkopos, 13–14, 17–18, 24, 103–6, 136, 139, 190, 192, 205, 209, 217–19, 229–30, 233–35, 239–50, 279, 281, 288, 295, 311–15
church office, 1, 17–22, 174–75, 179, 184, 239, 240, 242, 290, 312–13
church order, 3, 18–20, 184, 193, 232, 235
deacon, 14, 17–18, 24, 88, 190, 203, 217–18, 229–30, 243–50, 288, 295–96, 308–11
elder, presbyter, 13–14, 17–18, 24, 88, 139, 141, 203, 207–10, 224–30, 233–42, 246–50, 265, 271, 277, 279, 296, 301, 308–14
evangelist, 48, 153, 169, 170, 174, 178, 208, 230, 236
impeachment, 13, 296
prophet, 89, 174, 209, 236, 296
shepherd, 174, 297
teacher, 12–14, 25, 28, 32, 41, 46, 62, 77, 80, 83–86, 89, 100, 102, 107–8, 117–18, 122–24, 128–38, 146, 148, 151, 158, 161, 164, 168–71, 174–80, 192–93, 203–19, 222–27, 231–36, 240–41, 246–51, 254, 261–81, 285–87, 291–304, 310, 314, 316, 318, 345
threefold ministry, 18–19
Leadership Theory, 1, 7, 16, 26–29, 76, 141, 252, 290, 321, 322–23
charismatic leadership, 11–12, 15, 19–22, 65–70, 109–10, 139, 142, 172, 174, 177–80,

235–37, 278, 281, 283, 291, 295–96, 303–5, 310
social identity model, 6–7, 10–11, 31–35, 58–59, 63–64, 73, 75, 105, 147, 211, 290, 307, 312, 319, 323–24, 337
transformational, 58, 65
letters of recommendation, 12, 118, 123, 127, 292
linguistics, 13, 16, 143–44, 196, 200
list, 88, 106–7, 169, 174–75, 205, 218, 223, 230, 239, 241, 269
Literary Criticism, 13, 41, 189, 192, 200
Locations
  Achaia, 4, 77, 88, 93, 104, 255
  Alexandria, 181, 190
  Antioch, 4, 5, 173, 181, 190, 316–17, 329, 344–45
  Asia Minor, 4, 143, 148–51, 169, 180, 190, 250, 344
  Berea, 93
  Cenchreae, 87
  Colossae, 181
  Corinth, 3–6, 12–15, 18, 24, 28, 30, 32, 43–44, 52, 58, 73–98, 101–17, 120–39, 146, 151, 154, 161, 166, 170–73, 178, 180–84, 201, 205, 209, 211, 214–15, 223, 235, 255–56, 264, 273–74, 290–94, 298–312, 315, 317, 320, 323, 327, 330, 339, 342–45
  Crete, 189, 197, 255, 309
  Dalmatia, 198, 255
  Ephesus, 3–6, 12–15, 32, 43–44, 52, 58, 68, 73–78, 113, 134, 140–53, 161, 164–85, 197, 199, 201, 203, 205, 209–10, 214, 219, 226–28, 232, 235–38, 249, 253–57, 262, 265, 267, 270–84, 290–91, 295–12, 315, 317, 323, 327–28, 334, 336, 339, 342–44
  Galatia, 5, 98, 255, 319, 343
  Macedonia, 4, 93, 115, 129, 201, 255, 305
  Miletus, 255
  Nicopolis, 197, 254–55
  Philippi, 93, 181, 314
  Rome, 4, 20, 29, 143, 145, 154, 163, 165, 171, 180–83, 190, 198, 253–54, 317, 331–32, 337–38, 341, 343
  Spain, 198, 253
  Thessalonica, 77, 93, 146, 180, 255
  Troas, 201, 255
love, 97–98, 106, 118, 138, 154–55, 158, 161, 170, 193, 219
loyalty, 49, 78, 80, 86, 89–92, 99, 102–3, 111, 117–18, 123, 133–38, 148, 170–71, 177–78, 202, 204, 207, 235–38, 249–50, 257–58, 262–70, 277, 304, 318

mandata principis, 249, 283
manipulation, 81, 128
marital state, 82, 92, 99, 203, 212, 221–22, 246
master, slave, 79, 102, 126, 193, 203, 224, 288–89, 294
meal, 82, 84
meat, 82, 90, 92, 96, 99, 150
Mediterranean culture, 10, 43, 76
mentorship, 61–62, 179
meta-contrast, 40, 213, 222, 268, 322
methodology, 6–8, 23, 29, 32–33, 94, 202, 290, 307, 312, 321
military language, 148, 163–65, 182, 213, 225, 231, 264

Missio Dei, 217, 219
mission, calling, 13, 15, 66, 93–94, 98, 113, 121, 137, 145, 198, 207–11, 215–23, 226, 229–30, 237–38, 242, 250–51, 254–56, 261, 269–70, 288, 292, 296–99, 305, 307, 312, 317, 321, 324
missionary hubs, 4, 116, 139, 270, 317
missionary team, 3–4, 75, 78, 93, 127, 170, 253, 301, 305, 316
model, exemplar, 6–7, 10–14, 23–24, 28–29, 32–35, 44, 48, 50, 52, 58, 61–63, 68–69, 73, 75, 102–8, 112, 120, 125, 131, 136, 138, 147, 159, 161, 172–75, 196, 200, 208–9, 212, 222–23, 226–29, 232, 237–38, 246, 249, 263–68, 273–76, 283, 288–90, 304–7, 310, 314–15, 319, 322–24
monepiscopacy, 15, 19–20, 184, 234, 240, 307, 312–16
morality, 81, 85, 96, 99, 103, 139, 159, 161, 174, 221, 268
myth, 203–4, 212, 222–23, 297

Names NT
  Achaicus, 87, 89, 106
  Alexander, 34, 206, 209, 215, 253, 269, 334
  Apollos, 78, 79–80, 94–95, 101, 103, 107, 111, 114, 118, 123, 134, 138, 189, 256, 291, 294, 341
  Aquila & Priscilla, 268
  Artemas, 189
  Chloe, 87, 89, 90
  Crescens, 269
  Crispus, 87, 89
  Erastus, 87, 268
  Fortunatus, 87, 89, 106
  Gamaliel, 259
  Hermas, 194, 338
  Hermogenes, 262
  Hymenaeus, 206, 209, 215, 253, 265, 266, 272
  Jambres, 267, 275
  James, 306, 327–35
  Jannes, 267, 275
  Luke, 128, 222, 230, 268, 336, 338
  Lydia, 230
  Mark, 230, 253, 268, 336, 341
  Onesimus, 179
  Peter, 79–80, 94–95, 123, 256, 327, 329, 333, 335, 337, 339, 341–42
  Philetus, 265–66, 272
  Phoebe, 87, 181, 248
  Phygelus, 262
  Pilate, 226
  Sosthenes, 87, 89
  Stephanas, 87–89, 104–11, 120, 125, 136–39, 292
  Timothy, 4–5, 11–15, 18, 21, 25, 68, 75–78, 88, 90, 107–10, 114, 117, 120, 126–27, 136–37, 146, 169, 178, 183–91, 196–291, 295–6, 309–17, 320, 323, 328, 332–33, 336–46
  Titius Justus, 230
  Titus, 5, 12, 25, 113–16, 125–28, 132–33, 136–37, 188–90, 196–202, 207, 218, 223, 234, 242, 244, 252–55, 261, 264, 268–69, 273, 282, 291, 313, 318, 320, 332, 336–37, 344, 346
  Trophimus, 268
  Tychicus, 189, 253–55, 268
  Zena, 189

Names OT
  Aaron, 266, 267
  Joshua, 14, 260, 263, 266, 274, 277, 296
  Korah, 266
  Moses, 12, 14, 97, 100, 116, 117–18, 123, 126, 130–34, 252, 260, 263, 266–68, 274–78, 292, 294, 296, 301, 338
Names Other
  Aristotle, 192
  Basilides, 190
  Clement, 15, 17, 139, 148, 190, 194, 293, 317
  Clement of Alexandria, 190
  Dionysius, 193
  Enoch, 193
  Ignatius, 148, 173, 190, 194, 198, 243, 314–17, 329, 338, 342–45
  Irenaeus, 17, 190, 192, 232
  Marcion, 144, 190
  Papias, 192, 194
  Philo, 79–80, 345
  Polycarp, 190, 194, 198, 329, 334
  Serapion, 192
  Tatian, 190, 193, 340
  Tertullian, 190
  Thecla, 194
Neo-Pythagoreans, 193
nested identity, see Social Identities
network, 4, 15, 77, 98, 116, 123, 129–31, 136, 139, 143, 146, 151, 154, 163, 171, 181–83, 198, 202–3, 254–55, 269, 305, 309–10, 316–20
normative fit, see Social Comparison
norms and values, 1–2, 11–12, 14, 24, 43–48, 51, 53, 55, 66, 69, 79, 80, 83–86, 89, 91, 94, 97, 101, 105–6, 111, 119, 124, 134, 136, 138, 140, 150, 152, 158, 160, 165, 205–14, 221, 224–27, 245–49, 256, 259–62, 271–73, 282–85, 289, 293, 298–303, 310–11
NT studies, 1–2, 7, 41, 43, 57, 76, 312, 319, 322

opposition, 8, 13–14, 19–23, 37, 41, 57, 67, 97, 98, 110, 114, 127–29, 134–39, 143, 163, 173, 189, 192, 197, 200–1, 204, 208, 222, 225, 227, 229, 247, 255–58, 266–68, 275–83, 295, 297, 299, 317–19
oral tradition, 13, 78, 145, 192, 194, 196, 200, 263, 291, 302
ordain, see appoint
organizational psychology, see Psychology
outsiders, 8, 33, 59, 61, 96, 128, 150, 155, 203, 206, 228, 229, 273

paraenesis, exhortation, 25, 105–6, 122, 130, 157–60, 169, 186, 204, 215, 223, 232, 252, 260, 267, 275–76, 279
participation, 12, 60, 66, 83–84, 97–98, 107, 122, 129–30, 150, 212, 215–16, 248, 285, 296, 300–1
Pastoral Epistles, 13, 17, 21, 25, 28–29, 143, 184–91, 195–211, 218–19, 222, 224–25, 229–34, 242–44, 247–48, 252–53, 263–64, 267, 270, 282, 284, 286, 327–28, 331–40, 344
patriarchalism, 160, 224, 246
patronage, 12, 24, 44, 79–80, 86, 90, 105, 111, 114, 118–19,

122–25, 129–33, 138, 156, 162, 183, 205, 207, 218, 225, 228, 271, 273, 282, 292, 294, 301–2, 313, 315
Pauline corpus, 5, 27–28, 43, 45, 141, 143, 145, 176, 184–85, 190, 192, 195, 197, 289, 321
peace, 156, 161, 164–65, 182, 216, 230
personal identity, 34, 38
piety, 216, 219, 220
pillar, see Architecture
polemics, 108, 197, 199, 222, 225, 318
poor, 78, 84, 99, 246
post-apostolic, 168, 243, 279, 314, 317
post-Pauline, 4–5, 173, 261
prayer, 203, 207–8, 211–12, 215–17, 222–26
pressure, 45, 85, 163, 182, 203, 205, 237, 261, 283, 287, 289
privilege, 82, 85, 96, 99, 106, 126, 157, 207, 233
proactive, 55, 59, 299–301, 320
prototype, 40–41, 48, 50, 59, 60, 66, 68, 102–9, 127, 138, 147–48, 173, 178, 207, 212–15, 226–27, 231–32, 242, 246, 257, 268, 275–76, 280, 284
prototypical, 9, 11, 40–41, 53–60, 63–74, 89, 100, 106, 110–11, 125–28, 132–38, 147, 168–70, 176–77, 215, 221–25, 231–32, 237–38, 246, 249–51, 257, 266, 269, 271, 278–81, 284, 287, 295, 300, 316
Pseudepigraphy, see Authorship
Psychology
    cognitive psychology, 6–7, 10, 34, 50
    organizational psychology, 10, 34–36
    social psychology, 7, 33–40, 68, 290, 320
purity, 18, 81, 96, 117, 158–59
purpose, 52–53, 63, 71, 95, 150, 163, 173, 185, 211, 213, 219, 223, 226, 232, 238, 250–51, 258, 269, 277, 312, 321

reactive, 299–1, 320
reception, 100, 110, 119–20, 133, 173, 187, 191–92, 292, 294
reconciliation, 12, 82, 113–16, 125–33, 136–39, 142, 209, 295, 318
reinterpretation, 164, 166, 173–74, 182–83, 219, 267, 303
repentance, 115, 133, 136, 138, 265–66, 276, 280
resurrection, 33, 85, 86, 92, 100, 102, 121, 126, 142, 161, 292–93
reveal, revelation, 47, 51, 108, 131, 162, 167, 169, 172–74, 178, 202, 231, 293–95, 303, 310, 324
rhetoric, 7, 14, 41, 57, 60, 79, 80, 93–95, 98–100, 119–25, 128, 131–34, 138, 147–52, 155, 158–61, 165–66, 187, 199, 213, 223, 227–28, 237, 254, 256, 258, 265, 274–89, 300, 306, 315–21
riches, see Finances
ritual, 48, 56–57, 63, 69–73, 83–86, 92, 96–97, 100–1, 128, 131, 140, 150, 179, 268
rivalry, divisions, 24, 78–80, 84–98, 102–3, 110, 112, 118, 121,

132–35, 190, 207–10, 228,
   256, 273, 292, 323
Roman imperial ideology, 12, 91,
   131, 143, 148–51, 154, 156,
   159, 162–66, 181–83, 216–20,
   261, 330–31, 336

salvation, 94, 125, 197, 208, 216,
   219, 231, 260–63
scribes, see Authorship
secretaries, see Authorship
self-categorization, 34, 37
self-concept, 34, 38, 45, 51
self-reference, 109, 118, 123,
   172–73, 187, 189, 235, 284–87
Septuagint, 18, 266, 268
serve, servant, 9–12, 14, 24, 27, 30,
   45, 48, 54, 56, 58, 69–74, 79,
   87–89, 95, 99, 104–11, 118,
   128, 130, 138, 156, 160, 166,
   169, 177, 179, 181, 183, 201,
   205–12, 218, 222, 225–26,
   229, 232, 235, 237, 242–50,
   253–54, 260–66, 270–72,
   278–81, 287–88, 293–300,
   310, 315–16, 322–23
shame, see honor
SIMOL, see Leadership Theory:
   social identity model
social change, 1, 30, 55, 60, 66–67,
   70, 92, 102–3, 115, 152, 238,
   323
Social Comparison, 11, 14, 38–41,
   45–51, 57, 91–96, 101, 125,
   138, 151–54, 157, 186, 204,
   229, 243, 262, 280–81, 284,
   287, 291
   category accessibility, 46–47,
      51, 80–81, 85–86, 102–3, 111,
      119, 134, 145, 161, 164, 170,
      205, 223, 238, 242, 288
   comparative fit, 40, 42, 46–47,
      51, 59, 80–82, 86, 93–96,
      101–3, 111, 119–20, 123–24,
      205, 207, 316
   normative fit, 1, 10, 19, 46–47,
      122–23, 134, 164, 172, 223,
      225, 291, 307–11, 324
social competition, 2, 28, 39, 49,
   51, 69, 79–81, 86, 90–91, 98,
   102, 105–8, 111, 114–16, 129,
   131, 148, 154, 165, 205–10,
   215–18, 226, 250, 264, 292,
   298, 302–5, 308, 315
social creativity, 49–50, 94, 126,
   129, 154–57, 160, 163–64,
   173, 216–17, 220, 261, 323
social mobility, 49, 155
social context, 2, 7, 23–24, 34, 40,
   46–49, 54–57, 60, 66, 99–100,
   104, 143, 145, 147, 166, 188,
   213, 259, 308, 312, 321
Social Identification
   cohesion, 11, 13, 15, 51, 57, 63,
      70–71, 74, 82, 91, 97, 102–3,
      108, 111, 120, 159, 170, 173,
      179, 206, 226, 231, 235, 258,
      292–95, 309–11, 314, 325
   commitment, 8, 11, 56, 60, 69,
      71, 126, 134, 157, 164, 206,
      246
   consolidation, 49
   differentiation, 43, 67, 78, 94,
      107, 155, 174, 176, 179, 184,
      312
   embedding, 11, 57–58, 61, 63,
      72, 77, 98, 130, 139, 150–51,
      178–79, 188, 210, 223, 226,
      233, 235, 261, 274–75, 280,
      310–11, 316–17, 324
   group identity, 1, 9, 16, 33, 51,
      53, 67, 81, 214

group norms, 11, 43, 55, 65, 150, 157–58, 205–6, 211
group processes, 2, 9, 11
identity construction, 146
identity narrative, 11, 50–51, 57, 60, 83, 85, 94–98, 108, 118, 135, 139, 159, 172–76, 179–80, 208, 217, 221, 224, 235, 258, 260–63, 267, 269, 274, 295–98, 303, 311, 317, 321
identity performance, 47–51, 57, 59, 61, 78, 82, 85, 91–92, 100, 116, 127, 158–63, 211, 217, 220–28, 249, 261, 267–70
imitation, 26, 106, 108, 127, 132, 159, 160, 190, 193, 198–99, 268, 275, 314
mobilization, 14, 48, 50, 54–57, 99, 163, 261, 267–70, 297, 303, 321
stability, 15, 51, 57, 63–64, 70–71, 74, 82, 91, 102–3, 109–11, 120–21, 150, 159, 169–70, 178, 206, 214, 219, 226–27, 256, 293–94, 298, 309–11
stereotyping, 11, 40, 128, 150, 155, 158, 185, 213–14, 226, 258, 261, 286, 287, 298–99, 318
Social Identities
  civic identy, 81–83, 96, 216, 236
  cross-cutting identy, 39, 80–86, 97, 100, 119, 150, 154, 158, 166, 206, 217, 256, 293, 296
  ethnic identity, 1, 39, 44, 45
  gentile identity, 9, 29, 149, 150, 155–58, 180–81, 259, 268, 277, 286, 295, 298, 303, 322
  Greco-Roman identity, 13–15, 18, 24, 29, 73, 114–19, 138, 148, 156, 159–61, 164, 179, 184, 203, 205, 211, 228, 256, 261, 273, 283, 291–300, 303, 311, 313, 322, 336, 339
  Jewish identity, 7–15, 18–21, 24, 29, 33, 71, 73, 80, 85–86, 92, 97, 101–3, 111, 114–38, 142, 148–51, 155–59, 164, 170, 174, 180–81, 197, 203–6, 209, 211, 220–22, 226, 255–56, 259, 261, 267–68, 273–74, 277, 280, 285, 291–305, 311, 313, 318–22, 327, 332–38, 344, 346
  kinship identity, 44–45, 96, 236, 289
  nested identity, 39, 78, 83, 86, 97, 118–19, 150, 154, 166, 206, 256, 285, 296
  superordinate identity, 39–40, 78, 86, 90, 94–95, 99, 117, 149, 150–51, 156, 164, 206, 285–86, 295–97, 321–22
social identity theory, 7, 10–11, 29, 33, 35, 37, 41–43, 52, 58, 68, 74–75, 78, 146–48, 173, 188, 229, 245, 255, 306, 308, 319–22
social memory, 50, 62, 95, 108, 118, 135, 139, 146, 148, 151, 168, 170–73, 178, 224, 228, 259–60, 286–87, 317
social psychology, see Psychology
social science methods, 1, 23, 26, 30, 36, 42–43, 75, 173, 278, 307
social tension, 45, 83, 97–100, 111, 120, 124, 152, 293–94, 299–303, 313
sociology, 6, 10, 16–17, 21–23, 31, 36, 45, 65–68
Socratic letters, 25, 186, 332

Subject Index

sophists, 79, 86, 111
speech, 13, 84, 233–35, 250, 301
spirit, 18–19, 85, 129, 208, 223, 256, 260
spiritual, 19, 21, 26, 107, 148, 150, 292, 322
stability, see Social Identification
stereotyping, see Social Identification
steward, 79, 107
stigmatization, see Deviance
subversion, 90, 165
suffering, 95, 106, 114, 122–27, 131, 134, 138, 142, 162, 172–73, 256, 260–67, 271, 281, 291, 300–3, 323
superordinate identity, see Social Identities
synagogue, 9, 18, 23–24, 87, 119, 236, 313

temple, see Architecture
tradition, 13, 17–20, 36, 50, 67, 83–86, 97–100, 107, 114–19, 124, 134, 138–39, 144–45, 148–51, 155–58, 161, 164, 173–74, 178, 186–94, 199, 207, 213, 220, 228, 230, 233, 235, 238, 251, 254, 259–262, 274, 277–81, 286–87, 294, 298, 300, 314
transformational leadership, see Leadership Theory
Trinity, 97, 336–37, 341
trito-Pauline, see Authorship

uncertainty, 42, 45, 58, 78, 80, 162, 209, 211
unity and diversity, 13, 16–17, 26, 64, 79–80, 90, 94, 97, 113, 124, 127, 132, 134, 138, 143, 149–52, 157, 159, 170–71, 174, 177–78, 182–83, 199, 208, 213, 217, 249, 259, 271, 285, 292–95, 299–302, 314, 321–22

value, 8, 38, 49, 56–58, 83, 94, 96, 99, 136, 153–57, 160, 165, 172, 174, 182, 187, 198, 200, 204, 220, 225, 261–62, 271, 321–22
victory, 122, 126, 138, 182
vilification, see Deviance
vocabulary, 117, 143, 195–97, 202

weakness, 80, 109, 123–27, 131, 138, 173
wealth, see Finances
widows, 14, 203, 210, 215, 224, 226, 245–47, 250, 288
work, 2–4, 13, 20, 32, 34, 39, 44, 52, 58, 62, 64, 67, 69, 76, 83, 87, 94, 102, 110, 122, 151, 167, 169–70, 183, 185, 192–93, 196, 205, 209, 216–18, 223–25, 229, 233–34, 250, 256, 277, 281, 290, 313, 316, 320, 323
worship, 1, 82–83, 148–51, 181, 197, 216, 221, 227

Scripture Index

Numbers
16:5   266

Deuteronomy
31:6–8   263
31:23   263
34:9   260

Joshua
1:6–9   263
1:18   263

Isaiah
  164

Ezekiel
  164
37   156, 343

Matthew
10:11–14   230
28:16–20   121

Mark
  190
6:10–11   230

Luke
  265
9:4–5   230
10:5–7   230

23:32–33   265
23:39   265

Acts
  13, 76, 179, 189, 197–99, 201, 230, 245, 287
13:2   218
14:26   218
15:38   218
16:1–3   287
16:3   255, 259
16:4   230
16:11–18:18   76, 93
16:15   230
17:5–7   230
18:1–2   182, 230
18:7–8   87, 171, 230
18:17   87
18:19   230
19:1   236
19:8–14   236
19:9–10   241
19:9   171, 233
19:23   77
20:28–31   180
20:29–30   180
22:3   259
28   253

369

Romans

	5, 29, 151, 181, 195, 255, 311, 320
1	29
7	29
12:8	169
12:1–15:13	332
15:24–28	298
15:30–32	181
16	29
16:1	87, 181, 248
16:3	181
16:3–15	182, 198
16:7	168
16:21–23	87, 103, 181, 198
16:22	191

1 Corinthians

	4, 11–12, 28, 75–112, 114–17, 120, 125, 134, 136–37, 139, 142, 144–45, 147–49, 151–52, 155, 164, 166–67, 171, 173, 176, 180, 195, 201, 214, 216, 270, 274, 276, 284, 286, 288, 290–95, 300, 306, 309, 312, 320–21, 323
1–4	78, 99, 119, 121
1–6	76
1:1	87, 89, 145
1:1–16	87
1:2	77, 93
1:10–11	78
1:11	87, 89–90
1:12	79
1:14	87, 89
1:14–16	87, 107
1:16	106
1:17	80
1:18	80, 94
1:18–25	79
1:18—2:5	122
1:20—2:16	93
1:23–24	94
1:26	87
1:26–30	94
1:29	99
2:1	80
2:1–5	79, 106–7
2:3	80
2:6–8	94
3:1–4	79
3:1—4:21	94
3:3	79
3:5–9	79, 94
3:6–9	107
3:9–10	79, 107, 294
3:12–15	94
3:16–17	79, 94, 220
3:21	99
3:22–23	80, 177
4:1	107
4:1–5	79, 94
4:7	98
4:8–13	95, 106, 122
4:14	99
4:15	107
4:16–17	106, 110
4:17	90, 107, 109, 137, 201
4:18	95, 102
4:18–19	110
4:19	109
5–10	81
5–6	85, 99
5	114
5:1–13	81
5:2	81
5:3–5	96
5:4–5	99
5:5	98
5:6	81
5:7	118
5:12–13	96

1 Corinthians (continued)

6:1–3	96
6:2	96
6:5	82, 98–99
6:7	96
6:8	96
6:11	96
7	285, 288
7:1	82, 90
7:17	98
7:17–24	82
7:39	246
8–10	85
8:1	82, 90
8:1–3	99
8:7	99
8:10	82
8:13	82
9:1	218
9:1–27	82, 98, 100
9:3–19	106
9:7	264
9:9	118
9:15–17	294
9:24	264
10	155
10:1–13	100
10:2	118
10:14–22	155
10:20–22	96
10:23–33	155
10:25–27	96
10:32	98
11	85
11–14	150
11–15	83
11:1	106
11:2	83, 107
11:2–17	83
11:7–12	97
11:14	84
11:16	98
11:17	103
11:18–19	84
11:21	97
11:23	83, 100, 107
11:23–26	97
11:29	97
11:3	84, 98
11:33	97
12	88–89
12:4–11	97
12:8–10	84
12:12–26	97
12:21–25	84
12:28	88, 168–69, 174
12:28–30	84, 88, 107
13	97
13:1	84, 106
13:1–3	100
13:1–7	106
13:11–12	100
14:1–4	84
14:6	100
14:11	100
14:14–15	100
14:18–19	100, 106
14:26	103
14:32	98
14:33	98
15:1–3	83, 107
15:1–4	85
15:3	83
15:3–8	100
15:5–7	85
15:8–9	294
15:8–10	100
15:12	85
15:24	83
15:32	180
15:32–33	85
15:34–36	98

1 Corinthians (continued)

16	89
16:1–4	98, 130
16:6	181
16:8–9	77
16:10	90, 107, 109, 137, 201, 218
16:10–11	110
16:15	87–88, 104
16:15–16	170, 218
16:15–17	104, 106
16:15–18	28, 76, 87–88, 141
16:16	87, 89, 104–5
16:17	87–88
16:17–18	89–90
16:18	104–5
16:19	98
16:22	98
16:23	181

2 Corinthians

	4–5, 11–12, 75, 78, 99, 109, 112–140, 142, 144, 145, 147–49, 151–52, 166–67, 171, 173, 176, 180, 195, 201–2, 214, 216, 270, 273–74, 276, 284, 286, 290, 293, 295, 300, 303, 305–6, 309, 320, 323
1–7	131, 133
1:1	77
1:1–2	145
1:5	127
1:5–7	125
1:8	180
1:8–10	102
1:8–11	77
1:9	125
1:15–23	113, 127, 201
1:16	181
1:17	126
1:18–19	126
1:23—2:3	113
2:1–6	114
2:3	113
2:3–13	115
2:6	113
2:13	113
2:13–14	113
2:14–16	122
2:16–17	126
2:17	127
3	116
3:1	123
3:1–2	116, 118, 123
3:1–3	127
3:5–18	116, 126
3:18	122, 126
4:1	126–27
4:4–6	126
4:7–14	122
4:7—5:5	122, 126
4:10	126–27
4:14	126–27
5:12	133
5:16	131
5:18–20	127
5:20	142, 294
6:4–10	122
6:11—7:4	117
6:13	129
6:13–14	113
6:14—7:1	117, 129
7:1–2	113
7:2	129
7:4–5	113
7:6	113
7:8–12	115
7:12	113–14
7:13	113
8–13	121
8:1	113, 129
8:1—9:15	129

2 Corinthians (continued)

8:16	137
8:23	137
9:2–3	129
10–13	114, 120, 133, 318
10:1	113, 127, 129, 172
10:4–5	118
10:5–6	133
10:7	123, 127
10:10	118, 123
10:12	118, 123
10:12–13	118
10:13–15	127
10:13–16	121
10:18	118
11:4	119, 122, 128
11:4–6	113–14
11:6	118, 123
11:7	118
11:7–9	123
11:11	118
11:12–14	127
11:13	123
11:16—12:10	126
11:18–19	118
11:19	119
11:20	118, 123, 128
11:21–29	122, 294
11:22	123, 127
11:22–23	114
11:23	123
12:1–4	127, 142
12:1–12	294
12:11	119, 127
12:12	128
12:14	113
12:14–15	118
12:18	113, 137
13:1–2	113
13:3	131

Galatians

	5, 120, 143, 151, 195, 320
2:9	121
5:2	172
5:13—6:10	332
6:11	191

Ephesians

	4–5, 8, 11–13, 22, 68, 75, 78,
	141–185, 195, 202, 217, 220,
	223–25, 239, 256, 260, 264,
	277, 284–85, 288–90, 296,
	300, 302–6, 309, 311, 320–21
1	146
1–3	156, 161
1:1	142, 144, 164, 180
1:3–14	153, 157, 161
1:9	153
1:12–13	170
1:15–23	153
1:17–19	153
1:18	151
1:20	161
1:20–23	151
1:21–23	149, 153, 161
2	155–56
2–3	146
2:1–2	155
2:1–3	149
2:1–10	154
2:4–6	155, 161
2:11	149, 155, 170
2:11–13	149, 153, 155
2:11–22	149, 155, 157
2:13	149, 151, 155
2:14–15	156, 161
2:17	155
2:19	156
2:19–22	156, 167
2:20	150, 167, 172, 178, 220, 296

Ephesians (continued)

3	163
3:1	149, 172
3:1–7	162, 167, 172, 178
3:2	162
3:2–13	149
3:4	161
3:5	162, 167
3:7–9	295
3:8	161
3:9–10	162
3:13	162
3:14	154
3:14–15	149
3:15	297
3:16	154
3:18–19	154, 161
4:1	157, 172
4:3–6	174
4:4–6	150
4:5	151
4:7–11	150, 297
4:11	150, 168–69, 174, 295, 312
4:11–12	179
4:12	170, 218
4:12–16	173
4:13	170
4:13–16	150, 170, 174
4:17–19	149–50, 222
4:17—5:1	150
4:17—5:21	157
4:17—6:9	157
4:22–24	151, 158
4:25–32	159
4:30	151
5:1–2	159
5:3–14	159
5:8–16	151
5:15—6:9	160
5:19–20	150
5:21–33	150, 156
5:21—6:9	150, 159, 285, 288
5:22–30	224
6	164
6:10–20	150, 163, 225
6:20	172

Philippians

	5, 195, 214, 320
1:1	28, 151, 169, 309
1:6	218
1:22	218
1:23	253
2:17	253
2:30	218
4:2–3	28

Colossians

	5, 22, 120, 141, 144–45, 195, 260, 285, 320
1:23	172
3:8—4:1	285
4:7–17	198
4:16	145

1 Thessalonians

	5, 86, 320
5:12–13	141, 169, 218
5:14–22	28

2 Thessalonians

	5, 320

1 Timothy

	4–5, 11, 13–14, 18, 21, 68, 78, 146, 184–256, 258, 264, 274, 277, 279, 282–90, 295, 298–300, 302–6, 309, 314, 320, 323
1	211–12, 225
1:1–20	187, 212
1:2	237

1 Timothy (continued)

1:3	189, 210, 206–7, 210, 227, 235
1:3–5	219
1:3–7	211
1:3–20	212
1:4	203–4
1:4–7	212
1:6	206–7
1:7	203–4
1:7–11	206
1:8	231, 264
1:8–9	203
1:10	204, 219
1:11	212, 231, 237
1:12	243
1:12–15	212
1:13	212
1:14–16	213, 231
1:15–17	207
1:16	212, 222, 237, 263
1:16–17	212
1:17	207, 210
1:18	189, 211, 237, 264
1:18–19	213, 231
1:18–20	212
1:19	206
1:19–20	206, 227
1:20	189, 206, 209, 253, 266
2	226
2–3	208
2:1	215–16
2:1–7	207, 215, 223
2:1–15	208
2:1—3:16	212, 215
2:2	219
2:2–5	220–22
2:3–7	217, 238
2:4	216, 219
2:5–6	216
2:7	215–16, 237, 295
2:8	207–8, 215
2:8–9	205–6
2:8–15	203, 288
2:9	215
2:9–10	208
2:11–12	215, 248
2:11–15	248
3	220, 229–30
3:1	205, 209, 227–29, 232–33, 239–42, 281, 296, 314
3:1–13	203, 230, 238, 285, 288
3:1–16	217
3:2	218–19, 241–42, 247–48, 313
3:2–3	229
3:2–7	205, 239, 241
3:3	207, 229
3:3–4	218
3:4–5	210, 229, 241
3:6	207, 218
3:7	218, 229
3:8	207, 218, 243, 247
3:8–13	243
3:9	219
3:10	218, 229
3:11	247–48
3:11–16	248
3:12	210, 218, 241, 247–48
3:13	229, 244
3:14	198, 201
3:14–16	208, 219, 238
3:15	210, 220, 282
3:15–16	220, 244
3:16	210, 216, 219, 221
4	211–12, 225–26
4:1	206, 222
4:1–3	211, 221
4:1–16	221
4:5	222
4:6	222, 237, 243
4:6–8	211, 223
4:6–10	222

1 Timothy (continued)

4:6–16	238
4:7	222–23
4:7–10	220
4:10–11	223
4:11–16	211, 219
4:12	222–23, 232, 237
4:13	222–23
4:14	210–11, 230, 232, 237, 239, 314
4:15	222, 237
4:15–16	212, 223
5:1–2	288
5:1–3	203
5:1—6:2	212
5:1—6:4	206
5:3–16	245, 288
5:3–23	203
5:4	224, 245, 258
5:5–6, 7–8	224
5:8	245
5:9–10	246
5:10	224
5:10–11	245
5:11–16	246
5:12	224
5:13	247
5:14	246
5:14–15	224
5:15	206–7, 247
5:16	245
5:17	210, 224, 229–30, 233, 235, 239–40, 241, 312
5:17–18	239
5:17–25	223, 241
5:18–19	224
5:19	210
5:19–21	240
5:20	209, 224
5:22	209–10, 239, 279, 296
5:24	206–7
6	211–12
6:1–2	224
6:3–10	211
6:3	207, 211
6:3–19	212
6:4	207
6:4–5	206
6:5	225
6:5–10	205
6:7	190
6:10	206
6:11	237
6:11–14	211
6:12	211
6:13	212
6:15–16	212
6:17	207, 225
6:17–19	207
6:17–21	212
6:18–19	225
6:20–21	191, 212
6:20	264, 311
6:21	206

2 Timothy

	4–5, 11, 14, 21, 68, 75, 78, 120, 183, 185, 189, 196–97, 199–200, 202, 252–290, 298–300, 302–6, 309, 320, 323
1–2	267
1:2	259
1:3	258
1:3–5	260, 265
1:5	267
1:5–7	255
1:6	260, 273
1:7	256
1:8	260
1:9–11	261
1:11–12	260

2 Timothy (continued)

1:12	260–61, 263, 311
1:13	263
1:14	263, 311
1:15	254–55, 262
1:15–18	189, 253, 267
1:16	254
1:16–18	198, 262
2:1	260, 262
2:1–2	263
2:2	255, 263, 270, 278, 296
2:3	256
2:3–4	264
2:5	264
2:6	264
2:8	260, 265
2:8–10	265
2:8–13	265
2:10	255
2:11	295
2:11–13	265
2:14	255, 260, 265, 270, 272–73
2:14–26	265, 270, 274, 278
2:15	265, 270, 272, 279
2:16	265, 270
2:16–18	255, 270
2:17	189, 253
2:18	270, 272
2:19	260, 265–66, 272
2:20–21	256, 270
2:21–22	272
2:23	265
2:23–26	255
2:24	260, 265–66, 272
2:24–25	272
2:25	256, 265, 276
2:25–26	255, 266
3:1–2	255
3:1–9	267
3:1–17	267
3:5	255
3:6–9	255
3:8–9	260
3:9–10	267
3:10–11	268, 275
3:10–13	267
3:12	255–56
3:13	255
3:14	267
3:14–15	255, 260
3:15	189
3:17	260, 267
4:1	273
4:1–5	268
4:1–22	268
4:2	255
4:3–4	255, 268
4:4	254
4:5	169
4:6	253, 268
4:6–8	268
4:9	253, 262
4:9–13	189
4:9–22	268
4:10	198, 269
4:10–13	269
4:11–14	253
4:14–15	269
4:16	253, 255
4:16–17	198
4:17	255
4:18	262
4:19–20	269
4:19–21	189

Titus

	5, 25, 196–97, 201–2, 242, 244, 252, 320
1:5	189, 197
1:5–9	190, 309
1:7	313
3:12–13	189, 197, 254

Philemon

19   172

1–3 John

284

Revelation

284

Other Early Christian Literature

1 Clement

15, 139, 148, 190, 194, 317, 338
42–44   17, 293, 302
44:3–6   139

2 Clement

194

Ignatius

148, 173, 190, 194, 198, 243, 314–17, 329, 338, 342, 343–45
Ign. *Eph.*   284
Ign. *Eph.* 2–4   315
Ign. *Pol.* 4   190

Polycarp

190, 194, 198, 329, 334

Mart. Pol.

194

Didache

194

Barnabas

190, 194

Hermas

194, 338

Diognetus

194

Papias

192, 194

Acts of Paul and Thecla

194

3 Corinthians

192